Foundations of Comparative Politics

This student-friendly introduction to the key theories and concepts of comparative politics now provides even broader coverage of the world's democracies, with examples drawn from across the globe. *Foundations of Comparative Politics* contains a wealth of information, clearly structured and easy to read, with clear definition of Key Terms. It covers all the important themes in the field, including constitutional design and institutions; mass and elite politics; policy-making and implementation; and the future of the state and democracy in a globalising world. A new chapter on studying comparative politics, and new 'What Have We Learned?' and 'Lessons of Comparison' summary sections help students pull together the lessons of each chapter. Combining facts and theory throughout, debate is stimulated through the use of Controversy boxes, and Fact Files and Briefings give students interesting data that illustrates the key issues in the text. Online resources, including MCQs and Powerpoint slides, complete the package.

KENNETH NEWTON is Emeritus Professor of Comparative Politics at the University of Southampton and Visiting Professor at the WZB, Berlin.

JAN W. VAN DETH is Professor of Political Science and International Comparative Social Research at the University of Mannheim.

CAMBRIDGE TEXTBOOKS IN COMPARATIVE POLITICS

Series Editors:
Jan W. van Deth, *Universität Mannheim, Germany*
Kenneth Newton, *University of Southampton, United Kingdom*

Comparative research is central to the study of politics. This series offers accessible but sophisticated materials for students of comparative politics at the introductory level and beyond. It comprises an authoritative introductory textbook, *Foundations of Comparative Politics*, accompanied by volumes devoted to the politics of individual countries, and an introduction to methodology in comparative politics. The books share a common structure and approach, allowing teachers to choose combinations of volumes to suit their particular course. The volumes are also suitable for use independent of one other. Attractively designed and accessibly written, this series provides an up-to-date and flexible teaching resource.

Other books in this series:
RICHARD GUNTHER & JOSÉ RAMÓN MONTERO
The Politics of Spain

JAMES L. NEWELL
The Politics of Italy

Foundations of Comparative Politics

Democracies of the Modern World

SECOND EDITION

KENNETH NEWTON and JAN W. VAN DETH

CAMBRIDGE UNIVERSITY PRESS
Cambridge, New York, Melbourne, Madrid, Cape Town, Singapore,
São Paulo, Delhi, Dubai, Tokyo

Cambridge University Press
The Edinburgh Building, Cambridge CB2 8RU, UK

Published in the United States of America by Cambridge University Press, New York

www.cambridge.org
Information on this title: www.cambridge.org/9780521136792

First published 2005
Second edition 2010

Printed in the United Kingdom at the University Press, Cambridge

A catalogue record for this publication is available from the British Library

Library of Congress Cataloguing in Publication data
Newton, Kenneth, 1940–
   Foundations of comparative politics / Kenneth Newton, Jan W. van Deth. – 2nd ed.
      p.   cm. – (Cambridge textbooks in comparative politics)
   ISBN 978-0-521-19988-9 (Hardback)
   1. Democracy.   2. Comparative government.   3. Representative government
   and representation.   I. Deth, Jan W. van.   II. Title.   III. Series.
   JC423.N484 2009
   320.3–dc22   2009029187

ISBN 978-0-521-19988-9 Hardback
ISBN 978-0-521-13679-2 Paperback

Additional resources for this publication at www.cambridge.org/newton

This book is dedicated to Konstanza and Joke

Contents

Contents

Contents

Briefings

Fact files

Controversies

Tables

Figures

Preface to the second edition

This second edition has been extensively revised and updated, based, in large part, on the comments and suggestions of anonymous readers contacted by Cambridge University Press. We could not follow all of their suggestions but have acted on most of them, resulting in a great many changes to the book, some major, some minor. We also had very useful feedback from Matthijs Bogaards and his students at the Jacobs University, Bremen, from Wolfgang Müller at the University of Mannheim, from Henk van der Kolk at Twente University and from the very helpful students at the University of Southampton who 'road tested' some of the chapters for us. Ursula Neumann and Benjamin Engst at the University of Mannheim checked many of the entries and provided updated information. Also, Benjamin Engst pitched in at the last stages of the revisions and helped us to meet our deadline.

Ken Newton would also like to thank Wolfgang Merkel and his colleagues in the DSL Research Unit in the Wissenschaftszentrum Berlin for their continuing support and for providing a wonderful working environment. Susanne Fuchs was especially helpful and deserves special thanks.

As political scientists, not politicians, we cannot blame any faults and errors in this second edition on anybody but ourselves, least of all those named above.

Ken Newton and Jan W. van Deth
January 2009

Acknowledgements

This book is the result of our discussions and contacts with many people at various places in the last few years. Ken Newton would like to thank the Wissenschaftszentrum Berlin for time spent there researching and writing early drafts of chapters. Wolfgang Zapf and Roland Habich made this possible with a kind invitation to join their group as a visitor. Tom Cusack, Jan Delhey, Wolf-Dieter Eberwein, Dieter Fuchs, Rick Hofferbert, Ron Inglehart, Max Kaase, Hans-Dieter Klingemann, Christiane Neumann, Marion Obermaier and Edeltraud Roller all combined to make the visits both delightful and productive.

Ken Newton would also like to thank colleagues at the University of Southampton, who have provided friendship and intellectual stimulation in the past few years. Though they don't know it, some of the ideas in this book were first tried out over our sandwiches and a great many cups of really bad coffee at lunch time. Sadly, most of the most brilliant theories and insights were shot down in flames in these discussions, by colleagues who based their criticism on no more than acute intelligence, hard information, a thorough knowledge of the subject and a sharp eye for a weak argument. Special thanks are due to Fritz and Mocha Metzeler who, with habitual kindness and generosity, made the Mulina available for work on this book, and for rest and recuperation afterwards.

Jan van Deth would like to thank his collaborators at the University of Mannheim and the Mannheim Zentrum für Europäische Sozialforschung (MZES) for similar friendship and intellectual stimulation. In Mannheim, too, many ideas were shot down with good arguments based on an excellent knowledge of the subject matter of comparative politics and a firm grasp of its methods.

Finally, we would like to thank Jana Jughard for preparing the final version of the manuscript.

Ken Newton and Jan W. van Deth
August 2004

Abbreviations and acronyms

AfDB	African Development Bank
ASEAN	Association of South East Asian Nations
AV	Alternative Vote
Benelux	Belgium Netherlands, Luxembourg Economic Union
CA	Consumer Association
CBA	Cost-benefit analysis
CEO	Chief executive officer
CIS	Confederation of Independent States
CND	Campaign for Nuclear Disarmament
CoR	Committee of the Regions (EU)
DARS	Democratic Arab Republic of the Sahara
DGB	Deutscher Gewerkschaftsbund (trade union association, Germany)
EAPC	Euro-Atlantic Partnership Council
ECHR	European Court of Human Rights
ECJ	European Court of Justice
ENA	*Ecole Nationale d'Administration*
EP	European Parliament
ESA	European Space Agency
ETUC	European Trade Union Confederation
EU	European Union
FBI	Federal Bureau of Investigation (USA)
GATT	General Agreement on Tariffs and Trade
GM	Genetically modified
IBRD	International Bank for Reconstruction and Development (World Bank)
ICJ	International Court of Justice
IDA	International Development Association
IISS	International Institute for Strategic Studies
ILO	International Labour Organisation
IMF	International Monetary Fund
IOC	International Olympic Committee
IOM	International Organisation for Migration
IPU	Inter-Parliamentary Union

IT	Information technology
JV	Joint venture
MCW	Minimum connected winning (coalition)
MITI	Ministry of International Trade and Industry (Japan)
MMP	Mixed-member proportional voting system
MNC	Multi-national corporation
MWC	Minimum winning coalition
NAFTA	North American Free Trade Association
NASA	National Aeronautics and Space Administration (USA)
NATO	North Atlantic Treaty Organisation
NGO	Non-governmental organisation
OAU	Organisation of African Unity
OECD	Organisation for Economic Cooperation and Development
OFCOM	Office of Communications (UK)
OPEC	Organisation of Petroleum Exporting Countries
OSCE	Organisation for Security and Cooperation in Europe
PAC	Political Action Committee (USA)
PPP	Purchasing power parity
PR	Proportional representation
R&D	Research and Development
SB	Second ballot (voting system)
SES	Socio-economic status
SMSP	Single member, simple plurality voting system
SNTV	Single non-transferable vote
STV	Single transferable vote
TI	Transparency International
TNC	Transnational Corporation
UK	United Kingdom
UN	United Nations
UNHCR	UN High Commission for Refugees
UNITAR	UN Institute for Training and Research
USA	United States
USSR	Union of Soviet Socialist Republics (Soviet Union)
WDIs	World Development Indicators
WEU	Western European Union
WHO	World Health Organisation
WTO	World Trade Organisation

Key terms and concepts

As key terms and concepts are introduced in the book, they are briefly defined in the margin of the text. Rather longer definitions, sometimes with qualifications and examples, are given in the Glossary at the end of the book and a fully searchable, electronic version is available on the companion website.

How to use this book

This book has many special features to help you work your way through the chapters efficiently and effectively and to understand them. This section shows you what these features are and how they help you work through the material in each chapter. Each chapter contains:

- An introduction with a brief account of the topics it covers, so that you know what to expect. For example, chapter 2 includes:
  - Why study states?
  - The modern state and democracy
  - The rise of democratic states
  - Redistribution and welfare states
  - theories of states and society

- Each chapter ends with a summary of its main findings and what we have learned from using the comparative approach to government and politics. For example, chapter 2 concludes with:

■ What have we learned?

- This chapter has dealt with the difficulties of characterising and defining states, and with the historical development of modern states, especially democratic ones.
- Democracy is a variable not a constant. Accepted ideas about what democracy is, and how it operates, are changing as standards rise.

■ The lessons of comparison

- Although states across the globe, from the strongest to the weakest, are increasingly confronted with other powerful organisations, especially international business (MNCs), non-governmental organisations (NGOs) and international agencies, they are still the most important political actors in the world.
- A concluding section reviews the main theories and approaches of political science towards the subject matter of the chapter. By the end of the

book you will have covered every major theoretical contribution to comparative politics from Plato to the most recent researcher in the field.

■ Theories of state and society

Broadly speaking, there are four major approaches to the relationship between 'state' and 'society':

- State supremacy
- State dependency
- Interdependency
- Separation and autonomy.

Democracy 'A political system whose leaders are elected in competitive multi-party and multi-candidate processes' (Freedom House).

- 'Key term' entries. When a new concept is introduced it is picked out in bold letters in the text and defined in brief and simple terms in the margin. All the key terms are then brought together in the 'Glossary of key terms' at the end of the book. This makes it easy to refresh your memory about concepts.

- 'Controversy boxes' provide you with an overview of the most contentious topics in comparative government and politics.

CONTROVERSY 2.1

Focusing on the state is ..... .

Area of debate	Right, because:	Wrong, because:
Euro-centrism	Although the idea of the modern state originated in Europe, every corner of the world is now claimed by states.	The idea of the modern state is Euro-centred and ideologically loaded, and should be replaced by concepts taking account of political arrangements in other cultures.

- 'Briefing boxes' give you a rich and concise account of important topics and material to illustrate them and bring them alive.

Briefing 2.1

Only the state can bail out private actors and guarantee financial security
In the first years of the twentieth-first century housing prices exploded in many countries and personal debts increased as people tried to raise their standard of living. Banks and other financial institutions provided easy mortgage credits and loans to finance this boom and make big profits. With the collapse... etc.

- In addition to the tables and figures, 'fact files' organise hard evidence to support the general accounts of comparative government and politics contained in the text.

Fact file 4.1

■ Constitutions

- The first codified constitution was San Marino's (1600), followed by Canada's (1774) and the USA's (1787).
- Between 1990 and 1995 ninety-six countries – more than a third of the world's total – adopted new constitutions. Twenty were in central and eastern Europe, but thirty-one were in central and southern Africa.
- Most countries have modified their constitutions at some point in their history, but Belgium, Canada, France (twice), the Netherlands, New Zealand, Sweden and Turkey have done so in major ways in recent decades. The Indian constitution…etc.

The end material of the chapters also includes:

- Two or three small projects that you can use to test your understanding and consolidate your learning.

Projects

1. Would you call the country you live in a 'nation' (or a 'nation-state')? What makes it a state, and when did it achieve statehood?
2. Draw up lists of:
   (1) the ten largest and smallest states in the world
   (2) the ten oldest and youngest states in the world
   (3) the ten richest and poorest states in the world.
   What do the oldest states have in common compared with the youngest, and what do the richest have in common compared with the poorest?

- A short list of further reading and details of useful websites.

Further reading

P. Dunleavy and B. O'Leary, *Theories of the State: The Politics of Liberal Democracy*, Basingstoke: Macmillan, 1987
An overview of discussions of the state and its development.

G. Gill, *The Nature and Development of the Modern State*, Basingstoke: Palgrave, 2003.
A concise overview of the state and its development.

Websites

http://countrystudies.us/
Extensive statistical information about many economic, social, political and
   demographical developments for virtually all states of the world.
www.un.org
Official website of the UN. Provides information on the UN as well as links to
   specific organisations.

The Introduction that follows spells out the main themes that run throughout the book. It tells you what to keep in mind and look out for as you work
your way through the chapters. Finally, at the end of the book we have added
a Postscript on the main methodological questions in comparative politics.

Extensive online resources, including all the material listed above, are
available on the book's website. You can search this material for yourself at
www.cambridge.org/newton.

For **students** additional material includes an updated reading list, websites and advanced further reading. Multiple-choice questions allow students
to test their understanding of each chapter.

For **instructors**, all figures and tables from the book are available along
with lecture slides. Additional student questioning includes exam and essay
questions.

Introduction

This introduction does three things. First, it explains why we should bother to study comparative politics at all. Why is it important to know how foreign political systems work? Second, it considers the strengths and weaknesses of the comparative approach to political science. It argues that, in spite of its problems, comparative politics adds something of great importance to our ability to understand what goes on in the political world. And third, it provides some signposts to guide you through the book to make it easier and more interesting for you to understand and absorb its contents.

■ Why comparative politics?

Why do we bother to study comparative politics and government? There are many good reasons but three of the most important are: (1) we cannot understand our own country without a knowledge of others; (2) we cannot understand other countries without a knowledge of their background, institutions and history; and (3) we cannot arrive at valid generalisations about government and politics without the comparative method.

Understanding our own country

To understand our own country we must study other countries as well. This may sound like a strange statement, but it has some powerful logic to support it. We often take the political institutions, practices and customs in our own country for granted, assuming that they are somehow natural and inevitable. Only when we start looking around at other countries do we understand that our own ways of doing things are sometimes unique, even odd or peculiar. It is said that fish will be the last form of life on earth to realise the existence of water: since they spend their whole life in water with no experience of anything else, they have no reason even to imagine that anything else exists. For this reason the writer Rudyard Kipling wrote, 'What knows he of England, who only England knows?', making the point that people who have no knowledge of other countries cannot begin to understand their own.

Understanding other countries

It is obvious that we cannot begin to understand the politics of other countries unless we know something about their history, culture and institutions. And this, in turn, is important because what these countries do often affects us directly or indirectly: they impose import duties on our goods, refuse to sign trade agreements or agree to pollution controls, do not contribute to international peacekeeping forces, threaten us with military force, or are unhelpful in trying to solve international economic problems. Why do they act this way? Knowing their history, culture and institutions helps us to understand and explain their actions and perhaps change the situation for the better. Ignorance is a recipe for complication and failure; knowledge can help us improve matters.

Constructing valid generalisations

The purpose of science is to arrive at valid generalisations about the world. Such generalisations take the form of 'if–then' statements – if A then B, but if X then Y. Aeroplane designers need to know that if their planes exceed the speed of sound they will break the sound barrier, affecting how the planes handle and the stress on their structures. Doctors need to know that if a certain drug is administered then a patient's disease is likely to be cured. Chemists need to know that if two substances are mixed then a third substance may be produced that is useful to us.

To arrive at these if–then statements, scientists carry out systematic experiments in their laboratories, comparing what happens under different circumstances. Aeroplane designers have wind tunnels; drug companies and chemists have laboratories in which they manipulate the conditions of their experiments in a careful and systematic manner. Political scientists also try to arrive at valid generalisations about the world of government and politics by means of comparison, but unfortunately they can rarely experiment. For example, political scientists are interested in the effect of different voting systems on election results, and it would be nice if we could order our government to use a new voting system to see what happens. Obviously this is not possible. An alternative might be to set up a quasi-experiment that tried to measure how people behave using different voting systems, but laboratory experiments can only approximate the conditions of the real political world. They cannot reproduce them exactly. And political scientists have to be exceedingly careful in their experiments not to break any moral rules or do harm to their experimental subjects. For the most part, controlling variables in an experimental manner, much less in laboratory conditions, is not an approach open to political science research.

What political scientists can do, however, is compare things that happen 'naturally' in the real world. For example, different countries have different voting systems and we can compare them to estimate their effects. We note that countries with voting system A have a higher voting turnout than countries using system B. However, we cannot immediately conclude that A causes a higher voting turnout than B until we are sure that this effect is not caused by factors other than voting systems. Perhaps system A countries happen to be smaller, wealthier or better educated than system B countries and it is size, wealth or education that influences voting turnout. We cannot control (hold constant) all other variables, as laboratory scientists do, but we can use methods to simulate the holding constant of variables. In this way we can make statements such as: 'All other things being equal (size, wealth, education), if a country has a type A voting system, then it will tend to have a higher voting turnout than countries with type B voting systems.'

It would be unwise to try to make general 'if–then' generalisations based on a study of only one country, or even a small handful of them. It is easy to jump to false conclusions when studying one or a handful of cases. In fact, this frequently happens when people with an inadequate understanding of the subject conclude that something must be true based on their limited experience of what happens in their own country (see briefing 1). What we need to do is compare a range of countries of different size, wealth and education to estimate the independent effects of these and voting systems on turnout. Studying one or a few countries might not be enough; we need a range of countries with a spread of characteristics that we think might influence voting turnout.

Comparative politics has increasingly turned to the comparison of either a few carefully selected countries or a large number of them. To study a number of countries using both type A and type B electoral systems we can concentrate on a few countries which are very similar in most of their characteristics but organise their elections differently. In this way we can conduct a 'natural experiment' that provides us with a few countries that have different electoral systems but little variation in other respects that might affect voting turnout. Alternatively, comparing a large number of countries with different voting systems and with a wide variety of other characteristics can reduce the chances of arriving at false conclusions. In this way we can see if countries with one particular kind of voting system have higher turnout than countries with other voting systems, irrespective of other variations.

Briefing 1

Is widespread gun ownership in the USA responsible for its high gun crime figures?
It is commonly claimed that the widespread ownership of guns in the United States is responsible for the country's high gun crime and murder rate. Yet both Switzerland and Israel have a high proportion of guns, partly because they train all men (in Switzerland) and all men and women (in Israel) for military service and because, depending on their duties, those in service routinely carry small arms or keep them at home.
Law-abiding citizens in both countries are entitled to own guns and in Israel a high proportion of people carry concealed weapons in their everyday life. In Switzerland shooting is a popular sport. In Israel gun crime and the murder rate is low by international standards and in Switzerland it is so low that there is no need to keep records and gun control is not an issue. Comparison shows that widespread gun ownership is not the only explanation for the country's high gun crime and murder rate.

Is the very high population density of Manhattan responsible for its high crime rate?
Experiments with rats shows that over-crowding causes aggression and compulsive eating. Does the high population density of New York (especially Manhattan) have the same effect on its population of increasing aggression, crime and obesity? Some other cities (Hong Kong, Singapore, Tokyo) with similar or higher density ratios have much lower violent crime and murder rates than New York, and relatively few obese people. The conclusions seems to be that: (1) it can be misleading to draw conclusions about human beings based on animal experiments: and (2) comparison of New York with other crowded cities suggests that population density cannot be a powerful cause, if it is a cause at all, of New York's high level of aggression, crime and obesity.

■ The strengths and weakness of cross-national comparative political science

Political scientists can compare in different ways; they can compare across time, across countries and across different places or population sub-groups within a country. For example, if we want to generalise in an if–then manner about the effects of age, gender and religion on voting turnout we might compare, within our own country, the voting turnout of old and young people, males and females, and different religious groups. This would be using the comparative method but not the cross-national comparative method. As things have developed in political science, however, the term 'comparative politics' has come to mean research on two or more countries. Although all scientists rely upon comparisons, when political scientists use the term 'comparative politics', they are most generally referring to the comparison of political patterns in different countries. Sometimes this is referred to as 'cross-national' research.

Cross-national comparative research has some great strengths. Although we can compare within a given country as well as across different countries, we have already noted that one-country studies can run into problems. For example, in conducting a perfectly good comparison of different electoral systems in our own country, we may not be able to examine the effects of different parties or party systems on turnout simply because our country always has the same parties and the same party system in its elections. When we take a broader view of countries with different parties we might see that these parties also have a big effect on turnout. The cross-national method is more reliable because it allows us to test generalisations about politics in one set of circumstances against those in a wide variety of circumstances. This means we can put greater confidence in the reliability of our generalisations.

■ The pros and cons of cross-national comparative politics

In spite of these advantages, comparative politics has its fair share of deficiencies:

- It cannot answer questions of values
- It lacks evidence
- It deals in probabilities, not certainties or laws
- It suffers from the fatal flaw that what it can measure is not worth studying
- Every country in the world is unique so comparisons are impossible.

We will look at these in turn.

It cannot answer questions of values

Questions such as 'Is democracy the best form of government?', 'Should we value freedom more than equality?' and 'Which party should we vote for?' are matters of values and subjective judgements. They are not, in the final analysis, a matter for empirical research. Like all sciences, comparative politics can never answer value questions or matters of subjective opinion, although it may provide evidence that helps some people to make up their mind about them.

It lacks evidence

Although comparative government deals in facts and empirical evidence, it often lacks even an adequate supply of facts and data. Rarely do we have adequate or comparable measures for a large number and variety of countries. By and large we have more evidence about the wealthiest countries in the world because they are better organised and equipped to produce statistics about themselves. For the same reason we have more evidence about recent years. But even in the most advanced societies we often lack even the minimum quantity and quality of evidence necessary to answer our research questions satisfactorily. This state of affairs will improve as data becomes more plentiful, but meanwhile the data problem remains a severe one.

It deals in probabilities not certainties or laws

Comparative politics does not provide us with laws about how government and politics work. It can only make if–then statements of a probable or likely kind. We can reach the conclusion that one voting system is likely to encourage a higher voting turnout than another, but cannot say that this will always or inevitably happen in every case. First, there is the unpredictable human factor, and second, there are a large number of causal factors involved, some of which can interact in a complex way. Rarely are matters so simple that we can say that A produces B. Most usually it is A, interacting with X, interacting with Y, interacting with Z, that produces B, or something like it. As a result, comparative government cannot tell us what will happen with a high degree of certainty but only, at best, what is likely to happen under certain circumstances, and the circumstances may not be present in any given case. Therefore, comparativists are fond of the qualifying words 'tends to', 'often', 'in some cases', 'probably', 'likely', 'may', 'in a percentage of cases'. Comparativists rarely use the word 'never' and rarely use the word 'always'. In the political world there are almost always exceptions to the general rule, and usually a significant number of them.

We should not be put off by the fact that comparative politics is not a laboratory subject and cannot manipulate its variables at will. Quite a few sciences suffer from the same problem. The human body is such a complex thing that doctors can rarely be certain that a given drug will cure a disease and are often unsure about its side effects. Similarly, the world's climate system is so complicated that climate specialists cannot tell us whether it will rain or not on a given day, so they talk about the probability of rain. Cosmologists cannot tell us whether the universe will continue to expand, contract or reach a steady state. Civil engineers cannot be sure that their buildings and structures will survive earthquakes, hurricanes and terrorist attacks. Note that in all these cases, as in comparative politics, scientists cannot control their variables in a laboratory, either because of moral limits (experiments on human beings) or the inability to manipulate the world's weather or, indeed, the universe. Comparative politics struggles to be as scientific as possible, but like some other sciences it falls short of the ideal.

It suffers from the fatal flaw that what it can measure is not worth studying

Some critics argue that the information used by comparativists is misleading, false or meaningless and that what can actually be studied using such information is of little or no value. The strongest criticism claims that empirical social science is limited to counting manhole covers – something that can be done with great precision by people of the meanest intelligence but is of little interest to anybody and little importance for anything.

It is certainly true that comparative politics is limited in what it can study, and that it can say little or nothing about the important value questions of political theory and philosophy. But comparative politics has things to say of interest and importance about many subjects of concern in modern society. For example, to continue with our examples of voting turnout, politicians and political commentators are worried that low or declining turnout shows that something is wrong with the democracies, and comparative politics can say something about whether and why this might be true. The critics might respond with the 'lies, damned lies and statistics' argument that voting turnout figures are of little use because they are inaccurate, misleading or fake – they overlook the possibility of corrupt election practices, compulsory voting, totalitarian countries with a 99 per cent turnout, or the fact that turnout can be calculated in different ways to produce different conclusions. The comparativists would reply that this is all the more reason for knowing about the problems of turnout figures, which means understanding how they are produced in different countries and when the statistics lie and deceive, and when they reliable and useful for study.

In the end the debate boils down to how one evaluates the different kinds of questions that political science can tackle. Critics argue that comparative politics cannot deal with the big issues of truth, beauty, freedom and justice; comparativists know this but claim they can study some factual matters that throw light on important questions. The critics argue that comparative politics deals with trivial and measurable issues; the comparativists acknowledge that this is sometimes true, not always, and that in any case science does not always advance in giant leaps and bounds but by inching along in tiny steps before making its big breakthroughs.

Every country in the world is unique so comparisons are impossible

One argument against comparative politics is that since every country is unique, all cross-national comparisons are like comparing apples with oranges. We cannot, according to this thinking, ever learn from other countries because everything is different there. We cannot benefit from studying how the Swedes subsidise their political parties, how the Japanese manage their national economy or how the New Zealanders reformed their political system because these countries are uniquely different. There is some truth in this argument. The practices that work well in some countries do not always travel well to other places. Nevertheless, it is worth noting that we can often borrow from other countries without much modification: the idea of the Ombudsman (see chapter 4) has been adopted successfully in many countries; the basic ideas of proportional voting systems (chapter 12) have spread throughout the world after its first use in Belgium in 1900; the principle of the separation of powers (chapter 4) as discussed by Montesquieu (1689–1755) is now found in every democracy in the world.

It is true that every country is unique, but it is also true that all countries are the same at a general level. At first sight this is a strange statement, and how do we explain it? An analogy is helpful. Every human being is unique with respect to DNA, physical appearance, personality and abilities. At another level, human beings are exactly the same: they are all (or the huge majority of them) *homo sapiens,* warm-blooded primates, vertebrate mammals able to walk upright on two legs, able to communicate complex and highly specific messages by voice, and they all have four fingers and an opposing thumb on each of two hands, and large, problem-solving brains. At a still more general level, human beings are similar to other primates, especially chimpanzees, gorillas and orang-utans and share no less than 96 per cent of their DNA profile with them. At a still more general level, human beings have something in common with pigs, to the extent that pig organs can be transplanted into human beings.

In short, what is unique and what is comparable depends on the level of analysis and what is being compared. A silly-but-serious question asks, 'Is a mouse more like a frog or a whale?' The critic of comparative politics might answer that these creatures are all different and unique and cannot be compared. The answer of the comparativist is that it depends on what you want to compare. The frog and the mouse are of similar size compared with the whale, but the frog and the whale can live in water, and the mouse and the whale give birth to live young. In some ways Costa Rica is more like the USA than Sweden because Costa Rica and the USA have presidential systems of government (chapter 5). In other respects Costa Rica is more like Sweden because both have unitary forms of government, whereas the USA is federal (chapter 6). At one level each political system is unique; at another level some systems are similar in some respects. What countries you select for comparison depends crucially on what you want to study. This makes comparative politics both more possible and more complicated than its critics assert.

■ The themes that run through the book – what to watch for

Although each and every system of government is unique, there are broad similarities between different groups of countries. This makes the job of the comparative political scientists easier because instead of reciting the particularities of each system, which would result in a mind-boggling list of detailed variations rather like reading through a telephone directory, we can often reduce this great mass of detail and complexity to a few general themes. These themes run through the book. The themes are:

- The importance of institutions
- History matters
- The social and economic basis of politics
- The importance of politics
- The way in which the infinite variety of detail combines with a few general patterns.

The importance of institutions

Much of the most recent comparative politics focuses on the attitudes and behaviour of individuals: how they vote, their political values, political culture, the ways in which they engage in politics, and so on (see chapter 9–11). At the same time we should not lose sight of the great influence and importance of institutions – the structures of government that distinguish federal and unitary systems, presidential and parliamentary systems, pluralist and corporatist systems, and so on. As you progress through the chapters you can note the ways in which institutions matter, and how and why they do so.

History matters

History throws a long shadow. Major events centuries ago, and the outcomes they produce, can affect us strongly even now. Sometimes, it seems, a political decision or turning point can create what is known as path dependency. By this we mean that decisions taken in the past can narrow the options that are available to us today, and decisions taken today may limit options in the future. For example, institutions tend to develop a life of their own and to preserve themselves because of institutional inertia. This means that an institution that has developed strong roots in government in the past may well influence current events. As we move through our chapters we will see how historical events, sometimes a long time ago, have implications for political patterns and practices today.

The social and economic basis of politics

One school of thought in political science explains political patterns in terms of social and economic patterns or prerequisites. It points out that different social groups think and behave in different ways and draws the conclusion that social conditions have a strong influence on politics (see chapter 2). Some writers go further than this and claim that all politics can be explained in terms of economic models. The chapters that follow will explain the social and economic basis of politics, but they will also deal with the limitations of these explanations.

Politics matters

The social and economic explanations of politics are limited because they tend to ignore or overlook the importance of political institutions, events, ideas and cultures. Social and economic factors may have a powerful influence, but so also do political considerations – how political elites react to events, how political ideals affect the way people think and behave, how political institutions have an impact, how electoral systems influence electoral outcomes. It may seem like trying to have one's cake and eat it when we insist that social *and* economic *and* political factors influence government and politics, but, in fact, this simply acknowledges the fact that the social, economic and political are tightly interwoven aspects of the same thing in the real world.

From a mass of detail to general types

As we have emphasised, every political system is unique in many ways, but fortunately for the student of comparative politics we do not have to keep track of each and every particularity because, at a more general level, political systems tend to cluster around a few general types. Whether we are discussing executive and legislative power, multi-level government, pressure group systems, electoral systems, the mass media, party systems, party ideologies, and so on, we will see how a huge variety of detailed and particular differences between countries most generally break down into a few general types. This is a blessing for comparative political scientists because it turns a job that would be like reading the telephone directory, where every entry is different from every other in some crucial but boring detail, into the more exciting task of constructing general models and theories that apply to a wide variety of democratic nations across the world. Instead of describing each and every political system, we can analyse their contrasts and similarities in terms of a few general characteristics. We can see families of similar political systems among the huge and bewildering variety detail. The chapters that follow describe these patterns, types and clusters of characteristics when they arise.

PART I

The state: origins and development

It was already late at night on 4 August 1789 when the French National Assembly continued its debates. The situation was disastrous. A new wave of social unrest, upheaval and looting had swept the country and people were near starvation in many cities. The problems seemed insoluble and the three classes – nobility, clergy and bourgeoisie – were fighting each other and the king. If no reconciliation could be reached soon, the country would collapse into chaos and civil war. Instead of dealing with these burning problems directly, the Assembly argued about a list of principles that should be used as a guideline and benchmark for political activities. On 26 August 1789, the 'Declaration of the Rights of Man and of the Citizen' was proclaimed. It sought to smash the ancient institutions and end privilege. From that moment on, the power of the state was to be based on the consent of its citizens and the protection of individual rights.

Until the National Assembly declared these principles, France was ruled by the king and his royal clique. The heated debates in August 1789 mark the rise of a new type of government and politics. Political power was no longer based on some 'natural order', God's will, or long-established rights of the nobility. As a citizen, every person had basic and equal rights, and the state was the property of its own citizenry. This double recognition indicated a radical break with previous think-ing. Power, government, politics, the state – all these had existed long before the Declaration was proclaimed, but in August 1789 the Assembly knocked down many conventional ideas and replaced them by new interpretations consciously focusing on the crucial position of 'the people'. In this way, the much older idea of the state was given a radically new interpretation.

We start our treatment of comparative politics with an overview of the historical development of the 'state concept' as well as the actual establishment of states around the world. Part I consists of three chapters. Chapter 1 examines the emergence of the state, its main characteristics, and its spread and variety in the latter half of the twentieth century. As will become clear, states are the most important agencies for the organisation of political power. In chapter 2, we will take a closer look at democratic states and welfare states as they originated in the last two centuries. The transition of states into democratic states is discussed in chapter 3. Although the number of states has constantly risen in the last few decades, democracy remains a fragile thing in some places and several states that were initially democratic returned to less democratic arrangements.

The three chapters of the first part of this book deal with states in general and with democratic states in particular:

- The idea of the state and the development of the modern state
- States and democratic states
- Democratic change and persistence.

1 The development of the modern state

Watch any newsflash or open any newspaper and you will see headlines such as 'France and Britain agree on migration', 'Reforms in Costa Rica problematic', 'US presents new plan for the Middle East', or 'Germany objects to Dutch tomatoes'. These phrases are shorthand. They refer to an agreement among French and British diplomats to check the passports of passengers from Paris to London, or to an initiative of the German minister for agricultural affairs to reduce the import of watery vegetables. Messages such as these are the alpha and omega of politics and current affairs. And states are always at the centre.

Indeed, the study of states and the similarities and differences in their political institutions and forms of government are at the centre of the study of comparative politics and government. Even fashionable debates about the 'withering away' of the state in an era of globalisation are possible only if we are clear about the concept of the state to start with. Nor can we understand the politics of the European Union, a form of political organisation that is above and beyond individual states, unless we understand what states are and what they do. This does not mean that states are the only things that matter, nor does it mean that 'the state' is a perfectly clear and straightforward concept. But it does mean that the centrality of states in the modern world cannot be neglected, and that the 'state concept' is one of the most important building blocks of comparative politics. The starting point of our account of comparative government and politics is therefore the nature of the modern state. And the starting point of our account of the state is a pragmatic approach to the question: How do we recognise a state when we see one?

In this introduction, we shall deal with the emergence of the state and the state concept. In spite of the common use of the term, it is not easy to distinguish states from other organisations and institutes.

The five major topics in this chapter are:

- What is a state?
- Territory, people and sovereignty
- The rise of the modern state
- Catalysts: warfare and capitalism
- Growth after 1945.

■ What is a state?

The state is only one of many different ways of organising government. In the eighteenth century, when the French Assembly issued its 'Declaration of the Rights of Man and of the Citizen' (see briefing 1.1), states were not widely spread across the globe. Other forms of political organisation such as city-states, empires, princedoms and tribes were much more widespread. The state is a relatively recent political invention. Today, however, the whole world is divided into states, and the concept of the state has triumphed as a form of political organisation. With the exception of the high seas and Antarctica, every place on earth belongs to a state (see figure 1.1). Several areas are disputed among states and wars over territory are waged, but in general there is no quarrel about the fact that states are the main actors in these disputes.

Declaration of the Rights of Man The seventeen articles, describing the purpose of the state and the rights of individual citizens, proclaimed by the French National Assembly in August 1789. A similar list had been proclaimed in the USA in 1776.

Though states are universal, they still present a puzzle. Philosophers, politicians, jurists and political scientists have argued about them for centuries. It goes without saying that France, Denmark, Uruguay, or South Africa are states: all are independent political entities and each of them is recognised by the others as a state. You can find them on maps, their representatives meet in New York or Paris and you hear their national anthems on various occasions. Still, six key difficulties can arise when we try to characterise states in general terms:

- States vary hugely, ranging from France under Louis XIV to Montenegro, recognised in 2006 as one of about 193 independent states in the world. Modern democratic states range from India and Canada, to Denmark and New Zealand, and from Stalin's Soviet Union to Germany under Hitler. How can we put such a diverse collection of political phenomena into the same box labelled 'states'?
- Some forms of government look like states in some respects, but they are not actually states. The European Union and the Russian Federation

Briefing 1.1

First three articles of the 'Declaration of the Rights of Man and of the Citizen' (Paris, 1789)

1. Men are born and remain free and equal in rights. Social distinctions may be founded only upon the general good.
2. The aim of all political association is the preservation of the natural and imprescriptible[1] rights of man. These rights are liberty, property, security, and resistance to oppression.
3. The principle of all sovereignty resides essentially in the nation. No body nor individual may exercise any authority which does not proceed directly from the nation.

(www.yale.edu)

[1] 'Imprescriptible' means self-evident and obvious, and not derived from or dependent upon any external authority.

perform many state-like functions, but are they the same as states such as Argentina, Latvia, or Taiwan?

- The Vatican, Luxembourg, Monaco and San Marino look like states in some respects, but they are not the same as their neighbours, France and Italy.
- Some states have been recognised for centuries, but others, such as Israel and Palestine, are highly disputed. Is the latter a state simply because it calls itself one?
- Even for undisputed states such as France it is not easy to reach agreement about the exact date of its beginning. Was it in 1789? Or should we go back to the Treaty of Verdun in 843? Did states exist in Africa or Asia before European colonisers drew borders, almost haphazardly, through these continents? Were Babylon or Ancient Rome states as we understand them today?
- The term 'state' is quite close to other but different terms, such as country, nation, political system, nation-state and empire. To make things even more complicated, these terms are often confused or loosely used as synonyms.

We do not get a clear picture of what is meant by the term 'state' by simply looking at the different ways it is used (or misused) today. We have to be more systematic, and we can do this by following in the footsteps of the Greek philosopher Aristotle (384–322 BC). He began with the question: What distinguishes a state from other forms of social life? In the opening sentences of book I of his *Politics*, Aristotle remarks:

> Every state is a community of some kind, and every community is established with a view to some good . . . But, if all communities aim at some good, the state or political community, which is the highest of all, and which embraces all the rest, aims, and in greater degree than any other, at the highest good.
>
> *(Louise R. Loomis, ed., Aristotle: On Man in the Universe, Roslyn, NY: Black, 1943: 249)*

Figure 1.1: States of the world, 2007

Source: www.lib.utexas.edu/maps/world_maps/world_pol_2007.pdf

This characterisation contains a number of important assertions. First of all, a state is not some abstract construct, but a variant of human social life (a 'community'). It is, furthermore, not just any variant of social life, but the most important one ('the highest of all') and it can also be called a 'political community'. Finally, all other communities are included in the state because it 'embraces all the rest'. Modern states still claim to be the dominant force, just as Aristotle noted. In order to obtain and keep its place as the highest and most encompassing 'community', a state must be in charge: that is, it must be more powerful than any of the 'communities' it incorporates. This characterisation immediately suggests that **power** is vital for any discussion of states and politics. And yet even this focus on power, important though it is in defining the state, is not sufficient. States also have other characteristics to do with territory, people and sovereignty (controversy 1.1).

> **Power** The ability to make other people do what they do not want to do. Power is the ability to apply force.

CONTROVERSY 1.1

What is a state?

1. Do we have a clear idea about the state?

   What is a (or the) nation? No satisfactory criterion can be discovered for deciding which of the many human collectivities should be labelled in this way.

   (Eric Hobsbawm, Nations and Nationalism since 1780, *Cambridge: Cambridge University Press, 1990: 5*)

   As a concept the state has been somewhat overlooked in the political theory and research of the last century, especially in the Anglo-Saxon world, and still creates a good deal of confusion and uncertainty.

   (David Robertson, ed., The Penguin Dictionary of Politics, *Harmondsworth: Penguin, 1985: 308*)

2. Is the rise of states self-evident?

   Of the many theories addressing the problem of state origins, the simplest denies that there is any problem to solve. Aristotle considered states the natural condition of human society, requiring no explanation. His error was understandable, because all societies which with he would have been acquainted – Greek societies of the fourth century B.C. – were states. However, we now know that, as of A.D. 1492, much of the world was instead organised into chiefdoms, tribes, or bands. State formation does demand an explanation.

   (Jared Diamond, Guns, Germs, and Steel, *New York: Norton, 1999: 283*)

3. Where do states come from?

   If we now ask, where the state comes from, the answer is that it is the product of a long and arduous struggle in which the class which occupies what is for the time the key positions in the process of production gets the upper hand over its rivals and fashions a state which will enforce that set of property relations which is in its own interest. In other words any particular state is the child of the class or classes in society which benefit from the particular set of property relations which it is the state's obligation to enforce . . . the state power must be monopolised by the class or classes which are the chief beneficiaries.

   (Paul M. Sweezy, The Theory of Capitalist Development, *New York: Monthly Review Press, 1942: 242–3*)

■ Territory, people and sovereignty

States collect taxes, provide schools and highways, wage wars, control the opening hours of shops, regulate the sale of alcohol and cigarettes, and promote economic growth. They erect police stations and Inland Revenue offices, municipal swimming pools and embassies abroad, mints and hospitals and they employ fire fighters and soldiers. Some states improve the living conditions of their citizens and provide services for the young and old, the sick and disabled, and the poor and unemployed. But it is not difficult to find examples of states that behave quite differently – ranging from the protection of illegal money deposited in Swiss banks to war and the genocidal killing of innocent millions for 'reason of state'. How, then, do we recognise a state if virtually anything can and has been done by them?

In spite of confusion and continuing debate about the 'nature' of the state, it seems to be rather easy to recognise a **state.** Almost every state calls itself a 'state' and emphasises its uniqueness by having a national anthem, a flag, a coat of arms, a national currency, a national capital and a head

> **State** The organisation that issues and enforces binding rules for the people within a territory.

of state. States are acknowledged by other states as 'states', and they exchange ambassadors. These are, however, the symbols of statehood. At the heart of the matter lie three core features of the state:

- A state entails a **territory** that it considers to be its own. This area can be as huge as Canada or India, as small as The Netherlands or Switzerland, or even as tiny

  > **Territory** Terrain or geographical area.

  as Slovenia and Tuvalu. It can be an island or a continent (or, in the case of Australia, both), and its borders may have been undisputed and secure for centuries or constantly challenged. To the territory of a state belongs the air space above it as well as its coastal waters. The only restraint on the territorial aspect of the state is that it has to be more or less enduring; an ice floe – even one as large as France or Uruguay – does not

  > **Country** An imprecise synonym or short-hand term for state or nation-state.

  count. Sometimes the label 'territorial state' is used to underline the importance of this geographical feature. Less precisely, we commonly use the term *'country'*.

- A state entails a **people**, that is, *persons living together*. Here, too, numbers are irrelevant (think of China, India, the Palau Islands and Iceland). To be a people, the individuals concerned must have some-

  > **People** A group of people whose common consciousness and identity makes them a collective entity.

  thing in common, but exactly what they must share to be called 'a people' – language, religion, a common history, a culture – is a highly contested matter. Minorities who do not speak the same language, or share the same religion or culture can be found in almost every state in the world. For instance, 30 per cent of the citizens of Latvia are Russians. For the moment, we shall stick to the requirement that any state requires a population, and say nothing about minimum numbers or what they have in common. In other words a deserted island may be part of a state, but it cannot itself be a state. Equally, not all individuals are citizens of a state. As the number of exiles, migrants, and asylum seekers increases, so the problem of the stateless becomes ever more acute (briefing 1.2).

- A state is sovereign, that is, it holds the highest power and, in principle, can act with complete freedom and independence: it has **sovereignty**.

Sovereignty The highest power that gives the state freedom of action within its own territory.

Aristotle had something like this in mind with his remark that the state is a community 'which is the highest of all, and which embraces all the rest'. Sovereignty is a claim to ultimate authority and power. Usually, two types are distinguished: (i) internal sovereignty, meaning that within its own territory every state can act as it wishes and is independent of other powers and (ii) external sovereignty, referring to the fact that the state is recognised as a state by other states. Sovereignty means that a state is independent and not under the authority of another state or 'community'. Here, we must distinguish between power and sovereignty: the USA and Mauretania are equal as sovereign states, though the USA is vastly more powerful. States are also sovereign in principle, as we noted above. This does not necessarily mean that they are free to do whatever they want, because all sorts of factors may limit their powers – other states, the global

Briefing 1.2

Not every human being is a citizen . . .
Citizens are protected and supported by the state. They can usually get a passport, a licence to drive a car, admission to elementary education, a job, or assistance if they are unemployed or ill. Yet quite a number of citizens are forced to leave the state they were born in, because they are refugees, exiles, or asylum seekers. Those of us lucky enough to be secure in our citizenship are likely to take it for granted, but its great importance in our lives can be seen in the plight of those who are deprived of citizen rights – no residency rights, no working rights, no passport, no welfare services, no driving licence and perhaps no bank account. More and more people are in this situation as the number of migrants, exiles and asylum seekers grows. Which

state should provide a stateless person with a passport, work rights, or unemployment support? Many are very reluctant to take in citizens of other states and offer them the same rights as their own citizens.

In 1950, the UN created the High Commission for Refugees (UNHCR), a special organisation to deal with exiles and refugees. Its main aim was to find new places to live for about 400,000 people who had been forced to leave the place they lived in Europe after the Second World War. Initially, UNHCR was founded for three years, but in 2007 it was working harder than ever, faced with the problems of more than 31.7 million people: refugees, internally displaced persons (IDPs), returning refugees, the stateless and others of concern. (www.unhcr.org)

economy, even the weather. Moreover, states may voluntarily limit their power by signing international agreements, although if they are sovereign states they may also decide to revoke these agreements if circumstances change. Especially after the genocides in Bosnia (1992) and Rwanda (1994), states increasingly accept the idea that sovereignty cannot be invoked when genocide, ethnic cleansing and crimes against humanity occur. Nor can states ignore those events beyond their borders simply because action does not suit their national interests (see briefing 1.3).

Each state is characterised by these three features; each claims sovereign power over its people and its territory. More specifically, we can speak of a state as an organisation that issues and enforces rules for a territorially defined area that are binding for people in that area. Sovereignty does not mean that the state is above the law. Indeed, most states constrain their sovereign power by subjecting them to the rules of a constitution (see chapter 4).

Straightforward as this definition of a state may seem to be, there are still complications. Some regions in the south of Italy are, in effect, controlled by the Mafia in a state-like manner. Multi-national companies (MNCs) such as Nike or Shell, and organisations such as the IMF, are also hugely powerful. Did the states of The Netherlands and Belgium disappear when they were occupied by Germany in the 1940s?

Briefing 1.3

R2P: sovereignty entails responsibility

Each individual State has the responsibility to protect its populations from genocide, war crimes, ethnic cleansing and crimes against humanity. This responsibility entails the prevention of such crimes, including their incitement, through appropriate and necessary means. We accept that responsibility and will act in accordance with it.

(Resolution adopted by the UN General Assembly:
60/1. 2005 World Summit Outcome)

... recognising that this responsibility lies first and foremost with each individual state, but also that, if national authorities are unable or unwilling to protect their citizens, the responsibility then shifts to the international community; and that, in the last resort, the United Nations Security Council may take enforcement action according to the Charter.

(Statement by Kofi Anan, UN Secretary-General to the General Assembly,
21 March 2005 (www.un.org/largerfreedom/sg-statement.html))

The *Responsibility to Protect* means that no state can hide behind the concept of sovereignty while it conducts – or permits – widespread harm to its population. Nor can states turn a blind eye when these events extend beyond their borders, nor because action does not suit their narrowly-defined national interests.

These principles were set forth in a report entitled *The Responsibility to Protect* (R2P), and continue to evolve and develop new meaning as the international community comes to understand that sovereignty entails responsibility.

(www.responsibilitytoprotect.org/index.php/pages/2)

In order to deal with those complications, the notion of the state is further specified by looking more closely at sovereignty. The German social scientist Max Weber (1864–1920) did this stressing, first of all, that the abstract term 'sovereignty' meant that the state possessed the monopoly of the use of physical force. Only if the state controlled the use of physical force could it impose its rules and realise its claims as the most important 'community'. Weber moved one crucial step further. In his view, the control of physical force was not sufficient for statehood. Also required was a 'monopoly' that was accepted as right – a monopoly that was not only legal, but also has **legitimacy**. The Weberian definition of the state, then, consists of four elements:

> **Legitimacy** The condition of being in accordance with the norms and values of the people. 'Legitimate power' is accepted because it is seen as right.

- Weber accepts the three conventional characteristics of a state – territory, people, sovereignty.
- He specifies the meaning of 'sovereignty' by referring to the distinction between 'legal' and 'legitimate'. It is not sufficient to base physical force upon the law (legality). The use of physical force must also be accepted as right, and morally legitimate by citizens.
- The use of physical force alone, therefore, does not distinguish between states and other organisations. Organisations such as Microsoft, the World Bank, the IMF, the Mafia and the European Union are powerful, and may be more important for many people than, say, the state of Latvia or Iceland. Some of these organisations use physical force, but none of them claims the monopoly of the legitimate use of this force over its people as states do.
- Finally, Weber points to the fact that some actor or institution must monopolise the legitimate use of physical force if the state is to avoid the danger of anarchy and lawlessness. Usually, we call this actor or institution the **government** of a state.

> **Government** A government has a monopoly of the legitimate use of physical force within a state. Securing internal and external sovereignty of the state are major tasks of any government.

We can see these elements in Max Weber's definition of the state:

> A compulsory political organisation with continuous operations will be called a 'state' insofar as its administrative staff successfully uphold the claim to the *monopoly* of the *legitimate* use of physical force in the enforcement of its order.
> (Max Weber, Economy and Society: An Outline of Interpretative Sociology, eds. Guenther Roth and Claus Wittich, New York: Bedminster Press 1968: 54; emphasis in the original)

Can we recognise a state if we see one with the help of Weber's characterisation? Most of the time it will not be too difficult to grasp that a trade agreement between Chile and Argentina will involve two states, or that Romania's application for EU membership is an act of state. Similarly, traffic regulations are enforced by the police in the name of their state, as are invitations to participate in public elections. All these are based on the claim of a monopoly of the legitimate use of physical force over people living in a specific area – and so all are acts of state.

We mentioned earlier that other terms are sometimes used in place of 'state'. States are often referred to as 'countries' or 'nations' or as 'nation-states', so we now examine what makes a country a state and a state a nation-state, by looking at the development of the modern state and the processes of state and nation building.

> **Nation-state** A state based on the acceptance of a common culture, a common history and a common fate, irrespective of whatever political, social and economic differences may exist between the members of the nation-state.

■ The rise of the modern state

The state emerged in medieval Europe, between about 1100 and the sixteenth century. In that period, territorially based rulers claimed independence and created their own administrations and armies. At the same time, the idea of sovereign power was developed. However, each state has its own unique historical patterns in its progress towards modern statehood, and none follows quite the same path. Any discussion of state formation and the development of states must therefore start from a two-fold assertion: (i) the state concept is inextricably bound up with European history and Western political theory, and (ii) there is no uniform or general law that governs the appearance, or disappearance, of states.

Historical origins and development

States originate in many different ways and their development follows no single pathway. There are three general patterns, however:

- *Transformation* First, states arose on the basis of the gradual transformation of existing independent political units – mostly medieval monarchies. Major examples were Britain and France, whose independence goes back to the Middle Ages and whose development as states took several centuries. In Europe the Treaty of Westphalia signalled the final triumph of the state as a form of political organisation, as well as settling the borders of many states (see fact file 1.1).
- *Unification* Second, some states arose by the unification of independent but dispersed political units. This process was mainly concentrated in the nineteenth century and major examples were Germany and Italy.
- *Secession* Finally, states arose from the secession or break-up of independent political units – mostly empires or large heterogeneous states – into one or more states. The break-up of the Austro-Hungarian Empire and the Ottoman Empire after the First World War are examples. In Africa and Asia decolonization after the Second World War resulted in many new states after former occupied territories gained independence. More recently, Czechoslovakia was split into two independent states: the Czech Republic and Slovakia.

Fact file 1.1

The Treaty of Westphalia (1648)
The first decades of the seventeenth century were characterised by a series of wars between Spain, France, Sweden, Bavaria, The Netherlands, Denmark and countries in central Europe, known as the *Thirty Years War* (1618–48). It destroyed about 2,000 castles, 1,600 cities and more than 18,000 villages across Europe. The population of the war-torn area declined about 50 per cent in rural areas, and up to 30 per cent in urban regions. This changed the economic, demographic and political landscape in Europe profoundly and eventually led to a settlement that, in effect, created the state system of the modern world.

In a situation of continual wars and conflicts, it slowly became clear that a solution could be based on a 'package deal' between different sides. In 1648, delegates from the warring factions met in the cities of Osnabrück and Münster in Westphalia to negotiate an all-encompassing peace treaty. The final set of agreements is called the *Treaty of Westphalia* or the *Peace of Westphalia*. It had very important consequences for the division of power – and therefore for the development of states – in Europe. The agreements recognised the rights of states and their sovereignty, settled the religious disputes in Europe and provided solutions for a number of territorial claims. Most important, the Treaty established a system of states, and of diplomatic relations between them, that has lasted more or less intact until the present day.

Most new states today, such as those born out of the collapse of the Soviet Union and Yugoslavia, are the product of secession. Few states are now the result of successful attempts to unify formerly divided or dispersed independent units.

State formation and nation building

One of the best-known efforts to account for the different historical paths taken by the modern states of Europe is presented by the Norwegian political scientist Stein Rokkan (1921–79). In his view, the formation of modern states proceeded in several phases, which are closely linked to basic societal conflicts ('**cleavages**'). Rokkan also distinguished between state formation and nation building. The first concerns the creation of state institutions, especially an army, a bureaucracy, and a system of government. The second involves welding the population of the state into a single 'people' with a shared sense of belonging that often comes from a common language, religion, education, historical heritage and culture.

> **Cleavages** Cleavages are deep and persistent differences in society where (1) objective social differences (class, religion, race, language, or region) are aligned with (2) subjective awareness of these differences (different cultures, ideologies and orientations).

Rokkan discerned four stages in the development of the modern state. The first two are generated by powerful elites who attempt to consolidate their power and territorial independence. The second two are of a quite different nature and concern the internal restructuring of established states.

The four stages are:

- State formation
- Nation building
- Mass democracies
- Welfare states.

State formation: penetration

In the first phase, elites took the initiative for the *unification of a given territory*, usually the elites of major urban centres who consolidated their control over peripheral and rural areas. Territorial consolidation was achieved mainly by economic and military means. In order to control these territories and secure their compliance, institutions were built to provide internal order and deal with disputes (police and courts), to provide external security (armed forces and diplomatic services), to extract resources (taxes and tolls) and to improve communications (roads and bridges), often for military reasons. Clear demarcation of territory was crucially important. Broadly speaking, the period of state formation in Europe started in the high Middle Ages and lasted until the foundations of the western European state system, enshrined in the Treaty of Westphalia (see fact file 1.1).

Nation building: standardisation

During the second phase of nation building the main concerns were cultural issues of a common language, religious differences and compulsory education. The aim was to create feelings of a common identity and a sense of allegiance to the political system among the often disparate populations of the new states. A common, standardised language was spread by compulsory education for every child. Military conscription for young men strengthened feelings of identity with the nation. The central idea of the nation-state is the acceptance of a common culture, a common history and a common fate, irrespective of any social and economic differences between people. If the historical roots of this common fate were not self-evident – and usually they were not – national myths about shared experiences and historical destinies were often created and spread through the school system. In order to heighten national identity, 'system symbols' – such as a national hymn, national flag and national heroes – were emphasised. By developing this sense of 'belonging', elites tried to transform their states into nation-states.

Mass democracies: equalisation

Although the nation-state is now the 'property' of its citizenry it was elites, not masses, who originally created and ruled it. In the third phase the masses conquered the right to participate in governmental decision making, and hence democratic states (or democracies) were created. Political parties were founded to link citizens with elites in assemblies and parliaments. Less visible – but certainly not less significant – was the institutionalisation of opposition parties: gradually these political systems accepted the idea that peaceful opposition to the government was legitimate, and even the idea of peaceful change of groups or parties in government. The idea of the alternation of parties in government was associated with the belief in the principle of the legitimacy of popularly elected government. Hence universal adult suffrage was introduced at a fairly early stage, although women usually had to wait much longer to vote. In mass democracies, political power is legitimated by mass participation and elections. The earliest mass democracies arose in Europe towards the end of the nineteenth century.

Welfare states: redistribution

The last phase in the development of the territorial state is the explicit endorsement of policies to strengthen economic solidarity between different parts of the population. Public welfare services were created to support the young and old, the sick and disabled, and the unemployed and poor. Progressive taxation and state contributions facilitate the transfer of resources from the wealthier to the less fortunate parts of the population. **Welfare states**, characterised by redistribution and equality of opportunity, were created, particularly in north-western Europe after the Second World War.

Welfare states Democracies that accept responsibility for the well-being of their citizens, particularly by redistributing resources and providing services for the young, old, sick, disabled and unemployed.

Few states went through these four stages from the medieval period to the third millennium in a more or less regular and ordered way (France and Britain are exceptional). In many cases, the order of the four stages was interrupted by revolution, war or foreign occupation (as for Germany) and it is not easy to say when some phases started or how long they lasted. When, for example, did Italy become a welfare state? In some instances, phases overlapped or coincided. Spain combined the last two phases after its transition to democracy in the 1970s. Some phases are very long for some states, but hardly discernible for others. In other words, the history of each state is too complex and diverse to be covered by a simple, uniform scheme. Rokkan's four phases help us understand the process of state and nation building not because each state follows exactly the same pattern but because we can compare and understand how they developed by describing how each deviates from, or conforms to, the general pattern. In spite of their differences, however, the early developments of almost all states were in the early stages driven by two fundamental and enormously powerful forces: warfare and capitalism.

Catalysts: warfare and capitalism

The initial phase of the state building process in Europe, as we have seen, is focused on securing the compliance of territories with the wishes of centralising elites. Military might was important in this process. Military technology changed in the late medieval period, replacing the heavy cavalry with massed infantry and, later, with artillery and guns. Small private armies with an obligation to a feudal lord were replaced by large standing armies serving the state. The rights and powers of local landowners and of the nobility were replaced by centralised state power and resources. At the same time, the need to wage war against internal and external enemies functioned as catalysts for state formation, because only states were able to organise and pay for the large armies and the wars they fought. War was a normal state of affairs for the emerging states of the sixteenth and seventeenth centuries: great powers such as Spain, France, England, and The Netherlands were very frequently at war during this period. Persistent involvement in wars and the long-term struggle for domination of territories over centuries of European history can thus be seen as the primary factor behind the emergence of the modern state with all its powers and capacities.

The rise of capitalism in the eighteenth and nineteenth century also facilitated the emergence of the modern state. The capitalist mode of production brings together two important factors – labour and capital – for the creation of goods that can be sold at a profit. But this production process depends on the availability of a secure infrastructure; that is, investment and profit depend on social and physical security and stability. The infrastructure necessary for capitalism and profit includes not just roads, bridges, harbours, canals and railways but also educational and health facilities, as well as police to protect property and a legal system regulating contracts and commercial disputes. Some of these can be produced only by a central power, while others require central regulation and control.

Capitalism, then, requires an agency capable of the following four tasks:

- To secure investments
- To provide social and physical infrastructures
- To control and regulate conflicts between capitalists and other classes
- To protect the interests of capitalists and other classes against competition from abroad.

The obvious institution to perform these functions is the state with its territorial boundary, its monopoly of the legitimate use of physical force, and its power to tax and provide collective facilities and services. No other institution can perform these functions as effectively, and without the state there could be no capitalism.

Was the state created to wage war and promote capitalism? In large part, yes, but this interpretation is too simple for the complex, difficult and varied process of state formation. Warfare and capitalism are certainly very important factors in the formation of states and the development of states in Europe. Yet none of these factors accounts for the initial rise of independent territorial units and the idea of sovereignty. The demands of war and profit certainly strengthen the formation of territorially defined political units that became known as states, but equally they were also important catalysts rather than direct causes of state formation.

Growth after 1945

From Europe, the idea of the state rapidly spread over the world, but it was not until the second half of the twentieth century that the number of states suddenly increased. After the First and Second World Wars, states founded special organisations to deal with relations among themselves, especially with regard to international conflicts. Some observers even looked forward to the creation of a single 'world state'. The League of Nations was created in 1919, but not all those eligible applied for membership and the organisation remained rather weak. After the Second World War a new organisation of states was set up: the United Nations (UN). UN membership is an unambiguous sign of internationally recognised statehood, and virtually all states have joined. Only the Vatican, DAR Sahara, the Palestinian Territories, Kosovo and Taiwan are not members of the UN, although they can be considered states. For a long time Switzerland declined membership to underline its international neutrality, but it joined the UN in 2002.

The spread of states over the world is illustrated by the steady growth of UN membership. Figure 1.2 shows the increase from about fifty states in 1945 to 192 in 2007. Three stages of growth are evident:

- A first occurs in the second half of the 1950s, when a first wave of decolonisation (e.g. Ghana, Morocco, Tunisia, Libya, Laos) took place. In addition, the recognition of 'spheres of influence' for the USA and the Soviet Union (USSR) allowed a number of states (e.g. Albania, Austria, Finland, Japan, Romania) to become UN members.
- Decolonisation also marks the second wave of the spread of states, which started in the early 1960s (including Algeria, Gabon, Senegal, Chad) and lasted until well into the 1970s (Surinam, Mozambique, Vietnam). By 1980, more than 155 states were UN members.
- The last rapid increase took place after 1989, when the collapse of the Soviet Union and the end of communist rule in central and eastern Europe caused a fresh wave of nation-state creation in places such as Hungary, Latvia, Lithuania and Poland. The spread of states, however, continued because of the foundation of new ones (including Bosnia-Herzegovina, the Czech Republic and Slovakia in the 1990s and Kosovo in 2008) and because of the search for recognition among existing countries, such as Kiribati and Tonga.

Occasionally states disappear. This was the case with the unification of East and West Germany in 1990 and North and South Yemen in the same year. Attempts to obtain independence by regional or ethnic separatist movements in some parts of the world probably mean that states will continue to increase in number in the coming decades.

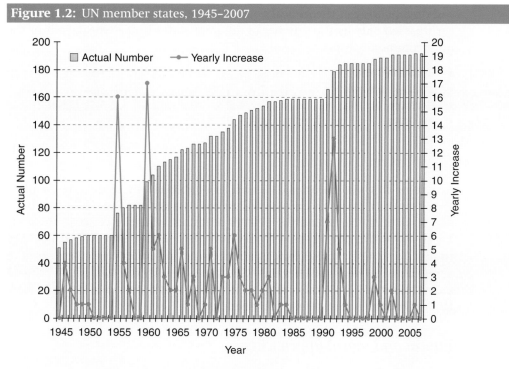

Figure 1.2: UN member states, 1945–2007

Based on: United Nations: Growth in the United Nations Membership, 1945-present (www.un.org/members/growth.shtml#1940).

■ State theories

The state has fascinated political theorists since the rise of the Greek city-state and the writings of Aristotle and Plato more than 2,400 years ago. Modern theories fall into two very broad categories. First, there are **normative political theories**. These are based on values and judgements about how the world should be, and what governments ought to do. Normative theories of the state are discussed in some detail in chapter 13.

> **Normative political theories** Theories about how the world should be or ought to be.

Second, there are **empirical political theories**, completely different from normative theories, about how the state actually operates and why it operates that way.

> **Empirical political theories** Theories that try to understand, by examining the evidence, how the political world actually works and why it works that way.

We shall present a systematic overview of empirical theories of the state based on the relations between states and societies at the end of chapter 2. For the moment, it is enough to note that political scientists, historians and philosophers have presented a very large and diverse array of theoretical approaches to the state and its origin, which is surpassed only by the number of different states in the world. Four of the most common approaches are:

- Constitutional
- Ethical and moral
- Conflict
- Pluralist.

Constitutional approaches

According to these theories, the state is established by some agreement or social contract between citizens and rulers that defines the major functions and tasks of the state and the powers of its rulers. Social contract theorists know very well that there never was an actual 'contract' of this kind, but they conduct a sort of mental experiment in order to understand what sorts of agreements between citizens and rulers are necessary to establish an ordered and stable state. The main concern of these theories is the question of how the *legitimacy* of the state is established.

Ethical and moral approaches

The starting point of these theories is how we can organise society so that individuals can live together as peacefully and satisfactorily as possible. Some take the view that society consists of individuals who should be as free as possible to do what they wish. Others view society as a collective entity that should ensure the collective well-being and welfare of its individual citizens. A variant of such views is the religious theories that argue that the state should establish the rule of God on earth, or else ensure that the state conducts its affairs according to God's intentions and rules.

Conflict approaches

These theories stress the conflicting nature of interests and values in society and see the state as a device to exercise the power necessary to regulate these conflicts. Marxist theories are one version of this approach. They emphasise the unavoidable struggle between different classes and their incompatible economic interests, and claim that the state is nothing other than an instrument by which property owners maintain their power over the great mass of the working class. As we have already seen, capitalism and state building were closely connected, and from this it can also be argued that the state is the means by which capitalists control other classes in society in order to secure their own interests. Feminist theories of the state are similar in some respects to class theories, but instead of seeing the world in terms of classes they see it as divided between male and female interests. Feminists argue that the state has been used by men to control women, and that it should now become the battle ground for women's liberation.

Pluralist approaches

Like conflict approaches, pluralist theories see the state as the main instrument for the regulation of conflict and the reconciliation of competing interests. But rather than arguing that the state is the instrument of the ruling class, pluralists see it as a kind of referee that uses its legitimate authority (force if necessary) to make sure that the interests of all groups are treated reasonably fairly. The state is a battle ground for many competing groups, not an instrument of class control and oppression.

Other theories

This does not exhaust the main theories of the state, nor the many variations on each of the main approaches, and you will inevitably encounter other theories and other variations. It will be helpful to ask four questions about any new theory in order to get an idea of its main content and concerns:

1. Is the theory a normative one that deals with the ideals and goals of the state, or is it an empirical theory that tries to describe and understand the nature and organisation of the state – the way in which the state actually operates as opposed to how it should operate?
2. Does the theory start from individual rights and duties and the importance of preserving them (in which case it is probably an individualist one)? Or does it start from the mutual obligations and interdependence of citizens (in which case it is probably a collectivist one)?
3. Does the theory emphasise the laws and the formal structure of institutions of the state (in which case it is likely to have its roots in organisational or constitutional approaches)?
4. Does the theory concentrate on the competing interests of classes, ethnic groups, or men and women (in which case it is likely to be a conflict theory), or does it emphasise the capacity of the state to reconcile and integrate the interests of different social groups (in which case it is likely to belong to the pluralist family)?

■ What have we learned?

This chapter has dealt with the difficulties of characterising and defining states, and with the historical development of modern states.

- Although globalisation is widely said to be reducing the power and importance of the state, or even causing its death, the number of states in the world is still rising. With the exception of Antarctica and the high seas, every spot on earth belongs to one of the 195 or so states in the world today.

- States are characterised by three features: territory, people and sovereignty.
- Ultimately, states are based upon the power of their armies, police and the law but to be stable and democratic the use of state force must be regarded as legitimate by its citizens. That is, the use of power should be in accordance with the norms and values of its citizens. The term 'legitimacy' is especially used by Max Weber in his definition of the state.
- Globalisation is widely claimed to cause the declining power of the state, even its death, but in spite of this, states retain a huge amount of power over their citizens and as actors in the international system.

■ Lessons of comparison

The historical perspective produces several important conclusions:

- States are only one of many forms of political organisation. They developed in Europe in the late medieval period and their rights and sovereignty were recognised by the Treaty of Westphalia (1648). From Europe they gradually spread over the rest of the world.
- States arise out of the transformation of existing political units, from the unification of different political units and as a result of the secession of political units that become independent. Historically, the creation of each state has followed a unique path, but in general, four main stages of development can be discerned: state formation, nation building, mass democratisation and welfare development.
- Warfare and capitalism have played a major role in most cases.

Projects

1. Would you call the country you live in a 'nation' (or a 'nation-state')? What makes it a state, and when did it achieve statehood?
2. Draw up lists of:
   (1) the ten largest and smallest states in the world
   (2) the ten oldest and youngest states in the world
   (3) the ten richest and poorest states in the world.
   What do the oldest states have in common compared with the youngest, and what do the richest have in common compared with the poorest?
3. Why is it so difficult to combine sovereignty with R2P (*Responsibility to Protect*) measures?
4. Why is the number of states in the world still increasing?

Further reading

P. Dunleavy and B. O'Leary, *Theories of the State: The Politics of Liberal Democracy*, Basingstoke: Macmillan, 1987.
An overview of discussions of the state and its development.

G. Gill, *The Nature and Development of the Modern State*, Basingstoke: Palgrave, 2003.
A concise overview of the state and its development.

H. Spruyt, 'The origins, development, and possible decline of the modern state', *Annual Review of Political Science*, Vol. 5, Palo Alto, Ca. 2002: 127–149.
An excellent review of the main streams of thought.

T. Ertman, 'State formation and state building in Europe', in T. Janoski *et al.*, *The Handbook of Political Sociology*, Cambridge, Cambridge University Press, 2005: 367–383.
A review of work on the origins and development of the concept of the state and the major theoretical approaches to it.

A. Vincent, *Theories of the State*, Oxford, Blackwell, 1987.
A concise general account of state theories.

Websites

www.un.org
Official website of the UN. Provides information on the UN as well as links to specific organisations.
www.countrystudies.us /
Statistical information about many economic, social, political, geographical, historical and demographical developments in many states.
www.state.uni-bremen.de
Academic research network on the changes of the state under the pressure of globalisation and liberalisation.
www.nd.edu/~apsacp/data.html
Overview of the most important databases available for comparative politics.

2 States and democracy

With only a few special exceptions, the entire surface of the world is divided between states. Yet it is not self-evident that comparative politics should focus on states as the main form of organised politics. After all, in the increasingly globalising world there are many other forms of organisation that have a big impact on politics and on daily existence in general. The European Union, Microsoft and al-Qa'ida are more powerful than many states and affect the lives of millions of people. If it is true that the European concept of the state is in decline, then why should we try to understand the state and its actions when newer political actors appear to be so important? This chapter starts with the question of why we continue to regard states as the most important building blocks of comparative analysis, when some writers claim that they are being replaced in importance in an increasingly global society.

The second problem is that even if we concentrate attention on states as a form of political organisation, there are a great many of them in the world and they come in a huge variety of shapes and sizes. Some are as old as France or as new as East Timor and Montenegro; some are large like Canada and India or small like Estonia and Namibia; some are as rich as Sweden or as poor as Mali. To cover all of them in a satisfactory manner is not possible within the covers of a single book, so in this one we concentrate on democratic states. But how do we recognise a democratic state when we see one?

In theory, one of the defining characteristics of **democracy** is a form of government in which the great mass of citizens can participate in political decision making and policy making. Nevertheless, even in tiny communities, such as the classical city-state of Athens or a Swiss commune of a few thousand people, it is very difficult to base government on the direct political participation of many people. For this reason government is usually in the hands of a comparatively small number of elected representatives who are supposed to exercise their power in the interests of the much larger number of people they represent. Therefore modern democracy immediately raises all sorts of questions about the ways in which the elected representatives are to be held responsible and accountable to citizens, and about the civil and political rights and duties of citizens that elected representatives should respect and preserve. We can judge the state of democracy according to the degree to which these civil and political rights are observed and the degree to which elected representatives are responsive and accountable to citizens.

> **Democracy** 'A political system whose leaders are elected in competitive multi-party and multi-candidate processes' (Freedom House).

Democracies do more than guarantee formal civil and political rights, however. They also accept responsibility, to a greater or lesser extent, for the welfare of their citizens: for the young and the old, the sick and the disabled and the unemployed and the poor. Sometimes their welfare services are extensive, sometimes minimal, but all democracies have adopted them to some extent. Since support for the less-advantaged social groups is based on the redistribution of resources among various groups, political decision making in welfare states can be very complicated and controversial.

The five major topics covered in this chapter are:

- Why study states?
- The modern state and democracy
- The rise of democratic states
- Redistribution and welfare states
- Theories of state and society.

■ Why study states?

It is a paradox that the power and importance of states seems to be in decline at the very time that states have captured almost every corner of the world's surface and when the number of states is at an all-time high. Nonetheless, new technologies have made it possible to locate the production of goods and services almost anywhere on the globe. Transport and communications, and especially information technology (IT) have created a 'global village'. Even wars are no longer restricted to conflicts between neighbouring states, but involve terrorist groups and special forces all over the world. As a result, the powers of states are increasingly limited by growing international interdependencies and interconnections, and by thousands of collective inter-national arrangements and agreements that limit the freedom of any one state to control its own affairs. The world, it is argued, is increasingly forming a single system, a trend described as **globalisation**.

Globalisation The growing interdependencies and interconnectedness of the world that reduces the autonomy of individual states and the importance of boundaries between them.

Part of the globalisation process involves the emergence of international organisations that challenge the pre-eminence of states. The United Nations and the European Union are perhaps the most conspicuous, but they are not alone, for there are other transnational organisations such as the North American Free Trade Association (NAFTA) and the Association of South East Asian Nations (ASEAN), as well as bodies such as the World Bank (IBRD – International Bank for Reconstruction and Development), and the International Monetary Fund (IMF). In recent decades a wave of new organisations known as non-governmental organisations (**NGOs**) such as Greenpeace, Transparency International, and Médecins Sans Frontières have joined the long list of older organisations that include the Catholic Church, the International Labour Organisation (ILO) and the Red Cross that operate on a world-wide scale to try to influence the policies and actions of states. Nor should we forget the growth of huge and powerful multi-national business corporations (MNCs). Microsoft is wealthier and more powerful than quite a few member states of the UN. If multi-national companies, non-governmental organisations and international bodies are now beyond full state control and regulation, then perhaps we should pay less attention to states and concentrate on the really important and powerful actors on the world stage (see controversy 2.1)?

NGOs Non-profit, private and non-violent organisations that are independent of government but seek to influence or control public policy without actually seeking government office.

Could it be that the European state, first given its seal of approval in the Treaty of Westphalia (see fact file 1.1), is now as outdated as the horse and carriage? Though this idea may seem realistic and up to date, it fails to take account of the fact that states are still the most important single group of actors in politics. They continue to be sovereign within their own territory, even if this sovereignty (chapter 1) is now more limited and circumscribed by international forces than it used to be. Even international terrorism is directed towards states and their representatives. Moreover, genocide, war crimes, ethnic cleansing and crimes against humanity all are directly linked to states and struggles for state power and independence. States have the main responsibility to protect their populations against those crimes. States have governments with supreme power within their borders and international relations continue to be conducted on this basis. Only states have the funds to bail out private financial institutions in times of huge financial crisis, and only states have the necessary credibility to offer their populations security in such times of crisis (see briefing 2.1). In short, states remain pre-eminently important, and they remain, therefore, the main focus and point of departure for the comparative approach to politics and government.

CONTROVERSY 2.1

Focusing on the state is …

Area of debate	Right, because	Wrong, because
Euro-centrism	Although the idea of the modern state originated in Europe, every corner of the world is now claimed by states.	The idea of the modern state is Euro-centred and ideologically loaded, and should be replaced by concepts taking account of political arrangements in other cultures.
National sovereignty and globalisation	States still claim sovereignty and only a very small part of the world (covered by the EU in Europe) has succeeded in establishing a trans-national form of government that may render the state obsolete.	The rise of regional and trans-national forms of government (EU, NAFTA and ASEAN/UN), of international government agencies (IMF, World Bank), of international NGOs (Greenpeace, ILO) and MNCs (Microsoft, Ford) shows that national sovereignty is losing its relevance.
Legacy and impact	States developed over several centuries and they continue to exercise a powerful influence on social, political and economic life.	States are based on old ideas and practices and should be replaced by more appropriate concepts for the present world, and especially to understand future developments.
Number	The number of states increases continuously.	The number of powerful states does not change; the newest states are small and unimportant.
Power	States are the most important actors in politics and they are in charge of military and economic power.	Only a few large states are important. Organisations such as the EU, Microsoft and the World Bank have more power than many states.
Financial liability and security	Only states can regulate markets and are able to accept liabilities when private actors and NGOs fall short.	Market failures and crises show the lack of power of states to protect their citizens. Only international action can deal with these problems.
Regional separatism	Many serious conflicts in the world – the Middle East, Caucasus, etc. – are a direct consequence of the struggle for independence and recognition as a state.	Restricting political independence to the founding of states is the cause of these conflicts and hampers more innovative approaches.
Terrorism and crime	States are the most important objects of international terrorism.	International terrorism and crime is not state organised and is a threat to state power.

Genocide, war crimes, ethnic cleansing, crimes against humanity	Conflicts about state power cause these problems and states are responsible for the protection of their citizens.	The spread of these problems shows the lack of power of states to protect their citizens. International action is the only solution.
Waning importance	Growing interdependencies between states confirm their crucial role. Interdependencies are best understood in terms of changing relations between states, rather than their decline.	Growing interdependencies show that states are losing their central position. It is more appropriate to focus on interdependencies and contacts and accept the decline of the state.
War	Wars are waged between states.	International terrorism means that the most important acts of violence are no longer restricted to states.

Briefing 2.1

Only the state can bail out private actors and guarantee financial security

In the first years of the twentieth-first century housing prices exploded in many countries and personal debts increased as people tried to raise their standard of living. Banks and other financial institutions provided easy mortgage credits and loans to finance this boom and make big profits. With the collapse of the housing and finance markets in the USA in September 2008 many of these credits and debts appeared to be virtually worthless and even the largest and wealthiest banks could not avoid the threat of bankruptcy. The result was not only massive loss of money and capital value but also loss of confidence in the whole system. The whole American finance system was instantly endangered – and with it almost every other financial system in the world. Only states had enough resources and credibility to bail out private actors and restore confidence in the financial system, and in these extraordinary circumstances governments and central banks injected huge amounts of money in order to stabilise the financial system. This underlines and reaffirms the uniqueness of states among the large organisations of the world:

- *United States*: issued a bail-out package of $700 billion (that is 700 with nine additional zeros) and took over some major investments banks and insurance companies;
- *United Kingdom*: acquired controlling stakes in some large banks in exchange for a $64 billion capital infusion. In addition $430 billion were provided as loan guarantees;
- *France*: injected $54 billion in banks in return for equity. As in Britain $430 billion were provided as loan guarantees;
- *Germany*: made $108 billion available to recapitalise banks and provided $540 billion as loan guarantees;
- *Iceland*: the country became *de facto* insolvent due to the run on its banks, and so the state approached the IMF and Russia for very large loans.

Source: International Herald Tribune, *October 14, 2008.*

States exist in such a huge variety of forms that we cannot deal satisfactorily with all of them within the covers of a single volume. Therefore, we concentrate on that especially important and increasingly widespread group of states that are democracies. Concentrating in this way on democracies enables us to compare and contrast a group of similar states: we are able to compare apples with apples, and not apples with oranges. At the same time, many of the democracies are found in European, Anglo-Saxon and North American countries and, therefore, these are inevitably overrepresented in our analyses. We will return to this difficulty in the Postscript.

■ The modern state and democracy

Mass political involvement transformed states into 'mass democracies' when the rights of opposition were recognised and general suffrage granted. Stein Rokkan emphasised the fact that the internal restructuring of the state converts subjects of the state into citizens, collectively known as the 'masses' or 'the people' (see chapter 1). But how do we distinguish between democratic and non-democratic states in the first place? Usually, this question is answered by referring to citizens' rights, elections and parliamentary accountability.

Citizens' rights

Discussions about political power and the rights of citizens have always been at the centre of debates about democracy. As the members of the French National Assembly confirmed in August 1789, the struggle for political power is not an aim in itself. It is what can be done with that power that matters. After all, Article 2 of the 'Declaration of the Rights of Man and of the Citizen' published in Paris (briefing 1.1) talks about the goal of all political institutions being 'the natural and inalienable rights of man'. In a similar way, the Virginia 'Bill of Rights' – published in 1776, thirteen years earlier than the French document – stressed the universal nature of these rights. A first characteristic of democracies, then, is the acknowledgement that it is not power but the protection of rights ('**human rights**') that is of prime concern.

> **Human rights** The innate, inalienable and inviolable right of humans to free movement and self-determination. Such rights cannot be bestowed, granted, limited, bartered or sold away. Inalienable rights can be only secured or violated.

Following this line of reasoning, the constitutions of many states start with an enumeration of human rights before political institutions and powers are defined (see chapter 4). Some constitutions even borrow heavily from the documents published in Paris and Virginia in the late eighteenth century.

The most common rights include:

- Freedom of speech and the press
- Freedom of religion and conscience
- Freedom of assembly and association

- Right to equal protection of the law
- Right to due process of law and to fair trial
- Property rights to land, goods and money.

Protecting these rights is the first aim of democratic political systems. Apart from anything else, they have a special political importance for both ordinary citizens and political leaders. If human rights are protected, citizens and leaders can engage in peaceful political conflict without fear of reprisals so that free competition for political power should result, on election day, in government by those winning most popular support. Competition alone is not sufficient to guarantee this, however; challengers must be allowed to join the struggle and losers should not be victimised because they were on the losing side. In this way democracy can gain the consent of losers and winners alike and so it can also be 'government of the people, by the people, for the people', as the American president Abraham Lincoln (1809–65) stated in his famous Gettysburg Address.

Elections and parliamentary accountability

The development of mass democracies began in a few countries in the nineteenth century. The basic idea at the time was not that citizens should be directly involved in politics, but should rely on being represented by elected political leaders. The main political task of citizens was to elect representatives (see chapter 11) who would govern on their behalf (representative democracy). Although this was an important step towards democracy, it was not 'democracy' as we would define it today. Only after long struggles between factions and competing elites was it recognised that democracies must function with the consent of their citizens, and later still with their active participation (participatory democracy). This meant that the principle of parliamentary accountability to citizens came to be incorporated into the democratic ideal. It was accepted in France in 1870, in Germany in 1918, but not until 1976 in Spain (see table 2.1). In several countries it took a long time before the new constitutional rules were realised in practice, often because autocrats and elites had to give up their privileges first. The Dutch constitution of 1848 formulates the principle of accountability, but it was not actually put into practice until 1866.

Representative democracy That form of democracy in which citizens elect leaders who govern in their name.

Participatory democracy Democracy in which citizens actively and directly participate in government.

Similarly, voting rights were extended only slowly and in stages. Several democracies completed universal male suffrage in the nineteenth century and many followed directly after the First World War in 1918. But only in a few countries were men and women given voting rights in the same year. In France, for instance, women had to wait almost a hundred years (until 1946) before they had the same voting rights as men.

Table 2.1 Parliamentary accountability and universal suffrage, selected countries

	Parliamentary accountability		Universal adult Suffrage	
	Accepted	Constitutionalised	Male	Female
Austria[a]	1918	1920	1907	1918
Belgium[b]	1831	1831	1893	1948
Denmark[c]	1901	1953	1901	1918
Finland[d]	1919	1919	1906	1906
France[e]	1958 (1870)	1958	1848	1946
Germany	1918	1919	1869	1919
Greece	1974	1975	1877	1952
Iceland[f]	1904	1944	1915	1915
Ireland[g]	1922	1937	1918	1918
Italy	1948	1948	1912	1945
Luxembourg	1868	1868	1919	1919
Netherlands	1848 (1866)	1983	1917	1919
Norway[h]	1905 (1814)	1905	1897	1913
Portugal[i]	1910	1976	1911	1931
Spain	1976	1976	1869	1931
Sweden[j]	1809	1975 (1809)	1909	1921
Switzerland	1848	1848	1919	1971
UK	1215 (Magna Carta)		1918	1918

Notes:
[a] Austria: The constitution of 1918 was considered 'provisional' until 1920. The rights of parliament to elect the cabinet were modified in 1929.
[b] Belgium: Constitutional monarchy in 1831 with a potential for further parliamentarisation.
[c] Denmark: Parliamentary accountability from 1901 onwards, constitutionalisation in 1953.
[d] Finland: An autonomous Russian district until 1919.
[e] France: Only for Fifth Republic. Parliamentary accountability for the Third Republic from 1870–5 to 1940 and for the Fourth Republic from 1946–58. In the Third and Fourth Republic, the parliament had more control than during the other periods.
[f] Iceland: Independent of Denmark since 1944.
[g] Ireland: Independent of Great Britain since 1937.
[h] Norway: Enforced political union with Sweden, 1814–1905.
[i] Portugal: An unstable, semi-presidential, parliamentary republic, 1910–17.
[j] Sweden: The 1809 constitution was formally effective until 1975.

Sources: Parliamentary accountability: Jan-Erik Lane and Svante Ersson, *Politics and Society in Western Europe* (London: Sage, 1998); Suffrage: Jan-Erik Lane, David McKay and Kenneth Newton, *Political Data Handbook* (Oxford: Oxford University Press, 1997: 118).

■ Democracy and the rise of democratic states

The crucial importance of free political competition and a real chance of taking over the powers of government are found in the definition of democracy applied by Freedom House. This independent institute, which monitors political developments in the world (see fact file 2.1), defines democracies as:

> political systems whose leaders are elected in competitive multi-party and multi-candidate processes in which opposition parties have a legitimate chance of attaining power or participating in power.
>
> *(www.freedomhouse.org/reports/century/html)*

There is certainly no inevitability about a state becoming democratic, and many reasons why non-democratic elites resist giving up or sharing power, but nevertheless the number of democratic states is rising. If we use the definition presented by Freedom House we find that:

- In 1900, not one of the fifty-five states in existence could be called 'democratic' according to current Freedom House standards. Even the most democratic, such as the USA or Britain, restricted the voting rights of women or black Americans. Monarchies and empires were the dominant state forms.
- The picture changed dramatically in the second half of the twentieth century. By 1950, the total number of states had risen to eighty, and twenty-two of them could be characterised as 'democracies', which meant that about 31 per cent of the world population was living under democratic rule.

Fact file 2.1

The Freedom House rating of states

Freedom in the World is an institutional effort by Freedom House to monitor the progress and decline of political rights and civil liberties in 192 countries and in major related and disputed territories . . . The Survey assesses a country's freedom by examining its record in two areas: political rights and civil liberties. A country grants its citizens political rights when it permits them to form political parties that represent a significant range of voter choice and whose leaders can openly compete for and be elected to positions of power in government. A country upholds its citizens' civil liberties when it respects and protects their religious, ethnic, economic, linguistic and other rights, including gender and family rights, personal freedoms and freedoms of the press, belief and association. The Survey rates each country on a seven-point scale for both political rights and civil liberties (1 representing the most free and 7 the least free) and then divides the world into three broad categories: 'Free' (countries whose ratings average 1–3); 'Partly Free' (countries whose ratings average 3–5.5); and 'Not Free' (countries whose ratings average 5.5–7).

The ratings are not only assessments of the conduct of governments. They also reflect the reality of daily life. Thus a country with a benign government facing violent forces (for example terrorist movements or insurgencies) hostile to an open society will be graded on the basis of the on-the-ground conditions that determine whether the population is able to exercise its freedoms. (*Freedom in the World 2002: The Democracy Gap*, The Freedom House Survey Team; www.freedomhouse.org/research/freeworld/2002/about.htm)

- After the decline of colonial rule in Africa and Asia, changes in Latin America, and the collapse of communist rule in Eastern and Central Europe, the number of democracies rose to 119 states by 2000. At the beginning of 2008, some 47 per cent of the 190 or so states respected a broad array of human rights and political freedoms and were labelled 'free' by Freedom House. About three billion people – 46 per cent of the world's population – lived in these states and enjoyed the protection of a broad array of political and human rights.

The twentieth century, then, was not only an age of devastating wars, genocide, bloodshed and totalitarian ideologies; it was also the 'Democratic Century'. Table 2.2 shows all the states of the world that have reached the highest democracy scores on the Freedom House scale and have more than one million inhabitants. The democracy score combines the two major characteristics of democracies mentioned earlier: the protection of basic civil and political rights. Low-scoring countries are the most democratic.

Although the Freedom House scores are based on civil and political rights as the two crucial features of democracy, other definitions and measures have been developed that include these and other criteria. Most of them refer to democracy as a system of government and use labels such as 'political democracy' or 'liberal democracy' as synonyms for what are here called 'democracies' or 'democratic states'. The political scientist Seymour Martin Lipset (1922–2006) provided one of the clearest definitions, explicitly spelling out the main features of a democracy as a system of government:

> First, competition exists for government positions, and fair elections for public office occur at regular intervals without the use of force and without excluding any social group. Second, citizens participate in selecting their leaders and forming policies. And, third, civil and political liberties exist to ensure the integrity of political competition and participation.
>
> *(Seymour M. Lipset, The Encyclopedia of Democracy,*
> *London: Routledge, 1995: iv)*

Democracy is a variable, not a fixed phenomenon; it changes and develops over time, so that what was regarded as good democratic practice a hundred years ago may not be now. There are disputes about whether states differ in their degree of democracy – as the Freedom House index suggests – or whether democratic states can be clearly distinguished from other forms of government (see chapter 3). Debates like these remind us of the difficult problems of applying the abstract concept of 'democracy' to actual political systems. Different measures and definitions give us different results when we try to classify states as 'democratic' or not, or if we try to grade them on a continuum. Nevertheless, the Freedom House and other approaches all agree: the number of democratic states in the world has expanded since the mid-1970s. By now, democracy is widely accepted as the preferred way to organise states (see briefing 2.2).

Table 2.2 Free and independent states, 2008 (only states with more than 1 million inhabitants are listed)

State	Freedom House Index	Population (million, 2008)	Area – total (000 km²)	GDP[a] (US$, 2007 est.)
Argentina	2.0	40.677	2,767	13,300
Australia	1.0	20.601	7,687	36,300
Austria	1.0	8.206	84	38,400
Belgium	1.0	10.404	31	35,300
Benin	2.0	8.295	113	1,500
Botswana	2.0	1.842	600	16,400
Brazil	2.0	191.909	8,512	9,700
Bulgaria	1.5	7.263	111	11,300
Canada	1.0	33.213	9,985	38,400
Chile	1.0	16.454	757	13,900
Costa Rica	1.0	4.196	51	10,300
Croatia	2.0	4.492	57	15,500
Czech Rep.	1.0	10.221	79	24,200
Denmark	1.0	5.485	43	37,400
Dominican Rep.	2.0	9.507	49	7,000
El Salvador	2.5	7.066	21	5,800
Estonia	1.0	1.308	45	21,100
Finland	1.0	5.245	338	35,300
France	1.0	64.058	643	33,200
Germany	1.0	82.370	357	34,200
Ghana	1.5	23.383	239	1,400
Greece	1.5	10.723	132	29,200
Hungary	1.0	9.931	93	19,000
India	2.5	1.147.996	3,288	2,700
Indonesia	2.5	237.512	1,919	3,700
Ireland	1.0	4.156	70	43,100
Israel	1.5	7.112	21	25,800
Italy	1.0	58.145	301	30,400
Jamaica	2.5	2.804	11	7,700
Japan	1.5	127.288	378	33,600
Korea, South	1.5	49.233	98	24,800
Latvia	1.5	2.245	65	17,400
Lesotho	2.5	2.128	30	1,300
Lithuania	1.0	3.565	65	17,700
Mali	2.5	12.324	1,240	1,000
Mauritius	2.0	1.274	2	11,200
Mexico	2.5	109.955	1,973	12,800
Mongolia	2.0	2.996	1,564	3,200
Namibia	2.0	2.089	825	5,200
Netherlands	1.0	16.645	42	38,500
New Zealand	1.0	4.173	269	26,400

Table 2.2 *(cont.)*

State	Freedom House Index	Population (million, 2008)	Area – total (000 km²)	GDP[a] (US$, 2007 est.)
Norway	1.0	4.644	324	53,000
Panama	1.5	3.293	78	10,300
Peru	2.5	29.181	1,285	7,800
Poland	1.0	38.501	313	16,300
Portugal	1.0	10.677	92	21,700
Romania	2.0	22.247	238	11,400
Senegal	2.5	12.853	196	1,700
Serbia	2.5	10.159	77	10,400
Slovakia	1.0	5.455	49	20,300
Slovenia	1.0	2.008	20	27,200
South Africa	2.0	43.786	1,220	9,800
Spain	1.0	40.491	505	30,100
Sweden	1.0	9.045	450	36,500
Switzerland	1.0	7.582	41	41,100
Taiwan	1.5	22.921	36	30,100
Trinidad and Tobago	2.0	1.047	5	18,300
Ukraine	2.5	45.994	604	6,900
UK	1.0	60.944	245	35,100
USA	1.0	303.825	9,827	45,800
Uruguay	1.0	3.478	176	11,600

Note: [a] PPP *per capita* (PPP: Purchasing power parity).

Sources: Freedom House (2008), *Freedom in the World. Combined Average Ratings – Independent Countries*, www.freedomhouse.org/template.cfm?page=410&year=2008.
Central Intelligence Agency (2008), *The World Factbook. Rank Order*,
https://www.cia.gov/library/publications/the-world-factbook/rankorder/2119rank.html
https://www.cia.gov/library/publications/the-world-factbook/rankorder/2147rank.html
https://www.cia.gov/library/publications/the-world-factbook/rankorder/2004rank.html.

Briefing 2.2

Democracy: universal principles and limitations

"We reaffirm that democracy is a universal value based on the freely expressed will of people to determine their own political, economic, social and cultural systems and their full participation in all aspects of their lives. We also reaffirm that while democracies share common features, there is no single model of democracy, that it does not belong to any country or region, and reaffirm the necessity of due respect for sovereignty and the right of self-determination. We stress that democracy, development and respect for all human rights and fundamental freedoms are interdependent and mutually reinforcing."

Resolution adopted by the UN General Assembly: 60/1. 2005 World Summit Outcome
(http://unpan1.un.org/intradoc/groups/public/documents/UN/UNPAN021752.pdf).

■ Redistribution and the welfare state

As states move gradually towards political freedom and democracy, so they will be confronted, as Rokkan points out, with growing citizen demands and a need to strengthen national identification by redistributive policies. This helps to turn subjects of the state into citizens of the state by giving every citizen a stake in public services and hence a sense of common national purpose and identity. It also turns states into welfare states to a greater or lesser extent.

As can be seen in the right-hand column of table 2.2, democratic states vary enormously in their level of economic development. A widely used indicator for economic development – the **gross domestic product** (GDP) per citizen – ranged in 2006 from US$1,300 in Lesotho to US$53,000 in Norway.

GDP The value of all final goods and services produced within a state in a given year. In order to compare the wealth of states the measure used is normally GDP per capita.

Most democratic states are wealthy, though not all of them are, but what most of them have in common is a rapid expansion of state activities since the Second World War. Even a cursory look at economic trends in democracies over past decades shows a remarkable growth of state spending and public employment. Many of them abandoned traditional laissez-faire policies and free-market economics after the traumatic experiences of the Great Depression of the 1930s and the post-war economic problems of the late 1940s. As they increasingly accepted responsibility for the young and old, the sick and disabled, the unemployed and poor, and for education, housing and pensions, these states developed into welfare states (chapter 1).

The expansion of state activities can be illustrated with a few basic figures. For example, average state revenues and expenditures among the industrialised countries rose from 26–27 per cent of GDP in 1960 to 45–47 per cent in 1997. On average, total spending of the twenty-seven member-states of the European Union had reached almost 47 per cent of their GDP in 2006! Even more striking, the growth of public expenditure and public services are directly linked to the consolidation of democracy in many states. State spending varies very considerably from one country to another, but the longer a state is a democracy, the higher its public spending is likely to be. Once a high level of spending is reached it becomes very difficult to reduce the state's spending in a democracy: large parts of the population benefit from these measures and it is hard to find a majority favouring cuts and reforms.

Although the upward climb in state spending levelled off in many countries after the early 1990s, state services of one kind or another continue to play a major role in the life of the average citizen. The reverse side of this coin is, of course, that welfare states are also tax states with state revenues growing almost as fast as public spending. As a result modern states function as huge redistribution agencies collecting taxes and supporting parts of the population in complicated ways (see chapter 17). In this sense there is no escaping the state, its taxes and its services in modern society. As the saying goes: in this life only death and taxes are certain.

■ Theories of state and society

As we saw in chapter 1, modern political theories about the state fall into two very broad categories: normative theories about what the state ought to do and empirical theories about how the state actually operates and why it operates that way. We shall discuss empirical theories now. As the relationship between democracy and state spending shows, the nature and functioning of the state is closely related to the society it governs. In fact, one way of distinguishing between different theories of the state is to look at how they conceptualise the relationship between state and society. Broadly speaking, there are four major approaches to the relationship between 'state' and 'society':

- State supremacy
- State dependency
- Interdependency
- Separation and autonomy.

State supremacy

Some theories presume the supremacy or dominance of the state over society. According to these theories, the state does not so much reflect the characteristics of broader society but is independent of them and above them. This idea is found in legal theories that stress the formal sovereignty of the state. Aristotle, for example, saw the state as a political community 'which is the highest of all, and which embraces all the rest'. According to this view the state is a self-regulating and supreme power. It is not the product of society or the social and economic groups within it; on the contrary, they are part of the state from which they arise. Such theories are summarised under the label 'Etatism'. Although some writers regard state supremacy as a threat to individual rights and liberty, others reach very different conclusions, regarding the state's main role as the preserva-

> **Etatism** A very strong emphasis on state power and an accompanying reduction of social and individual rights.

tion of law and order (the 'night watchman' role) and the defence of the full independence of the private sector, whether individual or collective.

The view that the state is an independent and dominant power has become more and more problematic as we have gained a better understanding of government. At first sight, the huge increase in the activity and powers of the modern state may, indeed, suggest that it invades society as a conqueror that gains greater and greater control over the lives of citizens. But a closer look reveals a more complicated development in which the relationship between state and society is mutually interdependent: the state influences society and helps to mould it, but society also creates the state, giving it powers but also setting limits on these powers. Besides, states are not single or monolithic entities that control societies as a field marshal might control his troops on a battlefield. They are highly complex 'communities' made up of different institutions and organisations with their own histories and interests, and expressing the outcomes of all sorts of past and present political battles between competing social and economic groups. Most political scientists today therefore do not see the state as something 'above' or controlling society, which leads us away from the notion of a dominant state and towards the idea of an interdependent one.

State dependency

Some theories see the state not as a supreme agency that dominates society, but, quite the opposite, as dependent on society, especially in its economic relations. Disputes about this view of the state and its relationship with social and economic forces have a long and complicated tradition in political analysis. The work of the German theorist Karl Marx (1818–83) inspired the idea that the state is only and always the expression of the struggle between classes in society – or, more specifically, that the power of the state is always an instrument of the dominant class. According to Marx, the state is nothing more nor less than 'a committee for managing the common affairs' of the dominant class. In modern society, this is the capitalist class, who own and control the means of production. According to this theory, the state is not a neutral referee that adjudicates between the competing interests of different classes or social groups, nor is it an agency that is above and independent of society. It is, and can only be, an instrument to strengthen the dominant position of specific groups in society – in a capitalist society, this means the interests of the capitalist class.

Marxists argue about whether and to what extent the state can be independent of economic forces and the interests of the capitalist class. The earlier writings of Marx argued that the state is merely a 'superstructure' whose shape and power is the inevitable product of the economic substructure. Later, Marx seems to have allowed for a degree of independence of the state, and twentieth-century Marxists have picked up this idea. Usually they emphasise particular 'structural tensions' in capitalist societies arising from the fact that modern states have conflicting, and even contradictory, tasks. On the one hand they are expected to protect the free market necessary for making profits but, at the same time, they are also expected to maintain social order and ensure that the population is educated and healthy enough to provide an efficient workforce. This means taxing business, which reduces profits. Another tension results from the great increase in state activities, which overstretches and overloads the state apparatus, and leads it into all sorts of activities that it cannot afford or perform well. As a result, the state becomes increasingly intertwined with social and economic forces and becomes increasingly dependent upon them. This leads us away from the notion of a dependent state towards an interdependent one.

Interdependency

A third set of theories stresses the interdependence of state and society, or the relationships of exchange between them. In these approaches the modern state has become ever more and ever deeper involved in social and economic regulation. At the same time, as society has become increasingly complex and differentiated it requires more state co-ordination, regulation and arbitration. These developments are different sides of the same coin, and it is not possible to say that one causes the other or that one dominates the other. They are mutually interdependent.

Neo-corporatist theories stress the close mutual dependency of state agencies, on the one hand, and major economic interest groups on the other. In traditional variants of this approach, trade unions and employer associations negotiate directly with state agencies about economic policies. More recent theories of governance stress the participation of a wide range and variety of organised social groups in making and implementing public policy of all kinds. We shall say more about the interdependency of state and society in our later discussions of governance and neo-corporatism (especially chapters 4, 10 and 15).

Separation and autonomy

Finally, some theories depict state and society as distinct and autonomous areas, each with its own rules and development, and each with its own imperatives and 'logic'. Deep social forces produce social groups, interests and organisations that neither can nor should be controlled or regulated by the state. Equally, the state cannot and should not be captured by any particular interests or class (as the Marxists claim) because the state is a battlefield occupied by many conflicting groups and interests. State activities have their limits, just as social interests and organisations do, and to try to exceed these limits is to undermine the democratic principles of a proper balance between the state and private interests. Pluralist and civil society theories stress the need for an area of social life and organisation outside the power of the state (see chapter 10).

The four approaches are only a brief beginning to our analysis of state and society. We will have much more to say about each as we progress through the chapters that follow and add greater breadth and depth to our understanding. Meanwhile, we can certainly conclude that modern states are characterised by complex connections with their society, and that it is difficult to say which of the four approaches is the best. Each seems to explain some aspect of the affairs of states better than the others. For instance, neo-corporatist and pluralist approaches explain the rise of welfare states in the 1960s in those states where welfare programmes and economic policies and practices were the result of close collaboration between the state and powerful economic interest groups. However, the spread of political dissatisfaction and frustration among large sections of society in some countries after the 1960s seems to be better explained in terms of 'structural tensions' between an increasingly active state that is also increasingly weaker in some respects. Only after looking more closely at the multifarious institutions, structures and activities of the modern state can we come to a more sensible judgement about the strengths and weakness of the various theories.

■ What have we learned?

This chapter has dealt with the difficulties of characterising and defining states, and with the historical development of modern states, especially democratic ones.

- Democracy is a variable, not a constant. Accepted ideas about what democracy is, and how it operates, are changing as standards rise.
- Democracy is a contested concept but most definitions stress the importance of universal citizenship with its accompanying political and civil rights and duties, political competition for support in regular and free elections, and parliamentary accountability with a mixture of representative and direct participatory democracy.
- Most democratic states are among the wealthiest in the world and hence they include a disproportionate number in Europe, North America and the English-speaking world.
- Growing political demands among citizens lead to redistribution and to welfare states that accept responsibility for the young and old, the sick and disabled, and the unemployed and poor. Not all democracies have developed their welfare provisions to the same extent, however.
- The number of democracies is still rising. Currently almost half of the world's states and population can be labelled 'free'.

■ Lessons of comparison

- Although states across the globe, from the strongest to the weakest, are increasingly confronted with other powerful organisations, especially international business (MNCs), non-governmental organisations (NGOs) and international agencies, they are still the most important political actors in the world.
- States and societies are intimately bound together in a wide variety of different ways.
- Comparative theories of the state can be distinguished according to how they conceptualise the relationship between state and society. Broadly speaking, there are four main theories of state and society: state supremacy, state dependency, interdependency, and separation and autonomy.

Projects

1. Collect information about Costa Rica, Denmark, Microsoft and the World Bank in order to describe their role and power in the world today. Use your data for a systematic comparison of the political impact that Microsoft and the World Bank may have, and why they are different from states.
2. Compare the figures for the government intervention measures presented in briefing 2.1 with the economic figures for states presented in table 2.2. Why are states the only organisations in the world able to finance these measures? When would you call a state bankrupt?
3. Do you live in a democracy? Present a systematic overview of the arguments to depict your country as more or less democratic.
4. Explain why all welfare states are democracies, but not all democracies are welfare states.

Further reading

R. King and G. Kendall, *The State, Democracy and Globalisation*, Basingstoke: Palgrave, 2003.
Presents a concise overview of the development of modern states and democracies.

G. Almond, 'The return to the state', *American Political Science Review*, 82(3), 1988: 855–74.
A critical evaluation of debates about the notion of the state in contemporary political science.

M. Levi, 'The state of the study of the state', in Ira Katznelson and Helen Milner (eds.), *Political Science: The State of the Discipline*, New York: Norton, 2002: 33–55.
A critical evaluation of debates about the notion of the state in contemporary political science.

M. L. van Creveld, *The Rise and Decline of the State*, Cambridge: Cambridge University Press, 1999.
Examines how the state came to replace rival forms of political organisation, and is now in decline.

F. Fukuyama, *State Building: Governance and World Order in the Twenty-First Century*, London: Profile Books, 2004.
Discusses the changing power of states in the modern world.

R. Dahl, *On Democracy*, New Haven: Yale University Press, 1998.
A short and clear account of democracy.

Websites

www.freedomhouse.org

Provides information about democracy and human rights for each state of the world.

http://freedom.indiemaps.com/

Interactive website covering large numbers of political indicators and countries

www.oecd.org

Official website of the Organisation for Economic Cooperation and Development (OECD). Provides information on the OECD and about the economic development of its member-states.

www.developmentgateway.org

Provides information about sustainable development and poverty reduction in many developing countries.

www.worldbank.com/data/

Statistical information about many economic, social, political and demographical developments in many states. Provides information about reduction in poverty, etc. and the World Development Indicators (WDIs).

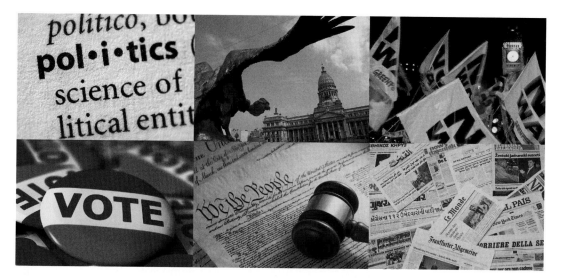

3   Democratic change and persistence

Democratic states appear in many different forms and stages of development. Some political scientists argue strongly for a clear line of demarcation between democracies and undemocratic states. Others claim that violations of citizens' rights and other democratic imperfections are a matter of degree and that states can be placed on a continuous scale ranging from the most democratic to the most undemocratic. The Freedom House index offers a middle-of-the-road position by distinguishing between democratic and non-democratic states on the one hand, and by grading democracies as being more or less democratic on the other.

The distinction between democratic and less democratic states is very important when we look at the rapid growth of democratic states. This growth is often called **democratisation** and is usually divided into 'waves'. The first wave, from the mid-nineteenth century to the 1920s, coincided with the rise of the nation-state. The second wave, starting after the Second World War and continuing to the early 1960s,

> **Democratisation** The continual process of transforming a political system towards more democratic arrangements.

was mainly the result of decolonisation. The third wave, from about 1975 to the end of the twentieth century, followed the spread of democracy in Latin America and Asia, and the disintegration of the Soviet Union. Although the third wave was expected by some to flow on irresistibly into the twenty-first century, transition to democracy is by no means inevitable and some countries have remained firmly against it while others have created partial, limited or illiberal forms of democracy. Neither North Korea nor Syria seem to be on the way to democracy at all, China and Cuba deliberately frustrate steps in this direction, and Zimbabwe and Russia have deliberately abolished some democratic institutions and practices. At the end of the twentieth century the third wave of the democratic tide seems to have ebbed away.

The end of the third wave and the appearance of faulty democracies have prompted a shift in the way that comparative political scientists approach democracy and democratisation. The earlier interest in the circumstances in which democracy is likely to put down firm roots has been complemented by an interest in the persistence and stability of democracy, and in a new set of states that are partially but not fully democratic. The terms 'failed democracy', 'partial democracy' and 'illiberal democracy' have been introduced to deal with the fact that democratisation can be reversed and that some states have not become fully democratic. Some violations of citizens' rights and other democratic imperfections are, it is argued, so fundamental that the resulting states are neither democratic nor undemocratic, but form a distinct category of their own known as 'defective democracies'.

In this chapter, democratic change and consolidation are discussed, first from the perspective of continual democratisation: What factors account for the success of the three waves of democratisation? Second, we focus on the stability of democracy: What makes democracy endure and why do some states reverse their democratic achievements? Finally, the rise of defective democracies and the return of undemocratic rule are considered: Are defective democracies really democratic, or do they simply try to cover their failings with false claims and democratic pretensions?

The major topics in this chapter are:

- Transitions towards democracy
- The limits of democratisation
- Embedded, partial and defective democracies
- Theories of democratic change and persistence.

■ Transitions towards democracy

As democracy spread across the world so it seemed to be the final, natural and inevitable point of political development – history was the story of progress from **authoritarian rule** to democracy. Stein Rokkan summarised these developments in very broad terms, stressing the changing circumstances of citizens and groups in society as the main driving force behind democratisation and the establishment of mass democracies (chapter 1). In this way, democratisation in many countries has been a long, long process lasting for decades – or even centuries. In other countries, however, revolutions, wars and foreign intervention have brought about rapid change. Each

Authoritarian rule Obedience and submission to authority; that is, the concentration of power in the hands of a leader or elite that is not responsible to parliament. No opposition is allowed to compete for power.

country has followed its own path, and just as with the rise of the state, complex historical processes and unique constellations seem to account for democratic transitions. And just as with the rise of the state, there are many different explanations of the process of democratisation.

In spite of these complications, some patterns of transition towards democracy can be seen. Most obviously, democracy is best established in economically developed countries. In fact, until recently it was difficult to find a democracy outside the select group of developed countries in western Europe and North America. As a result, many authors concluded that economic development is a necessary (and perhaps a sufficient) condition for democracy.

Some argue that the rise of a property-owning middle class is crucially important for economic development and democratisation:

1. These groups form a middle level between the traditional elites (land owners, the military and nobility) and the majority of working people (peasants, artisans, labourers, farm workers and paupers).
2. In the struggle to secure their economic position and political power, the rising middle class demands personal freedom and the right to participate in government affairs.
3. They also press for education, health care, improved housing and geographical mobility to improve the quality of their workforce.
4. The middle class forms its own associations and voluntary organisations, which form the backbone of civil society that further stimulates democratisation.
5. Finally, the middle class, with an interest in stability and predictability in economic and social affairs, had a moderating impact on social conflicts, preferring moderate solutions and rejecting extreme positions.

The shortest summary of this interpretation is: 'No bourgeoisie, no democracy'. This claim does not presume that the middle class is necessarily altruistic or concerned with the fate of others – all it needs to show is that this class favoured democracy for its own reasons.

Convincing as economic explanations of democratisation might be at first sight, a number of complications are obvious:

• Deviating cases are easy to find and cast doubts on the general validity of the relationship. Germany was economically highly developed, but succumbed to Nazi dictatorship in 1933. Several poor countries are democratic and democratisation preceded industrialisation in India. Apparently, economic development is conducive to democracy, but it is certainly not the whole story.
• A close correspondence of economic development and democracy does not mean that the former causes the latter. There might be a common background variable such as Protestantism or capitalism that causes both democracy and economic development. Protestantism has been picked out for its special role in promoting both economic development

(early Protestants saw wealth as a sign of God's favour) and democracy (Protestant theology sees every individual as equal in the sight of God).

- Economic development is an ambiguous concept which covers a large number of complex processes (such as industrialisation, urbanisation, stratification, bureaucratisation and rising levels of wealth, literacy and education). It is unclear how each of these contributes exactly to democracy or to specific aspects of democracy.

- Even if economic development is conducive to the early stages of democratisation it does not mean that economic factors count for the consolidation of democracy.

Explanations of political phenomena relying on economic forces always run the risk of being one-sided. So, too, do explanations relying entirely upon the power of political structures and institutions. States with perfectly good constitutions, and even those with an array of democratic institutions, have failed to sustain democratic practices. Democracy cannot be reduced to the material conditions of economic development, or to the institutional apparatus of the state, because the wishes, demands and expectations of people also have to be taken into account. In a seminal article on the 'social requisites of democracy' published in 1959, Seymour Martin Lipset (1922–2006) stressed the importance of economic factors for democracy. At the same time he pointed to the fact that the ideas and values of citizens on the one hand, and the ability of the political system to satisfy citizen needs and demands on the other, are very important too.

In other words, the ideal as well as the material interests of citizens matter for democracy, and this means investigating the importance of ideas in human affairs – ideas about liberty, equality, justice and the good life. The simple approach of explaining structures in terms of ideas and, vice versa, of explaining ideas in terms of structures, is unsatisfactory. For this reason, the transition to democracy must be approached from a variety of standpoints.

If combinations of economic, social and cultural factors are important for the spread of democracy, it is unclear which combinations are sufficient, and different combinations may work best in different times and places. This idea is implicit in the book *The Third Wave: Democratization in the Late Twentieth Century* published by the American political scientist Samuel P. Huntington (1927–) in 1991. He shows that democratisation proceeds not as a continuous process, but in surges and reversals – a kind of ebb and flow or two-steps-forwards, one-step-backwards process. In each 'wave' a relatively large number of non-democratic states make their first moves towards democracy:

- The first wave is very long and covers the second half of the nineteenth and the first part of the twentieth century. In this period many western nation-states were transformed into mass democracies. Yet even in this period a general pattern is not easy to detect – apart of the common processes of economic development and nation building, many peculiar historical factors are needed to explain the differences between, say, democratisation in Britain, Germany and Sweden. The first wave ends with the fascist reversal in Italy in the 1920s.

- The second wave is much shorter and starts with the end of the Second World War. In the direct aftermath of the war many states were newly founded (for instance Yugoslavia, West and East Germany, and China), a large number gaining independence with the collapse of colonial rule (for instance Indonesia, India and Algeria). Quite a number of these newly founded states tried to implement democratic rule, but not all survived as democracies, although India did. Democratisation in the second wave depended on political and economic opportunities as well as on the colonial legacies present in many countries. Foreign intervention and wars of independence appear to be important for the rise of democracy in many countries. The second wave ebbed away when some places reverted to authoritarian rule in the 1960s (Greece and several countries in Latin America).
- The third wave started in the mid-1970s and faded away at the end of the twentieth century. In this period, some of the non-democratic countries of Latin America and Asia were democratised, frequently on the basis of mass movements opposing ruling cliques and autocrats (for example in South Korea or the Philippines). The disintegration of the Soviet Union resulted in an additional growth of democratic states in Central and Eastern Europe. Here, too, mass pressure and opposition groups played a decisive role (for instance in Poland, Ukraine and Hungary).

Whereas democracy was a minority phenomenon until recently and mainly limited to north-western Europe and North America, the third wave changed this situation. By the end of the twentieth century democracy had reached every part of the world, South America, all of western Europe and considerable parts of Asia included. At the same time it is clear that these three waves are characterised by different processes and that there is no general explanation for the rise of democratic rule. Apparently, democracy can be reached by many different paths.

■ The limits of democratisation

What are the chances that new democracies survive their initial transformation? What makes them endure? Democratisation is a process that takes some time. It is not achieved by a single leap into a new form of government. Several phases can be discerned between the breakdown of an old system and the consolidation of the new one:

Consolidation Process of maturing and stabilising a new political system by strengthening and formalising its basic arrangements.

- *Initial phase* Opposition towards the ruling elite and undemocratic arrangements are mobilised; demands for more liberty are broadly accepted and generally seen as the main goal of political reform.

- *Emerging phase* The old undemocratic arrangements no longer function and new ones are set up; liberty is still the main common concern; a new constitution is declared and general elections are introduced for the first time; return to the old system is no longer easily feasible.
- *Advanced phase* Liberty is now taken for granted and attention shifts towards the achievements of the new democracy; providing liberty is no longer sufficient; group interests have to be satisfied; economic and public service performance become important; there is increasing stress on equality of rights and opportunities.
- *Phase of consolidation* The new arrangements are institutionalised and the system is able to meet the demands and expectations of large parts of the population. A balance between liberty and equality is reached and broadly accepted.

It is clear from this that successful democratisation depends on many factors and that progress can be halted, slowed or reversed at every stage. Moreover, the important factors prompting development change at each stage. Whereas formal rights, especially voting rights, are decisive in the early phases, the satisfaction of material demands is more important later. For the endurance of democracy, then, economic development appears to be an important factor once again. As it turns out, democracies can be jeopardised by large or growing inequalities: if the rich get richer end the poor suffer, democratic arrangements are less likely to survive the third phase. That is not to say, of course, that people forget about political principles in favour of economic performance. On the contrary, even if material and economic conditions are poor, citizens may defer gratification and maintain their support for democracy, as they did in many central European countries which managed to consolidate their democracies in the face of economic hardship in the 1990s.

Even if the starting point of democratisation can be easily identified – the end of a war, the expulsion of a dictator, a popular uprising – consolidation can take a long time, for nothing can be taken for granted until democratic principles are widely supported and entrenched in daily political life. Many aspects of the old non-democratic practices may live on during transition: senior positions in the bureaucracy may remain occupied by the same people who served the undemocratic system; continuing corruption is often a problem; and social and economic problems may persist in new democracies. Citizens may evaluate their political system in terms of its performance and if it fails over the long run they may turn into 'unsatisfied democrats' who retain a strong belief in democracy but believe that their own system of government fails to meet their expectations. In the long run, no system can survive if many people are seriously dissatisfied.

Dividing the process of democratisation in different phases and then identifying the different factors that operate in each phase helps us to deal with the many different paths taken in democratic consolidation. Yet concentrating in this way on how countries eventually reach a state of advanced and stable democracy runs the risk of assuming that this is an inevitable and preordained development that all countries will naturally follow. It assumes that democracy is the 'highest' and 'most sophisticated' form of government and that everything else is a deviation or a corruption of the 'normal' state of affairs. Undemocratic and unconsolidated systems are treated as not sufficiently developed, but it is assumed that, like small children, they will eventually grow up and become properly mature. There are certainly good reasons for preferring democracy to other forms of government but that is a different matter – a matter of values and judgements, not value-neutral empirical analysis. The task of empirical comparative government is to avoid value judgements about whether democracy is the best form of government and assumptions about whether it is the final, natural and inevitable point of historical development. Comparative government should try to understand how and why countries follow different historical paths and to try to develop general theories and models that explain these patterns.

The distinction between phases and the accompanying shifts in relevant factors help us to deal with the many different paths democratic consolidation takes. Yet stressing consolidation runs the risk of accepting democracy as a more or less self-evident end-goal and treating all factors as either conducive to or slowing down democratisation. Instead of trying to look at a political system in unbiased ways, undemocratic or unconsolidated systems are seen as 'not yet' sufficiently developed from the beginning. Moreover, democracy is implicitly taken as the 'highest' or 'most sophisticated' political system and all other systems are lumped together as negative deviations from this ideal. Such arguments have to be spelled out carefully. Using a simple phase model of democratisation and believing that democracy is our final destination and the paradise we all want to go to does not help us much to understand democratisation and the grounds for its importance.

■ Embedded, partial and defective democracies

As we have seen in chapter 2, there is much debate about the meaning and definition of democracy and its most important characteristics. As a result, there are different attempts to measure democracy using different indicators that are thought to be crucial (see briefing 3.1). In many cases the rankings produce very similar results so that, for example, a country that is high on the Freedom House index it is most likely high on the other scales as well. When democracy is highly developed and consolidated it can be labelled as an 'embedded democracy'.

> **Embedded democracy** A consolidated and stable system that is founded on a well-developed civil society, secure civil and political rights, a set of autonomous institutions of government that act within the rule of law, a system of free and fair elections, and a government with effective power to perform its duties.

At the other extreme, some countries are not democratic on any of the scales because they do not have any of the necessary basic characteristics. These are

Briefing 3.1

Comparing democracy and democratic development: major indicators

Name	Description	Scope	Source
Freedom House Index	Political rights and civil liberties.	Detailed country reports. Trends are pointed out. 193 countries.	www.freedomhouse.org
Bertelsmann Transformation Index (BTI)	Democratic and economic development and capabilities of the executive.	Detailed country reports. Trends are pointed out. 125 countries.	www.bertelsmann-transformation-index.de
Polity-Index	Monitors regime changes/political stability, authority, quality of executive.	Country reports point out specific developments. 162 countries.	www.systemicpeace.org/polity/polity4.htm
Polyarchy and Contestation Scales	Fairness of elections, freedom of organisation, freedom of expression, media pluralism, extent of suffrage.	Detailed country reports. 196 countries.	www.nd.edu/~mcoppedg/crd/datacrd.htm
Democracy and Development	Focus on political features and pure regime type determination.	Detailed country reports. 135 countries.	www.nd.edu/~apsacp/ACLPcodes.pdf
Unified Democracy Scores (UDS)	Synthesised indicator of democracy based on the ten commonly used indicators of democracy.	Worldwide democracy scores for the 1946–2000 period.	www.clinecenter.uiuc.edu/research/affiliatedresearch/UDS/

the totalitarian dictatorships and autocracies that are outside the scope of this book (see fact file 3.1). There is a third group of countries that appear to be democratic but are not completely so. No democracy is perfect and all have defects on one kind or another, but some countries seem to be neither developed and embedded democracies nor fully-fledged autocracies. They have been variously described as illiberal democracies, pseudo-democracies, limited

Fact file 3.1

The worst of the worst

Included in this report are eight countries judged to have the worst records: Burma, Cuba, Libya, North Korea, Somalia, Sudan, Turkmenistan and Uzbekistan. Also included are two territories, Chechnya and Tibet, whose inhabitants suffer intense repression. ... The report also includes nine further countries near the bottom of Freedom House's list of the most repressive: Belarus, Chad, China, Equatorial Guinea, Eritrea, Laos, Saudi Arabia, Syria and Zimbabwe. The territory of Western Sahara is also included in this group. ...

Massive human rights violations take place in nearly every part of the world. This year's roster of the 'most repressive' includes countries from the Americas, the Middle East, Central Asia, Africa,and East Asia; they represent a wide array of cultures and levels of economic development. ... The fundamental violations of rights presented in this report are all the more alarming because they stand in sharp contrast to the significant expansion of human liberty over the last three decades. In that period, dozens of states have shed tyranny and embraced democratic rule and respect for basic civil liberties.

Source: Freedom House, 'The Worst of the Worst: The World's most Repressive Societies 2008' (www.freedomhouse.org/uploads/special_report/62.pdf).

democracies, electoral democracies, defective democracies and diminished democracies.

These terms point to the fact that something is missing from such systems. In this way, undemocratic systems can be seen as 'partial democracies' or 'diminished sub-types' of democracy. How they are labelled depends on which particular feature is missing (see figure 3.1), the main examples covering:

(a) full suffrage for the population – where some groups are excluded from voting rights (e.g. Switzerland until 1971, when women were given voting rights, and the USA and Northern Ireland until recently, when all ethnic and religious groups were given voting rights).

(b) free electoral competition – where one or more political groups is excluded from elections.

(c) protection of civil liberties – where political liberties such as freedom of speech or association are limited, and where the rule of law is not firmly established or observed in all cases.

In other cases, democracies are flawed because while they take seriously the procedural rules for elections, the rule of law, civil rights, and so on, the government is unable to perform its proper role because anti-democratic forces are powerful. Sometimes this is the army, sometimes it is a church or religious group, and sometimes it is a traditional group of aristocrats, business interests or landowners. The terms 'guarded democracy' and 'tutelary democracy' have been used to describe such cases. Democratic failures of these kinds do not always occur in the early 'nursery school' stages of democratisation. They

Figure 3.1 Partial democracies: examples from diminished sub-types

1. Diminished from procedural minimal definition

(1a) Missing attribute: Full suffrage	(1b) Missing attribute: Full Contestation	(1c) Missing attribute: Civil Liberties
– Limited Democracy – Male Democracy – Oligarchical Democracy	– Controlled Democracy – De facto One-Party Democracy – Restrictive Democracy	– Electoral Democracy – Hard Democracy – Illiberal Democracy

2. Diminished from expanded procedural minimum definition

Missing attribute: Elected government has effective power to govern

- Guarded Democracy
- Protected Democracy
- Tutelary Democracy

Source: David Collier and Steven Levitsky, 'Democracy with Adjectives. Conceptual Innovation in Comparative Research, *World Politics* (April 1997), p. 440.

may emerge later when old elites reverse the process or, indeed, when new elites protect their privileges by cancelling elections or suppressing oppositions (see briefing 3.2).

It might seem that flawed democracies suffer from relatively minor problems that can be cured in time with some reforms and improvements. But it can also be argued that many countries of this kind suffer from such serious problems that they cannot be regarded as imperfect forms of democracy, even less as flawed examples of embedded democracy. Their failings undermine the whole arrangements of democracy, and therefore they constitute a special sub-set of systems that have been labelled **defective democracies**. They include Brazil and Mexico in Latin America, Russia and Bulgaria in central and eastern Europe, and South Korea in Asia. It should not be assumed that defective democracy is a temporary and transitional stage on the way to fully developed liberal democracy. The evidence is that a defective democracy is not a phase on the road to embedded democracy. It can stabilise itself and persist for a long time.

Defective democracies Systems of government that are neither democratic nor undemocratic, but maintain some democratic characteristics as well as some undemocratic ones that damage and disrupt the institutional logic of embedded democracy.

There are many reasons why a given country might stumble along the road to democracy, or even reverse its direction and become a failed democracy. The phase model of democratic consolidation suggests some of the causes. In the first phases, agreement has to be reached about the way new liberties and rights

Briefing 3.2

Expediency takes the place of democracy

After general elections in Zimbabwe and in Kenya in 2008, the ruling presidents refused to step down. In both countries a period of severe violence with many deaths ended as negotiations between the ruling party and the opposition started.

> "In Zimbabwe, as was the case in Kenya earlier this year, a government of unity is being pushed as an emergency measure to stop violence and a spiral down toward civil war. After peace is restored, the thinking goes, truth and reconciliation commissions, constitutional reforms, and finally democracy, will follow. But this is a pipe dream. A government that does not respect the people's vote will not concede power down the line. And an opposition that does not stand for the people, and for democracy when it matters most, is easily appeased with a nice chunk of the national cake. ...
>
> Corruption and underhanded political deals continue in Kenya. Already there have been calls for a general amnesty for the perpetrators of ethnic cleansing. The Truth and Reconciliation Commission that will be formed is more likely to forgive and forget. It is back to the usual business of bad leadership – at the world's insistence that expediency take the place of democracy."
>
> *Mikoma Wa Ngugi, 'Zimbabwe's misguided talks',*
> International Herald Tribune, *27 July 2008.*

are organised and how decision making is actually carried out. In this phase the existence of large or strong minority groups that are not satisfied with their treatment may be important. In the later stages the economic achievements of the new democracy and confidence in its future performance may be crucial. The good news is that democracies are able to rely on their initial consolidation as a significant factor for further development: democracies are clearly more likely to survive if they have already lasted a while. In spite of all the difficulties and dangers that can beset a new democracy, the fact remains that democracy has spread and become firmly rooted in many parts of the globe.

■ Theories of democratic change and persistence

Democratic transformation and consolidation are complex processes that are not easily explained and difficult to generalise about. For a long time the seminal work of Seymour Martin Lipset focused the debates on the importance of economic development as a necessary precondition for democracy. The more recent focus on **modernisation** theory takes a broader approach. This argues that economic and technological developments are closely linked and result in fundamental changes in every area of society (e.g. industrialisation, urbanisation, social and geographical mobility, and education), including the ways that people think about themselves and the social, economic and political world around them. Modernisation theory stresses the interactions between social, economic and political factors, rather

> **Modernisation** The dual processes of technological and economic development and the societal responses to these changes.

than the primacy of economic development. In this sense democracy may be both a cause and consequence of economic development. Usually, the rise of the middle class is seen as crucial for democracy – and a large and strong middle class is the result of the manifold processes called modernisation.

Although modernisation theory is a good starting point for explanations of democratic transformation and consolidation, it is clear that the theory relies heavily on European experience and is too broad and general to provide us with exact explanations for democratisation. Many aspects of modernisation (changing class structure, growing literacy and skills, spread of wealth, etc.) are clearly important for democratisation. But why would we refer to a rather vague theory of modernisation when transformations towards democracy might be explained by, say, changing class structures? Apparently, the wide scope of modernisation theory comes with evident analytical shortcomings.

Broadly speaking, two alternative approaches are available. Both accept the basic idea of modernisation theory that technological and economic developments are highly relevant for democratisation. Both attempt to avoid the European bias and try to specify the exact mechanisms that lead to democratic transformations and consolidation. Cultural theories stress the fact that the expectations and demands of citizens are crucial for democracy. The basis for this approach has been laid out by Gabriel Almond (1911–2002) and Sidney Verba (1932–) in *The Civic Culture*, published in 1963. In their view, democracy can only survive when citizens are characterised by a mixture of political and social orientations. These include, for instance pride in one's government and the expectation of being treated correctly by it. A democracy will survive with a mixture of pragmatism and commitment – not with the requirement that average citizens are expected to be involved in politics all the time, but with the idea that citizens can always participate if they wish and that their opinions will be heard by government if and when they express them. Since Almond and Verba's publication many different cultural theories have been presented, all characterised by the idea that the social and political orientations of citizens are crucial for democracy (see chapter 9).

Cultural theories have been criticised for neglecting the institutions of society. Institutional theory argues that citizens do not develop their attitudes and behaviour in a vacuum or by sitting down and working them out for themselves. They respond to the possibilities, opportunities and restrictions created by the institutional framework of government and politics. If the civil rights of freedom of assembly and association are protected, then citizens can form groups and political parties. If courts are independent of government and the rule of law is applied, citizens will be more likely to form peaceful opposition parties and to develop a sense of allegiance to the state. If government and its institutions are free of corruption, then citizens are more likely to engage with civic affairs, to participate in political life and to trust each other and their elected representatives. Institutional theories emphasise the relevance of these institutional arrangements for democracy and especially for democratic transformation and consolidation. Institutional theories are based on the idea that people make certain choices and develop certain attitudes and values because of the alternatives available, and these are strongly conditioned by the institutions of government and politics. We will revisit this argument in the next chapter.

■ What have we learned?

This chapter has dealt with democratic transition and consolidation. It has also examined democratic failure and defective democracy. The chapter shows that:

- Democratisation is not historically inevitable and its progress cannot be taken for granted. Some countries have never created democratic forms of government, some have partially succeeded, and some have failed and slipped back into dictatorship and autocracy.
- Understanding democratisation requires a careful consideration of the circumstances in which it takes root or fails in different countries.
- Some theories regard democracy as a continuum and assign graded scores to each country. Other theories see a sharp distinction between consolidated, established or embedded democracies at different stages of development, and defective, limited or partial democracies that suffer from a crucial democratic flaw that makes them fundamentally undemocratic, in spite of having some important democratic characteristics.
- Some theories of democratisation stress the importance of political culture and of citizens' attitudes and behaviour, others stress the importance of institutions and structures that encourage certain ways of thinking and behaving.

■ Lessons of comparison

- Just as there are different types of democracy so countries take different routes to democracy. This makes it difficult to explain the process of democratic transformation and difficult to produce generalisations about it.
- Economic development is an important factor, but it is certainly not the whole story. Not all economically developed countries are democratic and some democracies are poor. Some theories stress the rise of a middle class, some focus on the influence of international forces, some emphasise religion, revolution or war.
- The process of democratic consolidation can be divided into phases. In the early phases the creation of institutions that guarantee freedom, civil rights and the rule of law are important. Later, these are taken for granted and economic performance and social and economic equality become more important.
- Economic and social inequalities have threatened democratic consolidation in some countries.

Projects

1. Draw up lists of the democratic indicators employed by different organisations and publications (briefing 3.1) and apply their indicators to ten democracies. Do the different sets of indicators produce the same results when they are applied to the countries?
2. Explain why democracies are more likely to survive if they have lasted a while.
3. Discuss the pros and cons of the statement: 'Every democracy is a deficient democracy.'
4. Why is it so difficult to predict a 'fourth wave of democratisation'?

Further reading

R. King and G. Kendall, *The State, Democracy and Globalisation*, Basingstoke: Palgrave, 2003.
A concise overview of the development of modern states and democracy.

L. Diamond, *The Spirit of Democracy: The Struggle to Build Free Societies throughout the World*, New York: Holt, 2008.
A comprehensive, excellent and accessible overview of the many aspects of democratisation around the world.

D. Berg-Schlosser (ed.), *Democratization. The State of the Art*, Wiesbaden: VS Verlag, 2004.
Summarises the academic debates about democratisation from different points of view.

J. Markoff, 'Transitions to Democracy', in T. Janoski, R. R. Alford, A. M. Hicks and M. A. Schwartz (eds.), *The Handbook of Political Sociology*, Cambridge: Cambridge University Press, 2005.
A good general discussion of the transition to democracy.

W. Merkel, 'Embedded and defective democracies', *Democratization*, Vol. 11, No. 5, 2004: 33–58.
Elaborates the distinction between embedded and defective democracies, and the failings and persistence of the latter.

F. Zakaria, *The Future of Freedom: Illiberal Democracy at Home and Abroad*, New York: Norton, 2003.
Examines the spread of illiberal democracies.

P. Norris, *Driving Democracy: Do Power-Sharing Institutions Work?*, Cambridge: Cambridge University Press, 2008.
A comparative analysis of the relevance of institutions for democracy.

Websites

www.freedomhouse.org

Provides information about democracy and human rights for each state of the world.

www.ned.org/forum/internationalforum.html

Website of the International Forum for Democratic Studies, providing information for everybody interested in democracy and democratisation.

See briefing 3.1 for further websites with information about democratic developments.

PART II

The polity: structures and institutions

Part I of this book considered the nature and development of the modern democratic state in general terms. Part II looks more closely at internal structures and institutions – sometimes referred to as the 'machinery of state' or the 'nuts-and-bolts of government', because they are the permanent structures of the political system. They are important because they set the framework within which individuals and organisations behave in everyday political life. In this sense we can distinguish between government, with its formal structures and institutions, on the one hand, and politics, with its political behaviour and processes, on the other. Following this distinction, Part II concentrates on structures and institutions of government, while Part III focuses on the political behaviour of individuals, groups and organisations. Although this is a convenient and useful way of dividing up the book, we should not forget that structures influence and mould behaviour, just as much as behaviour helps to create structures. Although it is useful to distinguish between the institutions of government and the processes of politics, the two are simply different sides of the same coin.

Chapter 4 deals with the constitutional framework of modern democracies. Constitutions are sometimes overlooked in modern comparative politics, but the fact is that they are enormously important. They try to grapple with the basic problem of all democracies – how to balance the necessary powers of the state against the individual rights of citizens, and how to ensure that government does not become too powerful and remains responsible and accountable to its citizens. Constitutions are the blueprints of power in democracies.

Chapter 5 turns to the three main branches of most democratic governments – the executive, legislative and judicial branches. It shows how, in spite of the bewildering variety of constitutional arrangements, most states fall into one of two general types, either presidential or parliamentary systems, and how these work in practice.

Chapter 6, on multi-level government, looks at how government is divided in a different way. Few states are so small that they can be ruled by a single centre of national government. Most democracies are divided geographically with national government sitting on top of layers of regional, local and community government. Similarly, no democratic state can run its own affairs as if it were an island on its own. All have arrangements, agreements and treaties with other sovereign states. Chapter 6, therefore, examines multi-level government from the global and the international down to the local community.

Chapter 7 considers the two most important functions of government – the executive and the legislative. These two overlap to a considerable extent, but the executive is primarily responsible for executing (that is, carrying out) the affairs of state and the policies of the government, while the legislative is mainly concerned with representing the views of citizens, turning them into laws and keeping a watching brief on the executive.

Finally, Chapter 8 examines the administrative backbone of the state – the public bureaucracy. Bureaucrats are important, and potentially enormously powerful, because politicians rely heavily on the people who staff the government ministries to run the daily business of government.

The five chapters of Part II of the book, therefore, examine the main structures and institutions of government:

- Constitutions
- Presidential and parliamentary government
- Multi-level government
- Policy making and legislating
- Implementation.

4   Constitutions

Although the citizens of a given state may feel that theirs is the only or the best way of doing things, there is nothing natural or God-given about having a president rather than a prime minister, a unitary rather than a federal system, or two legislative assemblies rather than one. In fact, it is probably true to say that every modern democracy (chapter 2) has a unique set of government institutions, and combines them in unique ways. It is certainly true that there is no agreed formula or set of rules that will produce a democracy; each country follows its own special path and makes its own particular arrangements.

The particular configuration of institutions in any given state is defined by its **constitution**. This is the most basic set of laws that establishes the shape and form of the political structure. We start this chapter, therefore, by considering the nature and purpose of constitutions – what they are and why we have them. Constitutions try to create a complex set of **checks and balances** between the different branches of government, so that no one institution or person has too much power. We then introduce the three main branches of government – the executive, legislative and the judiciary – and outline their basic purpose and design. Constitutions, however, are only the beginning, not the end, of the story of comparative politics, so we also discuss the limits of constitutionalism and why it is necessary to go beyond formal laws to understand how democracies work in practice.

> **Constitution** A set of fundamental laws that determines the central institutions and offices, and powers and duties of the state.

Finally, we consider various theories of political institutions and how they help us to understand the structure and operations of the modern state.

The major topics in this chapter are:

- What a constitution is, and why we have them
- The division of powers
- The limits of constitutionalism
- Constitutional and institutional theories.

■ What a constitution is, and why we have them

In some respects government is like a game; before the players can even take the field to compete, they need to agree on a set of rules that decide how the game is to be played. Constitutions are the rules of the political game – who can vote, who can stand for office, what powers they are to have, the rights and duties of citizens and so on. Without these basic rules politics would degenerate into arbitrariness, brute force, or anarchy. If the rules work well, we tend to take them for granted and concentrate on the day-to-day game of politics, just as we take the rules of our favourite sport for granted and concentrate on today's match. Nonetheless, constitutions are important because they have a profound influence over how the game of politics is played, and therefore over the outcome of the game – who gets what, and when? For this reason, some theories of politics place great importance on constitutions, and on the political institutions that they create and shape.

Constitutions are sets of laws, but they are very special ones that lay out the most important institutions and offices of the state and define their formal powers (see briefing 4.1 and fact file 4.1). Consequently, they have four main features:

1. *Fundamental laws* Constitutions are laws about the political procedures to be followed in making laws. They are supreme laws, taking precedence over all others, and defining how all the others should be made. Some analysts call them 'meta-rules' (rules about how to make rules), but the German constitution calls them 'the Basic Law'.
2. *Entrenched status* Constitutions have a special legal status. Unlike other laws, constitutions usually state the conditions under which the constitution can itself be changed. These conditions are often very demanding in ways that are intended to make sure that the change is not hasty or undemocratic, and that it has widespread support.
3. *Codified document* Constitutions are written down, often in a single document that presents the constitution in a systematic manner.
4. *Allocation of powers* Constitutions outline the proper relations between institutions and offices of the state, and between government and citizens. This is probably the most crucial part because it allocates powers

Briefing 4.1

Constitutions

Constitutions vary so much that no two are likely to be the same in any particular respect. Some are long and detailed (India's has 387 articles and nine schedules), some short (the USA's has seven articles and twenty-seven amendments). Many are general, but others try to specify the kind of society and political system they aspire to – Sweden's sets out specific regulations for social security and labour laws, Japan's renounces war, and Croatia's states that some rights can be restricted in case of war. Some are contained in a single document, some refer to other documents or to international agreements such as the UN Declaration of Human Rights (1948). Some have been changed comparatively frequently, others rarely. Some are old, some new. In a few cases, the constitution is said to be unwritten (Britain and Israel) but, in fact, it is better to refer to them as 'uncodified', because while much is written down, it is not consolidated in one main document.

It is easy to obtain the constitution of every nation in the world from websites (see p. 90) so no examples are provided here. In spite of their huge variety, most constitutions fall into four main parts:

- *Preamble* The preamble tends to be a declaration about nationhood and history, with references to important national events, symbols and aspirations. The preamble tends to be inspirational rather than legal or rational.
- *Fundamental rights (Bill of Rights)* A list of civil and political rights and statements about the limits of government powers. Some constitutions refer also to economic, social and cultural rights. Many of the newer constitutions simply adopt the 1948 UN Universal Declaration of Human Rights.
- *Institutions and offices of government* The main structures or institutions of government are described, together with their powers and duties. Usually this means the executive, legislative and judicial branches of national government, and sometimes lower levels of government as well.
- *Amendment* The procedures to be followed in amending the constitution.

and functions to government and specifies the *rights and duties* of governments and citizens – who can do what, to whom, and under what circumstances.

Because constitutions are so important, they are often the focus of fierce political battles between different groups who want to frame the rules in their own interest. Democratic constitutions therefore try to impose rules that are fair and impartial to all groups and interests in society, so that all can compete on a 'level playing field'. They try to do this by incorporating a set of seven basic principles:

1. *Rule of law* According to Albert V. Dicey (1835–1922), the nineteenth-century British constitutional theorist, the rule of law underlies the idea of constitutionalism. The rule of law, not the arbitrary rule of powerful individuals, is the hallmark of democracy.

Fact file 4.1

Constitutions

- The first codified constitution was San Marino's (1600), followed by Canada's (1774) and the USA's (1787).
- Between 1990 and 1995 ninety-six countries – about half of the world's total – adopted new constitutions. Twenty were in central and eastern Europe, but thirty-one were in central and southern Africa.
- Most countries have modified their constitutions at some point in their history, but Belgium, Canada, France (twice), The Netherlands, New Zealand, Sweden and Turkey have done so in major ways in recent decades. The Indian constitution has been amended more than seventy times since 1950, but the American has been amended only twenty-seven times since 1787, and ten of these were contained in the Bill of Rights of 1791. France has had seventeen constitutions since 1789.
- About 70 per cent of constitutions date back no further than 1945.

2. *Transfer of power* Democracies are marked by a peaceful transfer of power from one set of leaders or parties to another. Democratic constitutions typically state the conditions for this – how and when government is to be elected, by whom and for how long. The peaceful transfer of power is so important that some political scientists define a 'democracy' in these terms – e.g. there have been three successive free and peaceful elections.

3. *Separation of powers and checks and balances* According to classical political theory, democracy is best protected by creating separate branches of government with different functions and powers, each checking and balancing the power of the others in a system of checks and balances.

Separation of powers The doctrine that political power should be divided among several bodies or officers of the state as a precaution against too much concentration of power.

4. *Relations between government and citizens* At the heart of any democracy is the relationship between citizens and their government, so constitutions often include (or refer to) a Bill of Rights that enumerates the rights and responsibilities of citizens, and the limits of government power over them. Those who are suspicious of government in any shape or form see constitutions as setting clear limits on the power of government in order to guarantee the rights of the citizens.

5. *Locus of sovereignty* Since there must be a governing body or office capable of making authoritative decisions, constitutions usually specify who or what is to be the ultimate authority to make and enforce law.

6. *Government accountability* Democratic governments are accountable to their citizens, and constitutions normally try to pin down the mechanisms of this accountability – who is answerable to whom, and under what circumstances.

7. *Final arbiter* Constitutions are sometimes disputed because none is fully clear, consistent, unambiguous, or comprehensive. The last job of a constitution is to say who is to be the final arbiter of its meaning and how it may be changed.

■ The separation of powers

Democratic constitutions attempt to create limited (not autocratic or totalitarian) government that is accountable to, and responsive to the will of, its citizens. According to classical political theory (John Locke (1632–1704), Montesquieu (1689–1755) and the *Federalist Papers* (1777–8) in the USA), this is best achieved by dividing power between the executive, legislative and judicial branches of government, and by creating checks and balances between them so that no one branch can become too powerful.

Executives

Most large organisations have a person, or small group, to take final decisions, decide policies and take ultimate responsibility. Businesses have company chairmen and chief executive officers (CEOs). Governments have political executives (from the Latin term 'to carry out') who do the same job, and who are usually known as presidents or prime ministers – President Obama of the USA, Prime Minister Aso of Japan, Chancellor Merkel of Germany, Prime Minister Singh of India, President Bachelet of Chile, President Khama of Botswana and so on. The **executive** branch of government, being at the top of the political pyramid, performs three main functions:

> **Executive** The branch of government mainly responsible for initiating government action, making and implementing public policy, and coordinating the activities of the state.

1. *Decision-making* – initiating government action and formulating public policy
2. *Implementation* – executives implement (apply) their policies, which means they must also run the main departments and bureaucracies of state
3. *Coordination* – coordination and integration of the complex affairs of state.

In most modern democracies the executive officer is called a president or prime minister. But, to complicate matters, presidents are not always political executives. For example, both the USA and Germany have presidents, but they do entirely different jobs. In America, the elected president is both the head of government and the head of state, which is an enormously powerful and important position, but the German president is only the head of state and a largely ceremonial figure who is, in some respects, rather like a constitutional monarch (see fact file 4.2). In what follows we are concerned mainly with the politically powerful presidents who, as both heads of state and government, are significant political figures, not ceremonial ones.

Fact file 4.2

Heads of state and heads of government

■ Presidential heads of government

- In presidential systems, the directly elected president is both head of state and head of government.
- In parliamentary systems, the head of state is a largely ceremonial function carried out either by a monarch or a president, while the head of government, a position of real power, is normally filled by a prime minister or chancellor.
- Presidential heads of state may be elected or appointed, but presidential heads of government in democracies are always directly elected.
- Surprisingly, quite a few heads of state in established democracies are monarchs – Belgium, Denmark, Japan, The Netherlands, Norway, Spain, Sweden and the UK. This is because these countries have often avoided revolution and adapted slowly to democratic pressures, leaving their kings and queens in place while adapting institutions around them.
- Apart from the monarchies, non-executive presidential heads of state, performing a largely ceremonial role, are found in Austria, Germany, Greece, Ireland, India, Israel, Japan and Italy.

■ Presidential heads of government

- Usually the president is a single person, but a few countries (Bosnia-Herzegovina, Cyprus and Uruguay) have experimented with joint presidencies, usually unsuccessfully.
- There are seventy-eight presidential systems in the world, making them the most common form of democratic government in the world. Fifty-five of these are new democracies formed since 1990, and it remains to be seen how many of these will remain presidential if these systems change.
- Presidential systems are found mainly in Latin America, which has been influenced by the USA, and in the new democracies of central and eastern Europe.

Legislatures

Executives are the decision-making branch of government, and **legislatures** are the law-making branch. The term derives from the Latin words 'legis' (law) and 'latio' (bringing). Legislatures evolved from the assemblies that medieval monarchs called to agree to some royal action – to levy taxes or wage war. These assemblies started meeting regularly, and eventually came to be elected by all citizens of the state and so they acquired legitimacy as representative parliaments or assemblies (see fact file 4.3). Technically, a legislature is any law-making body, however constituted, but in a democracy the legislature gets its legitimacy from the fact that it is directly and popularly elected by citizens.

Legislature The branch of government mainly responsible for discussing and passing legislation, and keeping watch on the executive.

Fact file 4.3

Legislatures

- The precursor of modern parliamentary legislatures is probably the *Althingi*, the assembly established by Viking settlers in Iceland about a thousand years ago.
- Legislatures can consist of any number of assemblies, but about three-quarters of contemporary legislatures have one chamber (unicameral) and the rest have two (bicameral).
- Unicameral legislatures include Bulgaria, Denmark, Estonia, Finland, Israel, New Zealand, Peru, South Korea and Sweden.
- New Zealand, Denmark, Sweden, Iceland and Peru have all moved from bicameralism to unicameralism since 1950. Although more countries have created second chambers than abolished them in recent decades, it appears that unicameralism has been successful in the established democracies.
- Bicameral legislatures include Australia, Austria, Canada, Brazil, Mexico, the USA, Germany, India, Italy, Japan, Spain, South Africa, Switzerland and the UK,
- The larger the population of a country, the larger its legislative body is likely to be. India, with a population of more than 100 million, has a lower house with 545 members. Brazil, with a population of 200 million, has a Chamber of Deputies with 513 members. At the other extreme, Trinidad and Tobago, with a population of 1.3 million, has a House of Representatives of 41 members, and Iceland, with a population of 300,000, has an Althingi with sixty-three members.
- The larger the country the more likely it is to be bicameral. On average, unicameral democracies have populations less than half that of bicameral countries.
- Four out of five federal states are bicameral, compared with one-quarter of unitary states. The representation basis of many second chambers in federal systems is often regional or local, as it is in Australia, Canada, Germany, India, Switzerland, Brazil and the USA.

Legislatures are known by a variety of names – assemblies, parliaments, houses and chambers – but all amount to much the same thing: assemblies are meetings of elected representatives who meet to discuss public affairs; parliaments are 'talking shops'; houses and chambers are the places where assemblies and parliaments meet – the House of Commons, the House of Representatives, the Chamber of Deputies.

Legislatures may be formed by one (unicameral) or two (bicameral) houses. If we remember that democratic government is already divided between three main branches, one might well ask why the legislative body should be further divided into two chambers. Indeed, two chambers may only complicate matters:

- Which of the two is to be the stronger and have the last word if they disagree?
- If the first is elected in a democratic fashion, how is the second to be constituted, and if it is also elected won't it inevitably clash with the first?

For these reasons, there is a great debate about whether unicameralism is better than bicameralism (see controversy 4.1), but it turns out that most

One chamber or two?

Pro-unicameralism	Pro-bicameralism
• Power is mainly located in one assembly. No confusion of roles, responsibilities, or accountability.	• Two chambers provide another set of checks and balances, with powers to delay, criticise, amend, or veto – a constitutional backstop.
• No overlap or duplication between assemblies. Two assemblies can result in rivalry and even deadlock between the two.	• Two forms of representation, usually direct election to the lower chamber, and another form of election (indirect) or appointment to the higher.
• There is room for only one elected, representative body. 'If the second chamber agrees with the first, it is useless; if it disagrees it is dangerous' (Abbé Sieyès).	• A second chamber can reduce the workload of the first by considering legislation in detail, leaving the first chamber to deal with broad issues.
• Most legislatures are unicameral, and the number is increasing. Many new states have adopted unicameralism with apparent success, especially in Africa and the Middle East.	• A majority of democracies have bicameral legislatures – Australia, Britain, Canada, France, India, Italy, Japan, Mexico, Brazil, the USA, South Africa and Switzerland.
• Unicameralism is particularly suitable for unitary states (three-quarters are unicameral).	• Bicameralism is suited to federal systems, where territorial units of government within the state can be represented at the national level: 80 per cent of bicameral systems are in federal states.
• Costa Rica, Denmark, New Zealand and Sweden have abolished their second chambers, without apparent adverse effects.	• Some claim the main defence of bicameralism is political – upper chambers are conservative bodies with the job of tempering the actions of the lower house.
• Unicameralism seems to work best in small countries.	• Bicameralism seems to work best in countries that are large or socially and ethnically diverse – it helps to resolve regional conflict.
• Second chambers with appointed members are often criticised as being places where 'has-been politicians' go to die.	

democracies are bicameral. This is because it is usually not too difficult to sort out a system that enables two houses to work together effectively. Whatever the abstract and theoretical problems may be, it is generally possible to solve them in a practical way.

Strong and weak bicameralism

Bicameral legislatures come in two forms: *weak* and *strong*. In the strong systems, both assemblies are of equal strength, but since this is a recipe for conflict – even deadlock – there are rather few cases of successful strong bicameralism. Many of them are found in federal systems (see chapter 6), including Australia, Belgium, Germany, Switzerland and the USA. Most bicameral systems are 'weak', which means that one assembly is more powerful than the other. To complicate matters the stronger (first chamber) is usually known as the 'lower house', while the weaker (second chamber) is the 'upper house', usually called the Senate (after the American Senate). Weak bicameralism is also known as 'asymmetric bicameralism' – i.e. the two houses are of unequal power. Typically in weak bicameral systems, the lower house initiates legislation and controls financial matters and the upper house has limited powers to delay and recommend amendments.

Membership of the second house

Since democratic lower chambers are directly elected by the population, many upper chambers are constituted on a different basis. Most are not directly elected by the population as a whole, but are either indirectly elected or appointed, or some combination of both. Some upper chambers, however, are directly elected, usually in federal systems (see chapter 6) but on a different basis than the lower house. If they are directly elected at all, upper houses are often based on different geographical constituencies.

Tenure and size

The terms of tenure of upper houses are usually different. They are often elected for a longer term of office (five–nine years, rather than the three–five years of lower chambers). Upper chambers sometimes have an older qualifying age, and they are usually much smaller than lower ones.

Judiciaries

Should politicians be the final judge of how the constitution should be interpreted? The danger is that the government of the day will try to manipulate matters in its own interests. Therefore, constitutions are, in the words of David Hume (1711–76), a set of 'institutions designed for knaves'. This does not presume that all politicians actually are knaves, but takes full account of the possibility that they might be, and that a constitution needs a safeguard against this danger. Since a constitution is primarily a legal document, it is argued that lawyers should be the final arbiter of it. Besides, judges (the **judiciary**) are often thought to be the best independent and incorruptible source of experience and wisdom on constitutional matters. This, in turn, requires judicial independence to protect judges from political interference and from the temptations of corruption. For this reason, judges are often appointed for life and paid well. Some

> **Judiciary** The branch of government mainly responsible for the authoritative interpretation and application of law.

Judicial review The binding power of the courts to provide an authoritative interpretation of laws, including constitutional law, and to overturn executive or legislative actions they hold to be illegal or unconstitutional.

countries have created special constitutional courts, but most use their regular courts (see fact file 4.4).

Not all democratic countries accept the principle of **judicial review** of the constitution. Some reject it, for two main reasons:

1. It is difficult to guarantee the political independence of the judges. In many countries, senior judges are appointed by politicians and conservative politicians tend to appoint conservative judges while liberal politicians are more likely to appoint liberal ones. Nor are judges entirely immune from the social pressures of public opinion and the mass media. Most important, judges usually come from conservative social groups and deliver conservative political judgements. In short, it is claimed that judges are not, or cannot be, neutral.

2. In a democracy, so it is argued, the democratically elected legislature should have responsibility for interpreting the constitution, not an appointed and unrepresentative judiciary.

Fact file 4.4

Judiciaries

- The principle of judicial review was originally limited to the USA in the nineteenth century. It became more widely accepted in the twentieth century, especially in federal systems where the courts were used to settle disputes not only between branches of government but between federal and other levels of government as well.
- A few democracies, such as Belgium, Finland, The Netherlands and Switzerland, do not have judicial review.
- Some states (Israel, New Zealand, the UK) have judicial review in practice, but not in theory. In the UK, the binding nature of EU law has given the courts the role of judicial review.
- Special constitutional courts have been created in Austria, France, the EU, Germany, Greece, Chile, South Africa, Italy, Portugal and Spain, and many of the new democracies of central and eastern Europe.
- Judicial review is carried out by regular courts in most countries including Australia, Canada, Denmark, India, Italy, Japan, Sweden, and the USA.
- The Federal Constitutional Court of Germany has become one of the most active in the west, rejecting some 5 per cent of all legislation on constitutional grounds, and becoming involved in issues ranging from freedom of speech and abortion to federal–state relations and public finance. The European Court of Justice (ECJ) is also active and powerful in EU matters.
- Obudsmen (also known as Parliamentary Commissioners, Inspectors General and Public Protector) are found in many western European states and the EU, as well as Brazil, Croatia, the Czech Republic, Estonia, India, Israel, Latvia, New Zealand, Peru, South Africa and the USA.

Judges are involved in more than constitutional law. The meaning of other laws may also be ambiguous and disputed, and sometimes this has political implications – electoral law for example, or tax law with implications that affect government's capacity to raise money for public services. In fact, some legislation is deliberately vague, because it was the only way out of political deadlock between competing groups. In such circumstances, it is the job of the courts to interpret the law and to decide how it should be applied to particular cases. In doing so, the courts may go beyond merely interpreting the law and actually modify or change it in subtle ways. In this respect, judges can play an important political role as the third branch of government.

Judicial activism

The role of the courts in government is tending to widen. The Supreme Court of the USA was not given power of constitutional review in the 1787 constitution, but had successfully claimed it by 1803. The USA then went through two notable periods of **judicial activism** in the 1930s (when it tried to stop Roosevelt's New Deal legislation) and again in the 1950s (when it promoted racial integration). There is a general tendency now for the courts to take a more active role in government across the democratic world where the judiciary has the right of judicial review. The five main reasons for the expanding role of the courts are:

> **Judicial activism** Involves the courts taking a broad and active view of their role as interpreters of the constitution and reviewers of executive and legislative action.

- An increasing volume of legislation and government actions
- The increasing complexity of government machinery, which means that there is greater chance of conflict between branches and levels of government, especially in federal systems or when new supra-national governments (e.g. the EU) are being developed
- An increasing emphasis on the rule of law and the rights of citizens, and the need to write these down in the legal form, such as in a Charter or Bill of Rights
- A willingness to use the courts (the 'culture of litigation') as a means of resolving conflict
- Possibly, an unwillingness or inability of politicians to deal with difficult political issues; they may be happy to pass on some political 'hot potatoes', especially moral issues, to the courts.

There are problems with judicial activism as there are with judicial review of the constitution. Striking down legislation and choosing between different interpretations of the law can amount to policy making, and sometimes even small differences of legal interpretation of the law can have large policy ramifications. Should judges have this power? And when there is a conflict between elected government and the courts, who should win?

Another quasi-legal development in modern democratic politics is the appointment of ombudsmen. An **ombudsman** is a 'grievance officer', or a state official to whom citizens can appeal if they feel wrongly treated by public bodies. Sweden, which invented the concept, has four ombudsmen covering different areas of public services. Although ombudsmen are found in many western European countries, most democracies (about 75 per cent) do not have them, preferring to use normal court procedures. For the most part, ombudsmen are not lavishly funded and their powers are usually limited, so they rarely have a big impact.

> **Ombudsman** A state official appointed to receive complaints and investigate claims about maladministration.

Unitary and federal states

We shall discuss **federal states** and unitary government at greater length in chapter 6, but it is appropriate to make an important constitutional point here. In federal systems, power is divided not only between the executive, legislative and judicial branches of government, but also between territorial units of government. These territorial units – states, or regions, or provinces – often have substantial powers and rights that are guaranteed by the constitution. In some ways, therefore, federalism is another form of the division of powers within the state – a geographical division between geographical areas, to complement the political division between the executive, legislative and judicial branches. Moreover, the territorial units of federal systems often repeat the division of powers found at the federal level because each unit has its own executive, legislative and judicial branches of government.

> **Federal states** Federal states combine a central authority with a degree of constitutionally defined autonomy for sub-central, territorial units of government.

This distinguishes federal from **unitary states**. In a unitary system, national government ultimately controls all layers of government below it, and can reform, reorganise, or abolish units of local or regional government without any special constitutional restraint. In federal systems, the rights and powers and existence of the federal units are protected by the constitution.

> **Unitary states** In unitary states the central government is the only sovereign body. It does not share constitutional authority with any sub-central units of government.

■ The limits of constitutionalism

Constitutions are not like cooking recipes that produce exactly the right result if they are followed to the last detail. They are, after all, only legal words on pieces of paper. How they work in practice is a rather different matter. Constitutions are important documents, perhaps supremely important, but there are seven key reasons why they should not necessarily be taken at their face value:

- They may be completely unimportant simply because they are not observed. Most dictatorships have democratic constitutions, and politicians in established democracies have been known to try to flout, break, or go around them.

- They may be incomplete. They are general documents that may not even mention some of the more important aspects of the constitution – electoral systems, political parties, or even the office of prime minister.
- A full understanding of a constitution sometimes requires reference to other documents – supreme court judgments, historical documents, or the UN Declaration of Human Rights.
- Written constitutions are often supported by conventions.
- Constitutions can develop and change, even if the documents do not. The American constitution of 1787 did not give the Supreme Court of the USA the right of constitutional review. The Supreme Court took this power for itself in 1803 when it ruled on the case of *Marbury* v. *Madison*.

> **Conventions** Unwritten rules that impose obligations on constitutional actors that are held to be binding, but not incorporated into law or reinforced by legal sanctions.

- Constitutions can be vague or fail to cover particular or exceptional circumstances.
- Constitutions can fail. History is full of failed democratic constitutions that have been supplanted by revolutions, autocrats and military dictatorships. The lesson is that successful democracy cannot be imposed by constitutional law, no matter how well thought-out this may be; democratic politics must also be accepted and practised by political elites and citizens alike. Constitutions are like fortresses – they must be well built and well protected by soldiers.

This leads us to the conclusion that constitutions are rather like maps or blueprints of the main institutions of government (for three examples see briefing 4.2), but actual operations may differ – even differ radically – from the legal documents. This leads to the debate about how important institutions are, and to what extent they actually determine the operations of a political system and the behaviour of political actors within it.

■ Constitutional and institutional theories

The 'old constitutionalism'

The interest of political theorists in constitutions dates back at least to Aristotle's famous commentary on the constitution of Athens. In the late nineteenth and first half of the twentieth century, however, the lead was taken not by political theorists but by lawyers and comparative political scientists. Their work was largely legal, descriptive and historical, and confined to a few western states, especially to the UK, the USA and France. After the Second World War this style of political science was fiercely criticised for being too descriptive and legalistic rather than analytical, for its failure to theorise and generalise, for being culture-bound by its narrow western origins and, above all, for its interest in formal and legal documents rather than 'going behind the scenes' to get at the real stuff of everyday politics.

Moreover, as we have already seen, constitutions do not always work as they are supposed to. As a result, many of the constitutions so carefully designed

Briefing 4.2

The Constitutions of Argentina, France and Japan

Argentina

Type of government	Presidential republic: federal state.
Date of constitution	1853, revised 1994
Head of state	President
Executive	Cabinet appointed by President
Legislature	Bicameral National Congress
	Senate: 72 directly elected, six-year term, half every three years Chamber of Deputies: 275 directly elected, four-year term, half every two years
Judiciary	Judicial review by Supreme Court
Sub-national government	23 provinces and one autonomous city (the Federal Capital of Buenos Aires)

France

Type of government	Republic: unitary state
Date of constitution	1958, amended in 1962, and in 1992, 1996 and 2000 to comply with EU requirements, and in 2000 to reduce presidential term of office from seven to five years
Executive	Head of State, President, directly elected Head of Government; Prime Minister nominated by National Assembly majority and appointed by President; Cabinet appointed by President at suggestion of Prime Minister
Legislature	Bicameral
	Senate: 321 seats, indirectly elected for nine years, one-third every three years
	National Assembly: 577 seats, directly elected for five years
Judiciary	Supreme Court of Appeal plus Constitutional Council for constitutional matters
Sub-national government	22 regions, 96 departments

Japan

Type of government	Unitary state with constitutional monarch and parliamentary government
Date of constitution	1947
Head of state	Emperor

Executive	Prime Minister; cabinet appointed by Prime Minister
Legislature	Bicameral
	House of Councillors: 247 seats, six-year term, half every three years
	House of Representatives: 480 seats, elected for four years
Judiciary	Judicial review of legislation by Supreme Court
Sub-national government	47 prefectures

Source: http://confinder.richmond.edu/

(mainly by constitutional lawyers for the newly decolonised and independent countries of Africa and Asia) collapsed and gave way to dictatorship and military government because they were not adapted to social, political and economic circumstances. The failure of these constitutions made it clear that democracy rests on more – far more – than constitutional design, no matter how good this may be on paper. Consequently, when an interest in constitutions was revived in the last quarter of the twentieth century, it went beyond the 'old' institutionalism of legalistic and descriptive studies of constitutions.

The 'new constitutionalism'

The 'new constitutionalism' tried to balance out three main concerns:

1. The protection of citizen rights and the limitation of government powers – in other words, the classical concerns of constitutional theory.
2. A concern with balancing the limited powers and maximum accountability of government, with the need for effective government action in a complex and fast-changing world. It is argued that constitutions are not abstract designs, but practical machines that need careful construction and engineering, and then to be judged by how effectively they work in practice.
3. An attempt to adapt the constitutional design of a country to its social and economic circumstances. It was realised that there is no single constitutional design that is best, but a variety of models to suit different conditions. Constitutional theory tried to solve the problem of how stable democracies could be established in previously undemocratic countries, especially in countries divided by ethnic, religious, linguistic and cultural cleavages. In central and eastern Europe, civil society theorists argued that it was vital that constitutions guaranteed the rights of citizen organisations, and their independence from government. Ethnically mixed societies, it was argued, needed a form of 'consensus' democracy that protected the rights of minorities and gave them effective power to participate in government. We will return to civil society theory in chapter 10 and to consensus democracies in chapter 7.

The 'new institutionalism'

Both the 'old' and the 'new' constitutionalism assumes that constitutions matter, and that they are not only a vital part of any democratic system but also an influence – perhaps even a decisive influence – on how political actors behave and how political systems works. This basic idea is expounded in what is known as the 'new institutionalism'. 'The new institutionalism' is not so much a theory as a general approach that focuses on the organisations, structures and institutions of government and politics. There are variations on the general theme, but there is a common argument underlying them:

- Institutions are the framework within which individuals behave. Political institutions not only constrain what individuals do, but also what they think is possible to do. As we have seen, actors in a system tend to take its basic structure and rules for granted – as given – and organise their behaviour accordingly.
- Institutions are the products of past political battles in which winners tend to create particular forms of organisation that work in their own interests, although they may be quite unconscious of this. Constitutions embody the outcomes of past political struggles over how the game of politics is to be played, and by whom.
- Institutions have a degree of inertia built into them. Once established, they will tend to persist, unless circumstances encourage attempts to change them, and sometimes they may be so firmly rooted that this is difficult.

In short, institutions matter. They are political actors in their own right. They are partly the products of the society in which they are embedded, but they also help to shape society and its politics. It has therefore been argued that political science should 'bring the state back in' by combining a concern with the major institutions of a political system (not just constitutions) with an understanding of their historical development. The idea of 'constitutional engineering' is based on the premise that institutions are important and that whether it concerns reforming an existing constitution or designing a new one from scratch, getting the right mix of institutions for a society is important for its democratic stability and quality.

However, this is all very general, and what we need now is some examples of how institutions work in order to put some flesh on the bones of the general theory.

The mobilisation of bias

The idea that institutions matter was caught (some time before the 'new institutionalism') by the American political scientist E. E. Schattschneider (1892–1971) in the phrase 'organisation is the mobilisation of bias'. This means that all organisations (institutions are one kind) have a built-in capacity to do some things better than others, which may well serve some interests better than others. Politics, therefore, is the organisation of bias in the sense that some issues are organised into politics, while others are organised out.

In some countries, second chambers are used to give membership of the upper house to geographical areas or to occupational groups. This means that some interests will find it easier to gain access to the highest levels of government than in a unicameral system. And since upper chambers tend to be conservative bodies (this is one justification for their existence), there is a tendency for bicameral systems, especially strong bicameral ones, to have a conservative veto-power built into them.

Institutional influence, rules and inertia

In an important article published in 1984 in the *American Political Science Review*, James G. March and Johan P. Olsen argued that institutions were basically a collection of inter-related rules and routines that defined how the members of an institution saw it and their own role within it. These routines included stock responses to problems that were automatically used before trying anything else. How people behaved within the institution, therefore, was determined by institutional rules and routines that defined what was appropriate action in the circumstances. Legislative assemblies, especially old ones steeped in tradition, for example, have their own rules and ways of doing things. New members must learn and accept their customs to have a successful political career.

The economist Douglass North has spent much of his life exploring the ways in which economic institutions, once created, can have long-term effects on the content and impact of economic policy. The political scientist Peter Hall also shows that institutions come to absorb and embody a set of policy ideas, such as Keynesian economic theories, that have a long life because they become institutionalised in particular structures which gives them a life of their own. To understand the policy choices made now, we have to understand institutional histories and the ideas they stand for. The political scientist Arend Lijphart has investigated the relationship between different types of government institutions and political policies, something we will come back to later in this book (see chapter 7).

Marxist structural theory

An early form of institutional and structural analysis was Karl Marx's (1818–83) account of the capitalist state which, he said, was simply a device that enabled capitalists to stay in power and exploit the workers. As he put it in the *Communist Manifesto* (1848), 'the executive of the modern state' is 'but a committee for managing the common affairs of the whole bourgeoisie'. According to Marx, capitalists create and use the institutions of the state for their own purposes: the police and the courts to protect capitalist property; schools, universities and established religion to indoctrinate people into a state of 'false consciousness' in which they cannot even recognise their own best interests; parliament to give an illusion of democracy; and the military to protect the empire as a source of profit. Marx thus employs a structural–historical approach that focuses not on the behaviour of individuals who happen to be capitalists or workers, but on the workings of the whole system and its historical development. He implies that capitalists are not to be blamed for their exploitation of the workers; they are simply following the logic of the situation they find themselves in.

Governance

Governance The act of governing; that is, the total set of government's activities in each phase of the policy making process.

The most recent form of institutional theory revolves around the concept of governance. Although the term '**governance**' can mean rather different things to different people, its core idea is that government no longer revolves around a few institutions of the central state, but consists of a much wider and looser network of organisations and institutions, some private, some public and some a partnership of the public and private. If government is about 'top-down', hierarchical power relations organised by public institutions, and if politics is about 'bottom-up' participation of individuals and groups, then governance is about bringing these two together by coordinating the activity of the large number of institutions, groups, individuals and organisations in the public and private sector. Government is no longer about a narrow range of organisations and institutions but about trying to give shape and direction to the complex multi-level activities of multifarious public and private political actors. In short, governance focuses not on a few institutions of the central state but on a wide variety of institutions, organisations and associations that blur the dividing line between government and the wider society.

■ What have we learned?

This chapter has dealt with how the institutions in a state are configured in its constitution. It argues that:

- Constitutions are a codified set of entrenched and fundamental laws (laws that determine the procedures to be followed in making other laws) that allocate powers between the main offices and institutions of the state.
- Democratic constitutions establish the rule of law and create limited government that is accountable and responsive to the will of its citizens.
- The best way of doing this is by dividing power between different offices and bodies, so that each acts as a check on the other and has its power balanced against that of the others.
- In most democracies, power is divided between three branches of government – the executive, legislative and judiciary, each of which checks and balances the others. All democratic governments follow this principle to a greater or lesser extent, but presidential and parliamentary, unicameral and bicameral, general courts and special constitutional courts, and federal and unitary forms of government do it in different ways.

Lessons of comparison

- Democratic constitutions come in a great many shapes and forms with many different institutions and many variations on their themes. All these forms can be democratic, and a comparison of them shows that there is no single route to democracy but different pathways arriving at roughly the same place.
- Different institutions have different combinations of strengths and weaknesses. Each do some things well, other things less well, and each differs in its strengths and weakness. None is perfect, so choosing this or that institution is a matter of trading off between a package of 'goods' and a package of 'not so goods'.
- Political systems rarely operate in the precise manner outlined by their formal constitutions, but most democracies operate roughly as the formal constitution requires. To a greater or lesser extent they all operate a system of division of powers, with checks and balances between the executive, legislative and judicial branches of government, all provide a more or less free and fair electoral system, all have a set of institutions that ensure a greater or lesser degree of accountability of the government to its citizens.
- Institutions have a life of their own, and they have an independent effect on society from that of politics. Among other things, they influence and shape the behaviour of individuals within them, a fact recognised by 'institutional' theories of politics.
- The study of failed constitutions shows that a democratic constitution on its own, no matter how well framed, is not enough. Constitutions are like fortresses; they must be well designed and well manned.

Projects

1. Assume you are a consultant brought in to advise on the creation of a constitution for Iraq **or** Afghanistan. Would you recommend:
   1. A unicameral or bicameral legislature?
   2. A federal or unitary system?
   3. A special constitutional court?
   4. An ombudsman/ombudsmen?
   Explain the reasons for your decisions.
2. How can institutions be political actors in their own right that constrain what people do? How can they shape what people think they can do?
3. If the French President visits The Netherlands, the Dutch Queen would normally welcome him, but the French Prime Minister will normally be welcomed by the Dutch Prime Minister. How do you explain this? Who would you invite to a meeting of 'heads of government' of EU member-states if the meeting was held in your country?

Further reading

R. L. Maddex, *Constitutions of the World,* London: Routledge, 1997.
Presents a summary of the constitutions and constitutional history of eighty nations.

V. Bogdanor (ed.), *Constitutions in Democratic Politics,* Aldershot: Gower, 1988: 1–13.
This introduction to an edited volume of essays on constitutions and democracy provides a useful general discussion of the subject.

P. Norton (ed.), *Legislatures,* Oxford: Oxford University Press, 1990.
A collection of classic work on legislatures.

R. A. W. Rhodes, 'The institutional approach', in David Marsh and Gerry Stoker (eds.), *Theories and Methods in Political Science,* Basingstoke: Macmillan, 1995: 42–57.
A good account of the institutional approach and of new institutionalism.

F. L. Wilson, 'The study of political institutions', in Howard J. Wiarda (ed.), *New Directions in Comparative Politics,* Oxford: Westview Press, 3rd edn., 2002: 189–210.
A good discussion of why and how political scientists study institutions.

B. G. Peters, *Institutional Theory in Political Science: The 'New Institutionalism',* London: Continuum, 1999.
A thorough, book-length treatment of different forms of new institutional theory.

Websites

http://confinder.richmond.edu/
This website provides the constitutions, charters, amendments and other related documents of the almost 200 nations in the world. Each country entry is linked to its constitutional text.
www.rulers.org
Contains lists of heads of state and heads of government of all countries and territories, going back to about 1700 in most cases. Also sub-divisions of various countries, as well as a selection of international organisations. Recent foreign ministers of all countries are listed separately.
www.servat.unibe.ch/law/icl/
The International Constitutional Law project website with a good collection of constitutional documents.

5   Presidential and parliamentary government

We have seen in chapter 4 that each democratic constitution has its own particular and special features, and that each combines them in a different way. This might produce a severe problem for comparative politics, for if every system was unique then all we could do would be to describe them in bewildering and endless detail. Fortunately for students of comparative politics, this is not the case. The great majority of democracies combine their three branches of government in one of three general ways – most of them fall fairly neatly into presidential or parliamentary or semi-presidential systems. Of course, each particular democracy retains its own special features, but most nonetheless conform to one of the three general types, and can be classified accordingly.

The first task of this chapter is to map out the three systems and the main differences between them. Since each has its own strengths and weaknesses, the second task is to consider their respective merits and deficiencies. Third, since constitutions do not exist in a societal vacuum, the next job is to try to sort out the form of government best suited to each kind of social and historical circumstances. Some forms of government are more likely to work better in certain conditions than others, and it is also possible that countries might do well to shift from one form to another as they develop over time.

The five major topics in this chapter are:

- Presidential systems
- Parliamentary systems
- Semi-presidential systems
- Presidential, parliamentary and semi-presidential systems compared
- Theories of parliamentary, presidential and semi-presidential government.

■ Presidential systems

Presidential systems A directly elected executive, with a limited term of office and a general responsibility for the affairs of state.

Directly elected Election by the electorate at large (popular election) rather than an electoral college, the legislature, or another body.

A great many **presidential systems** are modelled on the USA, and they reproduce many features of the American system, though not in every detail (see fact file 5.1). The main point about a presidential system is that its president is **directly elected** and his or her executive power is balanced by a legislature that is independent of the president because it, too, is popularly elected. The president, alone among all the officials of state, has general responsibility for public affairs. He or she may appoint ministers or cabinet members, but they are responsible only for their own department business, and they are accountable to the president, not the legislature. To ensure a real separation of powers (see chapter 4) neither the president nor members of the cabinet can be members of the legislature.

Presidential government is marked by four main features:

1. *Head of state and government* Presidents perform the ceremonial duties of head of state and are also in charge of the executive branch of government: they are usually chief of the armed forces and head of the national civil service, and responsible for both foreign policy and for initiating domestic legislation.
2. *The execution of policy* Presidents appoint cabinets to advise them and run the main state bureaucracies.
3. *Dependence on the legislative branch* Presidents initiate legislation but depend on the legislature to pass it into law.
4. *Fixed tenure* Presidents are directly elected for a fixed term and are normally secure in office unless, in exceptional circumstances, they are removed from it by the legislature.

The separation of executive and legislative, each with its independent authority derived from popular election, is a deliberate part of the system of checks and balances (see chapter 4). In theory both have powers and are independent of each other, but in practice presidents and assemblies usually have to share power. They must cooperate to get things done, and the result is not so much

Fact file 5.1

Presidential and parliamentary systems

■ Presidential systems

- Influenced by the USA, many Central and South American democracies have presidential governments – Argentina, Bolivia, Chile, Costa Rica, the Dominican Republic, El Salvador, Mexico, Peru and Uruguay.
- Most democracies in Africa are presidential including Benin, Botswana, Ghana, Namibia and South Africa.
- Presidential government is often found in the newly established democracies of the 'third wave' (see chapter 3), including Argentina, Croatia, the Philippines, South Korea and Taiwan.
- Switzerland is unique. It has a collective presidency formed by the seven members of the Federal Council (*Bundesrat*), one being selected to be the formal president each year.
- Most democratic presidents are restricted to one or two terms of office, a few to three and most set a minimum age for candidates that is higher than for other offices in order to get more experienced candidates.

■ Parliamentary systems

- There are currently fifty-six parliamentary systems in the world, including thirty-one constitutional monarchies and twenty-five established democracies.
- Parliamentary systems are most common in the older democracies of western Europe (including Austria, Belgium, Denmark, Ireland, The Netherlands, Norway, Sweden and the UK), and half of them are in British Commonwealth countries, including Australia, Botswana (where the Prime Minister is confusingly called the President), Canada, India and New Zealand.
- Israel is unusual in having a directly elected prime minister who, unlike a president, can be removed from office by the parliament, thus precipitating an election for both the prime minister and parliament.
- In contrast to presidential systems, the prime ministers or chancellors of parliamentary systems do not have limited terms of office, and in recent decades some of them have had successive election victories and have held on to power for a long time – Gonzales (Spain), Kohl (Germany), Menzies, Fraser and Hawke (Australia), Mitterrand (France), Thatcher (UK) and Trudeau and Mulroney (Canada).
- A large proportion of parliamentary democracies are smaller states (India is an exception) and many are small island democracies.
- Of the newly democratised countries of central and east Europe, Croatia, Bulgaria, Hungary, Latvia and Slovakia are fully parliamentary.

a separation of powers as a complex mix of them, consisting of a separation of institutions but a mix of powers in the daily give-and-take of their political relations.

Costa Rica is typical of the separation of powers in presidential systems. Its constitution provides for independent executive, legislative and judicial branches of government, with a clear division of offices and powers that check and balance one another. For example:

- The executive branch (president, vice-presidents and ministers in the Government Council) has the power to tax and spend according to law, but the legislative branch (the Legislative Assembly) has the power to amend the president's budget, and appoints a Comptroller General to check public expenditure and prevent overspending.
- The president has the duty to maintain order and tranquility in the nation and to safeguard public liberties, but the Assembly has the power to suspend (provided it has a two-thirds majority) individual rights if it believes there is a public need to do so.
- The president has the power to enter into agreements, public treaties and accords, and to enact and execute them according to the constitution, but the Assembly has the right to approve or disapprove international conventions, public treaties and concordats.
- The Legislative Assembly appoints members of the Supreme Court, which has used its right to enforce constitutional checks on presidential power.
- The Legislative Assembly appoints a powerful and independent Special Electoral Tribunal to oversee elections and ensure their free and fair conduct.

This division of powers has an important effect on the way that presidents work, because ultimately they are dependent on their legislatures. It is said, for example, that the American president has little power over Congress other than the power of persuasion. Some in the White House have found this inadequate, for the purposes of government. If Congress and the president are of a different political mind they may fight each other and get little done. One image likens the president, the House and the Senate to participants in a three-legged race – difficult to move along unless they move together, and easy to fall over if they pull in different directions. The problem is heightened if the presidency is controlled by one political party, and one or both houses of parliament by another. If, on top of this, the president is weak and the parties poorly co-ordinated or split, the majority party may be unable to pass its legislation. The result is that apparently powerful presidents are sometimes immobilised by elected assemblies.

For this reason, many presidential systems have failed the test of democratic stability and some experts believe that they do not make for effective government. The USA may be the only successful example, although Costa Rica has successfully maintained its presidential system since 1949.

■ Parliamentary systems

In **parliamentary systems** the executive is not directly elected but usually emerges or is drawn from the elected legislature (the parliament or assembly) and, unlike a directly elected president, is often an integral part of it (see fact

file 5.1). This form of parliamentary executive usually consists of a prime minister (sometimes called chancellor or premier)
and a cabinet or a council of ministers. The cabinet or council is the collective executive body.
Usually the leaders of the largest party in the
assembly, or the governing coalition within it,
take the executive offices. Unlike presidents,
who are the only officials with general responsibilities for government affairs, parliamentary
executives are supposed to share responsibilities among their members. This
means that the cabinet, including the prime minister, is jointly responsible
for all the actions of government, and the prime minister, therefore, is only
primus inter pares (first among equals). In fact, prime ministers in many countries have acquired more power than this, as we shall see.

> **Parliamentary systems** These have
> (1) a directly elected legislative body,
> (2) fused executive and legislative institutions,
> (3) a collective executive that emerges from
> the legislature and is responsible to it and
> (4) a separation of head of state and head of
> government.

Whereas the executive and legislative branches in presidential systems are
separated, this is not so clearly the case in parliamentary systems where:

1. The leader of the party or coalition of parties with most support in parliament becomes the prime minister or chancellor.
2. The prime minister or chancellor forms a cabinet usually chosen
   from members of parliament, and the cabinet then forms the core of
   government.
3. The government is dependent upon the support of parliament, which
   may remove the executive from power with a vote of no confidence. The
   executive (government) is also dependent upon the legislature (parliament), because the latter can reject, accept, or amend legislation initiated
   by the government. Equally, the executive can dissolve the legislature
   and call an election.

This means that the executive in a parliamentary system is directly dependent on, and accountable to, the legislature (i.e. the parliament), which can
veto legislation with a majority vote, and bring
down the executive with a vote of no confidence.
Since the executive has **collective responsibility**
for government (unlike a president), it must
stick together because public disagreement

> **Collective responsibility** The principle that
> decisions and policies of the cabinet or council
> are binding on all members who must support
> them in public.

within the cabinet or council on a major political matter will almost certainly
result in its being seriously weakened. The prime minister and the cabinet
must be closely bound together by mutual dependence and 'collegiality' if
they are to have a chance of remaining in office. The prime minister appoints
cabinet members and can sack them, but to remain in power the prime minister must also retain the confidence of the cabinet.

Presidential systems are usually modelled on the USA and often found in
Latin America, while parliamentary systems are often modelled on the British
system, and are widely found in the British Commonwealth, but also in western Europe (see fact file 5.1). While, in theory, presidential and parliamentary

systems operate in very different ways, in practice they tend to converge. Both depend on a close working relationship between executive and legislature. Although the power of a president is formally greater than that of a prime minister, in practice prime ministers in the modern world are said to be accumulating power so that they become more and more 'presidential'. For example, British prime ministers and German chancellors seem to have become progressively more powerful in the late twentieth century.

One of the advantages of parliamentary over presidential systems is said to be that the former produce strong and stable government by virtue of the fusion of executive and legislature. This has generally been the case in Australia, Britain, Canada, Denmark and Japan. But just as presidential systems are sometimes weak, divided or deadlocked, so also are some parliamentary systems – in Italy and in the French Fourth Republic (1946–58). The difference between stable and unstable parliamentary systems seems to lie less in their constitutional arrangements than in their party systems. Where there is a strong, stable and disciplined party majority (either a single party or a coalition) the result is often strong and stable government, because the executive can usually depend on majority support in the legislature. Where parties are fragmented, factious and volatile, or where majorities are small and uncertain, the parliamentary system is likely to be weak and unstable. This directs attention from constitutional arrangements to the role of political parties, a theme we will revisit again, especially in chapter 13.

■ Semi-presidential systems

Semi-presidential Government consists of a directly elected president, who is accountable to the electorate, and a prime minister, who is appointed by the president from the elected legislature and accountable to it. The president and prime minister share executive power.

The French Fourth Republic suffered from chronic instability caused by party fragmentation and deadlock in the assembly, running through twenty-seven governments in thirteen years. To overcome this problem the French Fifth Republic (1958–) created a semi-presidential system with a strong, directly elected president with substantial powers to act as a stable centre for government. The president was given powers to:

- appoint the prime minister from the elected assembly, and to dismiss him.
- dissolve parliament and call a referendum.
- call an emergency and substantial powers to deal with it.

The prime minister, in turn, appoints a cabinet from the assembly (the president may do this if he is from the same party as the prime minister) which is then accountable to the assembly. In this way, the French system of semi-presidential government combines the strong president of a presidential system with a prime minister and the fused executive and legislative of parliamentary systems (see fact file 5.2).

Fact file 5.2

Semi-presidentialism

- Relatively few countries have a semi-presidential form of government, and only Finland, France and Portugal have maintained one for more than a quarter of a century. Finland's semi-presidentialism has moved towards a parliamentary system.
- Among the new democracies the Czech Republic, Estonia, Lithuania and Slovenia have chosen the system, but there has been a tendency in the Czech Republic, Poland and Romania for the presidential office to be converted into a more prime ministerial one.
- Israel has a hybrid presidential–parliamentary system of government, including the semi-presidential characteristic of a directly elected prime minister.

This system worked smoothly in the early years of the Fifth Republic when the president (de Gaulle) and the prime minister (Debré) were from the same political party. During this time the president was the dominant force. To the surprise of many, the system continued to work well later when the president (Mitterrand) and the prime minister (Chirac) came from different parties – what the French call 'cohabitation'. In this period, the balance of power tended to swing in favour of the prime minister.

Semi-presidentialism is found in relatively few democracies (Finland, France and Portugal) but it has been adopted by some of the new democracies of central Europe (the Czech Republic, Estonia, Lithuania, Poland and Slovenia), which have tried to blend parliamentary systems with a comparatively strong, directly elected president. The attraction of an elected president in the ex-communist democracies is to have a single strong public figure who can act as (1) a focus of national feeling, important in a newly independent state that needs a strong central figure and (2) as the centre of executive power to help overcome extreme party fragmentation in the new legislatures.

There are indications of a tendency to move away from semi-presidentialism in some countries as political conditions change. In Finland, there have been attempts to reduce the power of the president. The central European states are still feeling their way, and if they develop strong party systems and consolidate their national identity, they may well move from a semi-presidential to more purely parliamentary forms of government.

■ Presidential, parliamentary and semi-presidential systems compared

We are now in a position to compare all three types of government. The main points of comparison are laid out in briefing 5.1. It is clear that there are things to be said both for and against all three as forms of democratic

Briefing 5.1

The three major forms of democratic government: main features

Presidential	Parliamentary	Semi-presidential
• Citizens directly elect the executive for a fixed term	• The executive emerges from a directly elected legislature and is an integral part of it	• Executive power is shared between a president (directly elected) and a prime minister who is appointed or directly elected
• Except for a few joint presidencies, the president alone has executive power	• The cabinet shares executive power and must reach compromises to maintain unity	• The prime minister appoints a cabinet, usually from the ruling party or coalition in the assembly
• The presidency is the only office of state with a general responsibility for the affairs of state	• The executive is a collegial body (cabinet or council of ministers) that shares responsibility, though the prime minister, premier or chancellor may be much more than *primus inter pares*	• The president often appoints the prime minister and has general responsibility for state affairs, especially foreign affairs
• The president shares power with a separate and independently elected legislature	• The office of the prime minister/premier/chancellor is usually separate from the head of state (whether monarch or president)	• The president often has emergency powers, including the dissolution of parliament
• Neither can remove the other (except in special circumstances such as impeachment)	• The prime minister and cabinet can dissolve parliament and call an election, but the prime minister and cabinet can be removed from office by a parliamentary vote of 'no confidence'	• The prime minister and cabinet often have special responsibility for domestic and day-to-day affairs of state
• The president is directly elected and therefore directly accountable to the people	• The prime minister and cabinet are responsible to parliament	• The president is directly elected and directly accountable to the people; the prime minister is responsible either to the president or to parliament
• Examples: USA, many states in Central and South America	• Most stable democracies are parliamentary systems – Australia, Austria, Belgium,	• Examples: Finland (until 1991), France and many post-communist states,

| (Colombia, Costa Rica, Dominican Republic, Ecuador, Venezuela), Cyprus, the Philippines, and South Korea | Canada, Denmark, Germany, Greece, Iceland, India, Ireland, Israel, Italy, Japan, The Netherlands, Norway, Spain, Sweden, Switzerland, UK | including Belarus, Poland, Russia and Ukraine |

government, but it is also clear that all three can work as effective democratic structures. Whether all three work equally well in countries with different social conditions and political histories is a different matter. One view is that presidential systems can be weak and ineffective, and run into problems of executive–legislative deadlock, leading to attempts to break through the problem by a 'strong man' who promises decisive and effective government. Not many countries have managed the presidential system as well as the USA.

At the same time, semi-presidential systems also have their problems. They can produce deadlock between presidents and prime ministers, leading to weak and ineffective government. Not many countries seem to be able to handle the problems of 'cohabitation' as well as France. Some parliamentary systems have also produced weak, divided and unstable government, while others have tended towards an over-concentration of power (see controversy 5.1). It is clear that we should look more closely at the arguments about parliamentary, presidential and semi-presidential government.

■ Theories of parliamentary, presidential and semi-presidential government

At the heart of debates about the three types of government lies one of the fundamental problems of any democracy: how can a political system balance the need for accountability to citizens and protection of their basic rights against the need for government that is strong enough to be effective? Too much government power means too little democracy, but too little government power means too little government. How do our three systems measure up to this dilemma?

At the outset, we have the problem of evaluating semi-presidential systems: there are too few of them, and only two examples in established democracies (France and Finland, which has moved towards a parliamentary system). Many of the new democracies of central and eastern Europe are semi-presidential, but these are rather special cases and some seem to be transforming themselves into parliamentary systems. Only time will tell whether they remain semi-presidential or for how long, and we have to set them aside for the time being at least.

CONTROVERSY 5.1

Presidential, parliamentary or semi-presidential government?

Presidential	Parliamentary	Semi-presidential
For		
• The USA is a model	• Most of the world's stable democracies are parliamentary systems	• In theory combines the best of presidential and parliamentary government
• Separation of the executive and legislative institutions of government according to classical democratic theory	• Fusion of executive and legislative can create strong and effective government	• The president can be a symbol of the nation, and a focus of national unity, while the prime minister can run the day-to-day business of the government
• Direct election of the president means direct accountability of the president to the people	• Direct chain of accountability from voters to parliament to cabinet to prime minister	
Against		
• Conflict between executive and legislation may be chronic, leading to deadlock and immobilism	• The fusion of the executive and legislative, and a large legislative majority, combined with tight party discipline, can produce leaders with too much power	• Conflict and power struggles between prime minister and cabinet, and between prime minister and president are not unusual
• Weak and ineffective presidents have sometimes tried to make their office much stronger	• Parliamentary systems without a legislative majority can be weak and unstable	• Confusion of accountability between president and prime minister
• Few presidential systems have survived long		

A leading writer on the relative merits of presidential and parliamentary systems is Juan Linz (1926–). He claims that presidentialism entails a paradox. On the one hand presidents are strong because they are directly elected and have popular support. They can rise above the petty in-fighting of parties and factions and speak for their country and its people. The president is also a single person who takes all the power of the presidential office. On the other hand, presidents are normally bound by all sorts of constitutional provisions that limit their power: they must have legislative support for actions, decisions and appointments; they have to deal with the independence of the courts; and they sometimes face a highly fragmented, undisciplined and ineffective party system that makes it difficult to shape and implement a coherent policy. Because presidents do not always have the support of the majority in the assembly, they may be unable to implement their policies. In a word, presidentialism is prone to **immobilism** (see briefing 5.2). In addition, unlike parliamentary leaders, presidents

> **Immobilism** The state of being unable to move (immobilised) or unable to take decisions or implement policies.

have a fixed term of office, which means it can be difficult to remove an unpopular president, but also means a sharp break in policies when a new one is elected.

According to Linz, parliamentary systems are more conducive to stable democracy. They are more flexible and adaptable because they do not impose the discontinuities of fixed terms of presidential office. Since the political executive is rooted in the majority party of the assembly, or in a coalition of parties, it is based on compromise and bargaining within or between parties. And since parliamentary executives are not limited to one or two terms in office, they can maintain a degree of continuity – the party leader may be replaced but the party or coalition may continue in power.

How does the theoretical argument about the superiority of parliamentary over presidential government measure up to the empirical evidence? At first sight, the evidence is compelling. The USA is the only example of long-lived democratic presidentialism, unless we also count Costa Rica, and there are a few notable failures – Argentina, Brazil and Chile. At the same time, a high proportion of western European democracies are parliamentary, as are many of the stable democracies of the British Commonwealth. It is estimated that of forty-three stable democracies in the world existing between 1979 and 1989, thirty-six were parliamentary, five presidential and two semi-presidential.

A second look at the evidence, however, suggests a more favourable evaluation of presidential government. First, while it is true that many presidential systems have failed, many of these are in Latin America, which raises the question of whether the explanation lies in inherent institutional design faults, or in the economic problems, lack of democratic traditions and fragmented parties of the countries which adopted the system in the first place. Would parliamentary government have worked any better in these countries?

It is impossible to know, but it is important to note that parliamentary systems failed in Greece and Turkey, and did not perform at all well in France and Italy.

There are also different sub-types of presidential government, some giving the office great powers and others limiting them. Similarly, some presidents operate within a cohesive and well-organised party system. It may be that presidents with strong party support in the main legislative body have a better chance of producing stable democracy than presidents with weak party support.

■ What have we learned?

This chapter has dealt with the three main branches of democratic government and the way in which they can be combined. It shows that:

- In spite of great constitutional variety, democratic states fall into one of three general categories – presidential, parliamentary and semi-presidential.
- Presidents are directly elected for a fixed term of office. The main examples are found in the USA, Latin America and Africa.
- In parliamentary systems the political executive (chancellor, premier, or prime minister and the cabinet or council of ministers) is not directly elected but emerges from the majority party or ruling coalition in the assembly. The executive continues in office as long as it has the support of the assembly, so there is no fixed term of office. Parliamentary systems are found mainly in western Europe and the stable democracies of the British Commonwealth.
- The semi-presidential system is a hybrid of the other two types, consisting of a directly elected president and a prime minister who appoints a cabinet from the assembly. There are not many semi-presidential systems in the world, and the best known is in France.
- Most stable democracies in the world are parliamentary. Relatively few are presidential or semi-presidential.

■ The lessons of comparison

- There is no single best formula for a stable democracy. Each of the three main systems has its advantages and disadvantages.
- Different systems may be suited to different national circumstances and the same country may change its system as it develops. The best system for any given country at any given time may depend on its particular historical, social and economic circumstances.
- The semi-presidential system seems to be well suited to the circumstances of the new democracies of central Europe, but this may change as they develop.

- Comparing presidential and parliamentary systems around the world suggests that it may not be the basic principles of presidentialism that tend to create unstable democracies so much as a history of authoritarianism in the countries that have adopted the presidential form and their weak party systems. It may be that presidents with strong and organised party support can sustain stable democracy.

Projects

1. Assume you are a consultant brought in to advise a newly independent state that wishes to set up a democratic constitution. Would you recommend (a) a presidential, (b) a semi-presidential or (c) a parliamentary system? Explain the reasons for your decisions.
2. Why is there no single best institutional design for democracy?
3. How could we decide, using the comparative method, whether it is the basic design of presidential government or the weakness of party systems that causes democratic instability?

Further reading

A. Lijphart (ed.), *Parliamentary versus Presidential Government*, Oxford: Oxford University Press, 1992.
The best collection of work on parliaments and presidents.

J. Linz and A. Valenzuela (eds.), *The Failure of Presidential DemocracyI*, Baltimore, MD: Johns Hopkins University Press, 1994.
A critical commentary on presidential government.

S. Mainwaring and M. S. Shugart (eds.), *Presidentialism and Democracy in Latin America*, Cambridge: Cambridge University Press, 1997.
A defence of some forms of presidentialism.

R. Elgie (ed.), *Semi-Presidentialism in Europe*, Oxford: Oxford University Press, 1999.
Up-to-date accounts of the three forms of government.

A. Siaroff, 'Comparative presidencies: the inadequacy of the presidential, semi-presidential and parliamentary distinction', *European Journal of Political Research*, 42(3), 2003: 287–312.
Discusses the inadequancies of the three forms of government and presents a different typology.

Websites

http://encyclopedia.thefreedictionary.com/presidential%20system
Basic introduction to the presidential system with links to related topics.

http://encyclopedia.thefreedictionary.com/Parliamentarism
Basic introduction to parliamentarism with links to related topics.
www.oup.co.uk/pdf/0–19-829386–0.pdf
Introduction to semi-presidentialism
www.ipu.org
The Inter-Parliamentary Union's website with information on parliaments in
the world.

6　Multi-level government: international, national and sub-national

Government in all but the smallest countries is organised like a set of 'Chinese boxes', or 'Russian dolls', one unit of government tucked inside another. The smallest units of community or neighbourhood government fit into local government:

- which (in federal systems) is contained by state/regional/provincial government
- which is part of the national system of government
- which is a member of various organisations of international government.

For example, a resident of Wilmersdorf-Charlottenburg lives in one of the twelve *Bezirke* (boroughs) that form the City of Berlin:

- which is one of the sixteen *Länder* (states) that make up the Federal Republic of Germany
- which is one of the member states of the EU in Europe, of NATO in Europe and North America and of the UN across the entire globe.

Government is organised on different geographical levels in this way because no single centre could possibly do everything itself. It must be divided, not only into different branches at the national level (executive, legislative, judiciary) but also into smaller territorial units of local administration and policy making at the sub-national level. Nor can countries manage their affairs entirely on their own; even the largest and most powerful must deal with other countries to solve international problems of security, diplomacy, the environment and trade.

Dividing government into geographical layers in this way makes sense, but it also creates questions of its own:

- What should be centralised and what decentralised to lower levels of government?
- How do we ensure that the resulting system is as efficient and as democratic as possible?

We touched briefly on this topic in chapter 4 when we discussed unitary and federal states, but the topic of multi-level government is so important that we will return to it now in greater depth.

There are usually three main layers of government within a country:

1. National, central, or federal government
2. A middle or meso-level that is variously called state, provincial, regional, or county government
3. Local or municipal government, which may cover anything from quite small areas to large metropolitan cities or regions.

Often there is a fourth and lowest tier of government for local communities and neighbourhoods, but it is rarely of very great significance and will not be discussed here. Layers of government below the national level are collectively referred to as 'sub-national' or 'non-central' government. In addition, there are many kinds of international and supranational organisations that have an important impact on the way that national and sub-national governments conduct their business, all the more so in an increasingly globalised world.

This chapter, therefore, discusses the multiple layering of government. It starts at the international level and works down to the most local level of sub-national government, as follows:

- Supra-national and international government
- The national level: federal and unitary states
- The inter-play of multi-level government
- The arguments for and against centralisation and decentralisation
- Theories of multi-level government.

Before starting into the chapter, however, we must clear up one possible source of confusion about the word 'state', which has three possible meanings. It can refer to the whole apparatus of the government, as in the phrase 'the state apparatus', which refers to all branches and all levels of government. It can also refer to the national or central government of a country, as in the phrase 'the central state'. And third, in federal systems it can refer to the level of government below the central government, where the federal government is nation-wide, and states are sub-divisions of the federal territory, as in the state of California, or the state of North Rhine-Westphalia in Germany. Sometimes the meaning of the word is only clear from its context – as in 'state and local government' (middle and local levels), 'the Japanese state' (Japanese government), 'the Indian states' (regional units), and 'the federal states of the world' (federal systems).

■ Supra-national and international government

Government above the national level is, for the most part, a matter of cooperation between countries that keep their national sovereignty, but nevertheless set up organisations to deal with problems that spread across national boundaries. We could not, for example, organise international flights without international air traffic control. International cooperation between governments of this kind is replete with an 'alphabet soup' of inter-governmental organisations (IGOs), including the UN, NATO, the IMF, the ILO, the OECD, OPEC, Interpol, GATT, the IBRD, the NAFTA, the OAU, the WTO. These are all agencies of government that are created by international agreements between countries, but they are not the same as governments or states. They are forms of confederation, so our first job is to distinguish confederations from their close cousins, the federations.

Confederations

The term 'confederation' is often confused with 'federation', because the terms sound similar and have much in common. **Confederations** are looser-knit than federations, and are formed by other organisations that want to cooperate with each other on a gererally specific matter, but that also want to preserve their

> **Confederations** Organisations whose members lend some powers to a body that manages affairs of common interest, while retaining their own independence.

independent identity and not merge completely into a single, larger body. Confederations do not encroach upon the sovereign autonomy of their members who can leave the confederation when they please, whereas federations are created by a pooling of sovereignty that binds their constituent units together. Confederations range from powerful and cohesive organisations to weak and loose-knit ones, but the great majority are weaker, less centralised and less stable than federal states and all have a narrow range of functions and duties (see fact file 6.1). The short-lived American Confederation Congress (1781–89) that prefigured the USA's federal system formed in 1789 highlights the main problem of such groupings – they are often too loose and powerless to achieve much, and sometimes they fall apart.

Confederations are formed by all sorts of organisations for all sorts of purposes, and they operate at all levels of the political system, from the most local to the most global. Trade unions, for example, often form confederations

Fact file 6.1

Confederations

- Confederations include international organisations such as NATO, the UN and the United Arab Emirates.
- One of the earliest confederations was the Swiss Confederacy, dating back to 1315 (some say even to 1291).
- When the USSR (a federation) collapsed in 1989–90, the Commonwealth of Independent States (CIS, a confederation) was created in 1991 as an emergency measure to tie twelve of the former Soviet Republics together.
- Many transnational confederations do not last long – the Czechoslovakian Confederation of the early 1990s, the League of Nations, various Middle East confederations of Arab states; but some have been successful – NATO, the UN and United Arab Emirates.
- The weakness of the confederal system of the USA lead to the creation of the Federal constitution of 1789.

Briefing 6.1

The Dominican Republic: membership of international organisations
The Dominican Republic is a member of 51 major international organisations, including the Food and Agricultural Organisation, the Inter-American Development Bank, the International Labor Organisation, the Inter-Parliamentary Union, the International Organisation for Migration, the Permanent Court of Arbitration, the Rio Group, the United Nations, the Universal Postal Union, the World Customs Organisation and the World Trade Organisation.

around their common interests, as do business associations, professional organisations, churches and sports clubs. However, international confederations are particularly well suited to the needs of countries that want to retain their independent identity and autonomy while cooperating with other countries on specific matters such as economic development, defence, environmental policy or cultural affairs. The World Trade Organisation (WTO), the World Bank (IBRD and IDA) and the European Space Agency (ESA) are examples of international government confederations. Briefing 6.1 lists just a few of the international confederal organisations to which the government of the Dominican Republic belongs.

Supra-national government goes one important step further than international government. It involves the cooperation of countries that are willing to pool sovereignty, at least on certain matters, along federal lines. Since the international system has long been based upon sovereign nations (the Westphalian system outlined in chapter 1), the creation of supra-national government is a rare thing. In fact, the European

Supra-national government Organisations in which countries pool their sovereignty on certain matters to allow joint decision making.

Union is the first and, by far and away the most advanced experiment with supra-national government in the world today.

The European Union: federation or confederation?

The European Union is a hybrid of confederal and federal features. Its federal features are a Commission (a quasi-executive), a powerful European Court (ECJ) whose verdicts take precedence over national law and some pooling of sovereignty on particular matters. Its confederal characteristics are an unwillingness of member countries to surrender sovereignty on some matters of economic and social policy, a weak parliament and weak coordination of foreign policy. Members can leave a confederation at any time (Greenland left the EEC in 1985), but the deep integration of the EU along quasi-federal lines makes this difficult. France withdrew its troops from NATO military command (a confederal organisation) in 1966, but it would find it a great deal more difficult to pull out of the EU or its currency, even if it wanted to do so.

It remains to be seen whether the EU strengthens its federal or its confederal nature. As things stand at the moment, however, its nearest equivalent is the North American Free Trade Association (NAFTA), but its limited concern with trade relations between the sovereign states of North America means that it is not contemplating the deep integration of the member states of the EU. NAFTA is unlikely to turn itself from an international body into a supranational one.

■ The national level: federal and unitary states

At the national level, government is organised on either a federal or a unitary basis. As we saw in chapter 4, federal systems contain middle-level territorial units of government (states, provinces, regions) which have a guaranteed status in the constitution that gives them a degree of independence and autonomy from the central government. In contrast, **sub-central** units of government in unitary states (chapter 4) are the creatures of central government, which creates them and which can reform, restructure, or abolish

> **Sub-central government** All levels of government below central/national government.

them without constitutional limitation. How central government changes local government in a unitary system is a sensitive political issue, of course, and there may be severe limitations to what it can do, but this is a political, not a constitutional, matter.

Though they vary considerably in the degree to which power is concentrated, unitary governments are still more centralised than most federal systems. The advantage of federalism is that it combines a degree of national government unity with a constitutionally entrenched degree of independence for lower levels of government, variously named states, regions, or provinces. We can see this in figures 6.1 and 6.2 and table 6.1, which show that

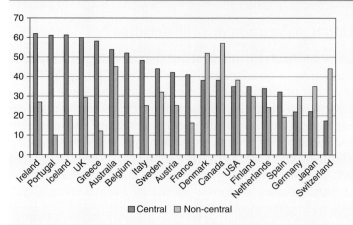

Figure 6.1: Share of total government expenditure: central and non-central government, 1994, per cent

Note: Central plus non-central plus social security spending = 100 per cent.

Source: OECD, *Managing across Levels of Government* (Paris: OECD, 1997: 35).

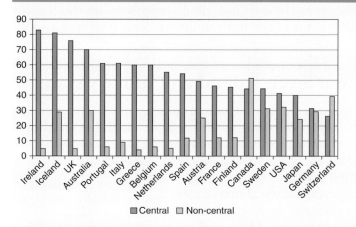

Figure 6.2: Share of total government receipts, 1994 per cent

Note: Central plus non-central plus social security spending = 100 per cent.

Source: OECD, *Managing across Levels of Government* (Paris: OECD, 1997: 35).

sub-central units of government in federal systems usually account for a greater proportion of public sector taxes, spending and employment, suggesting greater decentralisation of service responsibilities to lower levels of government.

Federal decentralisation is especially important in two situations – where a country is large geographically, or where different social groups in the population are concentrated in particular regions.

Table 6.1 Share of public employment, late 1990s, per cent

New Zealand	Central	90
	Local	10
Ireland	Central	87
	Local	13
Portugal	Central	86
	Local	14
France	Central	49
	Sub-national	31
	Health	21
UK	Central	48
	Local	52
Spain	Central	47
	Autonomous communities	31
	Local	22
Austria	Federal	45
	Länder	28
	Local	27
Denmark	Central	27
	Local	73
Finland	Central	25
	Local	75
Sweden	Central	17
	Regional	25
	Local	58
Canada	Federal	17
	Provincial	44
	Local	39
USA	Federal	15
	State	23
	Local	61
Australia	Commonwealth	15
	State	73
	Local	12
Germany	Federal	12
	Länder	51
	Local	37

Source: OECD, *Managing across Levels of Government* (Paris: OECD, 1997)

Geographically large countries

Large territories may be better organised as federations in order to give far-flung territories a degree of autonomy that reduces their dependence upon a distant centre of government. One of the founding fathers of the American

111

constitution, Thomas Jefferson (1743–1826), said: 'Our country is too large to have all its affairs directed by a single government.' Many of the largest countries in the world, in terms of area or population, or both, are federal (see fact file 6.2).

Countries with markedly different geographical regions

Many federal states have multi-ethnic or multi-national populations that are concentrated in different geographical areas (Belgium, Canada, India, Switzerland and the USA). A country with deep

Political cleavage A political division created when political organisations use social cleavages for their own purposes to mobilise support. Social cleavages are often more important politically if they coincide with regional divisions.

political cleavages of any kind, whether based on language, ethnicity, religion, culture or history, may have severe problems with its unity, and these problems will be compounded if the cleavages coincide with geographical divisions.

For example, in Canada the French-speaking part of the population is concentrated in Quebec. Federalism makes it easier to hold diverse areas together within a single country by giving regions a degree of control over their own affairs. Belgium turned itself into a federal system in 1993 to prevent its three

Fact file 6.2

Federal states

- Of the 193 states in the world, twenty-four are fully federal.
- Federal states include Brazil, Canada (sometimes described as quasi-federal), India, Malaysia, Mexico, Nigeria, Switzerland and the USA.
- The first example of federalism in the western world was the Achaean League in ancient Greece (251–146 BC). The first federal state in modern history was the Dutch Republic of the United Provinces (1579–1795).
- Modern federal states include some of the largest in the world – Brazil, Canada, India, Mexico and the USA – and cover 40 per cent of the globe's population and nearly half its land. But Switzerland is also a federal state.
- The number of states within federal systems varies. There are three regions in Belgium, six states in Australia, twenty-six cantons in Switzerland, twenty-six states and a Federal District in Brazil, and fifty states in the USA.
- Belgium is a new federal state, being created in 1993 out of the three linguistic areas of Brussels, Flanders and Wallonia.
- No truly federal system has ever evolved into a unitary system, but there are many examples of failed international federations (the West Indian Federation, 1962, the Central African Federation, 1963, the Malaysian Federation (Singapore left in 1965), the East African Federation, 1977 and Yugoslavia and Czechoslovakia, 1992).
- Though technically a unitary state, Spain grants greater powers to its autonomous regions than some federal nations give to their states.

major regions (French-speaking Brussels, Dutch-speaking Flanders and French-speaking Wallonia) from falling apart.

Federal systems all have a constitutionally recognised territorial division of political powers, but there are different forms of federalism: some have many units of sub-central government, others only a few (some names and numbers are given in table 6.2); some reserve powerful functions for the centre (Canada, India), others give them to the states (Australia, Switzerland, the USA); some specify carefully the functions and powers of each level of government, others assume that powers and functions not specifically assigned to one level will be the responsibility of the other. In some federal systems, the upper legislative house is reserved for representatives of the states, regions or provinces (the *Bundesrat* for the German *Länder* and the Senate for American states), which gives them a powerful stake in national as well as regional and local politics.

In theory, there is a distinction between 'cooperative federalism' and 'dual federalism'. In the cooperative type, federal and state government share powers and, consequently, are required to cooperate closely with one another (Germany, Switzerland). In a dual system, there is supposed to be a clearer separation of functions and powers (Australia, the USA), with each level of government having its own sphere of competence. In practice, however, federalism of both kinds requires close and constant cooperation, negotiation and bargaining between federal and state government. In theory, the USA draws a line between the responsibilities of the federal government and the states, but in practice they cooperate closely in many areas of domestic policy. The metaphor of 'the marble cake' is often applied to the USA: a cake where the layers are not divided by clear, straight lines, but mixed and melded in a complex partnership of shared responsibilities. The key fact about any federal system, whether of the Swiss/German or Australian/US type, is not the separation of powers, but cooperation, inter-governmental relations and interdependence. The study of 'inter-governmental relations' and 'fiscal federalism' (the politics of shared taxing and spending powers) is important in

Table 6.2 Federal states: names and numbers of regional units of government, 2000

Australia	6 states, 2 territories
Austria	9 *Länder*
Belgium	3 regions
Canada	10 provinces, 2 territories
Germany	16 *Länder*
India	25 states, 7 union territories
Mexico	31 states, 1 federal district
South Africa	9 provinces
Switzerland	20 cantons, 6 half-cantons
USA	50 states, 1 federal district

federal systems because government is not so much layered as intertwined in a way that makes it difficult to understand how it works in practice.

Federal systems usually have three main levels of government – national government, local government and a middle level between them. To make life complicated the main middle-level units are often called 'states'. To distinguish 'states' in a federal system from central government the latter are often called 'federal' or 'national' governments. Local government is normally under the general oversight of the states, not the federal government. This means that each state or province can determine its own system of local government, with the result that they can vary in a bewildering variety of ways. The picture is often complicated further where large cities are given special powers of their own. Some cities in the USA have 'home rule charters', which give them a special degree of autonomy. In many countries (Brazil, Australia, the USA, India, South Korea) the capital city is also treated as a special case.

Although federalism allows the degree of decentralisation and flexibility that is necessary for large and mixed populations, there is often a price to be paid for it. Inter-governmental relations between federal and state government can be complicated and sensitive, and special arrangements and understandings have to be created to allow them to operate effectively. These can be slow, complex and costly as different levels of government, each with its own powers and duties, work out a common programme of action between them. The growth of federal funding and regulation has often created a tangled mass of complicated inter-governmental relations.

Unitary and federal systems in practice

We have drawn a clear distinction between unitary and federal systems so far, but in practice there is less difference between them.

Quasi-federal features

In the first place, some unitary states have quasi-federal features such as a degree of 'home rule' for special areas. These include the island of Åland (Finland), Corsica (France), the Channel Islands and the Isle of Man (the UK), and the Faroe Islands and Greenland (Denmark). Special status is not reserved only for islands. Scotland, Northern Ireland and Wales have long had their own standing within the UK, as do the regions of Alto Adige and Val d'Aosta (as well as the island of Sicily) in Italy. Spain is a unitary state but it gives some regions (notably Catalonia and the Basque Country) so much autonomy that it might be called a semi-federal or regional system. In other words, unitary states can be rather variable and flexible, and not as highly centralised as they first seem (see fact file 6.3). In a word, they also **devolve** power to lower levels of government.

Devolution Devolution occurs where higher levels of government grant decision-making powers to lower levels while maintaining their constitutionally subordinate status.

Second, central and local government *depend upon each other*, even in the most centralised of states, such as the UK and France. Just as central government in

Fact file 6.3

Unitary states

- Among the democracies of the world with a population of a million or more, forty-four are unitary states, including most of the old and new democracies of western and central Europe, but also Benin, Chile, Costa Rica, the Dominican Republic, El Salvador, Ghana, Israel, Jamaica, Japan, Mali, Mauritius, Namibia, New Zealand, Peru, South Africa, South Korea, Taiwan and Uruguay.
- Unitary states are usually smaller than federal ones in terms of both population and territory. Japan is the largest unitary state (population 127 million), and Switzerland the smallest federal system (population 7 million).
- Fused local government systems (sometimes called 'Napoleonic systems') were found in their clearest form in France, Italy, Greece, Portugal and Turkey, though late twentieth-century reforms have tended to reduce central government's direct control of local government.
- Dual systems (sometimes referred to as the 'Westminster model') of local government are found in New Zealand, Ireland and the UK.
- The local self-government model is found in Denmark, Finland, Norway and Sweden.
- Since the 1970s, Finland, France, Greece, Ireland, Italy, Spain, Sweden and the UK have all created or strengthened their middle or meso-layer of regional government. This has reduced the difference between fused, dual and local self-government arrangements.

Paris relies upon the cooperation of local officials in the *communes* and *départements*, so local officials depend upon Paris for resources and support. Each has to negotiate and cooperate with the other to some extent, as in federal systems.

Third, federal systems are tending towards greater centralisation. As countries become internally more integrated, and as they face the pressures of globalisation, so federal governments have assumed greater control over some national affairs. Some federal systems have become more centralised in an attempt to reduce economic inequalities between regions, and in order to implement national minimum standards of service provision. Because federal government has greater financial resources it is increasingly funding local services through grants and transfers of various kinds. In doing so, it is exercising greater control over local policies and services.

Although there is a tendency for federal and unitary states to converge, they still remain distinct. Figures 6.1 and 6.2 and table 6.1 show that central government in unitary states usually accounts for a higher proportion of public expenditure and employment than central government in federal states: compare France, Ireland, New Zealand, Portugal and the UK at the top of table 6.1 with Australia, Canada, Germany and the USA at the bottom.

Unitary, federal and confederal government compared

Having described the operations of federal, confederal, and unitary government in theory and practice, we can now compare their advantages and disadvantages. This is done in controversy 6.1. We can draw three general

CONTROVERSY 6.1

Unitary, federal or confederal?

Unitary	Federal	Confederal
For		
• Central government is clearly accountable	• Another form of the separation of powers	• Permits states (or other autonomous political units) to cooperate while maintaining their sovereignty
• A single centre of power that permits coordinated and decisive state action	• Encourages consensus and compromise between federal and state authorities	
• Best suited to small states, or homogeneous states with similar regions	• Best suited to large states (either population or geographical area), and/or those with markedly different regions	• Best suited to cooperation in one sector or field of government activity – economic (IMF), diplomatic (UN), defence (NATO)
• Can help national integration by focusing on national politics	• Can protect the rights of territorially concentrated minorities	• May be the only form of cooperation possible
• Facilitates the equalisation of regional resources (through national tax system, for example)	• Can maintain the unity of the country by containing regional divisions, so deflecting and defusing potentially dangerous national conflicts	
• It is still possible to grant some areas special powers (e.g. Basque Country in Spain)	• Encourages small-scale experiment, innovation and competition between states: the efficiency argument	
• Helps the creation of a system of equal rights and duties for all citizens	• Creates opportunities to respond to the different needs and demands of groups in different regions	
Against		
• Can result in an over-powerful central state	• Can result in duplication, overlap and confusion of responsibilities and accountability	• Unstable – members can withdraw easily

• Can result in national major-ities exploiting or repressing regional minorities	• May lead to conflict, ineffi-ciency, or stalemate between levels of government	• Can be ineffective – when members can-not agree
• Can result in a rigid and hier-archical form of government	• Can result in complex, slow and expensive forms of government	
	• Can be inherently conservative	
	• Can strengthen tendencies towards national disunity and disintegration by encouraging breakaway of territorial units	
	• Can deflect political attention from national groups and inter-ests to geographical interests	

conclusions from a summary of the arguments for and against the three types of government:

1. Choosing between them is not a matter of deciding between good or bad, or even between better and worse, but trying to decide which is better for what purposes and under what circumstances.
2. Federal systems are better suited to large countries, especially where minorities are concentrated in geographical areas that can be given a degree of independence from central government. Unitary states are bet-ter suited to small, homogeneous countries.
3. Confederations are good at dealing with specific policy areas where those who participate in the confederation want to retain their own formal independence.

Local government

Why do we have local government? Why not allow central government to run everything, or perhaps restrict the system to two levels alone – national and regional? The answer is simple: most countries are far too large and complex to be run by a single centre, or even by a few regional units of government. Government must **decentralise some** of its operations in the interests of both democracy and efficiency. It makes no sense, for example, to have bureaucrats in the capital city deciding when to close park gates in some dis-tant town, or what books to buy for the local library. These are local matters that should be in local hands. As a result, most countries rely heavily on local government to deliver a wide range of services.

The difficulty lies not in justifying decentralisation in theory, but in decid-ing exactly what and how much to centralise and decentralise in practice. As

General competence The power of local government units to manage their own affairs, provided they observe the laws of the land and relatively few legally defined exceptions.

Fused systems The system of local government in unitary states in which central officials directly supervise the work of local government.

Dual systems The system of local government in unitary states in which local authorities have more independence than in fused systems but within the authority of central government.

a general rule, the 'high politics' of state (international diplomacy, defence, economic development, the distribution of national resources) are handled by central government, while local government has its own core services (its **general competence**, local planning and transport, refuse collection, sewage). Increasingly, however, there is a larger 'grey area' of services that are shared and mixed between levels of government to various degrees.

Local government in unitary states tends to fall into three broad categories – **fused systems, dual systems** and local self-government – ranging from the most to the least centralised.

Fused systems

The clearest example of the fused model is the centralised and uniform system set up by Napoleon in France. He placed agents of central government (*préfets*) in each local government unit (*département*) to supervise their work and ensure that central government policies were carried out. Variations on the centralised French system are found in Italy, Spain and Portugal and in their former colonies and spheres of influence in Africa, Asia and the Americas, as well as Japan and South Korea. Fused systems are also found in many of the new democracies where sub-central political officials were traditionally appointed by the ruling central government.

Dual systems

The classic example of the dual system is Britain, where central government retains a good deal of power, though it does not directly control local government through an army of *préfets*. Rather it 'manages' local government at arm's length, thereby giving it rather more autonomy. Many key public services (education, housing, health) are delivered by local councils but controlled and financed to varying degrees by central government. Local authorities are required by central government to provide some services and engage in some activities, but may have discretion over others services and activities. The dual system is found in the UK, the USA, Israel and India, and in many former British colonies in Africa, Asia and the Pacific.

Local self-government

The principle of local self-government with more freedom of local action characterises the Nordic countries. Local government is entrusted with the tasks allotted to it by central government, and has freedom of taxation within limits. As figures 6.1, 6.2 and table 6.1 show, local government in Denmark, Finland and Sweden accounts for a relatively high proportion of public expenditure and employment among the unitary states. There was world-wide approval in the 1980s and 1990s of local self-government, but good intentions were not always put into practice.

Whatever the local government system, it involves a degree of decentralisation of government and a degree of autonomy and legitimacy for local government. While decentralisation of this kind makes a lot of sense in many ways, it also creates two special problems of its own namely:

- central–local political conflict
- the dilemma of reconciling the needs of democracy and efficiency.

Central–local political conflict

Political conflict between central and local government is endemic in many states. If local government is to play its democratic role, it must be elected by, and accountable to, local citizens; but central government is also elected and accountable. Which level of government is to have the final word in decision making? The problem is likely to be aggravated if central and sub-central government are controlled by different political parties. This is often the case because local elections are usually held between national elections (mid-term elections) when there tends to be a reaction against the central government of the day. The result is that 'opposition parties' are often elected locally. Party political conflict is sometimes thus built into central–local relations. Usually this is resolved by negotiating, bargaining and compromising. In turn, this calls for a set of institutions which enable central and local governments to talk to each other and resolve their problems.

The problem of how best to fund local government is a permanent source of disagreement and conflict in most democracies. On the one hand, central government is ultimately responsible for national fiscal policy and the level of public spending – both local and national. It also controls most of the taxes that raise money (income tax, business and sales taxes) and it is the rare local authority that can fund its own services from its own revenues. In addition, the demands of equality between areas mean that central government redistributes money from rich to poor areas, otherwise the latter would have unacceptably poor public services. Transfers of money from central government are often the largest source of funds for local authorities. On the other hand, democratically elected local councils naturally wish to control their own affairs, which means minimising financial dependence upon central government. The Japanese say that their local government is '30 per cent free' because 70 per cent of its money comes from central government.

The resulting financial tensions between financial centralisation and decentralisation were heightened in the second half of the twentieth century by the sustained growth of the welfare state and by the increasing amount of public money spent by sub-national government – money that was often provided by central government grants and transfers. The situation was then compounded by financial problems and cuts in services in the last part of the century, and even more by the tendency for central government to delegate new service responsibilities to the localities without funding them adequately.

Democracy, size and efficiency

The second dilemma for local government is how to reconcile the often competing claims of *democracy* and *efficiency*. There are seven main aspects to this problem:

Subsidiarity The principle of democracy that decisions should be taken at the lowest possible level of government – that is, at the level closest to the people affected by the decisions. Usually the term subsidiarity is used in connection with the territorial decentralisation of government, but it is not limited to this form.

- Democracy in local government requires that it should be based, so far as possible, around small communities of people where participation is easiest and there is a common identity and set of interests among citizens. The **subsidiarity** principle requires that decisions are taken at the lowest possible level in the system.

- Some services are most efficiently provided on a small scale, some on a larger one. Parks, refuse collection, local libraries and local transport are small-scale, but refuse disposal, central reference libraries, higher education, urban transport, water and police services are larger-scale. This means that there is no single optimum size for multi-purpose authorities.

- Services are not isolated from each other. They need integrating so that, for example, residential areas, schools and hospitals are provided with public transport, and transport should be integrated with local economic development and environmental policies. This means that there is a need for a body that can plan and coordinate a wide range of services, some small-scale, some large.

- Local government units should be large enough to have a tax base adequate for their purposes, and they should probably be large enough to have a mix of rich and poor citizens so that the financial load can be equitably distributed.

- Some of the largest cities (Calcutta, London, New York, Tokyo) are bigger than some countries, and require large units of local government to run them, even if they have smaller sub-divisions nested within them. On top of this, there is a problem of where to draw the boundary around any large city. Should they be defined fairly narrowly to include only densely populated urban areas, or should they include the surrounding commuter suburbs and villages which depend upon the big city for work and recreation? Since suburban commuters use central city services for both work and pleasure, it seems sensible to draw wide boundaries around cities.

- Some features of local geography and history, such as rivers, mountains and historic divisions, suggest boundaries between local government units that may not fit neatly with the most efficient or the most democratic scale of service provision. Sparsely populated areas and islands are often combined into geographically large units of local government with small populations.

- Optimum sizes change according to technical developments and ideas about how public services should be organised. Sometimes this reduces scale, but in other cases it increases it. Computer networks, for example, make it possible to decentralise some town hall functions and create many little local offices that are more accessible to the public. At the same time, the capital and environmental costs of refuse disposal make it necessary to operate on a larger scale than before. As city populations grow or shrink, so the optimum size of service-providing units also changes – local schools are closed and their pupils sent to larger schools that are supposed to be more effective and efficient.

This means that there is no optimum size for units of local government, nor is there a 'natural' range of service functions for it: it is a matter of trying to balance economies and diseconomies of scale, and weighing up the often competing demands of large-scale efficiency and small-scale democracy. There are many different ways of organising local government, and the endless search for the best balance explains why local government across the western world has been subject to constant reform.

Most countries have experimented with three forms of local organisation and service delivery:

- General-purpose authorities
- Joint bodies
- Single-purpose authorities.

General-purpose authorities

These deliver a wide range of services and go under such different names as municipalities, communes, districts, prefectures, boroughs, councils and shires. They are invariably directly elected, but their function and population size varies enormously from one country to another. Some countries have a single tier of general-purpose authorities that divides the entire territory of the country into local government units with much the same powers and functions. Others divide local government into two or more tiers each with different powers and functions. For example, large cities may have a single overall authority to deal with area-wide services (transport, economic development, planning) and smaller units within them for local ones (libraries, parks, refuse collection). Sometimes large rural areas are run by top-tier authorities, but the towns within them by second-tier ones.

Joint bodies

Rather than create new, larger authorities by merging two or more smaller ones, some countries have kept their smaller general-purpose authorities but created a range of joint bodies to provide a range of special mutual services (economic development, water supply). This practice is increasingly common across the world.

Special-purpose authorities

In some countries, particular services are provided by special single-purpose authorities. These include school boards, river authorities, water boards, urban transportation and police authorities. Special-purpose authorities are most frequently found in the Third World, central and eastern Europe and in the USA.

The result of trying to match services and functions with different types and levels of local government units is often a complex and confusing struc- ture of authorities. Such a structure may have a logic of its own, but one that is difficult to understand. The USA is an extreme case because it is frag- mented into more than 85,000 units of local government in the shape of general-purpose authorities, special-purpose authorities, home-rule cities and cities without home rule and a bewildering range and variety of other agencies. The government of New York City, with its tangle of 1,500 local government and service units, has been called 'one of the great unnatural wonders of the world'.

Restructuring local government

For much of the twentieth century local government has struggled to keep pace with four key powerful social, economic, and political changes:

1. *Social and economic changes* National and local political institutions have had to adapt to huge population movements, large shifts in working pat- terns, increasing interdependence of urban and rural areas, the growth of huge metropolitan areas and increasing national and global integration. To take one example, road transport has been totally transformed by the speed and volume of traffic, and whereas roads used to be mainly the responsibility of local government national highway systems now require national planning and funding. International cooperation is necessary for rail and air transport, and even for roads.
2. *Financial pressures on central and local government* As the political demands and financial pressures on both central and local government grow, so both have to develop new modes of operating and relating to each other.
3. *Ideological pressure for decentralisation* Politics in the late twentieth century began to favour decentralisation and grass-roots participation.
4. *Technology* Transport, communications and computer technology have affected patterns of work, residence and leisure, and they have also made the decentralisation and devolution of local government easier, just as

they have helped to centralise other public functions (central police records, national standards for schools and hospitals).

The result of these changes is that local government has been the object of constant restructuring in many countries. In fact, few democracies have not reformed and restructured their local government system since 1945, and some have had several goes at it. Amid the huge variety of reforms and developments seven general trends stand out (see fact file 6.4).

1. *Consolidation* In many countries small units of local government have been amalgamated and consolidated into larger units. Sometimes central government has initiated reforms, but in others cases local units have voluntarily merged.
2. *Meso-government* Many unitary states have strengthened or created a middle level of regional government – **meso-government** – that fits between central and local government. In some cases this meso-level has been given substantial powers and service responsibilities so that it is the functional equivalent of state government in federal systems.

   > **Meso-government** A middle level or tier of government between central and local authorities, and often known as state, regional, provincial, or county government.

3. *Decentralisation* Local government in unitary states has often been given a broader range of responsibilities and powers. Since this happened at the same time as central governments were coming under intense economic pressure, some observers felt that this was, in effect, 'exporting' the economic problems of central government.
4. *Centralisation* Both federal and unitary states have become more centralised in some respects.

   Most of these reforms have been justified by the government of the day on the grounds that they improved rationality, efficiency and democracy, but there sometimes seem to be political interests at stake as well. For example, in some countries left-wing governments have implemented reforms favouring left-leaning big cities over more conservative and rural areas, while in others right-wing central governments have diluted the powers of 'leftish' urban areas or tried to outflank them by creating higher levels of urban and rural government that are likely to be more conservative. Politics is important in central–local relations and they account for the last two sets of changes in local government.
5. *Politicisation* Local government became increasingly political in the late twentieth century. As local authorities enlarged their size and responsibilities, parties and ideological groups penetrated the corridors of power and contested local elections.
6. *Central–local conflict* Politicisation of localities has sometimes brought them into direct conflict with central government, especially where different parties are in power and both levels claim democratic legimacy

Fact file 6.4

Sub-central government: patterns of change

Changes in the structure, powers and functions of sub-central government in the modern world are varied, complex and sometimes contradictory, as the following examples show.

■ Consolidation

- The population size of local government units various dramatically within and between countries. In Japan some municipalities have as few as 200 residents, the average in western Europe is 10,000 and in the UK it is 125,000.
- Many western European countries have reduced the number of municipalities substantially in recent decades, by up to 75 per cent in Sweden, Denmark and the UK. Consolidation has also occurred in countries as various as Canada, New Zealand, Australia, Thailand and Japan, much less so in France, Switzerland and the USA.
- Compulsory (and sometimes drastic) consolidation is more usually found in unitary states where central government has used its constitutional power to reorganise local government. Voluntary (and usually more modest) reorganisation is found in federal systems.

■ The growth of middle levels of government

- In western Europe, France, Finland, Italy, Ireland, Greece, Spain and the UK have introduced important regional layers of government.
- Belgium turned itself into a federal state, with three regions.
- Austria, Canada, Denmark, Sweden, Switzerland and the USA have strengthened their middle levels of government by removing restrictions from them or devolving services to them.
- In 1990, with the collapse of the Soviet Union, Hungary shifted power from regional to local authorities as part of its democratisation process.

■ Decentralisation

- Many new democracies have decentralised their political systems as part of their efforts to democratise. Examples include most of the ex-communist countries in central Europe, as well as Brazil, the Philippines, Mexico and South Korea.
- Austria, Canada, Finland, France, Italy, the UK and Spain have devolved some services from central to middle levels of government.
- Denmark, France, Hungary, Iceland, Ireland, Japan, Mexico, Sweden, New Zealand, Turkey and the UK have shifted some services from central to local levels.
- The number of local special-purpose authorities has increased in Canada, the UK, New Zealand and the USA.
- In some cases the powers and functions of cities have shifted downwards to the localities, communities and neighbourhoods – e.g. in Chicago and Montevideo.

■ Centralisation

- Sweden has shifted some powers from local to central government, and central control over local finances and service standards has increased substantially in the UK.
- In Australia, Canada and the USA the federal government has taken greater powers over state and provincial governments – over education in Australia, health services in Canada, and welfare, integration, minimum drinking age and speed limits in the USA.

from their elections. This has occurred in many parts of the world where national political struggles have spread to the local level.

7. *Contracting out and privatisation* Almost all democratic states have contracted out, privatised or created public–private partnerships to some extent. This is further discussed in chapter 8.

■ The interplay of multi-level government: the case of the EU

We have seen how the changing world has brought about greater interdependence between levels of government, and nowhere is this clearer than in the EU. The mere existence of the Union as a developed form of supra-national government means, of course, a degree of centralisation in Brussels. At the same time, the EU pays careful attention to its regions (as federal systems do), putting regional policy high on its agenda and spending a large proportion of its budget on regional aid. It has created the Committee of the Regions (CoR), which, though only an advisory body, gives regions a direct input into EU deliberations. The result is that the EU often manages to by-pass national governments – which can be a nuisance when they present obstacles to its policies – and deals directly with the meso-level of regional government. This enhances the power, importance and financial resources of the regions, and therefore represents a decentralising tendency. Consequently, the EU is both a centralising force, insofar as some national powers have moved upwards, and a decentralising one, insofar as it strengthens regional government, while encouraging regional dependence on Brussels for financial and political support.

■ The arguments for and against centralisation and decentralisation

Having considered the four main levels of government – international, national, regional and local – we are now in a position to form a judgement about the various merits and difficulties of centralised and decentralised forms of government. The basics of the argument are presented in controversy 6.2. This makes it clear that the debate has many sides. It is not a question of whether to have either centralised or decentralised government, but rather a matter of what to centralise and how much, what to decentralise and how much, and what to share between higher and lower levels of government and how much. There are no clear answers to these questions and the debate is likely to continue.

To centralise or decentralise?

Arguments for decentralisation

- *Democracy* Local government adds an important dimension to democracy by allowing people in small communities to participate in, and have some control over, their own local affairs. Because it is also closer to citizens, local government may also be more accessible and democratic.

- *Efficiency* Centralisation may be inefficient, as many large corporations and the highly centralised states of the communist era found, because it means that decisions are taken by people who are far removed from the implementation of the decisions and from first-hand knowledge of their effects. Centralisation may be too rigid and unresponsive to local needs and demands.

- *Adaptation to local circumstances* Should central government officials in the capital city decide what time to lock local park gates, or how to run the local library? Such things ought to be decided by local people according to their wishes and knowledge of local circumstances.

- *Local minorities* Decentralisation allows geographically concentrated minority groups to control their own local affairs.

- *Training ground for democracy* Local government is a citizen training ground for democracy.

- *Recruiting ground for national politics* Local politics help to develop a pool of politically interested and talented people who can be recruited into national politics. Many national politicians start off in local government.

- *Experimentation and development* State and local government can experiment on a small scale with new services and new methods of delivering services. Successes can spread quickly; failures are not large-scale disasters.

■ Arguments for centralisation

- *Democracy* Central government can claim to have stronger legitimacy and support (higher election turnouts), more media attention and a broader and deeper mandate (the whole country).
- *Efficiency* The small-scale provision of some public services can be inefficient if it results in duplication, wasteful competition and high capital costs, as many small units of production have found. Some services can be provided only nationally (defence, national economic planning), some are more efficiently provided this way (population censuses, motor registration) and some are so expensive that they must be provided nationally or internationally (building planes, space research).
- *Equality* Inequalities between areas can be reduced by the redistribution of resources (money, space, human capital) by national government. Central governments usually control the most productive taxes (income tax, business taxes) and they have the money and power to redistribute.
- *Protection of minorities* Decentralisation may allow local majorities to oppress their minorities. The defence of 'states' rights' in the USA has sometimes been a thinly disguised attempt to maintain racial segregation.

- *Local elites* Decentralisation can protect entrenched local elites.
- *Disintegration of the state* It is sometimes feared that decentralisation may lead to the break-up of the country (Basque Separatism, Quebec, Scottish Nationalism).
- *National identity* Focus on a national government can promote national integration. Some political identities are not local or regional but based upon national factors – class, culture, gender, language and national history.

■ Theories of multi-level government

Theories of multi-level government tend to fall into three basic types: first, there are philosophical and political defences of decentralised government, including pluralist theory; second, there are rational-choice theories of federalism and local government; and, third, there are the historical accounts of centre–periphery relations.

Philosophical and political theories: Mill and Tocqueville

The basic philosophical and political arguments for decentralised government were laid out by a French writer on American democracy, Alexis de Tocqueville (1805–59), and the British philosopher John Stuart Mill (1806–73). Developing basic liberal values, Mill argued that local self-government was important because, so far as possible, political decisions should not be imposed from above, but developed and accepted from below. Compared with central government, local government gives more people a first-hand experience of public affairs and, according to Mill, it is the chief instrument for educating people into their citizen duties. Tocqueville argues a similar case, but his writing concentrates on the citizenship benefits of local parties and voluntary associations rather than local government, ideas we shall consider in chapter 10.

Pluralist theory

Modern pluralist theory builds on Mill and Tocqueville. It argues that democracies should not have a single, monolithic centre of power but require many centres of power so that many people and groups can exercise influence on different issues, in different ways and in different political arenas. Democracies divide power vertically (into executive, legislative and judiciary) and horizontally (into different layers of territorial government) in order to create a variety of political arenas. Groups that lose a political battle in one arena can turn to another, and so live to fight another day. If they fail to get satisfaction in, say, central government they can take their causes to the courts, or local government, or perhaps international arenas.

Breaking the political system into geographical units with their own powers and responsibilities also has the advantage of decentralising political problems, and hence of not overburdened the centre with an accumulation of divisive issues. This is especially important where minorities (ethnic, linguistic, religious, or cultural) are geographically concentrated and where they have their own sub-central units of government to tackle their own problems in their own way. What makes local politics important is its very 'localness' – meaning that it is accessible to local people and that they are best placed to understand and deal with local issues (see controversy 6.2).

Economic theories

Rational choice

Rational-choice theories borrow heavily from economics and assume that politics is based upon the rational calculations of actors (individuals, organisations, governments) who are self-interested and try to maximise their own preferences. Many rational-choice theories start from the position that the political world consists of individuals, as against institutions with a culture and a history, who make rational choices that maximise their own utility – that is, their political behaviour is driven by calculations of what is in their own self-interest. Rational choice is a high-level general theory and it has been applied to many aspects of government and politics. Here we are concerned with its use to explain (1) the origins of federalism and (2) its defence of highly fragmented systems of local government made up of very small, competing, jurisdictions.

William Riker, Federalism: Origins, Operation, Significance (1964) According to William Riker (1920–93), the origins of federalism lie in a 'bargain' between national and local leaders, to the benefit of both, which enables them to expand the territory under their control, and to defend it against external enemies. Federalism is a rational solution to the problem of how to maintain a balance between the interests of a central power and of geographical regions so that each maintains control of their own affairs but can cooperate to deal with a common, external threat, and thereby increase their own power. In his book *Federalism: Origins, Operation, Significance* (1964), Riker claims that evidence about the origins of federal systems supports his hypothesis that military security and territorial expansion are the driving forces behind the formation of federations.

It might be argued that much the same explanation accounts for the historical origins of unitary states as well. Many were forged historically from smaller political units, city-states and princedoms when these were threatened by large, efficient and powerful enemies. A single authority brought together by centralising leaders had a much better chance of developing the economic capacities and military power to compete effectively with external enemies. In other words, the formation of both federal and unitary states is a response to external economic and military threats, and the need to create a larger and stronger political unit to deal with them. What distinguishes them is the historical circumstances of their development along either federal or unitary lines, something best explained by centre–periphery theory, discussed below.

Rational-choice theory of local government

Rational-choice theory also has its theory of local government, especially the highly fragmented and divided local government in the metropolitan areas of the USA. Splitting the government of a large urban area into many local jurisdictions, and giving each its own taxing and spending powers, means that citizens (the theory calls them 'consumer-voters') are provided with a choice of different 'packages' of public goods at different prices. Consumer-voters can move from one locality to another in search of their preferred 'package' of public goods, in much the same way that shoppers choose their supermarket for the goods it sells and the prices it charges. One municipality may have low taxes and few public services, another may tax in order to provide good education for young families, while a third may specialise in services for the retired.

This theory substitutes an economic logic for a political one: consumer-voters can move from one municipality to another to maximise their preferences, instead of using their vote to influence civic leaders and local public services. The economic argument is that a highly fragmented system of government is not inefficient, as many argue, but, on the contrary, produces a quasi-market that allows consumer-voters to vote with their feet. Some political economists find this approach helpful and insightful, but others doubt its value, for a string of reasons. First, consumer-voters are not free to move at will from one municipality to another. They are severely constrained by the needs of work, family, schools and house prices. Second, survey data shows that few people see local public services as very important when they are deciding where to live. Being near work, family and shops is much more important. Third, there is only a tenuous link between local taxes and services in many countries because financial transfers from higher levels of government pay a large proportion of the local service bill. And last, in most countries other than the USA, local government is not fragmented into many competing jurisdictions. It is consolidated and coordinated by higher levels of government which redistribute national tax resources and regulate local services.

Centre–periphery relations

Unitary states have typically emerged from old, centralised monarchies that kept their local government under the authority of central government as they gradually developed their modern democratic structures. Denmark, Finland, Japan, The Netherlands, Norway, Sweden and the UK are examples. In contrast, federal states are often formed by the merger of established and autonomous political areas that come together to form a political union, while retaining a degree of their original independence. In the case of Switzerland, federalism is designed to accommodate a history of autonomous localities created by mountainous geography and reinforced by language and cultural differences. In the case of Australia, Canada, India and the USA

129

federal governments cover large geographical areas that were not previously united under a single (monarchical) centre, but brought together by a colonial power.

According to the widely quoted theory of Rokkan and Lipset (see chapter 1) the historical process of state and nation building involved, among other things, the centralisation of regions and territories under a common central rule. In many cases, a powerful and modernising elite first conquered outlying areas and their local elites and then, by the processes of state and nation building, created a single political system with common political institutions and a common sense of national identity. The processes started many centuries ago in the case of some European countries, and took a long time to complete. Even so, one can often still see the historical imprint of centuries past in modern times, even in the most centralised and uniform unitary state, where the parties, voting and political/social patterns of peripheral regions are often rather different from the metropolitan centres.

However, the centre's attempts to incorporate the periphery has not always been altogether successful, as we can see from the nationalist movements in Italy (the Northern League), Spain (the Basque country and Catalonia), the UK (Scotland, Wales and Northern Ireland) and France (Corsica). In such cases, the unitary state may best be preserved by devolving powers to the peripheries. In the unusual case of Belgium, a unitary state turned itself into a federal one in order to maintain the integrity of the country.

Relations between the centre and the periphery are often relations between dominant and subordinate political groups. One variant of centre–periphery theory argues that the institutions of the central state were originally created by powerful interests (a class or ethnic group) that exploited the periphery for its resources, in much the same way that colonial powers exploit the natural resources of the Third World. According to some writers 'internal colonialism' of this kind exists in a subtle form in the UK (where England exploits Scotland, Wales and Northern Ireland) and the USA (where the north exploits the south), and in countries where the capital city region dominates and exploits the surrounding rural and agricultural areas.

■ What have we learned?

This chapter has dealt with the organisation of multi-level government. It argues that:

- The government and politics of the modern world consists of four main levels, with the lower levels nested in higher ones – local government nested inside middle or meso-government, nested in unitary and federal systems, and a layer of international and supranational government above them all.

- Most organisations at the international level are confederations that are looser than federations and do not encroach on the sovereignty of their members. The European Union is part federation, part confederation.
- Federal systems are more decentralised than unitary states, although to some extent federal systems have centralised and unitary states have decentralised since 1945.
- Federal systems are better suited to some circumstances (large countries with territorially concentrated minorities) and unitary states are better suited to others (small, homogeneous countries). There is a close association here between social and geographical circumstances and forms of government.
- Local government in all countries, federal or unitary, faces two insoluble dilemmas:
  a the conflict that often arises between different levels of democratically elected government
  b the problem of how to reconcile the conflicting claims of democracy and effectiveness.

■ Lessons of comparison

- There is not a single or a simple solution to the democracy versus efficiency dilemma because there is no single, optimal size for units of sub-central government. Each country has its own solutions, each with its merits and deficiencies.
- Attempts to solve these democracy versus effectiveness problem can take different forms involving the consolidation of units of local government into a smaller number of larger units, a shifting of service functions both up and down the political system, the creation or strengthening of meso-government, a degree of decentralisation in federal states and centralisation in unitary ones.
- The centralist/decentralist debate revolves around the problem of what to centralise, and how much, and what to decentralise, and how much, and what to share between levels of government. In most countries, there is a large area that is neither central nor local but involves close cooperation between central and sub-central government.

Projects

1. Draw up a table that assigns government functions (international relations, education, pollution control, libraries, parks, economic development, housing, transportation, police) to different levels of the political system (international, national, regional, local, community). What general lessons can you draw from this exercise?

2. Sub-central government is responsible for varying proportions of total government expenditure and employment in different countries (see figures 6.1 and 6.2 and table 6.1). Would you draw the conclusion that the higher the share of public expenditure and employment, the more decentralised the country?

Further reading

R. A. W. Rhodes, 'Intergovernmental relations: unitary systems', and Grant Harman, 'Intergovernmental relations: federal systems', both in M. Hawksworth and M. Kogan (eds.), *Encyclopedia of Government and Politics, Vol. 1,* London: Routledge, 1992: 316–35 and 336–51.
Two short, comprehensible, readable articles on federalism, unitary states and local government.

M. Burgess and A. G. Gagnon (eds.), *Comparative Federalism and Federation: Competing Traditions and Future Directions*, New York: Harvester Wheatsheaf, 1993.
A useful collection of essays on federalism.

L. J. Sharpe (ed.), *The Rise of Meso Government in Europe*, London: Sage, 1993.
On meso government in western Europe.

B. Denters and L. Rose (eds.), *Comparing Local Government: Trends and Developments*, Palgrave: Basingstoke, 2005.
An account of local government in western countries.

OECD, *Managing Across Levels of Government,* Paris: OECD, 1997 (also at www.oecd.org/dataoecd/10/14/1902308.pdf).
Compares multi-level government in twenty-six member states of the OECD.

Websites

www.forumfed.org
The Forum of Federations is an international network on federalism and related issues. General information about federalism, useful links and a list of countries with federal systems of government.
www.oultwood.com
Many links and much information about local government in twenty-one countries; the councillors, members of parliament, etc.
www.unescap.org/huset/lgstudy/comparison2.htm
On local government in Asia and the Pacific: a comparative analysis of fifteen countries.
www.coe.int/T/Congress/Default_en.asp
The website of the Local Government International Bureau from the Congress of Local and Regional Authorities of Europe. Covers forty-seven countries in Europe.

http://encyclopedia. thefreedictionary.com/Federalism
Basic introduction to federalism with links to related topics.
http://encyclopedia.thefreedictionary.com/Local%20Government
Basic introduction to local government with links to related topics.
http://encyclopedia. thefreedictionary.com/Unitary%20state
Basic introduction to unitary states with links to related topics. List of unitary
   states with links to general information about the state.

7   Policy making and legislating: executives and legislatures

Governments are there to get things done. At the highest level, the most important things they do are formulate public policies and frame the laws of the land, and at the heart of the policy and law-making process lie the two main branches of government – the executive and the legislative assembly. This means that the study of the relations between executive and legislative branches is a topic that lies at the very core of comparative government.

Sometimes the executive and the legislative branches cooperate and act together, sometimes they fight and struggle for power. Since democratic constitutions deliberately divide the powers of government between different branches, so that they check and balance each other, there is nothing wrong with the political struggle between them. However, some analysts argue that all is not well with the classical system of checks and balances because the golden age of legislatures, some time in the nineteenth century, has given way to the twentieth-century supremacy of executives. What were once powerful elected assemblies with a great deal of control over the affairs of state are now little more than rubber stamps for decisions made by their executives. If true, this has obvious implications for the state of democracy in modern executive-dominated government.

Others claim that presidents and prime ministers have not acquired such great power. They argue that legislative assemblies were never that powerful to start with, that the balance of power between executives and legislatures has not changed much and that executives are still dependent upon the support of their elected assemblies.

Another part of the discussion is concerned with correcting a common misperception about what the role of legislative bodies actually is, rather than how much power they have, or have lost. To 'legislate' means to make laws, and who should do this other than those who are elected to sit in the legislative chamber? Do not our national assemblies sit in endless discussion – sometimes solemn debate, sometimes angry and heated argument – about the policies and laws of the government of the day? Yet law making is not actually the main function of legislatures, and may not even be one of their most important functions. The curious fact is that legislatures, in spite of their name, are not mainly there to legislate. To understand why this is the case, we must examine the main functions of legislative bodies.

Since things rarely ever remain the same, we will also examine recent efforts of legislative assemblies to modernise. Many of them are in the process of reforming and streamlining themselves for modern government **administration**, so that they can do their work more efficiently and acquire the 'political muscle' necessary to exercise more control over their executives.

> **Administration** A term with two meanings. Either (1) a term synonymous with government – e.g. the Obama administration, the Merkel administration or (2) a term synonymous with the management processes of bureaucracies – e.g. the administration of the state through bureaucratic agencies. The term is used in the second sense in this chapter.

In this chapter, we analyse the relationship between executives and legislatures in the policy and law-making processes of modern democratic government. The major topics in this chapter are:

- Making laws: executives and legislatures
- The increasing power of executives
- The functions of legislatures
- The reform of legislatures
- Theories of democratic institutions: consensus and majoritarian systems.

■ Making laws: executives and legislatures

Classical democratic theory divides government into three main branches, the executive, legislative and judiciary, and gives them different powers and functions so that none can become too powerful. Each should have powers of its own, and each should operate a system of checks and balances to ensure that they are dependent on each other. In this way neither can do its job without the agreement of the other because they are bound together in a relationship of perpetual, mutual dependency (see chapter 4). In virtually all democratic systems **legislation** can be passed only when both the executive and legislative

> **Legislation** Legislation is the body of laws that have been passed by the legislature. Legislating is thus the act of initiating, debating and passing such laws.

branches agree. Indeed, this condition is formally spelled out in some constitutions. For example, Article 61 of the Dutch constitution states: 'Laws are decided on by government and States-General together.' It is this sort of formal requirement for agreement that tries to ensure that power is shared.

In real life, however, some democratic systems deviate to a greater or lesser extent from the classic formula. Because the two branches should work closely together there is inevitably some overlap and fusion of executive and legislative functions and powers, and it is more accurate to say that their powers are mixed rather than separated. This is most evident in parliamentary systems, but it also applies to presidential ones where, although there is supposed to be a clearer separation of powers, there is, as we saw in chapter 4, in reality a complex and subtle mix of executive and legislative powers.

Some have, however, argued that the classical system of executive and legislative checks and balances does not operate in modern government. They claim that modern executives have acquired so much power that they now dominate the processes of government, reducing legislative assemblies to the role of junior partners, even to little more than rubber stamps for executive decisions (see controversy 7.1). If this is true, then the lack of checks and balances may even pose a threat to democratic government itself.

The rise of executives

There are good reasons for believing that the balance of power between executives and legislatures may have shifted decisively in favour of executives. Six stand out as particularly important.

1. Government complexity

   The growing complexity and interdependence of the social, economic and political world gives a new importance and role to executives. As technical problems grow ever more complex (nuclear power, the environment, the economy), as society becomes ever more differentiated and difficult to manage, as demands on government grow and as international and global pressures increase, so complex government increasingly requires a single centre of coordination and control. In addition, one of the major problems in modern government is to keep the multifarious agencies, departments and units of government moving in the same direction, and this increasingly difficult job of coordination is an executive rather than a legislative function.

2. Delegated legislation

   The nature of legislation also changes. It is no longer possible to frame laws for specific and known circumstances – these change too quickly, in accordance with technological innovation, international forces and social pressures. It is necessary instead to devise more general laws, which inevitably leave much of the detail to be decided by executives. This is known as delegated legislation, and it gives executives more power.

Delegated legislation Law or decrees made by ministers, not by legislatures, though in accordance with powers granted to them by the legislative body.

CONTROVERSY 7.1

Parliaments and legislatures

What happened to parliaments?

Something has happened to parliaments. Parliaments were the key institutions of representative democracy. They translated the voice of the people into reasoned debate and ultimately into law. They also held governments to account, of all the checks and balances of power they were the most effective. They symbolised the constitution of liberty. For my father – and later for
me – becoming a member of parliament was an affirmation of our deep belief in democracy.

Much of this however has to be said in the past tense today. A number of developments have conspired to weaken parliaments:

- Governments have increasingly used orders, regulations and other secondary legislation which is not subject to parliamentary scrutiny.
- There is also a tendency for governments to turn directly to the people – by referenda, but more ominously by relying on polls and the views of 'focus groups'.
- This process goes hand in hand with phenomena like celebrity politics (candidates have to be telegenic), and snapshot or throwaway politics (what counts is the moment, not extended debate).
- Self-elected crowds and groups, demonstrations in the streets, non-governmental organisations, increasingly claim to be the people, to speak for the people.
- All this happens at a time at which important decisions have emigrated to political spaces for which there are no parliaments anyway. This is as true for internal decision making as it is for the role of economic markets.

*(Adapted from Lord Ralf Dahrendorf, speech at the Institute for
Human Sciences, Vienna, Newsletter, 72, Spring 2001)*

A decline of legislatures?

In what was the first truly empirical study of western governments, James Bryce, devoted a chapter to the subject of the 'decline of legislatures'. He argued that legislatures were weak and legislators incompetent or even corrupt. The idea of the decline of legislatures seemed confirmed in the twentieth century by the weaknesses of western European parliaments, not to mention those of most Third World countries.

While contemporary legislatures are often weak, there is some doubt as to whether they *declined* in quality and power during the period which preceded Bryce's investigation, let alone in the decades which followed. The view that there was a 'golden age' of legislatures seems at best exaggerated…

Legislatures are generally weak. Their weakness is due to general causes, many of which are structural and are connected with the complexity of matters and the need for urgent decisions. Only on a very few occasions did they realise the standards which Bryce, and indeed earlier Locke and Montesquieu, would have wanted them to display.

(Adapted from Jean Blondel, Comparative Government, London: Prentice Hall, 1995: 250)

3. Organisational advantages of executives

   Executives have significant advantages when it comes to organising for power. They are usually small in number – presidents and small cabinets – which makes it easier for them to unite around a common interest, and to react quickly and decisively to events. They are often supported by large and well-funded staffs in presidential and prime ministerial offices, and they are headed by highly visible political leaders who are able to appeal directly to the population, over the heads of the members of the elected assembly.

4. Mass media

   Modern executives have equipped themselves with effective press offices to help them exploit every ounce of favourable publicity they can get from the mass media. To some degree, the debating functions of legislatures have also been transferred to the mass media because more public debate about politics now takes place in TV studios rather than parliamentary debating chambers. In contrast, legislatures are rather large and cumbersome bodies consisting of hundreds of elected representatives, divided along party lines, and often unable to act quickly or with a single voice. In such circumstances executives take the lead and acquire power.

5. Party organisation

   Modern political parties are often tightly organised and highly disciplined. This helps executives to maintain control of their parties and ensure that their policies and **bills** are accepted by legislatures. By and large, the stronger the party system, the stronger the executive, and the weaker

   > **Bill** A formal proposal for a law put before a legislature but not yet accepted by it.

   the legislature. The major exceptions to strong executive power are usually found in countries with comparatively weak parties. Switzerland is probably the best example, but in Israel, the USA and the new democracies of central and eastern Europe, weak and fragmented parties help to undermine the executive and strengthen the legislature.

6. Emergency powers

   The threats of pandemics, natural disasters and terrorism require, some argue, greater power in the hands of political executives who are best able to respond quickly and effectively to emergencies.

There is evidence to support these general arguments. First, some executives have been given greater law-making powers in recent years (Australia and France). Second, the executives in many countries have made increasing use of the power of delegated legislation, which gives them more decision making autonomy. Third, some analysts argue that prime ministers in parliamentary systems have become so powerful as heads of state that they have, in effect, assumed the powers and status of elected presidents. This is said to be occurring in Australia and the UK, where a series of powerful prime ministers have accumulated decision-making authority that has transformed their office. Fourth, as we saw in chapter 6, power in federal systems, the most decentralised form of government, has become increasingly concentrated in the twentieth century, and in doing so has given the executive officers of their federal governments greater power than before.

Arguments about the rise of executives are strongly disputed by other political scientists, who claim that the trend is more apparent than real. They point to events that seem to show that even the strongest executives can be reined in by their legislatures. Nixon had to resign to avoid **impeachment**. Clinton was impeached, but not convicted of the charges. Thatcher was eventually toppled by her parliamentary party. The power of the 'Imperial presidency' in Mexico has weakened, and in Norway the influence of parliament has grown in recent years. There are examples of coalition govern-

Impeachment To charge a public official, usually an elected politician, with improper conduct in office before a duly constituted tribunal, usually the main elected legislative body, prior to removing the official from office if they are found guilty. Not known much outside the USA, and not often used there.

ments falling because they no longer had the confidence of their elected assemblies (see chapter 13). Consequently, it is said, the old executive systems of prime minister and cabinet continue to function more or less as they did in the nineteenth century, in the sense that power is shared and mixed between the two branches of government.

Increasing power of executives?

Is it possible to resolve the dispute about the increasing power of executives by reference to some systematic evidence? The figures in table 7.1 show what proportion of bills in fifteen western European countries were introduced by executives, and what proportion of these were duly accepted by legislatures and passed into law. The figures show two things quite clearly. First, most

Table 7.1 The source of legislation: governments and legislatures

	Government bills as % of all bills	% of government bills passed
Netherlands	98	85
Luxembourg	94	100
UK	92	92
Norway	90	99
Ireland	90	10
Greece	87	77
West Germany	74	100
Portugal	70	14
Austria	65	96
Denmark	59	84
Finland	48	100
Italy	29	51
Belgium	23	100
France	22	82
Spain	5	88

Note: The figures refer to various years in the late 1980s.
Source: Inter-Parliamentary Union, *Parliaments of the World* (New York: Facts on File, 1992).

bills are introduced by executives, not legislatures. Second, the overwhelming majority of bills introduced by executives are accepted by the legislatures and become law.

What can we conclude about the rise of executive power? Not much, some would say. The fact that legislatures invariably accept executive proposals for legislation simply shows how carefully executives sound out opinion in the legislative body before they present proposals. This argument is based on what Karl Friedrich (1901–84) has called 'The Law of Anticipated Reactions'. This states that wherever there are mutually dependent power relations, those involved will try to anticipate the reaction of others and modify their own behaviour accordingly. In terms of the executive–legislative relations, neither is likely to make a move or a proposal that is likely to be rejected by the other, so they sound each other out carefully before taking action. In fact, in most systems of government the two branches maintain an elaborate set of institutions and officials in order to maintain a constant dialogue to find out what each is prepared to accept. Unfortunately for the political scientist, much of this goes on behind the closed doors of party committee rooms, and we do not hear a great deal about the endless process of mutual bargaining and adjustment – what is sometimes termed 'wheeler-dealing' or 'horse-trading'.

Others, however, argue a different story. They agree that a good deal of legislation is based on shared powers and mutual accommodation between executives and legislatures. Nevertheless, the fact that most legislation is introduced by the executive, and that a very large majority of it is accepted by legislative assemblies suggests, to them, that executives are very powerful, even that legislatures have been reduced to little more than 'rubber stamps' and 'talking shops'. A key factor here, it is said, is the presence of increasingly centralised and disciplined political parties. Because party unity is so crucial to modern politics, and because a divided party is unlikely to do well in elections, party members in assemblies are under great pressure to comply with the wishes of their leaders. Strong parties make for strong executives; weak parties make for strong legislatures.

It may well be that the controversy about executive dominance will not be resolved. The executive seems to have gained the upper hand in some (Britain under Thatcher and Blair seems to be a good example), but mutual dependence seems to characterise others, especially where party systems are weak or fragmented and legislative committees are strong (Denmark, Switzerland, the USA).

Whatever the strengths of executives, or some of them, we should not slip into the assumption that legislative bodies are powerless in the face of almighty executives. It is one thing to claim that executives are increasing in power, quite another to say that legislatures are powerless. Indeed, elected assemblies still have an important role to play in government, and they are organising themselves to increase their influence and efficiency, as we will see now.

■ The functions of legislatures

Elected assemblies play many roles and have many functions, but these may be conveniently grouped under four general headings:

- The representation of public opinion
- The legitimation of government and the political system
- Law making
- The scrutiny of the executive and the administration of the state.

Representation of public opinion

Legislatures are the main representative body in democracies, and therefore the main assembly must be directly elected in order to reflect public opinion. In most cases, this means reflecting party political opinion, because most first chambers are elected along party lines. Some assemblies, however, represent the political interests of specific groups in society (farmers, workers, businessmen, churches, minority groups), or specific areas (cities, regions, or constituencies). No matter how they are elected or how they reflect public opinion, however, legislatures perform the common function of representing the electorate. In turn this means that legislative bodies must sort out and represent the main clusters of public opinion – a function known as **interest aggregation** – and then voice them in policy debates – a function known as **interest articulation**.

> **Interest aggregation** Sorting the great variety of political attitudes and opinions on a political issue, to reduce it to a more simple, clear-cut and agreed 'package' of opinion.

> **Interest articulation** The expression of political demands in order to influence public policy.

Elected assemblies are often criticised for not being representative of society, and it is true that many are not a social microcosm of the population they represent. Most are dominated by what might be called the four 'Ms' – that is, middle-class, middle-aged, majority group, males. In fact many elected legislatures are drawn heavily from a rather restricted set of occupations and social groups, most notably the professions (especially lawyers) and the better educated sections of society. Politics is becoming more 'professionalised' in the sense that elected representatives spend less time in ordinary jobs, but go into politics as young adults and stay there as they climb the 'greasy pole' of a political career. In sum: elected politicians in national government are not a good cross-section of society.

Against this, it might be said that it does not particularly matter whether the elected assembly is a microcosm of society or not. In the first place, politicians can represent the views of social groups other than their own. For example, middle-class individuals can reflect and defend the interests of the working-class people, and, indeed, many of the early pioneers of socialism were middle and upper class. In the second place, it might be argued that what counts most is to represent the views of political parties, which is how the electorate most usually divides itself when it votes. Most popularly elected legislatures do this fairly well, although exactly how well depends in large part of the voting system, as we shall see in chapter 12.

Legitimation

Whatever its composition and method of election, the fact that parliament is directly elected by the population and that it meets regularly in public to debate political issues, is important for the **legitimation** of the political system. Elected legislatures give governments their democratic legitimacy, and help stabilise the political system. This means that they not only legitimate the government of the day, but also the whole political system and the rules by which it works. This is important because it means that those who oppose the government will accept it because it is elected. Oppositions can wait patiently for the next election when they have a chance of taking over government themselves and being recognised as legitimate by those who have just been turned out of office.

> **Legitimation** The process of making something morally acceptable, proper, or right in the eyes of the general public.

Law making

We have already seen that most legislatures do not initiate bills, but they do consider them at some length. In many cases they change and modify details – sometimes important details – and in some cases are able to throw out bills or alter their fundamental intent. The intense pressures on parliamentary time means that some bills, or parts of them, are not scrutinised in any great detail. All, however, are processed according to a complex set of rules governing the passage of bills through parliament before they become law. This usually involves a sequence of debates or readings in one or both chambers, and a series of hearings in the committees, also in one or both chambers. Bills normally shuttle backwards and forwards between these debates and hearings and are subject to modification along the way before they are finally accepted (see briefing 7.1 for a Swedish example). To this extent, the mutual dependency of executive and legislative branches of government is a major feature of parliamentary systems. The legislative body is more important and powerful in the law-making process of some countries (Italy, Switzerland and the USA), but in all democracies the legislature does discuss and criticise new legislation, with a view to modifying it, or even rejecting it outright.

Scrutiny of the executive and the administration

A primary function of elected assemblies is to keep a close watch on the executive and on the administrative machinery of the state. Examining government bills is one method of doing this, but there are many others:

Briefing 7.1

A legislature at work: the Swedish Riksdag

- The *Riksdag* takes decisions on government bills, and on motions from its members concerning legislation, taxation and the use of central government revenue.
- Meetings of the chamber form an important part of the work of the members, but much also takes place in the party groups and in the sixteen *Riksdag* committees. The committees, whose members are drawn from the various parties, are working groups with responsibility for a particular area of business.
- All proposals for a *Riksdag* decision must first be considered by one of its sixteen committees. The committee publishes its conclusions in a report which may then be debated and decided by a plenary session of the *Riksdag*.
- Decisions in the chamber are often preceded by a debate.
- When the debate is over, the matter is decided, either by acclamation, or (if there are dissenting opinions) by vote.
- Occasionally the chamber will refer a matter back to the committee. When this happens, the committee has to reconsider the matter and draw up a new report.
- Members of the *Riksdag* are allowed to submit an interpellation – a question to a minister about the performance of his or her duties. Such questions enable the *Riksdag* to scrutinise and control the work of the government, to obtain information or to draw attention to a particular issue.
- Question time is held weekly for about one hour. The prime minister and six or seven other ministers answer questions put directly to them by members of the *Riksdag*.
- If a party group in the *Riksdag* wishes to debate a particular matter, which is unconnected with other business under consideration, it may request a current affairs debate. In 1997–8 five were held.
- Occasionally the government provides the *Riksdag* with oral information on issues of current interest. This is often followed by a debate.
- Much of the work of the *Riksdag* is regulated by the Riksdag Act, which regulates the chamber and its meetings, the election of the Speaker and the way in which business is prepared and decided.
- The *Riksdag* board is responsible for the overall planning of parliamentary business, including the selection of work procedures. The Board comprises the Speaker (chairman) and ten other members who are appointed by the *Riksdag* from among its members.

(Adapted from the Riksdag's website www.riksdagen.se/templates/PageWFrame_6577.aspx)

> **Interpellation** A parliamentary question addressed to government requiring a formal answer and often followed by discussion, and sometimes by a vote.

- *Veto powers* Some legislative bodies have powers to veto or modify policy proposals made by the executive.
- *Approving executive appointments* Appointments to high positions of state such as ministers, secretaries of state and national bank directors are involved here.
- *Question time* Most presidents or prime ministers are required to present themselves or explain themselves to their legislative bodies either in

person or writing. Normally questions are routine parts of the parliamentary timetable (see briefing 7.1), but they can be special (impeachment proceedings against the American president, for example, see below).

- *Debate* Debates are an occasion to consider government policy and actions in some detail. Some debates are concerned with specific pieces of legislation and may be quite technical, others are on general political issues, and some about emergency matters. The advantage of debate is that it subjects governments to the glare of public scrutiny and criticism, and can help to improve the quality of the legislation. The disadvantage is that debates in public assemblies are often reduced to party political 'shadow boxing' – ritual events staged for the public.

- *Vote of no confidence or impeachment* The ultimate power of legislative assemblies is the ability to remove the executive by a vote of 'no confidence' or impeachment. In parliamentary systems the government of the day can remain in office only as long as it has the support of a majority in the assembly. If it loses a vote of confidence in the assembly, it can no longer continue in control and will have to resign so that a new government with majority support can be formed. This is the cornerstone of the relationship of mutual dependence between the executive and the legislature, and we shall discuss it again in chapter 13, which considers the formation of party and coalition governments.

- *Committees* Perhaps the most important single legislative development in recent times is the strengthening of committees. In fact, committee work is now such a significant part of legislative operations, and so crucial to the scrutiny of executives that it needs to be considered in greater depth.

Legislative committees

Parliaments, including the European Parliament, are adapting to changing circumstances and trying to improve their effectiveness by streamlining their procedures, and by providing members with better facilities and resources (offices, secretaries, researchers, information). Most important they are increasingly concentrating on the scrutiny (sometimes know as '**legislative oversight**') of executive and administrative action. They have tried to do this by creating more effective and more powerful committees.

Legislative oversight The role of the legislature that involves the scrutiny or supervision of other branches of government, especially the executive and the public bureaucracy.

Close scrutiny of government cannot be done in large meetings. It is better performed by small committees with the time, experience and technical expertise to delve into the great complexities of modern legislation. Committees can also avoid the worst aspects of ritual party conflict that is often found in the main debating chamber. Effective and powerful committees, in turn, require their own expert advice and information, bureaucratic support and time for detailed work. If they are to have a major impact they must also be powerful, which means having a loud bark as well as sharp teeth – in other words they need real powers which enable them to influence government action.

Many legislatures are trying to assert their power, or regain lost powers, by developing an effective committee system for executive and administrative action, and reviewing legislation. This is often an uphill battle because committees depend on executives to grant them new powers and resources, and executives are usually unwilling to do this, because they know that these powers may well be turned against them. The clearest examples of powerful and powerless committees are in the USA and the French Fifth Republic. The former has a remarkably complex and powerful system of small and expert committees that can, and frequently do, exert a profound influence on executive appointments and policy. The French system is restricted to six committees, two of which have 120 members, and are therefore pretty ineffective. The Danish parliament also derives a good deal of its influence over government affairs from its effective committee system.

Effective committees tend to have a membership of fifteen to twenty-five or thirty people, with a good core of members who have served long enough to gain specialist knowledge and experience of a particular policy area. If there are enough of them, committees can cover a wide range of government business, including the close and detailed scrutiny of bills, public spending, foreign affairs, all the main aspects of home affairs and any other public matter they think should be reviewed. Each committee has a convener, or *chair*, who usually has a high standing and long experience in parliamentary affairs. The party composition of committees often reflects that of the assembly as a whole, with a majority of government members.

If they are to be influential and independent of the government, parliamentary committees will probably be constituted in the following ways:

- Their chairs should not necessarily be members of the governing party or parties
- They should have their own staff and expert advisors
- They should have powers to call witnesses and the right to question them closely, including leading members of the government
- They should have had time to build up their own knowledge and expertise in the business handled by the committee
- They should be able not only to issue public reports, which get publicity in the media, but also have the power to require government action following from their recommendations.

Committees may not have all these powers in full, and hence they may not often operate at maximum strength, but nevertheless they are one of the most effective weapons that legislative bodies have in their battle with powerful executives.

■ Theories of democratic institutions: consensus and majoritarian systems

On many occasions in previous chapters we have pointed out that there is an enormous variety of formal democratic arrangements and institutions, and that each country combines them in its own unique manner. We have also observed that this great diversity of constitutional characteristics usually resolves itself, in practice, into only a few general patterns shared by many countries. For example, in spite of their differences in length, detail and content, constitutional documents normally fall into four distinctive parts. Again, of all the different ways of combining executive–legislative relations, these usually revolve around only three types – presidential, semi-presidential and parliamentary. And although there are a great many different ways of organising territorial government within a country, there are only two main types in practice – federal and unitary – and only a few sub-types in each category. Fortunately for comparative political scientists, what might easily be a confusing mass of detailed country-specific differences turns out, in the end, to fall into a comparatively simple general pattern, albeit with exceptions to the general rule. This is good news for students of comparative government because it means that they can generalise about a number of similar democratic systems rather than point out the detailed differences between each and every one of them, although these undoubtedly exist.

In his ground-breaking comparison of thirty-six democracies, Arendt Lijphart (1936–) observes that despite their enormous variation, democracies tend to fall into two general categories. He calls these *majoritarian* and *consensus* democracies. Majoritarian systems, as the name suggests, give political power to the majority of citizens and the political parties that represent them, while consensus democracies try to represent as many people and groups as possible. The basic mechanism of the majoritarian model is to concentrate power in the hands of the political executive and to leave the exercise of this power relatively unconstrained. The majoritarian model concentrates executive power and places comparatively few restraints on its exercise, while the consensus model both disperses power and restrains its use.

The main characteristics of the two types of democracy are listed in table 7.2.

Majoritarian democracy, or the 'Westminster model'

This model:

- Concentrates executive power by giving it to whichever party (or, more rarely, combination of parties) controls a bare majority in the legislative assembly
- Fuses executive and legislative powers in the classic parliamentary manner

Table 7.2 The main institutional features of majoritarian and consensus democracies

Majoritarian democracy	Consensus democracy
Concentration of executive power	Executive power sharing
Fusion of executive and legislative power	Separation of powers
Single party government	Coalition government
Two-party system	Multi-party system
Simple majority electoral system	Proportional electoral system
Unitary government and centralisation	Federalism and decentralisation
Asymmetric bicameralism or unicameralism	Balanced bicameralism
Constitutional flexibility	Constitutional inflexibility
Absence of judicial review	Judicial review
Examples: Columbia, Costa Rica, France, Greece, New Zealand (before 1996), the UK	Examples: Austria, Germany, India, Japan, the Netherlands, Switzerland, and (arguably) the EU.

- Concentrates power by being either unicameral or, if, there are two chambers, by giving one assembly a clearly superior status
- Gives the courts no special powers to review legislation or decide constitutional matters, because this would diffuse power to another branch of government
- Has a degree of constitutional flexibility by allowing the constititon to be changed by majority vote in the legislature.
- Is often a unitary state and gives central government considerable powers not only over its own business but also that of the territorial units of government below it
- Has majoritarian and disproportional electoral systems favouring the emergence of two major parties, banks that are dependent on the executive and a pluralist interest group systems.

We shall discuss interest groups, electoral systems and party systems later (chapters 10, 12 and 13) but can now consider the formal constitutional and institutional features of majoritarian government that we have discussed earlier. It is no coincidence that the institutional characteristics of majoritarian government tend to go together, for they 'fit' with one another in a consistent and logical way. The British system is one of the best examples of majoritarian democracy, and it was based on the principle of parliamentary sovereignty, at least until membership of the EU changed this. If parliament is sovereign then it follows logically and inevitably that no other body or institution of government should be able to challenge parliament – not the courts, nor a written constitution, nor lower levels of government, nor a second chamber. The idea is to create a stable and effective government with power to get things done, but that is still accountable to the population through the elected legislature.

Consensus democracy

Consensus democracy also relies upon majority government, but rather than concentrating power, it shares it. Consensus democracies:

- Try to construct broad coalition government consisting not of a single majority party or a bare majority of them, but of a coalition of them
- Separate and balance executive and legislative power
- Are often federal – which, of course, means a degree of territorial decentralisation. In some cases safeguards may be built in for non-territorial language, ethnic or cultural groups, which are given a degree of governmental autonomy
- Have two legislative assemblies (bicameralism), often with balanced powers
- Have judicial review of political and constitutional matters, as a way of trying to sort out conflict between the different branches and levels of government
- Have a degree of constitutional inflexibility, because they try to maintain their diffusion of power and to include a wide range of opinion in any attempt to change the system
- Have proportional elections, multi-party systems, corporatist interest-group systems, and independent central banks.

These institutional features of government also 'fit' together logically, given the initial assumption that the job of democracy is to include and represent as many groups as possible. Such a government would share and separate power between the main parties and between two representative assemblies. It would also divide government territorially, especially if it were a large country in terms of geography, or population, or both. It would make sure that its arrangements were not easily changed by a few vested interests, and would reinforce the rights of all citizens by giving the courts the right to review constitutional matters and public policy. All this would be a particularly coherent package if the society in question were a culturally and ethnically mixed one, or what Lijphart terms a 'plural' society. These are particularly likely to be federal systems, and to have the other characteristics of consensus democracy. The basic idea is to create a form of government that is stable and effective, and works by distributing power, including most social groups in the political process and building a consensus acceptable to most of the organisations and parties involved.

Lijphart's study of democracy is widely discussed and has inspired much other research, but it is not without its critics. Some claim that the typology is too broad and general to apply to all cases, and that there are many exceptions that do not fit properly. The USA is neither majoritarian nor consensual, but a bit of both. Switzerland is a consensual system but it does not have judicial review. Canada is a consensus federal system in some respects, but has dominant one-party cabinets.

We will return to majoritarian and consensus democracies again later in the book (chapter 13) after we have considered voting systems, pressure group and party government, which are additional features of the two types of democracy not yet discussed here.

■ What have we learned?

This chapter deals with the roles of the executive and legislative branches of government, whose relationship is at the very heart of policy and law making. It argues that:

- In democratic theory, the executive and legislative branches should be separate, and each should maintain a system of checks and balances on the other. In practice, there is more of a mix than a separation of powers.
- There is a controversy about whether executives have increased their power in recent decades in response to a variety of social, economic and political pressures.
- Legislatures still have an important role in government. They represent public opinion, help the political system, review bills proposed by the executive and keep watch over the executive and state bureaucracy.
- Legislatures have tried to improve their efficiency and authority in different ways, but especially by developing committee systems that enable them to perform their function of scrutiny and oversight more effectively.

■ Lessons of comparison

- Powerful legislatures often have comparatively weak party systems (and vice versa) and a comparatively strong committee system.
- Although each democratic system of government has a unique combination of particular features, they often combine their general characteristics in only a few ways, so creating some general patterns and only a few general types.
- In spite of their infinite variety of detail, democracies tend to come in two main types, majoritarian and consensual.
- There are clear links between the social conditions of a society and its system of government. Consensus democracies are often large and pluralist societies. Many majoritarian systems are members of the British Commonwealth and show their British heritage in their government.
- Large plural societies tend to be consensual, suggesting that there is an important social basis to consensus forms of government.
- Historical background is important. Many majoritarian systems are British Commonwealth countries and developed their majoritarian institutions at the time of the Empire.

Projects

1. Does the composition of your own national parliament show that it is dominated numerically by the 'four Ms' – middle-aged, middle-class, majority group, males? What are the implications of your conclusion?
2. The website for your own national legislature is likely to have information about its committee system. What can you conclude from it about how the system works and how influential and important it is in the government of the country?
3. Has the power of the executive increased in your country over the past few decades?

Further reading

J. Denis and I. D. Derbyshire, *Encyclopedia of World Political Systems*, Vol. 1, Armonk: M. E. Sharpe, 2000: chapters 4 and 5).
A comprehensive overview of the world's executives and legislatures.

P. Heywood and V. Wright, 'Executives, bureaucracies and decision-making', in M. Rhodes, P. Heywood and V. Wright (eds.), *Developments in West European Politics,* Basingstoke: Macmillan, 1997.
An excellent overview of executive–bureaucracy relations in western Europe.

D. Olson, *Legislative Institutions: A Comparative View,* Armonk: M. E. Sharpe, 1994.
A good comparative study of legislatures.

P. Norton (ed.), *Parliaments and Governments in Western Europe,* London: Frank Cass, 1998.
A useful set of essays on western Europe.

L. Longley and R. H. Davidson (eds.), *The New Roles of Parliamentary Committees* (London: Frank Cass, 1998).
A good book on the role and development of parliamentary committees.

A. Lijphart, *Patterns of Democracy: Government Forms and Performance in Thirty-Six Countries,* New Haven: Yale University Press, 1999.
Lipjpart's account of his classic work on majoritarian and consensus democracies.

Websites

www.oecd.org/dataoecd/17/55/16212507.pdf
A document about the role of parliamentary committees in education policy.

www.ipu.org

Information on the structure and working methods of 265 parliamentary chambers in the 189 countries and the EU where a national legislature exists, with links to each country and the regional groups of parliaments.

www.ecprd.org/

The European Centre for Parliamentary Research and Documentation deals with European parliaments.

8   Implementation: the public bureaucracy

Governments make policy and pass laws but they are not and cannot be involved in the vast amount of routine implementation and daily administration of policy. For this, they rely on government ministries and the army of state bureaucrats who work in them. Like armies, the bureaucracy ranges from a small handful of very top officials down to office workers who carry out the routine work. The jobs of the highest officials (in the civil service, sometimes called 'mandarins', after the top officials of the ancient Chinese bureaucracy) are little different from those of the chief executive officers (CEOs) of multi-national corporations in the private sector, while many of the lower ranks are known as 'street-level bureaucrats' because they come into everyday contact with the general public.

Street-level bureaucrats The bureaucrats who regularly come into contact and deal with the public.

Whether they are mandarins or filing clerks, state bureaucrats are sometimes seen as lazy and inefficient. But alongside this stereotype there exists a completely different one that views bureaucrats as ambitious empire builders who want to expand their own departments in the interests of their own status and salary, and who conspire to take over the policy-making function of politicians to make sure that things are run according to the bureaucrats' wishes.

These contradictory images highlight an ambivalence that permeates the public **bureaucracy**. On the one hand, no democracy could even exist without effective bureaucracies to implement public policies and deliver public services. On the other hand, senior bureaucrats are often more experienced and highly trained than their political masters, and their role at the very heart of government gives them an enormous potential for power in the affairs of state. Yet they are supposed to be servants, not masters of the state.

> **Bureaucracy** A rational, impersonal, rule-bound and hierarchical form of organisational structure set up to perform large-scale administrative tasks.

In this chapter, we examine controversies about the role and power of public bureaucrats. The chapter outlines, first of all, the organisation of the state bureaucracy before looking more closely at the distinction between policy making and administration. It then considers the theory that it is permanent officials (bureaucrats) who run the state, not elected politicians. Politicians, of course, are fully aware of the potential power of their top civil servants, so the chapter continues by looking at how they have tried to counter this power. Finally, the chapter examines the wave of recent reforms that have tried to make the public bureaucracy more efficient.

The major topics in this chapter are:

- The organisation of the state bureaucracy
- Policy making and administration
- The dictatorship of the official?
- The New Public Management
- Theories of public bureaucracy.

■ The organisation of the state bureaucracy

The administration of the state – that is, the day-to-day work of implementing policies – is carried out by the bureaucratic departments or ministries of government. These are usually organised around the major functions of the state: economic affairs, foreign relations, defence, home affairs, transport and communications, education, welfare, the environment and so on. There is no logical or best way of dividing these functions, so the list of ministries varies from one country to another. In some, education is grouped with family matters, in others it is organised with employment and vocational training. Similarly transport, the environment and planning may be combined in the same ministry, or remain separate. Sometimes there is a special ministry for women and children. As a result, ministry sizes vary enormously from quite compact ones (Ministries of Justice are often separate and small) to huge super-ministries. Increasingly ministries combine a range of related functions under one umbrella in an attempt to integrate different aspects of policy – economic development, transportation and regional affairs, for example. The advantage is that related policy areas are combined under one organisational roof; the disadvantage is that the larger the department, the more cumbersome it may be.

The total size of the public bureaucracy also varies greatly from country to country. It is relatively small in Japan, Greece, and Turkey, and relatively large in the advanced 'Nordic welfare states' of Denmark, Norway and Sweden (see table 8.1). But even when it is relatively small compared with other countries, the **public sector** is often a rather large part of the economy in its own country. Japan, for example, has one of the smallest public sectors in the OECD countries, but it still accounts for an eighth of total employment. The largest public sectors account for a quarter of the workforce. Note, however, that the size of a ministry in terms of employment or its budget may tell us little about its power and importance. Japan's

Public sector That part of social, economic and political life that is not private but controlled or regulated by the state or its agencies.

Table 8.1 Public employment[a] as a percentage of total employment, OECD countries, 1990s

Country	'Limited' public sector[b]	'Extended' public sector[c]
Japan	6.5	7.0
Turkey	9.4	12.1
Greece	9.6	12.9
Netherlands	11.8	13.9
UK	11.9	16.9
New Zealand	12.1	14.2
Germany	14.1	15.4
USA	14.2	14.9
Australia	14.6	18.7
Portugal	14.8	17.5
Spain	15.1	18.0
Austria	15.8	22.5
Mexico	15.9	26.1
Ireland	16.8	21.1
Canada	17.4	19.9
Italy	18.2	23.2
Belgium	20.0	23.9
France	20.2	27.0
Iceland	21.1	
Finland	25.1	27.2
Norway	30.6	
Sweden	31.7	38.1
Denmark	35.4	39.3

Notes: [a] The OECD warns that it is very difficult to define and compare public employment across different countries, and that therefore care should be taken in interpreting these figures. They refer to slightly different financial years in each country.
[b] The 'limited' public sector column covers central and federal government, regional and state government, and local government and the municipalities.
[c] The 'extended' public sector covers the limited sector plus public enterprises.

Source: OECD, Measuring Public Employment in OECD Countries: Methods, Sources and Results (Paris: OECD, 1997).

Ministry of International Trade and Industry (MITI) is closely integrated with the country's business and political elites, and has played a very important role in Japan's economic success, but it is not a specially large ministry.

For all their power and importance in the affairs of state, departments and ministries are rarely even mentioned in constitutional documents, but nevertheless in the great majority of democracies they are governed by similar crucial principles. At the very top of each department or ministry – the terms are often used interchangeably – there is usually a politician who is ultimately accountable to the general public for its operations. These politicians may be directly elected and senior members of the representative assembly, or they may be appointed by, and accountable to, an elected politician. In parliamentary systems ministers in charge of departments are usually elected members of the governing party or coalition, and they constitute the cabinet or council. In presidential systems, the heads of the most important departments of state may also constitute a cabinet, but they are usually appointed by, and accountable to, the president, not drawn from the elected assembly or accountable to it.

In all cases, the theory is that the bureaucratic machinery of state should be under the control of elected politicians who are ultimately accountable to the general public, through the ballot box. Public sector bureaucrats are appointed to be servants of the state. They are not accountable to the general public but to their political masters. The policies of departments are supposed to be directed by elected politicians, and the day-to-day administrative work directed by professional bureaucrats.

The politicians in charge of departments work very closely with a relatively small group of the most senior bureaucrats in them. Although ministers are ultimately responsible for the work of their departments, they have to rely upon the experience and specialist knowledge of their civil servants (bureaucracy), both to make policy and manage the daily affairs of the department. Departments are vast machines, and because bureaucrats often know most about the complexities of both policy and its **implementation** they advise their ministers on both these aspects.

> **Implementation** The process of applying policies and putting them into practice.

There are three main types of senior bureaucrats with administrative and policy advisor functions:

1. *Permanent administrators* Some public bureaucracies are built on the idea that permanent officials should faithfully and impartially serve their ministers, whether or not they agree on policy matters. Permanent administrators are supposed to be politically neutral. The British system is based on this 'faithful servant' notion of an impartial bureaucracy, and for this reason its civil servants are not allowed to take any public part in politics. Some countries go to great lengths to select and train the best and the brightest for careers in the public service. France, for example, has an elite administrative corps trained at the Ecole National d'Administration (see fact file 8.1).

155

2. *Political appointments* Some countries do not believe in permanent administrators. They clear out the very top layers of departments when a new
government is elected, and appoint their own people. A new American
president typically appoints 3,000 people to posts in Washington, though
occasionally nominees are vetoed by Senate. One can see the sense in

Fact file 8.1

Public bureaucracies

- The term '*bureaucratie*' is said to have been used for the first time in 1764 in France to describe a
  new form of government by officials, which is completely different from democracy, autocracy, and
  monarchy. The term soon spread to Italy (*burocrazia*) to Germany (*Bürokratie*) and to Britain.
- As a political phenomenon bureaucracy predates the French invention of the word. It was necessary wherever the earliest empires created a need for the administration of large territories. The
  term 'mandarin' – referring to those at the very highest levels of the modern civil service – comes
  from the civil service of ancient China.
- The French Council of State is a special administrative court with the double function of protecting civil servants against attempts by politicians to manipulate them, and of ensuring that civil
  servants behave properly. Many other states have set up administrative systems of tribunals and
  law to regulate the public bureaucracy.
- State bureaucrats are known as civil servants in Britain (and many of the Commonwealth countries), 'apparatchiks' in the Soviet Union, Eurocrats in the EU and *Beamte* in Germany.
- Being a top civil servant in many countries is very prestigious, perhaps most of all in France
  and Japan. The French administrative elite are known as 'Enarques' after the Ecole National
  d'Administration (ENA), while most of Japan's senior civil servants are the products of the
  University of Tokyo's Law School. Spain has its prestigious system of *cuerpos*, and the British have
  traditionally recruited from the universities of Oxford and Cambridge.
- In the eighteenth and nineteenth century entry to the very highest levels of the civil service in many
  western countries was traditionally restricted to an upper-class elite. This is less true today now that
  top jobs are increasingly open to merit, and to recruits from working-class and minority backgrounds.
- Some state bureaucracies are run along 'generalist' lines, and recruit people of all-round ability
  and intelligence to work in a wide variety of top jobs – the UK, Ireland and, to some extent, Italy,
  Portugal and Spain. The more 'specialist' tradition is more technocratic and trains people for particular departments or jobs – France, Germany, The Netherlands and the Nordic countries.
- The practice of incoming governments appointing the top layers of the civil service is an old one
  in Finland, France, Germany and the USA, but it is now spreading to other countries. There are
  few political appointments in Japan.
- The most radical new public management (p. 160) reforms are found in the Anglo-Saxon countries of Australia, Canada, New Zealand, the UK and the USA, and in Denmark, Finland, Norway
  and Sweden. They are weakest in developing democracies.
- Almost all countries have implemented NPM since the 1980s, but these have taken different
  forms in different countries. In France, Sweden and Spain they were designed to strengthen the
  civil service; in Denmark, Norway and the UK to weaken and reduce it.

having people sympathetic to the government running its departments, but there is also the danger of **clientelism** and of using public office for private gain.

3. *Policy advisors* To counter the power of permanent officials, ministers increasingly appoint teams of their own policy advisors. They are distinct from appointed administrators because they are concerned with policy, not day-to-day departmental matters. There are two main reasons for appointing policy advisors. First, civil servants may not always be impartial in their advice because they have their own professional and organisational interests. Second, they may have worked so long and so closely with the private organisations they are supposed to regulate that they become 'captured' and 'domesticated' by these organisations and start representing their interests (see chapter 10). Outside policy advisors can bring a fresh approach to old problems.

> **Clientelism** A system of government and politics based on a relationship between patron and clients. Public sector jobs and contracts are distributed on the basis of personal and political contacts in return for political support.

Policy making and administration

In theory, elected and accountable politicians should make policy; appointed officials should implement it. In practice, however, the line between policy and administration is not that clear. It would be exceedingly foolish to try to implement a policy that could not be sensibly administered; at the same time the best administration in the world cannot save a fundamentally flawed policy; the way in which a policy is administered might well influence its capacity to achieve its stated goals, as some studies show clearly enough. Policy and administration are intimately bound together and cannot be neatly separated, a point made effectively in briefing 8.1.

Briefing 8.1

Policy making and administration

The relations between senior politicians and their civil servants would not seem to be promising material for a successful TV comedy, but it was the theme of the long-running *Yes Minister*, succeeded by the equally popular *Yes Prime Minister*, on British television. In one episode, the wily mandarin, Sir Humphrey Appleby, gives a lesson on policy making and administration to his new and inexperienced Minister, the hapless Jim Hacker:

> I do feel that there is a real dilemma here, in that while it has been government policy to regard policy as the responsibility of ministers, and administration as the responsibility of officials, questions of administrative policy can cause confusion between the administration of policy, and the policy of administration, especially where the responsibility for the administration of the policy of administration conflicts or overlaps with the responsibility for the policy of the administrative policy.

> *(Jonathan Lynn and Antony Jay, Yes Minister, London: BBC, 1982: 176)*

If there is no clear distinction between policy making and imple-mentation,how do we decide whether one has stepped into the role of the other? This is one of the oldest and most hotly debated controversies in government and in political science – the power of public bureaucrats.

■ The dictatorship of the official?

The power of the official

Like many other political institutions, the state bureaucracy is (a) essential and (b) dangerous. On the one hand, public bureaucracies are essential parts of the state apparatus to implement policies and deliver public services. Can you imagine any contemporary government without a small army of bureau-crats to organise public elections, collect taxes, administer state pensions, run schools and hospitals, provide welfare services, draw up contracts for mili-tary hardware, inspect the roads, ensure that public health and safety regula-tions are observed, run police and fire services and answer queries about all these from the general public? Whether these are public or private operations makes no difference to the fact that bureaucrats of some kind are indispens-able. Bureaucracies are also supposed to administer these services in a consist-ent, efficient and universal manner, rather than an arbitrary, idiosyncratic and corrupt one. In this sense, they are not only essential for the administration of large-scale government, but they promote equality and democracy as well.

At the same time, bureaucracies are also potentially powerful and anti-democratic. They have a reputation for being inefficient, rigid, bound by red-tape, secretive and impersonal. They can also nurture a 'bureaucratic ethos' that is managerial, technocratic, inflexible and undemocratic. Bureaucrats also have their own interests, which may conflict with those of politicians and the public. It is important, therefore, that public bureaucracies are con-trolled by elected representatives who, in turn, are accountable to the public. But are ministers in control?

According to the German social scientist Max Weber, it is the dictatorship of the official that is on the march, not that of the worker. He denies the Marxist theory that the workers can seize power by revolutionary action, and points to the enormous power of the permanent officials who actually run public bureaucracies whatever party is supposed to be in power. Among these, central government bureaucrats are especially important, although precisely the same argument applies to all forms of public and private bureaucracy – parties or large pressure groups (see chapters 10 and 13). Weber had three main reasons for claiming that civil servants are the masters rather than the servants of the state:

- *Qualifications and expertise* Politicians are not necessarily selected for their educational qualifications or managerial abilities. Senior bureaucrats are often hand-picked for their intelligence and ability and then highly trained.

- *Permanence* Politicians come and go as they move political jobs or lose elections, and their influence on any given ministry tends to be short lived. Career administrators stay in post for a long time and have a potential for exercising a long-term influence.
- *Experience* With permanence comes long-term and specialised experience as well as inside knowledge of how things work.

To these three considerations we can add two other factors that make it difficult for politicians to control their bureaucrats:

- *Secrecy* Civil servants sometimes protect themselves with powerful secrecy rules, which makes it difficult for politicians and the public to find out what is going on.
- *Fragmentation* We often think of the state bureaucracy as a single organisation shaped like a pyramid with power to control the smoothly working machine concentrated at the very top. In reality, it is often a highly decentralised – not to say ramshackle – structure of ministries, departments, agencies, commissions, units and offices, each with its own traditions, modes of operation, interests and powers. The 'ship of state' is not so much a huge oil tanker that takes a long time to change direction, as a whole fleet of ships and boats, all going in their own direction, and all handling the winds and tides in their own way. This makes it difficult to control and co-ordinate the public bureaucracies.

Mechanisms of control

To say that state bureaucrats may be difficult to control is not to say that they cannot be controlled. There are all sorts of ways of trying to enforce their compliance, if enforcement is necessary:

- *Politically appointed administrators and policy advisors* – see above.
- *Law* Bureaucrats are not above the law, and there is a rapid growth of administrative law regulating their behaviour, as well as a greater tendency to use the courts to overturn administrative action.
- *Recruitment and training* Training can be used to instil in bureaucrats a professional ethos of public service. However, this can cut both ways: intensive training can also result in a bureaucratic culture of isolation, secrecy and self-interest.
- *Representative bureaucracy* Some countries have tried to make their state bureaucracy representative of the general public rather than being a separate elite with interests of its own. The *Proporz* system which ensures a balance of recruits from the major parties is found in Austria. Another method involves **affirmative action** and equal opportunity policies that recruit from a broad cross section of the population and especially from women and minority groups. Many state bureaucracies now have affirmative action programmes of one kind or another.

> **Affirmative action** Policies designed to redress past discrimination. Affirmative action may require state bureaucracies to increase recruitment from women and minority groups.

- *Scrutiny, auditing and regulation* Financial controls are increasingly used to regulate and limit bureaucratic operations, as are elaborate procedures for scrutinising, auditing and monitoring them. Ironically, modern public bureaucracies have sometimes created small teams of bureaucrats to ensure that the bureaucracy is kept as small as possible. Parliamentary committees are also increasingly involved and, as we saw in chapter 7, have increased their efforts to keep a 'watching brief' over state bureaucracies.
- *Open government* Bureaucratic secrecy can be reduced by 'sunshine laws' to promote transparency and public scrutiny. Sunshine laws aim to shine light into the dark corners of state activity so that we can see what is going on.
- *Ombudsmen* These have been appointed to protect the public against mal-administration and abuse of power (see chapter 4).

■ The New Public Management: reinventing government

It is clear by now that there is an inevitable tension between (a) the bureaucratic goal of efficiency and the democratic requirements of participation and debate, and (b) the policy making roles of politicians and the administrative jobs of state bureaucrats. In addition there is sometimes, rightly or wrongly, severe criticism of public bureaucracy on the grounds that it is either inefficient and lazy, or imperialistic and expansionist – sometimes both simultaneously. As a result, a wave of **'New Public Management' (NPM)** reforms has swept across democracies since the 1970s. These reforms have taken two main directions (often at the same time).

> **New Public Management (NPM)** This refers to the reforms of the public sector in the 1980s and 1990s, based mainly on what was thought to be private sector practice and consisting mainly of privatisation, deregulation, business management techniques and 'marketisation'. Known also as 'reinventing government', it is said to have had the effect of 'hollowing out' the state.

Privatisation and market efficiency

Many public services have been privatised, which is assumed to make them more competitive and efficient. Some government departments have been transformed into private and semi-private agencies that are contracted by the state to deliver certain services at a fixed cost. Their CEOs are often not career civil servants but 'hired guns' on short-term, commercial contracts. Bureaucracies remaining in the public sector have often been decentralised, obliged to contract out some of their functions (e.g. computer maintenance and servicing), and adopt competitive internal markets in which divisions within the same bureaucracy 'sell their services' to each other. In other cases public sector agencies have cooperated with private organisations to provide public services by public–private partnerships. The purpose of these different reforms is to privatise the routine bureaucratic operations of the state, so that they are driven by the competitive forces of the market (or quasi-markets) to become more efficient. Another purpose is to separate those who *'steer'* (think about policy and plan future developments) from those who *'row'* (carry out the routine tasks), on the grounds that those who steer ought not to have to worry about the business of rowing.

Empowerment

A second set of reforms has been designed to change what were believed to be rigid, hierarchical, faceless and rule-bound public bureaucracies delivering 'one-size-fits-all' services into flexible, accountable and user-friendly agencies that are responsive to citizens' demands. Public participation in running public services has been encouraged by school boards, customer complaint arrangements, computer communication and user groups. Street-level bureaucrats who interact with the public have been given more discretion over individual cases, making decision more flexible and personal.

New Public Management reforms are highly controversial and the evidence for and against the them is inconclusive and ambiguous (see controversy 8.1). Moreover, their importance has been overtaken by the interest in electronic government and electronic democracy. This focuses on the potential for new forms of electronic communication to make it easier for citizens to inform themselves about and participate in politics, and easier for citizens to hold government accountable.

■ Theories of public bureaucracy

Theories of public bureaucracy (sometimes known as the **civil service**) take different views of the power of administrative agencies of the state. According to Weber, the bureaucracy is

> **Civil service** The body of civilian officials (not members of the armed forces) employed by the state to work in government departments.

powerful, but he has little to say about how the bureaucrats will use their power. According to rational-choice theory, the bureaucracy is capable of controlling public policy, and does so to promote its own interests. According to clientelist theory, however, some bureaucracies are used by politicians for their own political purposes.

The rational-legal ideal-type

Max Weber argues that society modernises itself by becoming more bureaucratic. Bureaucracy itself expresses the ethos of modern society because it is based upon legitimate power, and organised in a rational way according to formal rules. Weber defined bureaucracy as the most efficient method of performing large-scale administrative tasks, and created an **ideal-type** of bureaucracy with

> **Ideal-type** An analytical construct that simplifies reality and picks out its most important features, to serve as a model that allows us to understand and compare the complexities of the real world.

CONTROVERSY 8.1

The New Public Management

Defenders of NPM argue that:

- Specialised agencies can concentrate on their core activity – the efficient delivery of good and cheap services to their clients – without the distraction of policy making and the general oversight of public services.
- Senior civil servants are not distracted by the supervision of routine operations and can focus on their main job of policy making, long-term planning and strategic thinking.
- A smaller and more efficient public sector releases resources for private economic development.
- Forced by market and quasi-market competition and by the new client focus, public services are more responsive to citizen needs and demands.
- Released from public bureaucracy rules and constraints, agencies are better able to recruit the best talents to their workforce.
- NPM management has 'depoliticised' public services by taking decisions out of the hands of politicians.

Critics argue that:

- The benefits and impact of NPM have been exaggerated. The established civil service model continues to dominate even with the most radical and far-reaching NPM reforms. Most government functions are still carried out by the hierarchical and centralised bureaucracies of government departments.
- Since we have few accurate or reliable measures of public service efficiency before NPM changes, we cannot know whether the public sector is more efficient now.
- NPM reforms are not as common in developing countries as in advanced ones, and it is said that the benefits in developing countries are smaller.
- The costs of reforming and dismantling old systems must be weighed against their sometimes rather modest benefits.
- The creation of many agencies providing public services has fragmented government into small pieces in a time when joined-up government is crucial to its coherence and success. Government is even less integrated and co-ordinated than it was.
- NPM has sometimes resulted in the privatisation of public monopolies, and the introduction of markets and quasi-markets in the public sector has not eliminated the mistakes and inefficiencies that characterise both private and public sectors.
- Some privatised and deregulated services have had to be re-regulated and taken back into the public sector in all but name. It is widely claimed that deregulation, particularly in the USA and the UK, contributed significantly to the collapse of the financial system across the world in autum 2008, so the whole approach is now questioned.

> **Privatisation** The process of converting public services and amenities to private ones.

- **Privatisation** has replaced the ethos of public service and professional care with the profit motive.
- Economic efficiency is not the only or best measure of some public services. Fairness, justice and equity also matter. We might want to judge public transport by its pollution, social services by their care, refuse disposal by its recycling, and education by its ability to develop individual talents and creativity.
- Agencies have not so much depoliticised services as made them more responsive to wealthy and powerful groups. Good services are more likely to be provided for those who shout the loudest and apply the greatest pressures.

rationality, legality, hierarchy and formal rules as its core features. An ideal-type bureaucracy is characterised by its:

1. *Hierarchy* (or pyramid) *of command*, with authority based on official position (as opposed to personal characteristics such as age, gender, race, party membership, or religion).
2. *Civil service* of salaried professionals appointed and promoted according to their specialised competence, training and experience.
3. *Formal rules* determining individual decisions and behaviour (rather than personal or arbitrary decisions) so that individual cases are treated in the same, predictable way.
4. *Rationality* – the choice of appropriate means to achieve given ends.
5. *Record keeping*, providing bureaucracies with an 'institutional memory' of what has been done in the past, and the rules and precedents governing this action.

It is often pointed out that no real-life bureaucracy can function in this way. In the first place, the mechanical application of rules is bound to create injustice and hostility if people feel themselves to be no more than numbers or cogs in a wheel. Life cannot be reduced to rules, precedents and routines, and a human element almost always intrudes into bureaucratic operations. Bureaucracies invariably develop an 'informal organisation' of short-cuts, personal contacts and unofficial procedures that help ease of operation and efficiency.

In the second place, it is said that bureaucratic means will become ends in themselves if bureaucrats blindly follow rules and refuse to take initiatives or responsibility – something known as 'trained incapacity'. What sets out to be an efficient way of running the modern state may becomes inefficient; it may even be anti-democratic if trained incapacity prevents the efficient and responsive delivery of public services. As a result, real-life bureaucracies may work very differently from the ideal-type, something that has given rise to a huge amount of empirical research.

In the best of all possible worlds, public bureaucracies would come close to Weber's ideal-type but combine it with a degree of informal organisation to improve efficiency and responsiveness to clients. However, the informal element must not lead to corruption, such as bureaucrats taking bribes to 'ease' the way for clients, and it is easy to slip into practices that are not at all compatible with democratic principles. This is the problem in some of the new democracies that suffer from clientelism and patronage, where civil service jobs are rewards for political loyalty, not merit.

Clientelism

In contrast to the impersonal, politically neutral, rule-bound and universalistic Weberian model, clientelism involves the political use of public office for personal gain – power, or money, or both. The clientelist government acts as a patron that distributes favours and benefits in the form of public jobs, money, contracts and pensions in return for political support. Jobs in the state bureaucracy are filled not necessarily according to merit, professional training or experience, but by those who support the government in power. Contracts are given not according to cost and quality of work, but for material and political gain. Voters are rewarded for their support with jobs, money or gifts, and those who donate money to the party are rewarded with jobs, contracts and special concessions. In other words, clientelism is an institutionalised form of *patronage* summarised by the old adage: 'To the victor belong the spoils.' It can easily become corruption.

Clientelism in the public service is found to a varying degree in most states, but it is strong in some, especially in some of the less well developed democracies of Latin America, Africa and central Europe. It is also found in Italy and the USA (where it is popularly known as 'the spoils system', or 'machine politics'). It is closely associated with poverty, inequality, corruption and the weak rule of law. In some countries it is more or less formalised and public, to the extent that it is known and accepted that members or supporters of a given party will get certain public jobs if that party is in power. In some countries, even professors in universities owe their job to the party they support. There are 'mass clientelist' parties in France, Italy and Mexico. Clientelism is found mainly in societies that are rapidly modernising, urbanising and industrialising, and in those that are struggling to throw off a recent history of authoritarian rule that rested on clientalism and patronage. Nevertheless, clientalism obstructs both democratic and economic development.

The new right, rational choice and the New Public Management

The 'new right' theory of bureaucracy is not so much a theory as a political argument about the need to reform government and 'roll back the frontiers of the state'. The argument was developed in the 1980s and 1990s by politicians (notably Ronald Reagan in the USA and Margaret Thatcher in the UK), who favoured a classical liberal belief in a minimal state, and therefore favoured cutting taxes and services and privatising the public sector wherever possible, with the exception of public support for such things as farming, business and the military. The new right's belief that government should be 'reinvented', and that the state should be 'hollowed out', borrowed heavily from rational-choice theories of the state and bureaucracy.

Rational choice and bureaucracy

In his two influential and widely quoted books (*Bureaucracy and Representative Government*, 1971, and *Bureaucracy and Public Economics,* 1994), William Niskanen argues that state bureaucrats are self-interested, like anyone else, and try to maximise their position by expanding their budgets and staff. The bigger their departments, the greater their power and prestige, the larger their salaries and the bigger their pensions. Their special knowledge and experience – Niskanen calls this the 'agency problem' – makes it difficult for politicians to resist these expansionist goals. As a result, public goods and services are over-produced at the public expense and the public sector grows fat.

The theory has been widely criticised for the oversimplified assumptions it makes:

- It assumes that bureaucrats are energetically self-seeking, but might we just as easily assume that they are lazy and want an easy life?
- It assumes that bureaucrats pursue their own self-interest, but might they not also be concerned about the public interest?
- It assumes that bureaucrats will not recognise or care about the problem of over-production, but might they equally be trying to combat this problem?
- It assumes that bureaucrats will not serve their political masters, but might they not have a professional ethic of public service?

Though it is an elegant theory, few attempts have ever been made to test it empirically. However, allied with the new right politicians and a revival of liberal free-market economics, rational-choice theory had a strong influence on the 'New Public Management'.

The New Public Management

Central to NPM theories of the public sector is the belief that bureaucracies are costly because they are not competitive, as the economic market is said to be, and because they interfere with the *efficient workings of the private sector*. Public bureaucracies should therefore be cut, privatised and decentralised, and market principles introduced wherever possible in order to reduce public spending and prevent government 'interference' with private enterprise. The incentives for public bureaucrats to maximise their spending should also be limited, to encourage small and efficient operations instead. Some government departments have been replaced by agencies that are supposed to be run along business lines to provide government with services and facilities under 'market-like' contractual arrangements. These are run not by career public servants but by business executives on fixed-term commercial contracts. The routine tasks of government (processing forms, emptying dustbins, maintaining public property, even running hospitals, schools, and prisons) can be privatised and decentralised, leaving a small core of top civil servants to 'steer, not row'.

On the consumer side of public services NPM reforms have tried to reduce what are believed to be the serious problems of bureaucratic inertia, secrecy and unresponsiveness to the public. It re-defines public service clients as 'customers' (like those of shops, car salesmen, and cafés), and tries to make public bureaucracies more responsive to the needs of ordinary citizens.

165

The NPM wave swept across many democracies in the 1980s and 1990s, but we have yet to find out whether it has resulted in real gains for the public sector. It will take many years for the benefits and disadvantages to emerge, and even then they will not be clear because of all the problems of measuring and comparing public and private sectors and services, and of lack of evidence about the situation before and after NPM. Besides, there are many side effects and **externalities** of market and public services, which are sometimes ignored, and are exceedingly difficult to quantify. More important, the failure of the deregulated financial market in autumn 2008 has resulted in a complete rethinking of deregulation and privatisation and strong calls for a return to public controls and even public ownership.

> **Externality** A cost or benefit that does not fall on those who are responsible for the decision or action that creates the externality, and which they do not take into account when they take the action.

■ What have we learned?

This chapter deals with controversies about the role and power of public bureaucrats. It argues that:

- Policy making is the job of elected politicians who head government departments and ministries, but the day-to-day administration of government business is carried out by appointed officials (otherwise known as bureaucrats, civil servants, public servants, or permanent officials).
- Appointed officials are accountable to, and work under the policy direction of, their political masters, the elected politicians.
- However, the distinction between policy making and administration is not clear or unambiguous, and the considerable overlap between the two makes for a confusion of roles, especially since the senior bureaucrats (mandarins) work closely with politicians and act as their policy advisors.
- Appointed officials are said to be able to exercise power over their nominal political masters by virtue of their superior ability, qualifications and experience. State bureaucracies are also known for their secrecy and fragmentation, which makes it difficult for politicians to control them.

■ Lessons of comparison

- Aware of the potential for bureaucratic power, politicians have tried three general methods of controlling their bureaucrats: (1) trying to enforce rules and a culture of bureaucratic political neutrality; (2) replacing the top level of the bureaucracy with political appointees favourable to a new government; and (3) recruiting the bureaucracy from a broad cross section of the population to make it politically and socially representative.

- More specific methods for controlling bureaucrats include appointing political advisors, introducing scrutiny and auditing, applying principles of 'open government', and appointing ombudsmen.
- The New Public Management (NPM) practices that have swept across many states since the 1980s privatised many public services, deregulated many private businesses and introduced market or 'quasi-market' practices to try to make public services more competitive and efficient. Attempts have also been made to empower public service 'customers' to make public bureaucracies responsive to public demands.
- The reforms of public bureaucracies are controversial, and their effectiveness is difficult to judge. The recent crisis in the deregulated financial system has lead to many demands for re-regulation.

Projects

1. 'State bureaucracy is essential and dangerous.' What do you understand by this statement, and how can we reconcile these two characteristics of bureaucracy?
2. Assess the nature and effectiveness of New Public Management (NPM) reforms in your municipality:
   - Who took the initiative?
   - What were the main reforms?
   - What were the main goals?
   - What were the consequences?

Further reading

D. Beetham, *Bureaucracy*, Buckingham: Open University Press, 2nd edn., 1996
A good general book on bureaucracy.

B. G. Peters, *The Politics of Bureaucracy*, London: Routledge, 2000.
A general book on government and bureaucracy.

E. C. Page, *Political Authority and Bureaucratic Power*, Brighton: Wheatsheaf, 2nd edn., 1992.
Deals comparatively with the problem of how politicians control state bureaucracies.

H. Bekke, J. Perry and T. Toonen (eds.), *Civil Service Systems in Comparative Perspective*, Bloomington: Indiana University Press, 1996.
A selection of useful comparative articles on public bureaucracy.

T. Christensen (ed.), *New Public Management: The Transformation of Ideas and Practice*, Aldershot: Ashgate, 2002
An evaluation of the NPM.

T. Verheijen and D. L. Coombs (eds.), *Innovations in Public Management: Perspectives from East and West Europe,* Cheltenham: Edward Elgar, 1998.
An evaluation of the NPM.

Websites

www.sosig.ac.uk/roads/subject-listing/World-cat/civilser.html
Links to a great many specialist reports on civil services around the world.
http://encyclopedia.thefreedictionary.com/Bureaucracy
Basic introduction to bureaucracy with links to related topics.
http://encyclopedia.thefreedictionary.com/Civil+service
Basic introduction to civil service with links to related topics.

PART III

Citizens, elites and interest mediation

Part II of this book has discussed the formal institutions of government. Part III now looks at the politics of everyday life as practised by people – ordinary citizens and political leaders. The division between parts II and III implies a distinction between the structures and institutions of government, on the one hand, and the political attitudes and behaviour of individuals, on the other. A similar distinction is drawn between government institutions and structures, which are relatively fixed, and political processes, which are dynamic. At other times, a distinction is drawn between macro- and micro-analysis. Macro-analysis is concerned with large-scale phenomena, and often compares countries or broad sweeps of historical change. Micro-analysis deals with parts of the whole, usually the smallest 'unit' of political analysis – the individual. For this reason much micro-analysis often studies individual voting behaviour, or uses survey analysis to study attitudes and behaviour.

The distinctions between institutions and behaviour, between structures and processes and between macro and micro, are useful for studying government and politics, but we must always remember that they are simply different aspects of precisely the same thing. Structures and institutions set a framework for everyday political life; political attitudes and behaviour help to shape structures.

Part III starts with an account of the political attitudes and behaviour of individuals. If we understand what people think and believe about politics we are better able to understand their behaviour. Or perhaps we should put it the other way round: unless we understand political attitudes and values, we will never understand why people behave the way they do. Besides, what people believe and how they behave can have a profound and direct impact on what governments do, and they can also help to shape the structures and institutions of the state itself. So the study of attitudes and behaviour is important in its own right, and because of the impact they have on governments and the state. Chapter 9 is therefore about political attitudes, values and behaviour.

However, few of us have much political significance as individuals on our own. Most of us join with others in voluntary organisations, pressure groups and social movements in order to achieve our political goals. What we cannot do as isolated citizens we can try to achieve through trade unions or professional associations, pressure groups or social movements, which try to exercise organised influence over government. Chapter 10 therefore, looks at the politics of pressure groups.

The mass media are crucial in political life because they are the means by which citizens, groups and leaders acquire political information and try to influence each other. The mass media are also thought to be powerful political actors in their own right. Accordingly, chapter 11 turns to the politics of the mass media and their influence.

Elections determine who is to take control of government. They are vital to the conduct of politics and tell us a lot about how ordinary citizens relate to politics. Electoral behaviour is probably one of the best topics for research on mass politics and an important part of comparative politics. Chapter 12 therefore pays attention to voters and elections.

And, last in part III, chapter 13 deals with a very special and particularly important type of voluntary organisation – political parties. Parties have a chapter of their own because they are so important.

The five chapters in part III examine the key aspects of political attitudes, institutions and behaviour:

- Political attitudes and behaviour
- Pressure groups and social movements
- The mass media
- Voters and elections
- Party government.

9   Political attitudes and behaviour

Everyone has their own view of politics, and their own interests and ideas and ways of behaving. But individuals do not exist in isolation and nor are they unique. If this were the case it would make no sense to talk about 'the working class' or 'youth cultures', or to make generalisations about 'left-wing intellectuals' or 'right-wing business interests'. At a still more general level, citizens of the same country usually share similar assumptions and views about politics, which makes the Swedes different from the Chileans, the Spanish different from the South Africans and the South Koreans different from the Irish.

> **Political culture** The pattern of attitudes, values and beliefs about politics, whether they are conscious or unconscious, explicit or implicit.

Political scientists find it useful to label these shared patterns of beliefs and attitudes 'the **political culture**'. The first part of the chapter discusses the political values and attitudes of individuals and groups, and examines how modern research has tried to understand and explain political cultures.

Values and attitudes are important in their own right, but they are also significant because they tell us something about how people are likely to behave, and behaviour has a big and direct impact on political life. In order to understand what people do, and why they do it, it is necessary to understand what they think. For example,

> **Values** Basic ethical priorities that constrain and give shape to individual attitudes and beliefs.

it is not enough to know that someone did not vote in an election: we need to know whether their inaction was caused by apathy, alienation, or contentment. In the right circumstances, the alienated may take to the streets in revolutionary action, leaving the apathetic at home watching television.

There is another good reason for trying to understand political cultures. The structures and institutions of government rest, it is argued, on cultural foundations. If most people are satisfied with the way their system of government works, then it is likely to be stable over time. If a large proportion is dissatisfied and takes political action, then the system may come under pressure to change. Democratic political institutions rest upon democratic cultures, and a combination of democratic cultures and institutions produces stable democracy. In other words, there are two good reasons for studying political culture: it helps to explain individual behaviour and it helps to explain the persistence of democratic institutions and structures of government.

In this chapter, we examine the political attitudes and behaviour of citizens and political leaders. The major topics in this chapter are:

- Political attitudes
- Political behaviour
- Theories of political attitudes and behaviour.

■ Political attitudes

Political interests and identity

We know from our own experience that political attitudes and behaviour are not random. People with the same background often have a lot in common politically: manual workers differ from managers and professionals, students from their parents and teachers, and men from women. Individuals build their political ideas around their personal circumstances and interests, and when we talk about political interests we mean two sorts of things:

- *Material* interests – money, promotion, taxes, security
- *Ideal* interests – political values and ideals, such as a sense of justice and freedom, religious beliefs, or a left–right political position.

We should not underestimate the importance of ideal interests and values in trying to understand what people think about politics, and why they act the way they do. Many of the most important events in political history have been brought about by people prepared to fight and die for their material and ideal interests, and this means political beliefs and values that may have nothing to do with their own material circumstances.

How people define their material and ideal interests, is in turn, closely connected with who and what they think they are. They may define themselves as a member of a social class, or an ethnic or religious group, or perhaps as part of a gender, or age, or regional group. How people see the political world depends on how they believe they fit into it, and how they see their own **political identity**. According to this approach, politics is a struggle between people and groups whose material and ideal interests vary according to their class, region, ethnicity, age, gender, language, or nationality.

> **Political identity** *The way that people label themselves as belonging to a particular group (e.g. nation-state, class or caste, ethnic group, religious group).*

Political culture

One of the most influential approaches to the study of political attitudes, values and behaviour in the post-war period has been built around the study of political culture. The concept is an elusive and complex one, and it can be loose and vague, but we can best see political culture as a sort of map of how people think and behave. A map is not the real thing, it deals only with selected and general features of the world, but it can be a useful guide to the real thing. In the same way, political culture does not reproduce every detail of what citizens know and think and feel about politics, but it can be a useful and simplified guide to the most important features of individual beliefs, values and attitudes. Used well, the concept helps us to focus on what is important and to see patterns in what would otherwise be a confused jumble of individual features (see controversy 9.1).

CONTROVERSY 9.1

Political culture as a tool of political science: for and against

For

- Studies of political culture have produced important empirical findings about political attitudes and behaviour – e.g. the role of education and the family, and the importance and origins of competence, social trust and national pride. These were often overlooked or underestimated in previous studies.
- Political culture is claimed to be a 'bedrock' variable – it changes slowly and provides continuity. As a foundation of democracy, political values and assumptions are more important than the more changeable political attitudes usually discussed by newspapers and opinion polls.
- Political culture is a key concept linking (1) the micro-politics of individuals with the macro-politics of institutions and states, (2) subjective (values and attitudes) with the objective (e.g. voting behaviour) and (3) history and traditions with current circumstances and events.
- Sample surveys reveal differences in attitudes and behaviour that may be better explained by 'soft' cultural variables (values, religious background, education) than by 'harder' variables (social class, wealth) or by structural variables (election rules, government powers).
- Political culture certainly does not explain everything, but it helps to explain quite a wide range of phenomena from economic development and political stability, to democratic development and political behaviour.
- The study of political cultures is often based upon 'hard' and extensive quantitative data drawn from surveys.

Against

- Political culture is said to be a 'soft', 'residual', 'dustbin', or 'fuzzy' concept that can be used to explain everything and therefore nothing, especially where it is used when other explanations have failed – since the event is not explained by economic, class, constitutional, or other variables it must be explained by culture. Culture is often used as a *post hoc* (after the event) explanation that is not put to an empirical test.
- Political culture explanations risk being circular: we infer what people believe from how they behave, and then explain why they behave from what they believe. For example: people behave democratically because they hold democratic values, and we know that they hold democratic values because they behave democratically.
- Political culture is closely associated with attitudes and behaviour because it is close to them in the long causal chain of their determinants. Political scientists should search for causes that are further away in the causal chain – e.g. historical, or economic, or psychological.
- Cultures and structures are mutually interdependent and tend to go together. It is not surprising, therefore that cultures and structures are associated, but which is cause and effect?
- Some argue for a 'bottom-up' explanation in which the system is shaped and moulded by mass opinions and behaviour, others for a 'top-down' explanation in which structures shape or constrain attitudes and behaviour. If both processes operate, as they well may, how can we ever sort them out?
- Research can show the existence of sub-cultures, but not their relative importance. For example, is the elite culture more important than the mass culture, and how can we tell? Similarly, how much citizen participation is necessary to describe a national culture as 'participant' – 33 per cent, 40 per cent, 50 per cent, or perhaps 66 per cent?
- Where does the political culture come from? It may be useful to describe a nation's culture as 'participant' or 'alienated', but why is it like this? Why do countries have different political cultures and where do they come from?
- One argument against political culture explanations is that they deal only with the *last* link in a long chain of causes of political behaviour. The real and basic causes of behaviour may be historical, or economic (Marxist and class theory), or perhaps lie in individual psychology.

Culture is not innate: we are not born with a genetic imprint of a political culture in our brains. Rather, we absorb the political culture that surrounds us through the process of **political socialisation**, which passes on culture from one generation to the next. Hence cultures persist over time. We also absorb the culture of our own social background and group. Hence political cultures are patterned.

Political socialisation The process by which individuals acquire their political values, attitudes and habits.

Persistence

Political cultures are passed on from one generation to the next so they persist over time. They do change, of course, but they usually change slowly according to the accumulation of events and experiences, unless there is some traumatic event (war, revolution, economic collapse) to bring about a major change.

Pattern

Political cultures are patterned because members of the same social groups tend to be socialised into the same set of attitudes and values. They are also patterned because beliefs are often connected in a systematic way. For example, those in favour of minority group rights are likely to approve of Third World aid, and to have liberal social attitudes as well.

The civic culture

The first and most influential study of political culture was the book *The Civic Culture* (1963) by Gabriel A. Almond (1911–2002) and Sidney Verba (1932–). They define political culture as a pattern of **political orientations** to political objects such as parliament, elections or the nation. They then divide orientations into three dimensions:

> **Political orientation** A predisposition or propensity to view politics in a certain way.

- Cognitive
- Affective
- Evaluative.

Cognitive

To participate in politics, citizens must be aware of, know about and understand something about their political system – its main institutions, historical events, election system, political figures and national background.

Affective

To participate in politics, citizens must believe that politics is important enough to take up their time. It is significant, for example, that two out of three citizens in Austria, The Netherlands and Norway claim an interest in politics, compared with fewer than one in three in Argentina, Chile and Spain.

Evaluative

To know how they should participate in politics, citizens must also evaluate the system:

> **Subjective or internal efficacy** The extent to which ordinary citizens feel that they can make their views and actions count in the political system.

- Should it be supported or reformed (political support)?
- Do ordinary citizens have enough influence (**subjective or internal efficacy**)?
- Does the system operate as it should (**system or external efficacy**)

> **System or external efficacy** The extent to which ordinary citizens feel that political leaders and institutions are responsive to their wishes.

The fact that almost nine out of ten Norwegians are satisfied with their government, compared with fewer than one in ten in Japan, tells us something about the state of politics in these two countries.

According to Almond and Verba, to measure a political culture requires collecting systematic information from a random sample of the population about the most important aspects of these three dimensions. On the basis of their study of (West) Germany, Italy, Mexico, the UK and the USA, they identified three pure types of political culture, and showed that these were combined in different proportions in the countries they surveyed. They also identified a fourth type that, they said, was the mixture that came closest to a democratic culture:

- *Parochial cultures* have a low level of awareness, knowledge and involvement with government. They are usually Third World and rural societies with poor education, low economic development and poor communications, but there are pockets of parochialism in developed countries as well. In *The Civic Culture*, Mexico came closest to the parochial model.
- In *subject cultures*, people are aware of government and what it does (its outputs) but do not participate much (citizen inputs). Subject cultures are mainly found in non-democracies that emphasise the power of government rather than citizen rights and duties. Subject cultures do not encourage enough democratic participation. *The Civic Culture* found West Germany in the 1950s to have elements of a subject culture.
- In *participant cultures*, citizens are knowledgeable about politics, attach an importance to them and participate because they feel competent and knowledgeable. *The Civic Culture* found the UK and the USA closest to this culture. The danger is democratic overload, in which too much participation produces too many political demands.

Therefore, the best political culture for a democracy is:

- The **civic culture**, in which subject and participant cultures are mixed to produce neither too much nor too little participation. Citizens are active and elites respond to their demands, but citizens also trust their political leaders and give them a degree of independence. Almond and Verba found that the UK in the late 1950s came closest to the civic culture.

Civic culture The term used by Almond and Verba to signify the balance of subject and participant political cultures that best supports democracy.

The Civic Culture argued that political culture was a crucial theoretical concept that mediated between the micro- and subjective properties of a political system, and its macro-, institutional features. Culture is shared by individuals, so aggregate individual statistics (i.e. national averages) describe the properties of the system as a whole. Cultures and structures are also mutually inter-dependent, so they must 'fit' each other. As we saw in chapter 4, democratic constitutions are like fortresses – their institutions must be well designed and well built, but they must also be well manned by democrats who believe in them. When the culture matches the structure they are said to be congruent, but when they do not fit, the culture is said to exhibit **political alienation**. According to

Political alienation A feeling of detachment, estrangement, or critical distance from politics, often because the alienated feel there is something basically wrong with the political system.

Almond and Verba, Italy in the 1950s had an alienated culture because the democratic attitudes and behaviour of citizens were not matched by a sufficiently democratic structure. Alienated cultures were likely to produce a demand for change and a degree of political instability. In extreme cases they could generate mass pressures for political change, perhaps even revolution, as they did in central and eastern Europe in the 1980s.

Materialism and post-materialism

Almond and Verba's work had a huge impact in its time and stimulated many similar studies in the 1960s, but the approach lost favour in the 1970s and 1980s. It was revived, in large part, by Ronald Inglehart (1934–) who conducted a series of social surveys in many countries over a thirty-year period into what he calls materialism and post-materialism. Whereas Almond and Verba were mainly concerned with the persistence of political cultures over time and their relationship with stable democracy, Inglehart is interested in cultural and political change. His work starts from two basic propositions:

- Rapid economic development in the last hundred years has taken care of the basic material needs of most people in the west. Consequently, their values are shifting from material concerns (food, health, physical safety, social order) to post-material ones (civil liberties, the environment, job satisfaction, political and community participation, self-expression and the quality of life). Rising levels of education and an improved standard of living have caused a fundamental transformation of political values from material to post-material cultures.
- The shift from material to post-material values is slow because most people acquire their political culture in early socialisation and change their views only slowly after that. The clearest signs of the shift show up in the younger, wealthier and better-educated generation.

Inglehart's culture shift from materialism to post-materialism is slow and silent, yet in the long run it changes politics completely. Therefore Inglehart speaks of *The Silent Revolution*, the title of his book published in 1977. He argues that it nonetheless has profound and far-reaching effects, because it is part of broader changes involving participation, equality, community and self-expression. Post-materialism also involves greater tolerance of abortion, divorce, euthanasia, sexual minorities, single parents and minority groups, and opposition to nuclear energy and weapons and to the exploitation of the environment.

Post-materialism first appeared in young, wealthy and well-educated groups in the most affluent parts of the USA and western Europe in the 1960s. Early signs appeared in the generation that produced the student revolutionaries of 1968 in Berlin, California, London and Paris. The shift towards post-material values therefore helps to explain the remarkable fact that the increasing affluence of the 1960s did not induce a sense of satisfaction with society but, on the contrary, resulted in a wave of political protest that tried to change the political system.

Post-materialism, Inglehart says, has now spread to other parts of the west and to other parts of the developed world, as these grow more affluent. As older, more materialist generations are replaced, so the proportion of post-materialists in these countries is rising, and it is predicted that they will be in a majority in many western countries by 2010. Among the democracies, the highest proportions of post-materialists are found in Australia, Austria, Canada, Italy, the Netherlands and the USA, the lowest in Estonia, Hungary, India, Israel and Latvia. Moreover, as the younger generation rises to positions of political power, so post-materialists will gain control of governments. Nor is post-materialism limited to the western club of affluent nations. It is now found in developing countries such as China, Poland and South Korea as they grow wealthier and better educated. In his 1995 book *Modernization and Postmodernization*, Inglehart finds a close association between democracy and an emphasis on trust, tolerance, participation and a sense of personal well-being. In contrast, populations with material and survival values centring on money, safety and job security are likely to have authoritarian governments.

Six far-reaching consequences of the shift to post-materialism are said to be:

1. **Cognitive mobilisation** Education and wealth bring greater awareness of politics and better skills to participate.

    Cognitive mobilisation The process by which increasing knowledge and understanding of the world helps to activate people to play a part in it.

2. *Replacement of class with cultural cleavages* Materialist versus post-materialist divisions based on political cultures will gradually replace the left–right divisions based on class.

3. *Increased religious conflict* Because post-materialists tend to oppose traditional religion, there may be a religious backlash against them, especially from religious parties of the right.

4. *More political participation* The cognitive mobilisation of post-materialists results in greater demands for grass-roots participation.

5. *New forms of participation* Post-materialists favour 'new forms' of direct participation, community politics and new social movements, which means the decline of 'old' forms of participation organised around bureaucratic and hierarchical parties and pressure groups (see chapters 12 and 10).

6. *New political issues* Post-materialists are less involved in the left–right politics, and more interested in the environment, community politics, feminism, individual freedom and racial equality.

The post-materialist thesis is supported by a good deal of survey evidence from around the world, but not all the findings are consistent with it. Some research on value change in western Europe in the post-war period shows a rather different pattern:

1. *Persistent left–right divisions* The old left–right divisions have persisted, although they have changed and weakened in some respects.
2. *Fusion not replacement* Post-materialism has not replaced materialism. Rather elements of the old have been fused with elements of the new.
3. *High tide of post-materialism?* The evidence suggests that the drift towards post-materialism among the youngest generations in western Europe may be slowing, as economic conditions get harder, but it is too early to say whether this a temporary or permanent trend.
4. *A missing ingredient?* Most post-materialists are young, well-educated and middle class, but most young, well-educated, middle-class people are not post-materialist. Is there something else that helps to produce post-materialism?

Sub-cultures and elite cultures

No country has a perfectly uniform political culture and there are often variations between sub-groups and regions. Indeed, the existence of materialist political cultures side by side with post-materialism in the same country is evidence of the existence of sub-cultures. Members of a sub-culture share in the larger culture, but they also have their own characteristics. For example, the Canadian political culture differs in some important respects from that in Finland and South Africa, but at the same time French- and English-speaking Canadians have their own political sub-cultures. Sub-cultures are typically aligned with important divisions in society such as class, gender, generation, religion, region or race. One of the most important sub-cultures in any society, however, is that of the **political elite**.

> **Political elite** The relatively small number of people at the top of a political system who exercise disproportionate influence or power over political decisions. If powerful enough it is a 'ruling elite'.

Elite cultures are normally different from mass cultures, partly because elites are often drawn from the best educated and more middle- and upper-class sections of the population, and partly because they interact so closely with each other over such long periods of time that they tend to develop their own world view. Compared with mass cultures, elite cultures are:

- *Abstract* They tend to be organised around abstract political ideas and ideals as well as dealing with the concrete policy issues of everyday political life.
- *Complex* They are more elaborate and systematic.
- *Informed* They are based on a good deal of information.
- *Broad* They cover most of the general and particular issues in politics.

Because of this, political elites are said to be 'ideologues' who have a broader, more sophisticated and better-informed view of the political world, compared with most ordinary citizens.

> **Ideologues** Those with an informed, broad, sophisticated and more or less consistent (systematic) view of politics.

179

Some political scientists argue that the social background and education of western elites make them more democratic and tolerant, and with more liberal and fewer **authoritarian attitudes** than the general population. According to this view, democracy relies upon the civilised and democratic values of educated elites and their capacity to compromise and accept the rules of the democratic game. Others argue, on the contrary, that elites are more conservative than the masses, and that their liberal, democratic rhetoric simply disguises an interest in keeping power. This view argues that elites prevent the mass from developing political skills and interests because this would bring an end to elite power. We shall return to this theme at the end of the chapter.

> **Authoritarian attitudes** A system or syndrome of attitudes based upon prejudice, dogmatism, superstition, low tolerance for ambiguity, hostility to out-groups (anti-semitism and racism) and obedience to authority.

Political cleavages

We discussed the concept of 'cleavage' in chapter 1, but we return to it now because it is important for an understanding of political attitudes and behaviour. The importance stems from the common observation that particular social groups (distinguished by class, religion, ethnicity, language, region, or some other social feature) often tend to be similar in their political attitudes and behaviour. This brings us to social and political cleavages. Social cleavages are not the same as political cleavages and social differences do not necessarily turn into political differences. For a social cleavage to become politically important, three conditions must be met:

1. *Objective social differences* Differences must be socially important and recognised by society – race, religion or language for example.
2. *Subjective awareness* It is not enough for objective differences to exist – social groups must be aware of their identity and express them in their social life.
3. *Political organisation* It is not enough for objective and subjective differences to exist. There must also be a capacity and willingness on the part of political organisations such as parties and pressure groups to organise those who are objectively different and subjectively aware of their identity, and to represent them and fight for their interests.

There is no automatic progress from (1) to (2) to (3). Tall people meet the first criteria but not necessarily the second, and certainly not the third. Women meet the first two criteria but not necessarily the third. Objective differences must produce a collective identity, and collective identities must produce organisations that defend collective interests before a social cleavage is transformed into a political one. This leaves plenty of room for political activists and political entrepreneurs to use social divisions for political purposes, and it may even be be that social cleavages will not take a political form until and unless political activists exploit them.

The association of voting behaviour with social differences such as class, religion and ethnicity is commonly understood and needs no more explanation here, but the analysis of cleavages can be taken an important step further. There is a significant difference between divisions in society that are superimposed one on top of the other (**reinforcing cleavages**), and divisions that cut across each other (**cross-cutting cleavages**). Where lines of class, religion, education and ethnicity coincide they are more likely to create deep social differences between groups such that conflict breaks out. The deep divisions between the black and white populations of South Africa is a case in point. But where social divisions overlap, they sew society together by its own internal divisions (see briefing 9.1). For example, if a working-class person belongs to a church and a sports club that has both working- and middle-class members, the church and sports club will build bridges that cut across class differences. This will tend to moderate working-class opinions because class influences will pull in different directions. But social cleavages will be reinforced and polarised in the case of a working-class person who belongs to a working-class church and a working-class sports club. This will tend to reinforce and polarise political differences, so forming the basis for political attitudes and behaviour, party membership, voting and political action in general.

> **Reinforcing cleavages** Cleavages that are laid one on top of the other, making them potentially more important.

> **Cross-cutting cleavages** Cleavages that are laid across one another, thereby reducing their capacity to divide.

Different cleavage lines

Historical developments in various countries resulted in different cleavages and in different combinations of these cleavages. Important cleavages are:

- *Religion* Religion has a close association with politics. The Protestant Reformation in western Europe in the sixteenth century has been described as a critical juncture in its political history, and the Catholic and Protestant divide remains a factor influencing political attitudes and behaviour in Europe and in parts of Latin America to the present day.
- *Ethnicity* Ethnic differences, often linked to religious, national, language and cultural differences, are often the basis of political cleavages, especially where they are associated with economic inequality.
- *Spatial separation* A social group that is concentrated in the same area is more likely to generate its own political identity than groups that are mixed together in the same place. Spatial separation reinforced the **centre–periphery cleavage** in the early development of western states in which modernisers and centralisers of the state, usually in the capital and other big cities, came into conflict with local elites and landowners of

> **Centre–periphery cleavage** The political cleavage between the social and political forces responsible for creating centralised and modern nation-states, and other interests, usually on the periphery of the state, which resisted this process. Centre–periphery cleavages are often, but not always, geographical.

Briefing 9.1

Reinforcing and cross-cutting cleavages: Belgium and Switzerland

■ Reinforcing cleavages

Belgium is divided between Flemish-speaking (Flemish is a version of Dutch) Flanders in the north (57 per cent), and French-speaking Wallonia (42 per cent) in the south (reinforcing language–regional cleavages), with Brussels, the capital city, a contested area in the middle. Belgium is over 90 per cent Catholic (a cross-cutting cleavage) but the north is wealthier than the south (a reinforcing cleavage) and the socio-linguistic/regional cleavage is so important that parties are split along regional lines (reinforcing cleavages) creating highly fragmented party systems and great difficulty in forming stable governments. The linguistic conflict became so intense in the 1970s and 1980s that constitutional changes produced a decentralised federal system of government in 1993. After severe political crises the autonomy of the three regions was strengthened even more in 2008.

■ Cross-cutting cleavages

Switzerland is divided by both language (German 65 per cent, French 20 per cent and Italian 8 per cent) and religion (46 per cent Catholic, 40 per cent Protestant). All but four of the twenty-six cantons are linguistically homogeneous (a reinforcing cleavage) but the same language groups have different regional dialects (a cross-cutting cleavage), and most cantons are of mixed religion (a cross-cutting cleavage). Different language and religious groups often have the same economic interests in tourism or banking (a cross-cutting cleavage). There is no dominant city – Basel, Bern, Geneva, Lausanne and Zürich share capital city functions – and most Swiss identify with their nation (which cuts across the cleavages). Switzerland (a federal system) is a highly stable and integrated nation.

rural areas and the periphery. The modernisers wanted to subject peripheral elites to the power and taxes of the centralising state, and the peripheral elites wanted to keep their power and wealth. Later this division was overlaid by the industrial–agricultural cleavage, where the interests of new, rich, industrial and commercial capitalists in the cities conflicted with the interests of the more traditional rural landowners and farmers in poorer rural areas.

Spatial separation is more likely to involve the concentration of ethnic, religious, linguistic or cultural groups in geographical areas. This sometimes produces separatist political movements that want self-government for their own area. We see this in the Basque and Catalan regions of Spain, in Scotland, Ireland and Wales in the UK, in the French-speaking population of Quebec in Canada, the Sikh population and Khalistan in India, the Flemish and Walloon regions of Belgium, the division of Czechoslovakia into Czech and Slovak states in 1993, and the dissolution of the Yugoslavian state amid horrific bloodshed and genocide in the 1990s. Political conflict can erupt into violence and civil war in places where social divisions coincide with spatial separation, and it is often difficult (though not impossible) to develop and sustain democratic government. Federalism is one way of tackling the problem (see chapter 6).

Cleavages in countries and world regions

Democratic countries show a great variety of cleavage patterns, but many of them can be grouped in a few general categories. Class and status formed the basis of the main political cleavage in many early democracies in the west (Australia, New Zealand, western Europe) for much of the nineteenth and twentieth centuries, especially were they were linked, as they often are, with religious and regional divisions. In recent decades, however, class has declined in importance and a variety of other social and economic differences have become relatively more important (see Changing attitudes and behaviour below). A first way to distinguish countries is:

- *Homogeneous countries* Some countries are relatively cleavage-free. Japan is a homogeneous country with few and rather weak social divisions.
- *Weak Cleavages* Strong class cleavages have not emerged in India, in spite of mass poverty, because the country is fragmented by race, religion, language and caste. Social identities are often regional and regional coalitions have strongly influenced national politics. Class cleavages in America have been been blurred by race and region (the North–South divide of the Civil War).

A second way to classify countries on the basis of their cleavage patterns is to look at regional similarities and distinctions:

- *Central Europe* There is some diversity in the cleavage patterns of central Europe, but twenty years after the collapse of communism, they resemble some in western Europe, being based mainly on class and status, ethnicity, religion and region. The difference is that there is a gap opening up in central Europe between those who gained from the dissolution of the communist states, especially those who profited from the privatisation of the economy, and those who did not. Some countries in south-central Europe also have important ethnic and religious divides.
- *Latin America* Social cleavages have a weaker impact on politics in Latin America than in western Europe because the development of group political identities and allegiances have been blocked by clientelism and the highly personalised politics of authoritarian political leaders. Where party systems are fragmented and party identifications are weak, leaders often try to gain support from different social groups by 'buying votes'. Consequently, class and economic voting is much lower in Latin America than in western Europe, while broadly based and inclusive parties are more common. One cleavage that does often appear, albeit relatively weakly, is the division between poor, rural and agricultural regions and the wealthier, urban and better educated ones.

Fact file 9.1

Political attitudes and values

- *Trust* Trust between fellow citizens is said to be a crucial underlying condition for democracy. The *World Values Study* of 2005 shows that the less democratic a system, the lower its social trust. Among the democracies, Ghana, Brazil, Chile, Serbia, Argentina and Slovenia have comparatively low levels of social trust (10–18 per cent), whereas Sweden, Finland, New Zealand, Auatralia, the Netherlands and Canada have high scores (45–65 per cent).
- *Interest in politics* varies substantially in the democracies of the world. Between 65 and 82 per cent of citizens described themselves as 'very or somewhat interested in politics' in Austria, the Czech Republic, Israel, the Netherlands, Norway and the USA, compared with fewer than 30 per cent in Argentina, Chile, Finland, Portugal and Spain.
- *Satisfaction with democracy* is higher in established democracies such as Austria, Canada, Germany and Luxembourg (all above 65 per cent), much lower in some of the new democracies, including Croatia, Lithuania, Romania and Slovakia (all below 30 per cent).
- *Post-materialism* The highest levels of post-materialist values are found in the comparatively wealthy democracies of Austria, Australia, Canada, Italy and the USA (all above 25 per cent), and the lowest in Estonia, Hungary, India, Israel and Slovakia (all below 5 per cent).
- *National pride* The Australians, Mexicans, Peruvians, Portuguese, South Africans and Uruguayans are proudest of their nation. The Dutch, Germans, Japanese, Lithuanians and South Koreans are the least proud.
- *Ethnic, religious and linguistic differences*, with correspondingly strong political culture differences, are found in Belgium, Canada, Mexico, Peru, India, South Africa, Switzerland and the USA. The most ethnically homogeneous democracies are Norway, Sweden, Denmark, Finland, Japan, South Korea and Portugal.
- *Ethno-nationalism* European examples of regional nationalism include Bulgaria (the Turkish minority), Bosnia (Serbs, Croats and Muslims), Northern Ireland (Catholic nationalism and Protestant unionism), Russia (Chechen and other Siberian minorities), Serbia (Albanian nationalism), Spain (Catalan, Galician and Basque nationalism) and Turkey (Kurdish nationalism).

■ Political behaviour

Political behaviour comes in a great many forms, including reading a paper, talking about politics and joining voluntary organisations that play no political role for much of the time (see briefing 9.2), as well as the most common of all, which is voting in elections. If we include actions that have an unintended effect on politics, the range broadens further to include such things as not paying taxes and not voting. After all, a large minority of non-voters is a cause for concern in democracies, and tax evasion has a direct effect on government

Political behaviour All political activities of citizens as well as the attitudes and orientations relevant for these activities.

policies. Even clothes, music and food can have a political connotation, as students know.

Modes of political behaviour

Research in the 1950s and 1960s suggested that the population of western democracies could be divided roughly into three groups, according to their level of political participation:

- *Gladiators* These are the leaders and activists who run parties, political organisations and campaigns, and who hold political office. About 5–8 per cent of the population falls into this group.

Briefing 9.2

Varieties of political behaviour

■ Conventional

- Voting
- Reading newspapers, watching TV news
- Talking about politics
- Joining a political group (voluntary organisation, party, or new social movement)
- Involvement with a client body or advisory body for public service (consumer council, school board)
- Attending meetings, demonstrations, rallies
- Contacting the media, elected representatives, or public officials
- Contributing money
- Volunteering for political activity (organising meetings, election canvassing)
- Standing for political office
- Holding political office

■ Unconventional

- Unofficial strikes, sit-ins, protests, demonstrations
- Civil disobedience
- Breaking laws for political reasons
- Political violence
- Boycotting products or a producer
- Buying products ('buycotting')

Figure 9.1 is a stylised representation of how political participation research has developed since 1940

Figure 9.1: Expansion of the political participation research agenda since the 1940s

- *Spectators* The great mass of the population is not engaged in politics beyond voting in elections, reading a paper, watching TV news and occasion political discussion.
- *Apathetics* The politically inactive who know and care little about politics, and do not vote.

Later research on comparative political behaviour confirmed the existence of a small group of political 'gladiators' (leaders) and a larger group of 'apathetics', but it also found something surprising about the great mass of people in the middle. Their political behaviour could not be placed on a single continuum of political activity ranging from the simple act of voting at one end to the most demanding and time-consuming forms of political activity at the other. Rather, citizens tended to specialise in different modes of behaviour. Individuals usually concentrated on a group of similar sorts of political activity that clustered together (see briefing 9.3), according to the goals and values of the individuals, and according to the demands that the type of behaviour made on them. Political activity was not cumulative, and knowing what type of behaviour a given individual specialised in could tell us nothing about what other type of activity they might be involved in. For example, community activists were no more or less likely to vote than protest activists, and protest activists were no more or less likely to be party members than those who made contact with specialists.

Briefing 9.3	

Modes of political behaviour

Inactives	Rarely vote or engage in any form of political participation
Passive supporters	Vote regularly, support the nation, tacit support for the political system
Contact specialists	Contact political and public office holders about personal matters
Community activists	Cooperate with others in their community, join local organisations, contact local officials about public matters
Party workers	Join parties, volunteer for campaign work, canvass at elections, give money, attend meetings, stand for election
Leaders	Fill major political and public offices – elected representatives in national and sub-national government, party leaders, leaders of pressure groups and social movements, political commentators
Protestors	Specialists in protest and unconventional behaviour

Conventional and unconventional political behaviour

Democratic political participation has traditionally been confined to voting, attending political meetings, signing petitions, joining a party or political group and so on. These are sometimes known as 'conventional' forms of behaviour, but in the late twentieth century the political repertoire expanded to include 'unconventional' activities such as protests, demonstrations, boycotts, occupations and unofficial strikes (see briefing 9.2). Surveys show that this type of behaviour is more widely accepted now, though it is still not widely practised. Fewer than 5 per cent in Turkey, Hungary, Latvia, Japan and Argentina have been involved in the occupation of a building. By comparison with this low figure, election turnout in these countries is more than 70 per cent.

Patterns of political behaviour

There are many different types of political behaviour, and these combine in varying proportion in different countries according to their political structures, cultures and histories. However, there are also some striking patterns in participation in the democratic countries of the world which enable us to advance some reliable generalisations.

Most people are not political

Most people do not know or care much about politics. They vote sometimes, and they become active when the need arises. But these people are not necessarily 'apathetic', because there are other reasons for being politically inactive:

- *Marginals* People categorised as 'marginals' or who have **political marginality** include lunatics and criminals who are deprived of citizenship rights; illiterates; immigrants and those who do not speak the majority language; the mentally handicapped; the very old and infirm. Students often do not vote in elections simply because they are at university on election day and not in their home town where they are registered to vote.

Political marginality The condition of being on the fringes of politics, and therefore of having little influence.

- *Conflict avoiders* Some people avoid politics because it can lead to disagreement, conflict and bad feeling.
- *Alienated* Some people do not get involved because they believe they have no influence in the system (low subjective efficacy), or think the political system is not democratic (system competence). Fewer than a third of the citizens of Japan, Romania, Argentina, Italy and Spain express confidence in their parliament, compared with two-thirds or more in Lithuania, South Africa, Estonia, Latvia and Poland.
- *Loss of political salience* With the huge expansion of income and education since 1945, many people have the personal resources to deal with the problems and opportunities of their daily life. This makes them more independent as individuals. Politics, on the other hand, is a collective activity, and become less important and less necessary in a world where individuals have their own money and personal skills to handle their lives. Politics is no longer **salient**: it becomes, as one observer noted, 'background noise' or 'elevator music'. This is not to say that politics is of no importance, but it does mean that, in comparison with other activities – work, family, leisure – it has less significance. This is not to say that people do not participate in political life any more. They participate sporadically when the need arises, but without committing themselves and their time to ideologies or conventional organisations such as parties and trade unions.

Salient Something that is important, significant, or prominent in people's minds.

- *Apathetic* Those who are simply not interested in politics. The term 'apathetic' is often used as a critical value judgement, which means it should be avoided, quite apart from the fact that many are politically inactive for reasons other than apathy.

Sporadic political involvement

Though most people are not politically active most of the time, many are involved some of the time: they read a paper, watch TV news and talk about politics. They participate in one way or another when they feel the need, usually because their personal interests are affected. These sporadic acts of participation cover a substantial percentage of the population, and, as table 9.1 shows, more than half and as many as three-quarters of the population of most western European democracies have been politically involved in some way, beyond the simple act of voting.

Table 9.1   *Rates of political participation,[a] western Europe, 1974–1990*

	1974	1981	1990
Britain	31	66	77
Sweden		58	74
Norway		58	68
Denmark		48	59
(West) Germany	34	48	57
France		52	57
Italy	34	50	56
Iceland		40	55
Netherlands	28	37	54
Belgium		27	51
Ireland		32	46
Finland	26	40	38
Spain		32	32

Note: [a] Entries are percentages of the adult population who engage in some form of political participation beyond voting.

Source: Richard Topf, 'Beyond electoral participation', in Hans-Dieter Klingemann and Dieter Fuchs, *Citizens and the State* (Oxford: Oxford University Press, 1995: 69).

Participation rates are rising

As table 9.1 also shows, rates of political activity are tending to rise in the western world, contrary to the common claim that democracies are increasingly apathetic and alienated. Many parts of the democratic world show a decline in the 'old' politics of parties and elections, but an increase in the 'new' politics of referendums, petitions, community groups, citizen lobbies and single-issue groups.

Substantial variations in participation

The percentages involved in political activity often vary greatly from one country to another. This is true of particular modes of participation as well as of overall rates of activity, as the figures in table 9.1 show. Participation in the highest-ranked country in 1981 and 1990 is more than twice as high as in the lowest-ranked one.

Voters are not fools

Some political scientists emphasise how little people know about politics, how little they are involved and how poorly prepared they are to perform their citizen duties. Some survey research concludes that voters are often ignorant, irrational and inconsistent and that, as a result, opinion polls and surveys are not to be trusted. Asked about a matter on which they have no opinion or information, many come up with a **'door-step' response**, saying the first

> **'Door-step' response** Where those with no opinion or information respond to polls and surveys with the first thing that comes into their head (sometimes known as 'non-opinion').

thing that comes into their head, or something that they think they should say. Contradicting this dim view of the electorate, the American political scientist V. O. Key (1908–63) argued that 'voters [are] not fools'. He produced evidence showing that American voters switched votes between candidates and parties according to their judgement of the political circumstances. They judged candidates and parties according to their past records and future promises. Subsequent research has tended to confirm this, in two ways:

- Electoral behaviour can be explained in terms of real political trends and events, especially taxation, inflation, unemployment, economic performance, and social policies, war, and international events. Support for NATO declined after the collapse of the Soviet Union in 1989 because people thought there was no longer a great need for military defence of the NATO type, but when other military conflicts occurred they revised their views again.
- Some research argues that citizens use **'low information rationality'** or 'gut rationality' in deciding how to vote and behave. It is not necessary to have full and detailed information to make sensible judgements; a rough idea is sufficient. If the issue is a complex technical one, people can take their cues from those they trust – party leaders, political commentators, friends, newspapers.

> **Low information rationality** Where citizens without great deal of factual political information have a broad enough grasp of the main issues to make up their mind about them, or else they take cues from sources they trust (sometimes known as 'gut rationality').

The 'standard model' of political participation

The 'standard model' applies across a wide variety of countries and times. It shows that class and status, plus the closely related factors of education, income and family background, have strongly influenced rates and types of political participation. Those with high class and status often have the education to be able to acquire political knowledge and skills, and they are likely to understand the relevance of politics to their own circumstances. They are more likely to have the resources (education, cars, computers, email, office support, money) to become effectively involved in politics, they have the social prestige to be influential and they often have family backgrounds with a political interest. Class and status is often abbreviated to 'SES' or 'social and economic status', where class is closely associated with occupation and income, and status with prestige in society. Some people make a lot of money but have low status (the owner of a string of porn magazines) while others have high status though not much money (aristocrats fallen on hard times). SES is a combination of these two things. Most research on political participation finds systematic differences along cultural and ethnic lines, as well as between religious groups. Family activism is also passed on from one generation to the next. For the most part, different rates of participation reflect unequal access to resources, with money and education being the most important.

Gender, age and length of residence

The 'standard model' is often modified, though usually only a small degree, by gender, age and length of residence in a community. In many countries, politics is still regarded as something of a 'man's game', and women tend to participate less. Young and old people are less active than the middle-aged, whose involvement with their children's schools, their colleagues at work and their community tends to draw them into politically related activities. The longer people live in their community, and the stronger their social networks, the more they tend to be engaged.

Political elites

Following on from the last point, it is generally true that the leaders of the political west are overwhelmingly of the '3-M' variety – middle-aged, middle class and male. Most have a university education, and many come from three professions – law, teaching and the civil service (fact file 9.2).

Changing attitudes and behaviour

The political attitudes and behaviour of the twentieth century are changing. New economic forms and technology, globalisation, population movements, social mixture and heterogeneity, secularisation, changing class structures, increasing affluence, higher levels of education, greater mobility, democratic reforms, different ways of making political decisions and electronic means of communication have created different social and political patterns. The class divisions that were important in many urban–industrial societies of the nineteenth and twentieth centuries are being weakened or replaced by new social cleavages, new forms of political activity and the new political interests of minority groups – women, Greens, the young, nationalists and post-materialists.

Where once attitudes and behaviour were associated with stable, structured and homogeneous social groups living in their own communities (mining villages, ship-building towns, middle-class suburbs, inner-city working-class areas), they are now associated with socially mixed, shifting and changing populations with a greater and less stable variety of political interests. According to some research the collective politics of centralised and hierarchical parties, trade unions and business associations are being replaced by the fragmented and individual patterns of **issue publics** that vary as issues and political circumstances change. There is a greater variety

> **Issue publics** Groups of people who are particularly interested in one political issue (or more), are well informed and likely to take action about it.

of issue publics and of life-style politics, greater volatility and greater demand for grass-roots and community participation. Moreover, growing numbers of citizens use their shopping power to exert political pressure when they refuse, for instance, to buy shoes or sweaters produced by child labour. Political attitudes and attachments are becoming weaker and less predictable and the standard socio-demographic model organised around a few variables (class and status, religion, education, family background) now work less well. Whether fragmentation, variation and constant change are to be the hallmarks of the new world, or whether this will precede the emergence of a new and stable social and political order, remains to be seen.

We will return to this topic in chapter 12, where we discuss voting and elections.

Fact file 9.2

Mass political behaviour
Evidence collected by the World Values Survey from thirty-four established democracies in the world presents some interesting figures about the political behaviour of their citizens.

- *Political discussion* On average, 70 per cent of people surveyed in thirty-four democracies claimed to discuss politics frequently or occasionally. Almost half the population of the UK, Turkey, Hungary, Portugal and Argentina claim never to discuss politics, compared with fewer than 20 per cent in the ex-communist countries of Croatia, the Czech Republic, Slovakia and what used to be East Germany.
- *Political inaction* Most people (60 per cent) do not think that politics is very or at all important in life. By comparison 95 per cent think the family is very or rather important. 30 per cent claim never to discuss politics with friends, less than 5 per cent belong to a political party, less than 3 per cent have done voluntary work for a political organisation and less than 4 per cent belong to a local political action group.
- *Direct action* Direct action in the form of strikes, sit-ins, boycotts, marches and occupations is now widely accepted as a part of the political repertoire, but a comparatively small proportion of the population have been engaged in such activities compared with conventional political action. Fewer than 5 per cent of have been involved in occupations and unofficial strikes, and fewer than 10 per cent in boycotts.
- *Democratic reform* Most citizens of democracies (90 per cent) believe that democracy is the best form of government but a sizeable (60 per cent) and increasing proportion express a lack of confidence in democracy as it works in their country. Sixty per cent are dissatisfied with the way that their democracy is developing.
- *Revolutionary action* Most citizens (80 per cent) favour change and reform. About half (48 per cent) want more open government and the vast majority (85 per cent) believe change is too slow. But very few (4 per cent or less) believe in revolutionary or radical action.

Source, World Values Survey, 2000 (www.worldvaluessurvey.org/)

■ Theories of political attitudes and behaviour

Marxist and class theory

Marxist theories argue that political attitudes and behaviour are shaped by capitalist institutions that ensure that the system 'reproduces' itself, and that the masses are indoctrinated into a state of **false consciousness**. Education conditions the workers to fulfil their economic function and little else. Religion, 'the opiate of the masses', teaches people their place in life and emphasises spiritual matters rather than the physical conditions of life. The mass media indoctrinate people with a mixture of political propaganda and popular distractions (sport, game shows, films, soap operas, gossip). Political culture is, therefore, largely the creation of the ruling class and designed to protect their economic interests. The Italian philosopher, Antonio Gramsci (1891–1937) used the term **hegemony** to refer to the way the ruling class exercised power not by force, but by subtle influence over the hearts and minds of ordinary people. Political culture, viewed this way, is merely a 'superstructure' built on the material substructure of the capitalist mode of production and its class system.

> **False consciousness** The state of mind of the working class induced by the ruling class to conceal the real nature of capitalism and the real self-interests of the workers.

> **Hegemony** Hegemony indicates a class, political interest or country that is so powerful that it does not have to rely upon force or power to maintain its rule because its values and attitudes have been accepted or because people dare not oppose it.

Rigid and 'vulgar Marxist' theories (that is, crude and over-simple Marxism) have nothing to recommend them. They are 'over-determined' in the sense that they do not allow for the many individual and group variations that exist within any political system. The concept of false consciousness also has its difficulties; who can tell others that they do not see the world correctly, or understand their own best interests?

At the same time, there is clearly more than a small grain of truth in the class theory of attitudes and behaviour. Empirically, the 'standard model' that combines class and class-related variables explains a good deal of the variation in political attitudes and behaviour, and it seems to have applied to a broad variety of countries and circumstances for much of the nineteenth and twentieth centuries. However, it certainly does not explain everything, and its explanatory power declined in the late twentieth century. The class model though far from defunct, seems to be on the wane.

Elite theory

Elite theory grew up in opposition to Marxist class theory and is associated mainly with the names of the German sociologist Robert Michels (1876–1936) and the two Italian political sociologists Gaetano Mosca (1858–1941) and Vilfredo Pareto (1848–1923). Both elite and class theory argue that politics is dominated by a small number of people, but whereas Marxists argue that the **ruling elite** or ruling class reproduces itself by passing on its privileges and power to its children, elite theory claims that elites cannot perpetuate themselves in the long run. They change and circulate because elites inevitably decay after a time in power, to be replaced by a new, more successful and more vigorous elite. New elite groups rise to the top because of their superior political skills of cunning, force, or popular appeal. There are different versions of elite theory, but all claim that mass democracy is impossible because a small group will always dominate politics. This is a rather startling claim, and Michels cast his theory as the 'Iron Law of Oligarchy', which states that minorities always rule organisations.

> **Ruling elite** A political elite that is so powerful that it can make all the important decisions in government.

Probably the best known empirical examination of a national elite is that of C. Wright Mills (1916–62), that argues that the USA is run by a small group of people representing the 'military–industrial complex' and consisting of military leaders (the warlords), top businessmen (the corporate directorate) and political leaders. Mills argues that this group comes from the same middle- and upper-class background of interconnected families, schools and universities, thinks and acts the same way, interacts closely and circulates among the top positions in public and private life. The power elite makes all the 'key decisions' in the USA, although less important decisions may be made by middle levels of power in a more or less democratic manner. Mills' theory is discussed in greater detail in chapter 16, and pluralist theory, the main challenger to elite theory, is discussed in chapter 10.

Rational-choice theory

Some applications of rational choice have already been discussed (chapters 6 and 7), but since the theory is mainly about individuals it should be particularly applicable to the study of individual attitudes and behaviour. One of the earliest and most influential books, by Anthony Downs, argues that rational, self-interested voters will support the party most likely to represent their preferences. For their part, the political parties will try to maximise power by appealing to the average (median) voter, who holds the typical, middle-of-the-road attitudes and preferences of the great majority of people.

Early rational-choice theory, following economic models in which consumers were assumed to have perfect knowledge of the market, assumed that individuals were well informed about politics. Since this is obviously implausible, given that many people know rather little about politics, later versions relaxed this assumption and accepted that most people had little political information, but perhaps enough to make political judgements. Indeed, rational-choice theory turned its earlier assumptions about perfect knowledge into a strength, arguing that it is not rational to spend a lot of time gathering political information. The chances of any ordinary citizen having the slightest effect on any given political outcome (e.g. an election result) is close to zero, so the costs of being well informed far outweigh any likely gain. Indeed, from a rational self-interested point of view even voting is a waste of time, and it is much more sensible to **free-ride** on others. The theory thus comes to the conclusion that very few people will bother to vote. Yet people do vote in large numbers, and they do get politically involved, even though they may gain little from it in rational-choice terms. They do so, in part at least, not because of rational self-interest but because performing civic duties is part of a culture that emphasises civic responsibility as an end in itself.

> **Free-ride** To extract the benefits of other people's work without putting in any effort oneself.

The second main problem concerns the discussion of what is 'rational' and what is self-interest. Was it rational and self-interested for the early Christians to allow themselves to be thrown to the lions? If you define 'self-interest' in terms of the soul and salvation, the answer is 'yes', but then everything can be rational self-interest. Besides, some people seem to vote for the public interest rather than self-interest. They are, in the jargon, not 'pocket-book voters' who are motivated by their own material self-interest but carry out **sociotropic voting**, and take the general interest and the public good into account. They may even vote for increases in their own taxes for the general good – as middle-class socialists do. However, rational-choice, social- choice and public choice-theorists can argue that it is rational and self-interested to vote in the public interest because this helps to maintain the social and political conditions of security, safety and economic stability that enable people to achieve their personal interests. Once again, if it is rational self-interest to vote for the public interest then perhaps everything is rational self-interest.

> **Sociotropic voting** Deciding which party to vote for on the basis of general social or economic circumstances. The opposite is 'pocket-book voting' that is based on private interests of the voter.

Social capital theory and civic participation

The most recent theoretical development in the explanation of political attitudes and behaviour concerns the concept of 'social capital', but since this approach is also tied up closely with voluntary associations, the topic of chapter 10, we shall leave it until then. Meanwhile, we need note only that social capital also has a good deal to do with attitudes and behaviour.

■ **What have we learned?**

This chapter deals with the political values and attitudes of individuals and groups, and examines how modern research has tried to understand and explain political cultures. It argues that:

- Although every individual has a unique set of political attitudes and values, and a unique pattern of political behaviour, people tend to show the typical forms of attitudes and behaviour of their social and economic group.

195

- Political attitudes and values are built around the material and ideal interests that individuals derive from their sense of identity. Hence attitudes and values are generally strongly linked to class, ethnic, language, religious and territorial identities. Another way of saying this is that attitudes and values are closely associated with the social, economic and political characteristics of individuals and groups. Different theories stress different characteristics.
- The concept of 'political culture' is claimed to be important empirically (it is associated with many important empirical findings) and theoretically (linking subjective and objective, and macro- and micro-features of the political system). Critics claim that it is a vague and unsatisfactory explanatory variable.
- An important distinction should be drawn between reinforcing and cross-cutting political cleavages, which can result in severe political conflict and violence.
- People tend to specialise in a particular mode of political behaviour (clusters of similar forms of activity). With the exception of a minority of political activists, most individuals do not cover the full range of activities, but combine them in their own particular ways.
- Voters are not fools.

■ Lessons of comparison

- Most people are not political: rates of sporadic political activity are relatively high and participation seems to be increasing.
- Research on materialism/post-materialism argues that younger generations in affluent societies are shifting their values from material ones (jobs, money, etc.) to post-material ones (self-expression, job satisfaction, the quality of life, etc.). Critics claim that this culture shift has slowed down, and that post-material values have not replaced material ones but have been combined with them.
- Participation is often associated with different forms of social stratification (class, status, caste) and stratification related variables (education, religion, ethnicity) and to a lesser extent with gender, age and length of residence in the community.
- Across the western world, class differences in attitudes and behaviour appear to be declining and other forms of social difference are becoming more important, notably religion, and, some claim, political values.

Projects

1. What are the most important features of the political culture of your country? Why? The figures in the World Values Studies (www.worldvaluessurvey.org/) and in Inglenhart and Basanez, 2004 (see further reading below) will be useful for this question.

2. Read the section in this chapter on materialism and post-materialism, and then assess the extent to which you and your friends are materialists or post-materialists.
3. Critically assess Marxist, elitist and rational-choice approaches to political attitudes and behaviour. Which do you prefer, if any, and why?

Further reading

R. J. Dalton, *Citizen Politics: Public Opinion and Political Parties in Advanced Industrial Democracies*, Chatham: Chatham House, 2nd edn., 2002.
The best general introduction to political attitudes and behaviour. It covers France, Germany, Great Britain and the USA.

G. A. Almond and S. Verba, *The Civic Culture: Political Attitudes and Democracy in Five Nations*, Princeton NJ: Princeton University Press, 1963.
The original and classic study of political culture.

G. A. Almond and S. Verba (eds.), *The Civic Culture Revisited*, Princeton: Princeton University Press, 1980.
The best appraisal of the concept of political culture and the research done on it since the publication of *The Civic Culture*.

R. F. Inglehart, 'The renaissance of political culture', *American Political Science Review*, 82, 1988: 1203–30.
Marks a revival of interest in political cultures.

R. J. Inglehart and C. Welzel, 'Political culture and democracy', in Howard J. Wiarda (ed.), *New Directions in Comparative Politics*, Boulder, CO: Westview Press, 3rd ed., 2002: 141–64.
On political culture and democracy.

R. J. Dalton, 'Citizen attitudes and political behaviour', *Comparative Political Studies*, 33, 2000, 912–40. (also at www.socsci.uci.edu/~rdalton/archive/cps00.pdf)
An excellent review of changing political attitudes and behaviour at the end of the twentieth century.

Websites

www.esds.ac.uk/International/access/eurobarometer.asp
The European Union's bi-annual survey, called the Eurobarometer.
www.worldvaluessurvey.org/
Website about the World Values Surveys.
www.europeansocialsurvey.org/
The European Social Survey website. It is particularly easy to use and allows students to generate their own tables.

10   Pressure groups and social movements

Few of us have much influence in politics as individuals on our own; we have to combine with others to have any impact. And that is exactly what people do in democracies. Using their rights of assembly and free association, they organise themselves into a huge number and variety of voluntary organisations – professional and business organisations, trade unions, charities, social clubs, environmental groups, churches, women's groups, community associations, youth clubs, consumer groups, arts, science, leisure clubs and sports clubs. In recent decades, they have also developed a new weapon in the struggle for political power, namely social movements, which are not the same as pressure groups in all respects but have a lot in common with them.

Voluntary organisations and associations, clubs and social movements play an enormously important role in social and political life, and are said to be one of the main foundations of modern democracy. Politically active groups voice the demands of their members and defend their interests in the political arena, as any peaceful group in a democracy is entitled to do. Many groups play a direct role in the consultative machinery of government. Even if they are not politically active, groups help to create a peaceful, integrated and stable social order in which democratic government can operate effectively.

Voluntary associations organise themselves around the interests of social groups and strata, which makes them another example of the way that government and politics are deeply rooted in social life. In fact, they play a special role in politics as mediating organisations. They organise individuals into groups, and then link these groups with the political system by expressing and defending their political interests when the need arises. In this sense, they act as 'input' agencies in the political system that express the demands and concerns of individuals, but they also act as 'output' agencies that help to implement public policy. This means that groups are mediating agencies in a two-way process that links society and government – a function they share with parties and the media, which have their own chapters in this part of the book (chapters 11, 12 and 13).

Voluntary associations and organisations are thus crucial to an understanding of government and society: they express the social and political interests of their members, they try to influence the public by putting pressure on government, they often play a direct role in the consultative machinery of government and they play a crucial role in democratic politics by organising, integrating and stabilising society.

The main topics in this chapter are:

- Political connections
- Pressure groups and social movements in action
- Determinants of power
- Corporatism, para-government and tri-partism/pluralism
- International NGOs
- Groups, pressure groups and democracy
- Theories of voluntary organisations.

■ Political connections

Voluntary organisations and pressure groups

Modern government is often big government with activities that extend into almost every corner of life and have an impact on the daily lives of citizens in many different ways. Therefore, social groups have an incentive to organise themselves to defend their interests and to influence government policies that affect them. Perhaps the most conspicuous, because they are often large, wealthy, active and powerful, are the organisa-

> **Interest groups** Sometimes know as 'sectional' groups, interest groups are the type of pressure group that represent occupational interests – business and professional associations and trade unions.

tions that represent people in their working lives – business associations, professional associations and trade unions. Known as **interest groups**, many of these groups are constantly trying to shape government economic policies and matters that affect their occupations.

The professional associations and trade unions representing state bureaucrats can also be powerful interest groups, and in most countries the army, although not organised as an interest group, also exercises a powerful influence over defence policy.

Occupational groups are not the only form of pressure group. Far from it. In addition there are huge numbers and a vast variety of other groups known as **cause groups** that fight for their non-occupational goals. Churches are active on moral, educational and social issues, community associations deal with a wide range of local matters. Environmental groups have their special causes, as do arts and cultural groups, sports clubs, youth clubs, scientific associations, pensioners organisations, women's groups, arts and cultural associations, welfare organisations, transport groups, consumer associations, humanitarian groups, and so on. The list is almost endless, and it is difficult to exaggerate their number and variety.

Cause groups Sometimes known as 'promotional' or 'attitude' groups, cause groups are a type of pressure group that do not represent organised occupational interests, but promote causes, ideas or issues.

The result is that at any given moment and on any given issue organised groups and associations are likely to be engaged in a political struggle with each other and the government for influence over public policies. This is hugely important in political life because organised political action is one of the main ways in which citizens can influence their governments, hold them accountable and make them responsive to popular demands.

Democracies vary greatly in the number, variety and influence of **pressure groups**. Established democracies with a long history of freedom of association and decades of social and political stability tend to have a greater density of politically active voluntary associations than new democracies, where free association has not been allowed or encouraged by authoritarian or totalitarian governments. For example, the World Values Survey of 1999–2004 shows that in eleven of the best established democracies of western Europe and north America, 5.5 per cent of the population are members of local political action groups, compared with 2.4 per cent in the newer Mediterranean democracies (Greece, Italy, Portugal and Spain), and 2.2 per cent in eight of the ex-communist democracies in central Europe, and 3.7 per cent in the four of the third-wave democracies of Latin America (Argentina, Chile, Mexico and Peru). In the new democracies, groups are less densely organised and there is a history of them being under government control, rather than autonomous political actors (see briefings 10.2 and 10.3).

Pressure groups Private and voluntary organisations that try to influence or control government policies but do not want to become the government. 'Pressure groups' is a general term to cover interest groups and cause groups.

From the point of view of governments there are three main types of pressure groups:

- *'Episodic' groups* Most voluntary associations are not at all concerned with public issues and avoid politics if possible because they are controversial and cause difficulty between people. A local football club or film club has no need to get involved in politics

'Episodic' groups Groups that are not usually politically active but become so when the need arises.

in normal circumstances, but if their football pitch or cinema is due for demolition to make way for a road, they may campaign to protect their amenities, but only as long as the issue lasts. Such groups are known as **'episodic' groups**. Their importance lies in the fact that, while most groups are not political most of the time, they are already organised and can be mobilised quickly to defend their interests if the need arises.

- *'Fire brigade' groups* Some groups are set up especially to fight a particular political campaign as **'fire brigade' groups**, and are disbanded when the issue is settled. For example, a local action group might be set up to keep a park as an open space, but fade away when the issue is won (or lost).

> **'Fire brigade' groups** Groups formed to fight a specific issue, and dissolved when it is over.

- *Political groups* Some groups are created to engage in politics. One major purpose of trade unions and business associations, for example, is to engage in politics and to influence the wide range of public policies that affect their interests.

At this point, it would be helpful to clear up a purely verbal matter. This chapter refers to voluntary organisations of all kinds that play a political role as **'pressure groups'**. It uses the term 'interest groups' to refer to those kinds of pressure groups that represent people in their occupational capacities – that is the business, professional and trade unions that are particularly important in the pressure group world. All groups other than occupational groups are called **'cause groups'**. Interest groups and cause groups together make up the whole of the 'pressure group world'. This is not how the terms are used in some studies, which refer to politically active groups of all kinds as 'interest groups'. This, however, rather confuses matters because it leaves us with no way of distinguishing between occupational and other groups. We shall see later why this distinction is so important.

This still leaves us with other problems of definition. We have already mentioned that pressure groups and social movements are alike in some respects, and in addition that pressure groups are like political parties in some ways. All three are voluntary organisations and all are political. How, then, are we to distinguish between them?

Pressure groups and political parties

The pressure group world overlaps with political parties but it is helpful to draw lines between them because they usually play a different role in politics:

- Pressure groups want to influence government, parties want to become government. Trade unions and business organisations want to keep a foot in the door of government, but they do not want to be part of it.

Briefing 10.1

Pressure groups in India, Ghana and the Dominican Republic

India: the rise of interest groups and social movements

- Political participation in India has been transformed in many ways since the 1960s by the creation and entry into the political system of many new interest groups and new social movements. Voluntary organisations and interest groups have proliferated and were estimated to number 50–100,000 in the 1990s, and to be rising rapidly.
- The state has energetically promoted the formation of groups. One survey found that almost half of them received funds from central government, which recognises their role in social, economic and democratic development.
- Some interest organisations help the decentralised implementation of government policies (poverty alleviation, for example), some act as political watchdogs, pressing governments to observe the spirit of the laws and fulfil their election promises, some are concerned with raising political consciousness and encouraging people to demand their rights, and others are innovators, experimenting with new approaches to social problems.
- In the 1970s, activists began forming broad-based social movements to advocate interests that were neglected by the state and the political parties. One of the most powerful is the farmers' movement, which has organised a long series of demonstrations pressing for higher farm prices and more rural investment. Castes and tribes at the bottom of India's social hierarchy (the Untouchables) that were excluded from politics have organised themselves into a huge social movement. A broad-based movement has been created to promote women's issues, and an environmental movement has struggled to redefine 'development' to include respect for indigenous cultures and environmental sustainability.

The Dominican Republic: 'falta de organización'

- The Dominican Republic does not have a large number of interest groups or an intensely competitive pluralist system. A growing number of private associations started to fill the vacuum, which many Dominicans held primarily responsible for their nation's history of instability. But the *falta de organización* (lack of organisation) is still a problem for political life.

Ghana: interest groups fill a gap

- Political parties in Ghana have been weak and the national political system unstable, so interest groups representing some of the most important sections of society have filled the gap, acting as sources of stability and continuity in government and public policy. These groups are enormously powerful, playing a major role in the transition to democracy after 1992 and in subsequent public policy. The most influential are the trade unions (with a membership of half a million), and associations of lawyers, churches, journalists, students and the chiefs of the many ethnic, linguistic and cultural groups. Successive Ghanaian governments have tried to co-opt or control, if not to intimidate, the leadership of these organisations, resulting in acute conflict. Interest groups have often argued not for their own narrow, sectional interests but for long-term policies in the national interest that support democracy and the rule of law.

Based on reports of the Federal Research Division, Library of Congress, USA (http://countrystudies.us)

- Most pressure groups are interested in only one policy area, party programmes cover all (or almost all) of them. Welfare groups are concerned with welfare, art groups with art. Neither have any particular interest with foreign policy.
- Parties are primarily political, most pressure groups are not. Parties are set up to win power by nominating candidates for public office and contesting elections. Rose growers' associations are not interested in politics unless they have to be.
- Parties fight elections, most pressure groups do not.

These are not hard and fast differences. The Labour parties of Australia and the UK were created by socialist, workers' and trade union pressure groups. Some pressure groups are aligned with or integrated into parties, especially in dominant single-party systems like Japan, and some contest elections, though often for the publicity this brings rather than the hope of winning. Some pressure groups operate as parties (agrarian parties in

> **Aligned groups** Pressure groups that ally themselves with a political party, the best examples being trade unions and left parties, and business organisations and right parties. Many groups try to maintain a non-aligned status if they can, because they want to work with whichever party is in power.

Scandinavia, and religious groups in Israel), or turn themselves into parties (the Greens), but most groups stick to being groups. Some are naturally **aligned groups** – business organisations with right-wing parties, trade unions with left-wing parties. In most cases, however, groups try to maintain a non-aligned status so that they can work with whatever party or coalition is in power.

Social movements

Social movements also have much in common with parties and pressure groups, but differ in some respects. Social movements:

- Bring together a range of different organisations and associations to work loosely together. They are not organised into a single bureaucratic structure like pressure groups and parties.
- Have a broader range of political interests than most voluntary associations, but a narrower range than most political parties. Social movements are concerned with a particular area of public life – the representation of working-class interests, or minority groups, or religious issues.

Probably the best single example of a social movement is the working-class coalition formed in many countries in the nineteenth century to protect and promote working-class interests. Formed by trade unions, cooperatives and collectives, savings clubs, worker educational organisations and socialist organisations of all kinds, they initially formed a broad coalition of forces. Later, many of them formed their own political parties, so they made the transition from groups, to movements, to parties. The suffragettes were another early social movement, though they rarely formed their own parties.

In the modern world, we hear much more about **'New Social Movements'** (**NSMs**). These differ from voluntary organisations and parties in several ways. They have:

New Social Movements Loosely knit organisations ('networks of networks') that try to influence government policy on broad issues, including the environment, nuclear energy and nuclear weapons, economic development, peace, women and minorities.

1. A different sort of political agenda insofar as they are counter-cultural, anti-politics and anti-state

2. A broader range of interests (human rights, minority groups, the environment, peace) than most groups, but a narrower range than parties

3. A broader range of members than most groups, but a narrower range than the largest parties. Some social movements have been called 'rainbow coalitions' because they try to link rather disparate social groups and organisations under a single political umbrella

4. A looser and more decentralised form of organisation than groups or parties – they have been described as 'networks of networks'. The 'old' organisations are hierarchical, bureaucratic and professionally run, the 'new' ones are based upon the grass-roots participation of volunteers

5. Political methods that are often innovative and unconventional, involving direct political action, community involvement and sometimes protest action or even violence.

Environmental movements illustrate these points well. They often pursue a self-consciously different style of politics than conventional parties and pressure groups, and they have a wider agenda than most groups, as well as attracting a broader range of social types. Most groups appeal to specific kinds of individuals for specific kinds of activities – they are sports clubs, or choirs, or mountain walkers' clubs. Environmental movements are often networks of interests that come together as loose-knit coalitions, rather than hierarchically organised and bureaucratically centralised organisations. That is why they are called 'movements'. Environmental movements also often use unconventional political methods, including direct action, grass-roots participation and eye-catching protests.

Social movements are not new. The Abolition (of slavery) movement, and the Chartist and the Suffragette movements of the nineteenth century were followed in the 1950s in Britain by the Campaign for Nuclear Disarmament (CND). However, the 1960s and 1970s saw a wave of 'new' social movements concerned with the environment, peace, women's rights, nuclear power and weapons, minority rights, animal rights and racism. Examples include Friends of the Earth and Greenpeace, the Black Power movement in the USA, peasant and land reform movements in South America and the loose alignment of right-wing and racist groups in Europe.

Initially it seemed that these New Social Movements threatened the established order of the state, and its conventional parties and pressure groups.

The causes they promoted were not always new, but the political methods they used were often direct and unconventional. But, as it turns out, 'new' social movements have quite a lot in common with 'old' social movements, political parties and groups. Each has tried to steal the other's clothes. The old have adopted some of the policy goals of the new and, in their quest for power, the new have sometimes adapted and compromised with the world by adopting more conventional and pragmatic methods. The Greens formed political parties to fight elections, and while they initially opposed the formal hierarchies of the old parties and tried to work with a rotating leadership, some gradually succumbed to the old ways of doing things and kept their leaders in power. Meanwhile, the old parties, realising which way the wind was blowing, started to adopt modified Green policies in order to head off their electoral threat.

■ Pressure groups and social movements in action

Pressure groups and social movements perform two main political functions:

- *Interest aggregation* The formation of a single policy programme from a set of rather different interests and views. Student organisations have to aggregate the interests of different students – first- and higher-degree, arts and social science and natural science, home and overseas, young and mature, wealthy and poor. Pressure groups have the important role of sorting and sifting opinions and presenting it as a single package.
- *Interest articulation* Expressing and publicising policies in order to influence government action. This is their 'voice' function, in which they try to make their views heard amid the great confusion of noise made by all groups equally concerned to stress their own point.

Groups and movements use many different methods of articulating their interests – from lobbying politicians and bureaucrats, producing pamphlets, doing research and organising petitions, to organising strikes, sit-ins, non-cooperation, rioting, violence and staging publicity events. But there are two general rules in choosing any one or combination of these methods:

- First, try to get into the policy formation process as early as possible, because this is when options are open, when parties have not yet taken a public stand and when government is still undecided.
- Second, to operate at the highest possible level of government to which you have access, because this is the best way to achieve the greatest amount of influence with the least possible expense and effort.

This, of course, is easier said than done, because groups have to take account of two sets of powerful constraints that determine how they operate in the political system and how much power and influence they have in it. The first set of constraints concerns the nature of the group and its interests; the second, the nature of the political environment they are working in.

Groups and issues

Some groups have a privileged 'insider' status that gives them direct access to high-level government officials. **'Insider' groups** and governments are some-times heavily dependent upon each other and are in close and constant contact: groups want to influence policies and receive advance warn-ing about them; governments sometimes depend upon groups for their technical information and expertise, and for their cooperation in the smooth implementation of policy (see briefing 10.1). A great deal of the busi-ness between groups and government does not involve major policy issues but technical matters and details; some groups are routinely consulted about these, but to preserve their 'insider' status, they must not disturb the rela-tionship by making extreme demands or attacking the government in public. A professional association of doctors may be very concerned about a health issue and have important information that it wants to feed into government policy making circles, for example. Doctors are a prestige professional group that governments will listen to, and often there are special consultative com-mittees to enable them to meet regularly with top health officials so that they can exchange views.

> **'Insider' groups** Pressure groups with access to senior government officials, often recognised as the only legitimate representatives of par-ticular interests and often formally incorporated into the official consultative bodies.

Many 'insider' groups represent business and professional interests – indus-trialists, farmers, doctors, bankers, food producers – which play a key role in the economy. This gives them political influence. In some countries close relations between government and private interests are promoted by similar elite backgrounds – Oxford and Cambridge University and the London clubs in Britain, the Grande Ecoles in Paris, the Tokyo Law School and the Law and Business Schools of Harvard and Yale. In Britain and Japan, it is not uncom-mon for ministers and senior civil servants leaving public service to work for the very businesses and organisations which they were regulating when in office – the so-called 'revolving door' in the UK and the USA, or 'the descent from heaven' in Japan.

'Outsider' groups do not have this special relationship. They are excluded from close consultation because they lack bargaining power, are too critical of government, are generally unpopular, or because they prefer to be outside and independent of gov-ernment. While 'insider' groups rely heavily on their close government contacts, outsider groups use other methods of pro-test, direct action and publicity-attracting demonstrations. One of the ironies of pressure group politics is that powerful 'insider' groups can operate most smoothly and quietly out of the public eye, while the 'outsider' groups, for all the noise of their public campaigns, are less powerful and effective: protest

> **'Outsider' group** Group with no access to top government officials.

Briefing 10.2

International peak organisations

International NGOs such as Amnesty International and environmental groups are often regarded as key organisations in international governance, but they are only a small part of a huge number. They attract a lot of media attention but it does not mean that they are as influential or powerful as some other NGOs that work effectively without much publicity, especially those in the economic, business, health and labour areas. The following gives a flavour of the range of international NGOs, and of the breadth of their organisation in the world:

- The *World Council of Churches* has a membership of about 400 million Christians representing more than 330 churches, denominations and fellowships in 100 countries and territories (www.wcc-coe.org).
- The *International Confederation of Free Trade Unions* is the world's largest trade union body, with 221 affiliated organisations and 155 million members in 148 countries on five continents. It maintains close links with other international labour organisations, such as the European Trade Union Confederation (ETUC) and the International Trade Secretariats (www.icftu.org).
- The *Olympic movement* consists of the International Olympic Committee (IOC), sixty-five International Sports Federations, 199 National Olympic Committees, the Organising Committees for the Olympic Games, national sports associations and clubs and their athletes and other organisations recognised by the IOC (www.olympic.org).
- *Rotary International* is a world-wide organisation with some 1.2 million members in more than 29,000 Clubs in 160 countries (www.rotary.org).
- The *World Association of Girl Guides and Girl Scouts* has over 10 million members in 140 countries (www.wagggsworld.org). The World Scout Movement has more than 28 million members in 216 countries and territories (www.scout.org).
- The *Union of International Associations* is a clearing house for information about more than 44,000 international non-profit organisations (www.uia.org). Its list of organisations includes: The Disinfected Mail Study Circle, The International Group of Priests for Circus and Showmen of All Confessions, The European Council of Skeptical Organisations, The International Goat Association, The International Institute for Andragogy, The International Union of Private Wagon Owners' Associations, Proutist Universal, The Society of Indexers, Toy Traders of Europe, The United Elvis Presley Society and The World Association of Flower Arrangers.

politics is a weapon of the less powerful. Perhaps the best-known 'outsider' protest politicians in the world were Nelson Mandela (1918–) and Martin Luther King (1929–68), which makes the point that protest politics can sometimes be both peaceful and successful.

The nature of government

The way pressure groups operate is strongly influenced by the nature of the political system they are dealing with, and the location of power within it.

Direct routes

So far as they can, groups start with the most powerful actors:

- *Executives* In presidential systems it is best to approach the president or a staff member, and in parliamentary systems the prime minister or cabinet. Since only a few, special groups have such high-level access, the rest must approach the less powerful points that they can reach.
- *Legislatures* Groups without access to their political executives may start with their legislature, which usually attracts a good deal of pressure group activity, especially in the USA where parties are weak, elections frequent and elected representatives are sensitive to special interest campaigns and funds. Powerful groups do not need to waste time in the **lobby** of the legislative body. They have privileged contacts in committees and consultative bodies of government, and prefer to use them rather than lobbying the legislature, which is crowded with many different groups all trying to win the ear of politicians, who may well already have a clear view about their policies. Some groups choose to employ professional lobbyists (see fact file 10.1), and some 'buy' their influence by contributing to campaign funds.

> **Lobby** A popular term for pressure groups (based on the mistaken belief that pressure group representatives spend a lot of time in the 'lobbies' or ante-rooms of legislative chambers).

- *Government departments* It is often effective to start with the top bureaucrats in government departments, especially if the political system is blocked by weak and fragmented parties, or by conflict between the executive and legislature. It is probably also best to start with bureaucrats on technical matters because they will probably handle them in the end. Having a friend or ally who is a top public servant is exceedingly helpful, just as it is to have the 'revolving door' or the 'descent from heaven' provide a retired official with special knowledge and contacts on your side.
- *State and local government* Many pressure groups deal with local matters, so their natural target is state or local government.

Indirect routes

Since many groups do not have good access to either elected or appointed government officials, they try more roundabout routes to gain influence (see briefing 10.3):

- *Political parties* Aligned groups have special, friendly connections with political parties, while others try to 'buy' influence by contributing to campaign funds (see fact file 10.1). At the same time, parties that have already taken a public stand on an issue will be hard to shift, so it is best to get in early before they have thought about the matter.
- *Public campaigns* Modern methods of advertising, desktop publishing and computer mail shots have made public campaigns more attractive, but they are still relatively expensive, time-consuming and uncertain in their effects. There are so many groups in the political arena that it is difficult for any one of them to have a big effect, but if a group has public opinion on its side then governments are more likely to treat it with respect.

Fact file 10.1

Pressure groups

- One of the first pressure groups was The Society for Effecting the Abolition of the Slave Trade, founded in 1787 in Britain by William Wilberforce, a highly effective pressure group leader (www.britannica.com/ ebc/article?eu=407999).
- The number of registered Washington lobbyists is over 15,500 and their estimated expenditure in 2007 was $2.83 billion (www.opensecrets.org).
- There are about 3,750 Political Action Committees (PACs) operating in Washington. Most represent business, labour or ideological interests. In 1999 and 2000 they raised $604.9 million and gave most of this to chosen election candidates. The biggest spenders were the National Association of Realtors ($3.4 million), the Association of Trial Lawyers of America ($2.6 million), the American Federation of State, County and Municipal Employees ($2.6 million), the Teamsters Union ($2.6 million) and the National Auto Dealers Association ($2.5 million).
- The European Union's Directory of Special Interest Groups lists 915 lobby groups, mainly in the sectors of agriculture (131), industry (301), services (331) and general interest (394). They range from the Association of European Fruit and Vegetable Processing Industries to the Youth Forum of the European Union.
- One the largest social movements in India is the National Campaign on Dalit Human Rights. The Dalits are the 240 million in India who are not one of the four castes – the untouchables.
- The Deutscher Gewerkschaftsbund (DGB) represents nearly 11 million trade unionists in Germany (www.dgb.de/sprachen/englisch/grundsatz.htm). It operates at the *Länder* and Federal government level in Germany, with the ETUC (www.etuc.org) in the European Union and with the International Confederation of Free Trade Unions on the global level (www.icftu.org).
- The UN has a Conference of 374 NGOs which it lists as official consultative bodies.
- The Union of International Associations estimates that the number of international NGOs grew from 176 in 1909, to 833 in 1951, 1,718 in 1972 and 42,100 in 1998 (www.uia.org/statistics/organizations/stybv296.php).

- *Mass media* Many groups court publicity with press briefings and events (see chapter 11). News reports may be cheaper and more effective than advertising, but the channels of mass communication are overcrowded and it is often difficult to get media attention. A big demonstration or an eye-catching publicity stunt may do the trick, but nowadays there is no shortage of these.
- *Courts* Groups can achieve their goals through the courts, especially since they now play an increasingly important political role. The litigious nature of American society means that pressure groups are constantly in court, but in other countries the courts are a last resort, because the legal process is slow, expensive and uncertain.
- *International and multi-national government* Pressure groups are increasingly operating at the international level, lobbying bodies such as the UN and the EU. The distinction between 'insider' and 'outsider' groups operates here as well.

A life of pressure: Peter Jenkins, a public affairs officer with the British Consumers'
Association

I wish I were taking people out to lunch all the time but it's not really like that. The Consumers'
Association is different from most lobbying organisations in that we are here to represent consumers'
interests and we don't have large budgets for entertaining in the same way as some of the private lobbying firms.

I campaign on food and communication issues and work as part of a team made up of specialist advis-
ers, lawyers and staff from our policy unit. Between us we form, draft and carry out strategies on a variety
of issues. At any one time I might be working on BSE, GM crops, food poisoning or consumers' problems
with the utility companies.

An example of the lobbying work we do would be the work we carried out in the run-up to the formation of the Food Standards Agency. The CA had long campaigned for such an agency to be put in place
and once it was announced, the focus of our efforts changed. During the drafting of the White Paper we
were in contact with civil servants writing the legislation; once it was published we worked in parliament
to produce amendments that we felt were in the public's best interest.

Because the present government has such a large majority in the House of Commons we have found
it easier to work in the Lords. It's a case of lobbying sympathetic peers, explaining what the impact of the
legislation will be if it is unchanged, and persuading them to table amendments.

Sometimes it involves stalking the corridors of parliament late at night; mostly it's about knowing the
right person to call, and picking up the phone.

The other side of my job is representing the organisation to the media. Part of the campaigning
involves writing press releases and being on call to do radio and TV interviews. On Monday I came into
work thinking I had a quiet day only to be told there was a car waiting to take me to ITN.

The thrill of the job is when you are working on a campaign that is getting MPs excited and there is the
perceptible feeling that things are really happening.

(Adapted from the Guardian, 12 May 2001)

Groups often use different combinations of access points into the political
system depending on their resources, characteristics and political connections, and they will often look for allies and build coalitions with like-minded
groups. The political arena is often so crowded that it is helpful to have other
groups that help the struggle. Sometimes this produces strange bed-fellows:
militant groups of alternative life-style ecologists have sometimes formed an
alliance with conservative landowners to protect the environment. There may
be a price to pay for coalition building if partners want help with their own
campaign as the cost of support. Some groups refuse to fight with others if
they think they are too militant and extremist, especially if they use violence.
Cooperation and coalition building help to moderate group demands.

■ Determinants of power

It is extremely difficult to estimate the power of pressure groups, or to compare one with another, because so many factors are involved. Environmental
groups seem to have been successful in recent years but they have been

helped by a shift in public opinion, changes in government and media coverage of nuclear accidents, oil spills and the 'greenhouse effect'. Has government policy changed because of environmental campaigns or because of a combination of these other factors? Of course, environmental groups have themselves helped to change opinion, just as they have used their media skills to publicise environmental disasters in order to bring pressure to bear on governments. These different factors are so closely intertwined that it is virtually impossible to sort them out and say how much is due to environmental groups and how much to other factors. Group influence does seem, however, to depend on two groups of considerations – the internal features of groups and their issues, and the political environment in which they operate.

Group features

Groups can be distinguished in eight main ways:

- *Income* Some groups are wealthy and have offices and a large staff, others are poor and rely upon a few voluntary workers. By and large, interest groups are wealthier than cause groups, because they represent the economic interests of their members, who have a strong material incentive to join and pay a subscription.
- *Membership size* Large groups can collect membership subscriptions from many people, and then use this income to pay staff to raise more money. Nevertheless, size is not always an advantage, for small but cohesive groups can defeat large and divided ones. Some small groups are in fact remarkably wealthy.
- *Organisational advantages* Some social groups are easier to organise than others – compare adults with children, producers with consumers, doctors with patients, the healthy with the chronically ill, professors with students, the rich with the poor, home owners with the homeless, the employed with the unemployed.
- *Membership density and recruitment* A group representing almost all its potential members is likely to have more influence than one representing only a small proportion of them. Professions (doctors, lawyers, dentists, musicians) often make membership of their association compulsory, so they have membership density of 100 per cent. Farmers' associations often have a high density. At the other end of the scale, organisations for the homeless rely on a few dedicated activists, most of them not themselves homeless.
- *Divided groups* A united group is likely to have more influence than a divided one, and a group that holds the field on its own more influence than one with a rival that competes to represent the same interests. Groups that are united with a common interest are sometimes coordinated by a single **'umbrella' organisations** or 'peak association'.

> **'Umbrella' organisations** Associations that coordinate the activity of their member organisations.

211

- *Sanctions* Some groups have powerful sanctions. Businesses that can move their capital abroad, professional bodies that can withdraw cooperation with the government and groups that have public sympathy and can influence voters. Other groups have weak sanctions, or none – children can't go on strike, hospital patients don't refuse treatment, the homeless can't withhold rent, the poor may not have access to lawyers. Often this boils down to how important the groups are in the economy, and their structural power within it.
- *Leadership* A charismatic leader (Nelson Mandela, Martin Luther King) is a great asset.
- *The issue* Governments and parties often have set opinions about big, controversial public issues. Many groups choose to work on policy details and technicalities.

The political environment

There are five key features of the political environment that can affect pressure group success:

- *'Insider'/'outsider' status* 'Insider' groups are more likely to be powerful than 'outsider' groups. Their access to top decision makers gives them a 'voice' and influence at high levels of the political system.
- *Public opinion* Governments are more likely to take note of groups with strong public support. To do otherwise is to risk losing electoral support.
- *Legitimacy* Groups representing legitimate interests in society (doctors, lawyers, teachers, businessmen, church leaders) often have more influence than marginal ones (drug addicts, prostitutes, ex-criminals, minorities and radical groups of many kinds).
- *Political parties* Groups that are aligned with the party in government can have 'inside' influence – only to lose it, of course, when their party is out of office.
- *Countervailing powers* Groups with the field to themselves are likely to be more influential than those which face opposition. Sometimes groups cancel each other out by competing on different sides of the issue (they veto each other). One theory argues that the pressure group world is a 'veto-group system', in which few groups can get what they want because other groups have a capacity to stop them encroaching on their own interests.

It is not difficult to think of an imaginary case to illustrate the influence of group and political factors on the success of a pressure group campaign. Imagine that students are campaigning for higher maintenance grants from the government:

- The student body in most countries is quite large but since most students are not wealthy, their representative associations do not have a great deal of money, although they may have a small, experienced and enthusiastic permanent staff to organise a political campaign.

- Unfortunately, student bodies are often divided internally because they represent groups from diverse social and political backgrounds, different political interests, and varying types and levels of study.
- Worst of all, students have few sanctions. Their strikes are symbolic; they cannot threaten to move their capital investments, shut down factories or paralyse the economy. Withdrawing cooperation with the government and its officials would have no effect.
- On the political side, student representative bodies may not be 'outsider' groups, exactly, but there are many 'insider' groups with more prestige and power. Their image in most countries is not one that wins them much public sympathy.
- Students themselves come in all sorts of political shapes and sizes, and it is doubtful if their representative body swings many votes in national elections.
- If it came to a battle about how limited funds should be spent on higher education it is probable that the heads of universities and professors would win, and if it came to a battle over limited funds for different public services, it is probable that doctors, businessmen, trade unionists, farmers, road builders, social workers, or pensioners would win.

■ Corporatism, para-government and tri-partism/pluralism

Corporatism

In some countries, the relationship between government and economic interest groups representing employers and workers was so closely organised within formal government structures that a special term, 'corporatist', has been invented to describe them. **Corporatism** in democratic states (sometimes called neo-, or liberal corporatism) requires:

> **Corporatism** A way of organising public policy making involving the close cooperation of major economic interests within a formal government apparatus that is capable of concerting the main economic groups so that they can jointly formulate and implement binding policies.

1. A small number of hierarchically organised **'umbrella'** or **'peak' associations** to speak authoritatively for all their members.
2. That such groups are recognised, licensed or even created by the government to ensure that it deals only with a small number of dependable, official representatives.
3. A wide array of formal decision making and consultative government bodies that covers all groups and issues in the policy area.
4. An ability to produce policies that are binding on all parties, and implemented by them.

Corporatism was strongest in the economic sphere where the main interests could be coordinated:

- Trade unions agreed to limit wage and other demands in return for full employment
- Employers agreed to maintain full employment in return for industrial peace and cooperation
- The government promised low inflation and social benefits in return for economic stability
- All were willing and able to impose these agreements upon their own members. They came together within formal government institutions to hammer out a compromise public policy which all accepted and stood by.

One danger of corporatism is that groups not in the system – students, immigrants, peace and anti-nuclear campaigners and (initially) the Greens, as well as extremist right-wing and racist organisations – are excluded from these closed circles of power, and hence may explode into direct action in order to make their voice heard. Some student and worker protest movements have referred to themselves as 'extra-parliamentary opposition' to stress the point that they are outside the formal arenas of power. Corporatism developed in the 1970s and 1980s in western Europe as a method of managing economic growth, but tended to break down in the 1990s under the pressures of economic stagnation. Strong corporatism was found in Austria, Denmark, Luxembourg, Norway and Sweden. Weaker forms were found in Belgium, Finland, Ireland, the Netherlands, Switzerland and West Germany. A different form of corporatism is found in new democracies, where pressure groups are often weaker and less well organised, and where, traditionally, they have been controlled by authoritarian governments (briefing 10.4). The new democracies are usually moving towards more open and pluralist systems but it takes time to build up a momentum.

Para-government

In some countries, large institutional groups play the role of *para-public agencies* that provide public services with financial and other help from the state. The result is an area of government that is neither purely private nor public, but a third sector that is mixture of both:

- The Catholic and Protestant Churches in Germany collect taxes through the state, and provide social services in return.
- Scandinavian housing associations are para-public organisations that cooperate closely with public authorities and receive money from them.
- Farmers, business organisations, professional associations, and churches are involved in close cooperation with the state in Germany and Scandinavia, in order to resolve conflict, regulate society and provide services.

Briefing 10.4

Corporatism, interest groups and democracy in Latin America

- Although democracy has a firm grounding in some Latin American states (see table 2.2) it should not be assume that they are identical to the democracies of North America and western Europe. Latin America's politics is rooted in the corporatist system in which leading social and economic groups had a privileged place in the political system – traditionally the aristocracy, the church and the military. Countries such as Costa Rica and Venezuela have succeeded in expanding the opportunities for political participation for new groups, but in other countries political power is more likely to be more tightly controlled by a few charismatic leaders, the socio-economic elites and the military.

- Latin American politics is more pluralist than before, but there are far fewer organised interest groups than in the USA: tens of thousands of interests groups are represented in Washington; far fewer are found in Latin American capitals. And whereas American groups are independent of government, in Latin America they are sometimes co-opted or organised by the state or by the ruling party.

- However, there has been an explosion of interest groups in Latin America in the past thirty to forty years. They now cover not just the elites of the army, the church and business, but also the middle class, professionals, workers, peasants, women, indigenous groups, students, government workers and international NGOs. Nevertheless, interest group pluralism still tends to be under-developed. Many new groups are poorly organised and weak, and the system typically favours the privileged few, rather than the many. Among the democracies, Argentina, Chile, Costa Rica, Brazil and Uruguay have achieved a low level of pluralism, but other countries have yet to approach this standard.

Based on Communications in Latin America, 'Report on Latin America: Politics and Economics' (http://iml.jou.ufl.edu/projects/ Spring2000/Calcote/latam_la.html)

Tri-partism/pluralism

Some countries without corporatist structures use a much less centralised and co-ordinated system of economic policy making known as **tri-partism**. Here, the three corners of the 'economic triangle' cooperate in a much looser manner through a variety of different formal and semi-formal committees, consultative bodies and meetings. In such systems it makes more sense to talk about **policy communities** or **policy networks** than about corporatism. France, Italy, Japan and the UK are examples, and have been joined by some of the new democracies of central Europe, and by Mexico and Chile in Latin America.

Tri-partism A looser and less centralised system of decision making than corporatism involving close government consultation – often with business and trade union organisations.

Policy communities Small, stable and consensual groupings of government officials and pressure group representatives that form around particular issue areas.

Policy networks Compared with policy communities, policy networks are larger, looser (and sometimes more conflictual) networks that gather around a policy area.

Canada, India, New Zealand and the USA tend to be even less centralised and co-ordinated, and more pluralist and open in their approach. Nonetheless, the relationships between government and private interest groups in some policy areas of the USA are sometimes so close that political scientists talk of the **'iron triangles'** formed by executive agencies, congressional sub-committees and pressure groups. For example, the farming lobby in the USA is wealthy and well organised and has close, intimate working relations with government policy makers.

'Iron triangles' The close, three-sided working relationship developed between (1) government departments and ministries, (2) pressure groups and (3) politicians, that makes public policy in a given area.

International NGOs

Pressure groups have never been confined to domestic politics, but international groups are now more visible and active than ever before. Barely a week passes without a major news story that involves Amnesty International, Greenpeace, Médecins Sans Frontières, Transparency International or the Red Cross. Organisations like these form an increasingly dense network alongside the growing number of agencies of international governance such as the OECD, the UN and the WTO. As with domestic pressure groups, the international NGOs we hear most about are not necessarily the most powerful. Environmental groups and Amnesty International are certainly not weak, but they can rarely match the power of business associations. We shall return to them in the concluding chapter of the book.

Groups, pressure groups and democracy

Freedom of assembly and association are essential parts of any democratic system, and all groups have a right to be heard and to try to influence public policy in a peaceful manner. Besides articulating demands (the input function) in the open political arena, they also play an indispensable role within government itself on official consultative committees, working parties, advisory groups and commissions. Most democratic political systems have an elaborate array of these, and rely heavily on groups for advice, information, specialist expertise and help with implementing policies. Groups also have an output function in producing services for their members and the general public. They deliver meals to the ill and the old, run community centres, raise money for schools, hospitals and overseas aid, provide sports facilities and organise exhibitions. In some countries they run, with government support and money, schools, hospitals and a wide variety of social services.

For these reasons groups play a central part in **pluralist democracy**, which is based on free competition between a plurality of organised interests and on supportive relations between groups and government. The opposite of pluralist society

Pluralist democracy A democratic system where political decisions are the outcome of the conflict and competition between many different groups.

216

is **mass society** which has a weak foundation of organised groups and which, it is said, is particularly susceptible to extremist politics because the population is not well organised into groups that can defend their interests.

> **Mass society** A society without a plurality of organised social groups and interests, whose mass of isolated and uprooted individuals are not integrated into the community and who are therefore vulnerable to the appeals of extremist and anti-democratic elites.

At the same time, pressure groups can also present a threat to democracy. They are often not particularly democratic internally, and they represent the narrow sectional interests of their organisation not the public interest. If they become too powerful, and if they get too close to the top levels of government, they may 'capture' and control government policy in their own interests. This is the wrong way round: governments are supposed to control private groups in the public interest (see controversy 10.1). Policy areas said to be under private control include agriculture (e.g. genetically modified (GM) crops), health (e.g. smoking for much of the twentieth century), the defence industry (e.g. arms manufacturers), business (e.g. finance capital, manufacturing and commerce).

It seems, then, that a successful pluralist democracy depends on a balance of power between government and groups. Too much pressure group power results in private interests running government, too little in autocratic government that pays insufficient attention to legitimate citizen demands. It is a matter of debate where one draws the line between 'too much' and 'too little'.

■ Theories of voluntary organisations

The very large body of literature on groups in politics tends to fall into one of three major theoretical camps – pluralist theory, Marxist/elitist theory and social capital/civil society theory.

Pluralism

Pluralists argue that:

- Many political issues are fought over by competing groups. Rarely is one of them so powerful that it can get its own way. Most have to compromise but they often get something they want, even if it is only to prevent other groups encroaching on their interests. This is called **veto-group** power.

> **Veto-groups** Groups with the power to prevent other groups or the government implementing a policy, although they do not necessarily have the power to get their own policies implemented.

- All groups have some resources to fight their political battles – money, numbers, popularity, 'insider' status, leadership skills, popular support, votes. Resources are not distributed equally, but nor are they distributed with cumulative inequality: all groups have some resources; none has all of them: no group is powerless; no group is all-powerful.
- Power is fragmented, fluid, or 'mercurial'. There is no fixed power structure or power elite, but different configurations of shifting coalitions and

CONTROVERSY 10.1

Do pressure groups sustain or undermine democracy?

Sustain

- Groups perform the essential democratic functions of aggregating and articulating public opinion.
- Voluntary organisations are indispensable ways of organising minority interests, and most groups are minority groups.
- Voluntary associations are the 'free schools of democracy', teaching people political and organisational skills.
- Groups are recruiting grounds for local and national political leaders.
- Groups encourage the politics of accommodation, understanding and compromise by bringing together different people with different backgrounds and opinions in the same organisation.
- Overlapping and interlocking networks of organisations tie society together, counteracting internal divisions.
- Groups give people a sense of belonging, community, and purpose.
- Groups act as channels of communication between citizens, and between citizens and government.
- Groups provide a network of organisations outside and independent of government. They are a ready-made organisational basis for mobilising public opinion against unpopular government action.
- Groups provide governments with technical information and specialist knowledge, and can help implement public policy efficiently and effectively.
- Mass societies are prone to extremist politics and totalitarian political movements.

Undermine

- As narrow, sectional interests they may conspire against the public interest.
- Groups can be exclusive, keeping out some sections of the population and not representing their views (e.g. women, minorities). Corporatism and policy communities are also exclusive and work with a limited number of groups.
- Private organisations are often oligarchical, representing the interests of only a few leaders, not their members.
- Pressure groups are responsible only to their own members, but governments are responsible to the whole population. If pressure groups have too much power, then representative and responsible government will have too little.
- Close cooperation between groups and government risks two dangers. (1) Groups may become too 'domesticated', losing their critical independence of government. (2) Governments may be 'captured' by private interests, losing their critical independence and accountability to the public interest.

> **Hyper-pluralism** A state of affairs in which too many powerful groups make too many demands on government, causing overload and ungovernability.

- Too many powerful groups making too many powerful demands on government may result in government overload and **hyper-pluralism**.
- Groups tend to fragment public policy, preventing governments developing coherent policies.

power according to the issue and the circumstances. Today's winners will be tomorrow's losers, and vice versa.

- Groups that fail in one political arena (national government) may be successful in others (local government, the courts, international arenas).
- Groups often look for political allies, which obliges them to compromise and cooperate with others.
- Groups cannot always get what they want, but they can often veto other groups' proposals they do not like.
- The main exponent of pluralist theory, Robert Dahl (1915–), argues that pluralist democracy does not work in a perfect 'textbook' manner, but it works reasonably well, 'warts and all'.

Marxist/elitist theory

Pluralist theory is opposed by Marxist and elitist theories, which claim that the pressure group system undermines democracy:

- The 'iron law of oligarchy' (chapter 13) means that groups are controlled by a few, unrepresentative leaders, because they are the people with the skill, knowledge and experience to run them, and because leaders make sure they control group resources and the means of communication.
- The group world is dominated by educated, wealthy, and upper-class 'joiners'. Survey research shows that people of higher social and economic status are more likely to join voluntary associations, and that the leaders of such associations are generally dominated by the upper strata.
- Some social groups are weakly organised, or largely unorganised – the very poor, children, the homeless, the mentally and physically ill, minority groups.
- Group resources are distributed with cumulative inequality. The class-based nature of the group world ensures that middle-class groups have most of the resources necessary to fight political battles.
- Groups with structural power in the economy (especially business interests) are particularly powerful.
- Groups fight within a political structure that is systematically loaded in favour of middle- and upper-class interests. Government is not a neutral 'referee' in the group battle, but part of a system that favours the wealthy and well organised.
- The group world reflects and reinforces the power structure in which wealthy interests with structural power in the economy dominate the political system.
- Some elite theorists argue that a 'military–industrial complex' controls key decisions, leaving less important issues to pluralist competition.

> **Military–industrial complex** The close and powerful alliance of government, business and military interests that is said by some to run capitalist societies.

Social capital and civil society theory

Social capital theory has a lot in common with pluralist theory. Drawing on Alexis de Tocqueville's (1805–59) influential study of *Democracy in America* (1831), and on modern social science evidence, the American political scientist Robert Putnam (1941–) argues that:

> **Social capital** The features of society such as trust, social norms and social networks, that improve social and governmental efficiency by encouraging cooperation and collective action.

- Voluntary associations – particularly 'bridging' associations that bring different social groups together – are crucial for the development of democratic attitudes, such as trust, reciprocity and satisfaction with democracy, and for democratic behaviour, such as civic engagement, voting and membership of parties. The social trust and the personal and organisational networks that groups create are what make up the social capital on which democracy rests.
- Voluntary organisations teach the political skills of a democracy – how to organise, how to run meetings, how to compromise and how to work and cooperate with others for collective goals.
- Not all social organisations generate 'good' social capital that is beneficial to society as a whole. The Italian mafia, for example, generates 'bad' social capital that is of benefit only for the mafia.
- Putnam's research on Italy and the USA suggests that economic success and democratic stability is rooted in networks of voluntary associations. Democratic malaise (falling election turnout and party membership, declining trust in politicians and government institutions, cheating on taxes, political fear and cynicism) is caused by a decline in the voluntary organisations that generate social capital.

Among the many possible causes of the collapse of civic engagement in the USA, television seems to be important because it pulls people out of their community and isolates them in their homes. TV is said to be responsible for many of the signs of civic and political malaise – distrust, fear, cynicism, alienation, apathy, low political interest and understanding.

Social capital theory has aroused a great deal of interest and controversy. Its critics claim that:

- The definition and treatment of the concept of social capital is vague and all-inclusive.
- Some survey evidence shows that voluntary organisations have rather little effect on political attitudes and behaviour. In any case, which is cause and which is effect?
- Some research suggests that television is not particularly responsible for eroding social capital – on the contrary, television news and current affairs programmes can inform and mobilise people.
- Social capital theory sometimes assumes a 'bottom-up' process in which individuals who join organisations help to create a culture of civic

engagement and democratic participation. A 'top-down' approach argues that governments help to create the conditions in which both voluntary organisations and a climate of trust can flourish.

Writing on **civil society** has much in common with pluralist and social capital theory. It has flourished in the new democracies of central and eastern Europe where the importance of free and independent citizen associations not controlled by the governing regime is emphasised as a basis of democracy. It argues that:

> **Civil society** That arena of social life outside the state, the commercial sector and the family (i.e. mainly voluntary organisations and civic associations) that permits individuals to associate freely and independently of state regulation.

- Strong and vibrant private organisations are essential both for a satisfying social life, and as a counter-balance to the power of the state.
- Transition to democracy depends on building autonomous, private organisations and creating a culture and tradition to sustain them, especially in societies where such organisations have been controlled or suppressed by the state.
- So far, civil society in central and eastern Europe has tended to develop in a different way from western pluralism, in that organisations have formed most readily around nationalist, ethnic and religious interests that have become a force for division and conflict, rather than compromise and integration.

■ What have we learned?

This chapter deals with the key modern pressure groups and social movements. It argues that:

- The importance of the dense network of voluntary organisations as the social basis of pluralist democracy. Politically active groups mediate between citizens and government by aggregating and articulating political interests. Politically inactive groups help to integrate and stabilise society, permitting democratic government to operate effectively.
- Although a vibrant group life is essential for democracy, groups that are too strong are a threat to it. They can 'capture' policy areas and make public decisions that favour their private interests. Strong group pressures from every side may also cause hyper-pluralism and overloaded government.

■ Lessons of comparison

- The ways in which pressure groups work and the influence they exercise are determined by the nature of the groups, their issue(s) and the political and governmental environment in which they operate.
- The difficulties of trying to establish how powerful groups are, because there are usually many factors at work at the same time.

- In most countries, groups have a close relationship with government, ranging from highly formalised and institutionalised corporatist arrangements, to para-government systems, the 'iron triangles' and tight policy communities of tri-partite politics and to the more open policy networks of the most pluralist systems.
- There are arguments both for and against pluralist, Marxist and elitist, social capital and civil society theories of pressure groups politics.

Projects

1. Each student in the group should take a daily paper of their own country and read it for a few days for news items mentioning voluntary organisations and pressure groups. Classify the groups according to whether they seem to be interest/cause, 'insider'/'outsider', peak organisations, episodic/fire brigade, aligned/non-aligned. What, if anything, does this tell you about the likely power of the groups?
2. Voluntary organisations and pressure groups often have good websites. Search the websites in your country for examples of, say, a dozen groups (or for some of the groups mentioned in this chapter), and see what you can find out about the political activity or inactivity of the groups, how they operate and with what success.
3. Do you think pressure groups are good for democracy or help to undermine it?

Further reading

Graham K. Wilson, *Interest Groups.* Oxford: Blackwell, 1990.
A good introduction to the comparative approach to the subject.

Todd Landman, *Issues and Methods in Comparative Politics.* London: Routledge, 2000.
Chapter 5 and 6 contain an excellent summary of some two dozen studies of social movements.

Clive S. Thomas (ed.), *First World Interest Groups: A Comparative Perspective.* Westport, CT: Greenwood Press, 1993.
One of the few comparative books on pressure groups.

Robert Putnam, *Making Democracy Work: Civic Traditions in Modern Italy.* Princeton: Princeton University Press, 1993; and *Bowling Alone: The Collapse and Revival of American Community.* New York: Simon & Schuster, 2000.
Two of the original and classic studies of social capital.

Websites

www.politicalresources.net/
Lists organisations in many countries, and has a long list of international
organisations.
www.uia.org/index.html
The Union of International Associations lists international organisations.
www.psr.keele.ac.uk/parties.htm
Website with many links to international and national parties, interest groups
and social movements.
http://lcweb2.loc.gov/frd/cs/
A useful website, though now slightly out of date, with brief accounts of the
pressure group system in about 100 countries.
www.psr.keele.ac.uk/sseal/index.htm
Another web portal with links to a large number and wide variety of political
organisations.

11 The mass media

The role of the mass media in modern democracy is one of the most controversial topics in politics. Politicians are usually locked in a 'love–hate' relationship with the political media, and the media seem to play an ever-larger part in political life. Political scientists dispute whether the mass media are powerful or not, and whether their impact on politics is good or bad for democracy:

- On the one hand, the mass media are supposed to play a crucial role in supplying citizens with a full and fair account of the news and a wide range of political opinion about it.
- On the other hand, the media are often criticised for being systematically biased politically, and for their growing but unaccountable power.

In theory, a free press and television should be the watchdogs of democratic politics; in practice, some analysts believe, they are as much a threat to democratic government as a protector of it.

The dilemmas posed by the modern media raise all sorts of political problems. What is the proper role of the media in democracy, and do they perform in the appropriate manner? Given their political importance, how should they be organised? They should certainly not come under the control of government because that would be undemocratic, and this leaves two main alternatives:

- They could come under the regulation of public bodies not controlled by the government, to keep them accountable and responsible to the general public
- Or they could be constrained only by the economic forces of the market.

To what extent are the mass media pluralist – in the hands of many owners who communicate a wide range of political opinion – or are they increasingly under the control of a few conservative media moguls and MNCs? Do the mass media wield great influence over public opinion and the fate of political leaders, or are they relatively weak because market forces oblige them to follow public opinion rather than mould it? What impact will the new electronic media play in politics, and will they hasten the trend towards globalisation?

The major topics in this chapter are:

- The mass media and democracy
- Regulating the media
- Ownership and control
- The impact of the new media technology
- Theories of the mass media.

■ The mass media and democracy

The mass media are supposed to play a vital role in a democracy. The great majority of us rely almost entirely on them for political news and opinion, and the role we are able to play as citizens depends heavily on the fairness, accuracy and balance of the news we get. We cannot make sensible judgements about politics if we are fed a diet of biased, superficial and inaccurate news, and if the range of political opinion expressed in the media is narrow and shallow. This means that the news media should provide citizens with a full and fair account of the news and a wide variety of political opinion about it. If democracy is founded on the peaceful struggle between competing interests and ideas, then we all need full information about these interests and ideas in order to make up our mind about the political issues of the day.

In the same way that the political system should be pluralist – permitting the competition of many political interests and groups – so also should the media be pluralist, reporting a full range of political opinion and interpreting the news from a variety of political standpoints. In turn, this means that the political media must not be controlled by governments, nor must they be dominated by a narrow set of commercial or social interests that presents only one political position. The news media should not only be accurate in their reporting of the news, but open and pluralist in their presentation of opinion about it.

The importance of the media is magnified by the fact that they are not just channels of communication that simply convey news, but major political players:

- There is so much news in the world that the media must choose what to report and what not to report, and what to make the headline article or tuck away on the back page.
- The news media help to shape the news. They want to influence the course of public affairs, not merely report them. In some countries, they take up strong political positions on issues, they support this or that party and they attack or defend this or that political leader. In others, their partisanship is more muted, but still present.
- The mass media are important socialising agents that have an impact on how people think and behave politically.
- The mass media, some claim, are replacing parties as the main means of informing and mobilising citizens (see chapter 13).
- The mass media are even said to be replacing legislatures as the main arena of political debate so that we are now living in 'teledemocracies'.

None of this is made any easier by the fact that the mass media would face contradictory dilemmas and demands even if they operated in a perfectly pluralist fashion:

- Democracy requires that citizens are provided with a comprehensive coverage of the political news, but the evidence suggests that many are bored by this and would rather watch films or game shows, or read gossip and sports columns.
- The news should be scrupulously accurate, but it is extremely difficult to achieve high standards, given increasingly rushed news deadlines.
- The news media must choose what to report, and what to ignore. What is important and, what is not, is a contested matter.
- The media must offer news and opinion – facts and judgements about the facts. The news should be detached and neutral, but opinion is engaged and subjective. How can the political media be both? The usual answer is that the media should separate facts (the news) from opinion (editorial and opinion pieces), but this is either difficult or impossible, depending on whether you think there can be objective reporting or not.
- The news media must resist the pressures of **spin-doctors** who work for governments, parties and groups, and try to get the media to report their views. It is quicker, easier and cheaper to rely on their nicely packaged press releases than to delve into issues and probe behind the spin-doctors' version of them.

Spin-doctors Public relations specialists employed to put the best possible light on news about their clients. The term often implies people whose job is to manipulate the news.

- The mass media should be critical of politicians, when they feel it necessary, but they are often criticised by politicians for not being 'fair and impartial'. The problem is that journalists may feel that being 'fair and impartial' means getting to the truth of the matter, while politicians feel that it means simply reporting accurately and fully what they say.

In sum, the mass media are very important in democratic politics, but their role is riddled with dilemmas, contradictions and problems. Individuals depend upon the fairness, impartiality and accuracy of the news in order to play their role as informed citizens in a democracy. At the same time, the mass media do not, and cannot, merely report news. They have to decide what it is – and, besides, many newspaper and TV stations want to be a power and influence politics, not just report it. They are active players in politics, and major ones at that, not just passive conveyors of political information. Their central part in democratic politics raises the question of how they should be organised to best play their role. Should they be controlled or regulated in the public interest, or should they be left to run themselves as they think best?

◼ Regulating the media

The public service model

There are two main answers to the question of how to organise the mass media. One recommends a **public service model** for the electronic media, the other a market model for all mass mediums, whether electronic or not. The merits of the public service and market models are a hotly debated topic in politics (see controversy 11.1).

> **Public service model** The system of granting broadcasting licences to public bodies, usually supported by public funds, for use in the public interest rather than for profit.

The media market has long been recognised as divided between the print and the electronic media. The print media consist of newspapers, journals and magazines, while the electronic media cover radio, television and the web. In principle, anyone can publish a paper, magazine or newsletter (many student organisations do), and desk-top publishing has made this easier. Electronic communication is different. Until recently, broadcasting frequencies for radio and television were limited by **spectrum scarcity**. Spectrum scarcity means that radio and TV broadcasting was a natural monopoly or oligopoly. Since broadcasting waves were a scarce public asset of great public importance it was argued that they should be regulated in the public interest. Consequently, in the early days of radio and TV, most democracies controlled and regulated broadcasting according to the public service model. This has six main characteristics:

> **Spectrum scarcity** The shortage of terrestrial broadcasting frequencies for radio and TV, which meant that there could be only a few channels.

> **Market regulation** The regulation of the media market by public bodies.

1. *Market regulation* Spectrum scarcity makes a competitive market in electronic broadcasting impossible, so the state set up **market regulation** for

CONTROVERSY 11.1

Public service versus commercial media?

For the public service model
- The market does not ensure that truth will prevail, or that the best ideas will survive, only that popular demand is satisfied.
- News and political opinion is not a commodity, like soap powder, or something that can be road-tested, like motor cars. It is not subject to the same laws of supply and demand as consumer durables or commercial services.
- Only regulation in the public interest can ensure balanced, accurate, and impartial news reporting. To leave the news media to the market is to hand it over to a few multi-millionaire media moguls, or to MNCs that are often right-wing, resulting in strong and systematic media bias.
- The dangers of state control of the media can be, and have been, avoided by using regulators that are not controlled by government or the state (QUANGOs, see below).
- Bad media drive out the good, or force the good to adopt low standards. Commercial news reporting is often of a low standard (tabloid newspapers and 'tabloid TV'). TV news is often poor in the most commercial countries (e.g. the USA), and best in those that have retained important elements of public service broadcasting (Germany, Scandinavia). The amount of 'hard news' on American TV has fallen, commercial pressures have cut budgets for news programmes, and there is little coverage of international politics.
- The state must step in to exercise market and content regulation where market failure or spectrum scarcity results in oligopoly or monopoly.
- The commercial media are not necessarily politically free. They can be subject to powerful commercial and political pressures.

For the market model
- The public service model stifles innovation and is patronising – it gives the public what broadcasters think they need, rather than what they want.
- Whatever their faults, the commercial forces of the market are better than government or independent regulation of the media.
- The end of spectrum scarcity means that the electronic media market is the same as that of the print media, and should be subject to the same regulatory principles – minimal content regulation and market regulation only to avoid market failure.
- Regulation of the political media is not consistent with free speech. Regulation by agencies that are theoretically independent of government merely means 'backdoor regulation' by government, if only because it controls funds for public broadcasting.
- Low standards of journalism and news reporting are better than government control, regulation, or manipulation of the mass media.
- Market competition ensures that all main bodies of opinion will get a hearing, and that there will be free competition of ideas.

radio and TV, usually by giving broadcasting licenses to organisations that are required to operate under public interest rules.

2. *Content regulation* When spectrum scarcity meant that there were only a few radio and TV stations, it was thought necessary to regulate not just the market, but also the content of public broadcasting. Since there were

only a few radio and TV stations, and since they operated under licences issued by public bodies, broadcasters were required to abide by **content regulation** – public interest rules about what they broadcast. In terms of politics this meant a full, fair and impartial treatment of the news and shared time for the political parties, especially at election time, so that all sides were given an equal hearing.

> **Content regulation** Regulation of the content of the media by public bodies in the public interest.

3. *Self-regulation, or regulation by QUANGOs* If public broadcasting agencies were to avoid the danger of state regulation of the news, they should be self-regulating or regulated by public bodies that are independent of government. Such bodies, known as **'QUANGOs'**, operate at 'arm's length' from government.

> **QUANGOs** Organisations that are partially or wholly funded by the government to perform public service functions but not under direct government control.

4. *Public funding* Public service broadcasting is funded, partially or wholly, by public funds, and is not dependent upon profit.
5. *Education, information and entertainment* Public service broadcasting involves a wide range of programmes, including news and current affairs and educational and cultural programmes, as well as entertainment. It serves the public interest, rather than responding to market forces.
6. *National broadcasting* The function of public broadcasting is to serve the nation, including its minorities (linguistic, cultural and regional) and to serve as a focus for national identity. It works best within states rather than over the global broadcasting system.

Broadly speaking, the public service model of radio and TV operated in many western democracies from the start of radio broadcasting in the 1920s up to the 1970s.

The market model

The print media, in contrast to radio and TV under spectrum scarcity, are usually subject to market regulation only when there is a danger of forming an oligopoly or monopoly. Newspapers in some countries are subsidised or protected by the state (see briefing 11.1) but in the great majority they are wholly commercial enterprises. The reason is that the print media are thought to be no different from any other kind of competitive commercial market, which means that they should operate without public regulation, except in cases of market failure. In these circumstances, a monopolies board or commission is entitled to intervene in order to establish a competitive market. Similarly, since the print media are thought to be open and competitive, their political content should also be unregulated, partly because there is no obvious need for content regulation, as there is for radio and TV under spectrum scarcity, and partly because of the principle of free speech (freedom of the press). The market

Briefing 11.1

Newspaper subsidies in Norway

Daily newspapers are considered an essential commodity in Norway, in their contribution not only to the workings of democracy but also to cultural life. In relation to its population, Norway probably has Europe's highest number of dailies, with each town, as well as more sparsely settled districts, provided with a local paper.

In order to sustain such a press, Norway has developed a resource-consuming system of public support, in the form of subsidies towards paper, government advertising, direct grants, loan arrangements and cheaper distribution. Certain newspapers may receive annual subsidies of up to 20 million Norwegian Kroner. In addition, the Norwegian daily press is exempt from VAT. It has been calculated that subsidies to the press as a whole account for about 20 per cent of all newspaper income.

(www.reisenett.no/norway/facts/culture_science/
culture_under_int_pressure.html)

model therefore recognises some need for market regulation to guarantee market competition but sees little or no need for political content regulation.

Since the 1980s, however, the distinction between the print and electronic media has broken down. New broadcasting technology has effectively ended spectrum scarcity. There are now many different national and local radio stations, an increasing number of terrestrial TV channels and a rapid growth of cable and satellite channels. If one adds to this the new forms of communication in the shape of DVDs, e-mail, the net and text messaging, then the electronic media market is increasingly pluralist and competitive. There is, so the argument goes, no longer any need for the market and content regulation of the old spectrum scarcity days. In principle, it is claimed, the market for news and political opinion is no different from that for washing powder or motor cars. News is a commodity like any other and should be produced and consumed, so far as possible, according to unregulated market forces. Indeed, increasingly global broadcasting makes it more and more difficult for states even to attempt such regulation. How can states regulate satellite TV or the internet?

Technological change has resulted in a rapid shift towards the organisation of the mass media according to market principles. This means that the news media are increasingly driven by the commercial pressures of profit. Many commercial radio and TV stations have been created and some of the old public services stations privatised. The electronic media have joined the print media in being largely unregulated so far as both market and content are concerned.

In many countries, however, this has resulted not in the wholesale adoption of the market model but in a mixed model that combines increasingly commercial principles with some forms of public service funding and regulation (see fact file 11.1 and briefing 11.2). The mixed model applies mainly to electronic media, with the print media left largely to the market. Even in

Fact file 11.1

The political media

- Public service broadcasting had a monopoly in most of western Europe and the USA until the 1960s, when it was increasingly commercialised. By 1990 there were more commercial than public TV stations.
- The public service model is strongest in Austria, Denmark, Finland, Norway, Sweden, Switzerland and Germany. Belgium, the Czech Republic, Greece, Japan, the Netherlands, Portugal, Turkey, Greece, Italy and the USA are largely private.
- Many of the second- and third-third wave democracies swept away rigid state control and censorship of the media in favour of commercial media. A few, however, retained elements of the old state system, running them in parallel with commercial radio and TV stations.
- Private and commercial media systems are not necessarily politically free. There are some wholly commercial systems in non-democratic countries (Ecuador) and some of the new democracies have commercial media that are influenced, heavily influenced or even intimidated by government pressure.
- Newspaper sales and the number of daily newspaper titles are increasing around the globe (2.7 per cent and 2.9 per cent respectively in 2007). A total of 532 million papers are sold in the world every day – 99 million in India, 68 million in Japan, 50 million in the USA and 20.6 million in Germany.
- Most media systems in the world's democracies are now a public–private mix, although a few are wholly private and commercial. Public service TV stations operate in many countries, and state laws and regulations are widely applied to the broadcasting of news and current affairs programmes to ensure a fair and balanced reporting of the news. For example, all TV stations in Mexico must give a certain amount of broadcasting time to the government.

Briefing 11.2

The mass media systems: Finland, Bolivia and Japan

■ Finland – a pluralist system

Finland has a tradition of an independent and pluralist press dating back to the late eighteenth century, and for a country of 5.2 million it has an amazingly large and diverse media system – 200 newspapers (30 dailies), a mixed set of public and private TV channels (12) and national and local radio stations (76), 12,000 book titles a year, and high use of the internet. Finland has one of the highest newspaper circulations in the world. More than 80 per cent of Finns read a newspaper every day, and 60 per cent say that they are their main source of news. The state helps with tax concessions for publishers and subsidies for party newspapers and other quality magazines. There is increasing concentration of ownership and control of the media, especially of newspapers. Two large newspaper chains had emerged by 2000. As more media outlets are created, so the audience for each one has declined and the total media market is more fragmented. There is a variety of news agencies, public, private and party affiliated. Audiences for public television are large by international standards, but all TV and radio stations devote a good deal of their time to news and current affairs. Citizens who feel injured by press reports can appeal to the Council for the Mass Media, which has the power to fine and order a rejoinder. International comparison suggests that Finland's media are of high quality and reflect the main current of Finland's political life. The tone is perhaps best described as consensus seeking and civilised rather than aggressive and muck-raking.

■ Boliva – from authoritarian control to semi-free, semi-pluralist media

Up to the mid-1980s the Bolivian media were subject to harsh censorship and state control, but when these were eased competing newspapers and radio and TV stations quickly appeared. Almost fifty TV stations were broadcasting in 1989, and together with five national daily papers they reflected the main party political and religious interests. The media system is largely private but ownership is concentrated and, with low literacy rates, radio is important, especially in rural areas. According to Reporters Without Borders, an organisation campaigning for press and journalist freedom, Bolivia enjoys greater formal press freedom than many of its Latin American neighbours, but journalists and editors are constrained in their reporting of party politics, drugs and corruption because they have suffered violence for doing so.

■ Japan – pluralism with self-censorship

Japan has one of the very highest newspaper readerships in the world and a rapidly diversifying media system, including six major national papers, over 100 local papers, and many public and private TV channels and radio stations. The daily circulation of newspapers is 72 million. TV and radio coverage of news is comprehensive, and the public stations are balanced and factual, avoiding editorialising and commentary. The private print media can be critical of the government and reports stories about corruption in high places among politicians, bureaucrats and businessmen, but at the same time the free reporting of news is restricted by the tight organisation of 'kisha clubs', which are private (and often, it seems, secret) clubs in government, business and politics. They exercise strong informal pressures on their members that amount to systematic self-censorship. Investigative reporting is comparatively rare and mostly done by journalists outside the main media corporations and kisha clubs.

Sources: compiled from a variety of sources including Reporters Without Frontiers (www.rsf.org/), the Federal Research Division of the Library of Congress (http://countrystudies.us/), BBC Country profiles (http:// news.bbc.co.uk/2/hi/country_profiles/default.stm), Pressreferences.com (www.pressreference.com/) and individual country reports.

the most commercial systems, however, there is still a fair amount of public regulation, which takes two main forms:

1. *Regulation to ensure market competition* Cross-media ownership is often restricted, parts of the mass communications system thought to be

essential to national interest are kept in national hands and attempts are made to prevent monopolies and oligopolies. The rules are being progressively relaxed because of economic forces.

2. *Content regulation* Some public service channels are required to observe strict rules to ensure political fairness and balance, and some commercial channels follow the same rules. There is still a lot of content regulation over things such as cigarette advertising, pornography and the amount, content, and distribution of advertising.

If the media market was, indeed, competitive, as the market model supposes, we might leave this part of the story happily at this point. Unfortunately, however, there is a very large fly in the ointment. Increasingly, the commercial mass media are moving towards greater concentration of ownership and control in a few oligopolistic hands.

■ Ownership and control

Since the 1950s, the mass media market has developed in six related ways, with far-reaching implications for the workings of democratic government:

1. *Fragmentation of specialist media markets* Modern technology has made it possible for small, niche media to become increasingly specialised and varied. Local TV and radio, satellite and cable broadcasting, desk-top publishing, and especially the web have made it possible to tap into ever-smaller and more specialised markets. A look at the magazines for sale in a high street shop will show how many specialised products there are.

2. *Concentration of ownership and control of the mass market* Modern technology has made it possible for the mass media to reach larger and wider audiences around the globe but this, in turn, has vastly increased the capital costs of production and distribution. In this respect, the mass communications business is like other industries that grow in size and costs. The motor industry, for example, is moving towards a few major global producers of 'world cars', which will force even huge companies to merge to be able to compete. So it is with the mass media. Their history is one of mergers and takeovers, increasing concentration of ownership and control, to the point where pluralist and competitive markets have been replaced by a small number of giant media empires.

> **Cross-media ownership** When the same person or company has financial interests in different branches of mass communication – e.g. when they own a newspaper and a TV channel, or a publishing house and a TV network.

3. *Multi-media conglomeration* Many media companies collect together many different media businesses that span the range of publishing, music, films, radio, TV and the net. This is known as cross-media ownership or **multi-media conglomeration** (see below).

4. *Horizontal and vertical integration* Conglomeration entails the vertical integration of the communications industry, so that the same company controls all aspects of the financing, production, distribution and marketing

of its products. It also means companies move sideways into closely related industries. Film, music, DVD, CD-Rom, radio, newspaper, the web and magazine businesses feed off each other economically, so media companies increasingly stretch to cover them all. They also expand to cover spin-off businesses such as theme parks, entertainment and leisure centres, professional sports clubs and chains of shops.

5. *The integration of the media with other business activities* There is nothing new about a few media moguls dominating press or TV, but in the past they have usually confined their interests to the communications business. Multi-media conglomerates are now increasingly incorporated into a wide range of industrial and commercial activities, making it difficult to distinguish between the mass communications business and 'big business' in general.

6. *Internationalisation* Communications technology has produced a borderless world. Media conglomerates are no longer limited to countries or continents, but span the whole globe.

These six interwoven trends are illustrated in briefing 11.3, which provides information about Time Warner, the world's largest communications conglomerate. Less detailed information about smaller media companies is in briefing 11.4.

There are two main democratic dangers due to increasing global concentration of ownership and control:

- First, giant communications corporations are increasingly beyond public accountability and wield growing power without responsibility.
- Second, pluralist competition is weakened, placing the news media in the hands of a few business corporations with similar social, political and economic interests: in some countries, competition has largely disappeared. It is pluralist competition that is supposed to ensure that the general public gets a diverse diet of news and opinion in the political media. Instead, the multi-media moguls and multi-national corporations that increasingly control the news media are likely to restrict the public agenda to one that favours their interests. In short the problem with the market model is that it assumes market competition, but this is in rapid decline.

Once again, we cannot leave our story here. Media technology is changing incredibly rapidly and it seems likely to revolutionise itself all over again in the next generation when the full potential of interactive multi-media is realised. Some experts argue that this will transform the political media.

■ The impact of the new media technology: globalisation and E-politics

Communications are no longer limited by national boundaries; they are no longer merely international, but global. Journalists can dispatch reports and

Briefing 11.3

Mass media ownership: the case of Time Warner

When the publishing and film company Time Warner merged with the internet company America On Line (AOL) in 2000, it marked the fusion of the 'old' media and the 'new' and the creation of the largest communications corporation in the world. With revenues of close to $44.7 billion, the company has interests in films, music, publishing, television, the internet, sports, leisure and entertainment and other commercial holdings across the globe. Its media interests (some in association with other companies) include:

Magazines

More than sixty-five magazines with almost 300 million readers including *Time, People*, MAD, *Sports Illustrated, Golf Magazine, Yachting Magazine, Money, Entertainment Weekly, In Style, Fortune, Asiaweek, Popular Science* and The Health Publishing Group and IPC (a large magazine publisher in the UK)

Television

Wholly- or partly-owned channels in the USA, Europe, Asia and Latin America: Warner Bros, HBO, Cinemax, CBS, TNT, Cartoon Network, Turner Classics, CNN

Cable

HBO, CNN, Court TV and Time Warner

Internet

America On Line, CompuServe, Netscape, ICQ, Spinner, Winamp

TIME WARNER

Films

Warner Bros, Hanna-Barbera Cartoons, The Warner Channel (on five continents), Warner Theaters (in twelve countries), the library of MGM, RKO, and pre-1960 Warner films

Sports

Atlanta Braves, Atlanta Hawks, Goodwill games, Phillips Arena

Music

More than 200 labels in fifty-four countries, including Warner Bros. Reprise, Elektra, Rhino, Atlantic, MCM, Nonesuch and music publishing, packaging and distributing companies

Books

Publishing houses including Warner Books, Time-Life, Book-of-the-Month Club, Little Brown

Theme parks

Warner Bros. Movie World Theme Park, Warner Bros. Recreational Enterprises

Other

Time Warner Telecom, Sportsline Radio, Studio Stores, iAmaze, Streetmail, DC Comics License Rights

Derived from www.cjr.org/tools/owners, www.fair.org/extra/9711/gmg.html; www.thenation.com/special/bigten.html.

Briefing 11.4

Global communications corporations

Much of what we see, hear, or read in the mass communications media is produced and provided by only a few gargantuan multi-media, multi-national media **conglomerates** (see below). Time Warner is the largest in the world (see briefing 11.3), but others have huge interests in the communications industry, either alone or jointly with other companies. Many of

> **Conglomerates** Single business organisations consisting of a number of different companies that operate in different economic fields.

the largest corporations are joint ventures (JVs). The following are among the largest after Time Warner:

- **General Electric** $176.6 billion revenues in 2008. Twenty-eight TV stations and networks in the USA, Europe and Latin America (including NBC and CNBC); TV production and programming; twelve film companies (Universal Pictures); leisure and entertainment in the USA and Europe; sports (New York Knicks, New York Rangers, Madison Square Garden); four large film production and distribution companies with rights to 4,000 films and 40,000 TV episodes; military production (F-16 fighter, Abrams tank, Apache helicopter, U2 bomber); consumer and commercial finance companies in thirty-five countries.
- **AT&T Corporation** $119 billion revenues in 2007. Television stations and networks; TV distribution in 175 countries; cable TV; forty-three radio stations; music; cell phones; theme parks.
- **Sony** $78.5 billion revenues in 2007. Financial interests in television networks (in India, Japan, Latin America, Spain and the USA) and eight TV stations; film production and distribution companies (Columbia Pictures); music (including Columbia, Epic and Sony) and recording studios; internet services; electronics equipment, games, tapes, disks; insurance and credit financing; shops.
- **Liberty Media** A spin-off from AT&T in 2001, this company has assets of $47.6 billion in 2007. Interests in TV networks (Discovery, Animal Planet, Fox International Sports, TV Guide Channel and in eight cable and satellite systems); fourteen TV stations; the largest cable operator in Japan and cable interests in Europe; TV production; seventy radio stations in north America; more than 100 magazines; films; sports clubs; internet services; other holdings in car hire, phone services and chains of shops in Europe, Japan and South America.
- **Vivendi** Originally French, now global, $37 billion revenues. Books (Houghton Mifflin) and magazines; TV production and distribution in Australia, Brazil, France, Italy, Japan and the USA (Canal Plus, Cineplex Odeon, United Cinemas); music (Decca, Deutsche, MCA, Polygram, Grammophon, Universal Music, which has the largest catalogue of recorded music in the world); the production and distribution of CDs, DVDs and video games and software; telecommunications and internet access in Britain, France, Germany, Hungary, Italy, Kenya, Morocco, Poland and Spain; websites and music subscription services; theme parks, hotels and entertainment centres; recycling and incineration plant; commercial and industrial cleaning; rail networks; bottled water; transport; heating; advertising agencies.

pictures from almost any part of the world which can be broadcast almost instantaneously to millions of people. TV audiences for the 2006 World Cup were as high as 400 million. Some soap operas have a world-wide appeal, and some programmes (*Big Brother, Idols, Dancing with the Stars*) are replicated in many countries. There are only three major news agencies in the world (Agence France Presse, Associated Press and Reuters), which distribute the vast majority of international news material to the national media. In this sense, the 'global broadcasting village' is a fact now, not something waiting just around the corner.

The consequences of this are sometimes said to be revolutionary. Soon, it is claimed, we will all be watching the same TV news coverage of the same international events, even as we now concentrate on the American election, the Iraq war, the Olympic Games and the financial problems of Wall Street. The new technology is also said to be transforming old patterns of political participation because new social groups adept with the new technology – especially the computer-literate young – will use it to become informed and involved. The newest technology will make it possible to use the interactive information super-highway to engage in direct democracy. It is also claimed in some circles that the new technology will fragment the mass media market as it has the specialist market.

These arguments are appealing, but we must be careful not to exaggerate the impact of global communications technology. Most of the world's population has yet to make its first phone call, much less send a text message, use a computer or call up a website. TV saturates the wealthy democracies, but not the poorer ones which still lag behind, especially in access to cable and satellite. Computer use is further behind, even in some of the comparatively wealthy OECD countries. In some of the poorer democracies internet use is still limited to a tiny minority (see table 11.1).

In the early years of international cable and satellite TV news (BBC World News, CNBC, CNN) it looked as if the English language would dominate the world. However, the trend since the 1980s has been to broadcast TV news in local languages and to tailor it to the interests of local populations (Arabic speakers in the Middle East, Cantonese-speaking Chinese, Hindi-speaking Indians and Portuguese-speaking Brazilians). The days when we all watch the same CNN–CNBC–BBC news in the same language are further away than before. Not only have international TV news channels opted for more regional broadcasting, but national TV is also becoming less international. A majority in most countries still watches national programmes of all kinds, especially national news. The penetration of global TV is still rather limited, and national TV stations are increasingly relying on domestic, not imported TV programmes. Although it has a 'global reach', the new communications technology does not have a 'global grasp', and, if anything, its grip on world markets seems at the moment to be weakening.

Although most people watch TV news in the advanced democracies, and increasing numbers access news on the web, the newspaper market is still strong and actually growing around the globe. Research shows that those who are most interested in politics generally rely more heavily on their paper than on TV news, and regular newspaper readers are generally better informed

Table 11.1 *Newspaper readership, TV ownership and internet users: selected democracies, 2000–2004*

	Newspaper circulation per thousand inhabitants	TV ownership (% of population)	Internet access (% of population)
High			
Denmark	283.2	59.4	69.4
Norway	569.0	46.2	69.2
Sweden	409.5	51.9	69.0
Australia	161.0	55.5	66.0
Netherlands	279.5	51.9	64.0
USA	196.3	80.6	64.0
Middle			
France	142.1	59.5	43.8
Greece	43.2	24.0	35.6
Estonia	191.6	41.8	30.7
Hungary	162.3	43.5	30.3
Bulgaria	172.9	39.4	21.8
Low			
Namibia	17.2	3.7	2.3
Botswana	24.9	2.0	2.1
Ghana	13.9	9.3	1.0
Bolivia	110.4	11.6	0.9
El Salvador	28.5	67.7	0.6
Benin	5.4	1.1	0.4

Source: Computer Industry Almanac, *World Factbook* (http://www.cia.gov/library/publications/the-world-factbook) and UNESCO Institute for Statistics (http://data.un.org/Data.aspx?d=UNESCO&f=srID%3A25650).

about politics. It should be noted (table 11.1) that newspaper reading is most widespread in the old democracies which are also the wealthy ones with the greatest density of television sets, computers and web access. The new media, it seems, have not driven out the old.

The old communications technology, especially the printed word, was associated with the 'knowledge gap'. This gap increasingly separates those with the education to understand and keep up with political developments, and understand them, from those who have neither the education nor the inclination to do so. Some commentators argue that new electronic communications will break down the 'knowledge gap' because different social groups will use them to inform themselves and become politically active. Some of the young who are not in the habit of newspaper reading will pick up political news and opinion from the net, and perhaps from

> **Knowledge gap** The gap between those with a good education and understanding of the world, which enables them to acquire knowledge and understanding at a faster rate than those with less education and understanding.

text messages and e-mail. Political parties have started to use text messaging websites in their election campaigns. Can the new technology break down the old patterns and bridge the knowledge gap?

So far, there is little evidence that it will. In fact, the new technology has generally reinforced the old patterns because the wealthy and educated have been the first to use it. Political elites in most democracies have so far also made rather little use of interactive, multi-media communications for political purposes. Some governments in the wealthiest democracies have started to explore some of the possibilities, but their efforts are modest and unimaginative so far. However, it is early days, and things may change as the new technology spreads and even newer technologies are introduced. One striking new pattern is that the youngest generations are using multi-media communications most and things may change as they move into positions of political influence. Meanwhile, E-politics has still to be fully exploited in modern democracies.

■ Theories of the mass media

Everyone is an expert mass media theorist because everyone is exposed to the mass media in huge doses. Unfortunately, everyone's theory differs from the others:

- Some claim that the mass media are extraordinarily powerful in political life, others that they are weak.
- Some believe that they are a 'good' thing because they inform and educate politically, others that they are nothing but a corrupting political influence.
- Some are convinced that the mass media have a left-wing or 'liberal' bias, others are just as strongly convinced of their right-wing bias.
- Many assume that the mass media affect others but not themselves, since they believe they are too intelligent and well-informed to be taken in by bias, propaganda and superficial sensationalism. It is always the others who are stupid.

Before we consider sorts of claims, however, we should pause to consider how difficult it is to establish clear-cut media effects on political attitudes, opinions and institutions. Four methodological problems stand in the way:

1. The mass media are only one of the many influences on our lives, which include the family, education, work and the community. Media effects are tangled up with these other influences and it is virtually impossible to sort out their independent influence. Educated people are usually better informed about politics and more active, and they also spend more time with their newspaper and TV news. Is their knowledge and activity the result of education or news media exposure, if either? Perhaps their political family background causes all three?

2. It is impossible to generalise about the impact of the media. There are many different media and they probably have different effects on different kinds of people. Watching TV news and current affairs programmes has a different political impact from watching entertainment TV. Reading a quality newspaper is different from reading a popular newspaper. Using the web's political pages is different from using its shopping and pop music sites. Most generalisations about 'the effects of the media' are too wide-ranging.

3. The mass media and their audiences are linked by interdependence. The media select their audiences and tune their messages to appeal to them. Some papers are designed for intelligent and educated readers, some for a different market. Audiences also select the paper they read, if they decide to read one at all, just as they select the TV they watch and the websites they surf. The mutual adjustment of media to audiences and audiences to media makes it difficult to know what comes first, the chicken or the egg.

4. It is very difficult to measure the effects of television, the most important of all the mass media, because we have so few control groups which are not exposed to TV. Just as fish will be the last form of life on earth to discover water because they are completely surrounded by it and know of nothing else, so we find it difficult to know the effects of TV.

Each of these methodological problems is severe, and all of them together make it difficult to say anything with much confidence about media effects. This helps to explain why we can all hold our pet theories of the media: who can challenge them with hard and conclusive evidence? It also helps to explain why political scientists themselves cannot agree: how can they design research projects to answer the key questions when there are so many methodological difficulties? This helps to explain why there are four distinct theories of media effects:

1. *Reinforcement theory* **Reinforcement theory** argues that the mass media have minimal effects. Bound by the 'golden chains' of the market, they reflect and reinforce mass opinion, rather than creating it. The theory is built around four points:

> **Reinforcement theory** The theory that the mass media can only reflect and reinforce public opinion, not create or mould it.

   (a) In the same way that supermarkets sell what their customers want and are willing to pay for, so the mass media give customers what they want.
   (b) Audiences select what they want from the media, often to fit their pre-existing attitudes and predispositions (self-selection).
   (c) Individuals have a wide range of psychological mechanisms for handling media messages, including projecting their own beliefs (projection), forgetting unwanted messages (suppression), misinterpreting (distortion) and refusing to believe what they don't like (rejection).
   (d) Competitive media systems have a wide variety of channels of communication and present a variety of political views, allowing audiences to pick and choose what they like best.

2. *Agenda setting* **Agenda setting** theory argues that the media cannot determine what we think, but they can and do influence strongly what we think about. The mass media often cover particular issues intensively for a time, and such 'feeding frenzies' help to put the issues on the agenda, or climb up it. Examples include the Monica Lewinsky affair in the

   > **Agenda setting** The process by which a multiplicity of political problems and issues are continuously sorted according to the changing priority attached to them.

   USA, the Iraq war, international terrorism, the death of Princess Diana and ecological disasters and famines such as the Bhopal chemical leak in 1984. The persistent interest of the press in crime is said to make people more afraid of it than is justified by the crime figures. There is some evidence that journalists create their own 'echo chamber' in which they follow each other's lead and concentrate on the same news items.

3. *Priming and framing* Recent theories argue that the mass media have an influence over how the public see and evaluate politics, but in a subtle and indirect way. Imagine an election in which party *A* is thought to be good on domestic matters, while party *B* is better at foreign affairs. If the press emphasises domestic matters then the public is primed to think about an issue that favours party *A*. This is called **priming**.

   > **Priming** The theory that the mass media can prime us to focus on certain things and in certain ways by highlighting some issues rather than others.

   Similarly issues can be presented in ways that affect their political impact. This is **framing**. For example, a TV programme on homelessness might be presented in terms of figures and trends that relate homelessness to unemployment, poverty, or housing supply. It might also present it as a human issue, presenting an in-depth life history of a homeless person. The former is more likely

   > **Framing** The theory that the way news stories are set up (framed) influences how audiences interpret them.

   to incline people to think that homelessness is linked to government policies, while the latter will present it as a personal issue associated with the characteristics of drunkenness, laziness, or individual inadequacy. Human interest stories, it is argued, tend to absolve politicians and governments of responsibility.

4. *Direct effects* A large body of literature argues that the mass media have a strong and direct effect on politics, especially on the attitudes and behaviour of citizens and political leaders, but there is strong disagreement about what the effects actually are. Some argue that the effects are beneficial, because increasing educational levels are allied with ever-increasing amounts of news and political information, at lower and lower prices. This has the effect of cognitively mobilising citizens and increasing political awareness and interest, at least for some sections of the population (see chapter 9). For example, there is evidence showing that, other things being equal, those who watch TV news regularly are better informed about politics than those who do not. Newspaper reading has a bigger

impact on political knowledge, but only for quality papers with their range of political information.

Others argue, on the contrary, that media effects are pernicious and have coined the term 'mediamalaise' to describe them. Market competition and the pursuit of profits force the media to adopt the worst standards of sensational, trivial and superficial journalism (soundbites and photo-opportunities). The obsession with bad news in the form of crime, political corruption, scandal, disaster and political incompetence creates a dismal view of the world (the 'mean world' effect). If journalists cannot find political conflict, they create it. Their highly critical style ('attack journalism') undermines politicians and political institutions. Since news is a highly perishable commodity the media are constantly searching for 'new news', so the public is presented with a bewildering flow of news and information that it cannot understand (the 'fast-forward effect'). Television is said to undermine both 'social capital' and community life (see chapter 10). In short, the modern media are said to create widespread political cynicism, distrust, suspicion, apathy and dissatisfaction with government, and even with democracy itself.

> **Mediamalaise** The attitudes of political cynicism, despair, apathy, distrust and disillusionment (among others) that some social scientists claim are caused by the mass media, especially TV.

One theory that assumes that the mass media have direct effects on attitudes and opinions concerns what is termed 'cultural imperialism'. In the nineteenth century, imperial nations enforced their rule with gunboats, now they use television, films and Western fashion in clothes, food and music. Sometimes referred to as 'soft power' the result, it is claimed, is that Third World cultures are dying out, mainly because of American cultural influences. Critics of the theory argue that it overestimates the penetration of American TV and films into Third World countries, and underestimates the cultural resistance of Third World cultures: drinking Coke and wearing baseball caps doesn't indicate that people think and feel like Americans.

> **Cultural imperialism** The use of cultural products, particularly films, books, music and television, to spread the values and ideologies of foreign cultures. The term was often used to describe the cultural power of the west, especially the USA, over other parts of the world.

> **Soft power** In contrast to 'hard power' based upon military and economic force, soft power uses popular culture and the media to influence the way that people think and feel and behave.

The controversy about the mass media and their impact on government and politics is not going to be resolved in the near future. The methodological problems of investigating media effects, plus the passion with which different views are held, ensure that the debate will continue for a long time.

■ What have we learned?

This chapter deals with the media in democracies. It argues that:

- The ability of the news media to deliver a full and accurate account of the news, and a wide range of opinion about it, is crucial for democracy. They should therefore be free from government control and not dominated by any particular set of social and economic interests.

- Radio and TV broadcasting in the era of spectrum scarcity was often run according to the public service model. This involved both market and content regulation. Broadcasting technology has changed this by making it possible for many radio and TV channels to operate. Consequently, many national radio and TV systems have been deregulated or privatised to a greater or lesser extent.
- The print media are not normally subject to either content or market regulation because they are presumed to constitute a competitive market.
- It is exceedingly hard to pin down the political impact of the mass media, and research is divided between four main schools of thought – minimal effects, agenda setting, priming and framing, and direct effects. Researchers are also divided between those who believe that media effects are either benign or malign.

■ Lessons of comparison

- Ownership and control of the media has become increasingly concentrated in the hands of a few giant, multi-media, multi-national companies with markets in every corner of the globe.
- The new media technology has had a huge impact in some respects (the spread of global news, the diffusion of the web), but less effect in others (the resilience of local news and local language, the slow progress of E-politics and the persistence of the 'knowledge gap' based on the old technology).
- There is no necessary connection between democracy and either a free market or a public service media system. Some of the most advanced democracies operate with a mixed public/private system, and some authoritarian states have a free market system.
- Comparison across countries suggests that the extent to which the media generate mediamalaise depends upon the kind of media system it has. Public service news seems to be associated with better-informed and less alienated citizens.

Projects

1. Think of five reasons why the mass media may have rather little impact on politics, and then think of five reasons why they may have a big impact.
2. In a group, compile a list of all the different channels of political communication (newspapers, radio, TV, the web, etc.) and then of who in the group has used what channel in the previous week.

Which are the most frequently used channels, and which do you think are the most influential politically?

3. Examine the following figures and discuss what conclusions they suggest about the impact of newspaper reading on voting.

	Left-wing voters	Right-wing voters
Left newspaper readers (%)	63	26
Right newspaper readers (%)	37	74
Total (%)	100	100

Further reading

P. Norris, *Virtuous Circle: Political Communications in Postindustrial Societies*, Cambridge: Cambridge University Press, 2000.
An excellent account of the way in which the media operate and impact on democratic politics.

J. Street, *Mass Media, Politics and Democracy*, Basingstoke: Palgrave, 2001.
A general discussion of the mass media and modern democracy.

R. Gunther and A. Mughan, *Democracy and the Media: A Comparative Perspective*, Cambridge: Cambridge University Press, 2000.
Essays on politics and the media in Britain, Germany, Italy, Japan, the Netherlands, Spain and the USA.

J. Downing, A. Mohammadi and A. Sreberny (eds.), *Questioning the Media: A Critical Introduction*, Thousand Oaks, CA: Sage, 1995.
A useful set of essays on the mass media.

Websites

www.cjr.org/tools/owners
Columbia Journalism Review website with detailed information about who owns what in the global media market.
www.fair.org/extra/9711/gmg.html
Interesting article about 'The global media giants: the nine firms that dominate the world'.
www.thenation.com/special/bigten.html
Website from *The Nation* with some information about 'The big ten' and links to these companies.
www.ejc.nl/resources.html
The European Media Landscape provides a comprehensive overview of the media situation in selected European states.

12   Voters and elections

Elections determine who is to take control of government. From the research point of view they also have the advantage of involving a large number of citizens and of producing a large volume of reasonably reliable statistics, so they are one of the best topics for research on mass political behaviour. They tell us a lot about how ordinary citizens relate to politics, what they think is important and how they make up their minds about governments and issues.

Given their importance in any democratic system of government, a great many questions can be asked about voting and elections: How are democratic elections best organised? Who votes and should we worry about declining turnout? Who votes for what party and why? How have voting patterns changed in recent decades?

In this chapter we tackle these questions in the following sections:

- Democratic elections
- Voting systems
- Voting turnout
- Party voting
- Theories of voting.

■ Elections

Democratic elections

The preconditions for democratic elections are demanding, and we should not take them for granted, even in advanced democracies. They include universal adult suffrage, a secret ballot, impartial administration of voting and vote counting, free and equal access to the polls, freedom for candidates and parties to contest elections and an absence of gerrymandering. Free elections also require basic democratic rights, including freedom of speech, association and assembly, access to accurate and fair news reporting and parties that are not too unequal in resources. Relatively few countries meet all these requirements. Indeed, the American presidential election in 2000 suggests that registration and vote-counting practices are far from perfect in the USA.

Suffrage The right to vote.

Gerrymandering Drawing electoral boundaries to favour a particular party or interest.

Voting comes in two main forms: a general election for different levels of the political systems, and a referendum. Referendums are particularly useful for expressing public opinion on a particular issue, and they often involve either a constitutional change or a major policy issue, often one that is morally and emotionally charged. Democracies have increasingly used referendums since the 1960s, but except for Switzerland they are far less frequent than general elections. Most of this chapter will be about general elections for executives and legislatures (see fact file 12.1).

Referendum The submission of a public matter to direct popular vote.

Voting systems

One of the most basic decisions for any democracy is what voting system it should have. Many have been invented (the main types are outlined in briefing 12.1), but it is no simple matter to say what is the best and most democratic. Each has its advantages and disadvantages, and the choice depends on what one wants from a voting system. Those who value **proportionality** more than anything else choose a proportional representation system (PR), but others say that the system should, above all, produce stable and effective government. Some emphasise clear lines of government accountability to the majority of citizens, and others argue for adequate minority representation, on the grounds that democracies are to be judged on how they treat their minorities. Consequently it may be less a matter of choosing the best voting system than of selecting one of them, knowing what its strengths and weaknesses are in the light of what is expected of a good system. In the democracies of the world the most favoured systems are the simple plurality system, which is believed to produce stable

Voting system The arrangements by which votes are converted into seats on representative bodies.

Fact file 12.1

Voters and elections

■ Referendums and elections

- The minimum voting age in the great majority of countries is eighteen.
- Referendums are still used relatively rarely, and often for constitutional changes, but they have been held in almost every democratic country in the world, the exceptions being Argentina, Germany, India, Israel and Japan.
- Referendums are most common in Australia, Denmark, France, Ireland, Italy and New Zealand, but Switzerland stands out with almost 300 since 1941.
- Voter registration varies from 42 per cent in Switzerland, 58 per cent in India and 66 per cent in the USA, to 91 per cent in Belgium, 92 per cent in Iceland and 96 per cent in Australia. It averages 75 per cent in established democracies.

■ Voting turnout

- Voting is technically compulsory in a few countries, including Argentina, Australia, Belgium, Costa Rica, Cyprus, Greece, Italy, Peru and the Netherlands (before 1970). Turnout is only about 4–5 per cent higher in these countries compared with non-compulsory systems. This is partly because the formalities of compulsory voting are sometimes not followed up in reality. Voting turnout in older, established democracies tends to be about 15 per cent higher than in all other countries (73 per cent and 59 per cent respectively), but the gap between them has been closing slowly since 1945, and is now less than 10 per cent.
- If one excludes the two deviant cases of very low turnout among the most advanced democracies – Switzerland and the USA – average turnout is close to 80 per cent. If one then allows for the fact that a proportion of the non-voters are old, or ill, or temporarily absent from their voting district, then some nine out of ten citizens in democracies normally vote.
- Average voting turnout in PR systems (68 per cent) is higher than in semi-PR systems (59 per cent) and in plurality–majority systems (59 per cent).
- Founding election turnout in central and eastern Europe in the 1990s was on average 12 per cent higher than in later elections, but in Africa, Asia, the Middle East and Oceania turnout was actually lower in founding than in subsequent elections.
- Elections where the largest party wins less than half the votes have a turnout 10 per cent higher than less competitive elections where the largest party wins more than 50 per cent of the poll.
- Turnout is not closely related to national wealth or population size, but it is closely associated with the UN **Human Development Index**.

Human Development Index A UN index of national development that combines measures of life expectancy, educational attainment and wealth into one measure.

Countries with the highest HDI ratings had an average turnout of 72 per cent, those with the lowest 56 per cent.

■ Class voting

- Britain has one of the purest class voting patterns in the western world but its **Alford index** fell from 41 per cent in the general election of 1951 to 18 per cent in 2005.

Alford index A measure of class voting that calculates the difference between the proportion of working-class people voting for a left party, and the proportion of middle-class people doing the same. The higher the index, the greater the class voting.

- In the same period the Alford index for Germany fell from close to 30 per cent to less than 10 per cent, and for Sweden from 50 per cent to less than 20 per cent.

■ Religion and voting

- Religion and politics are closely related in many democracies, as we can see in their elections, where voting often reflects religious differences and beliefs.
- In most of the predominantly Catholic countries of western Europe (Austria, Belgium, France, Ireland, Italy and Spain and in the south of Germany and the Netherlands), the largest centre-right party is a Christian Democratic one that relies heavily on Catholic votes. Christian Democratic parties are also found in Australia, Chile and South Africa.
- In the Protestant countries of western Europe (Scandinavia, the UK and the north of Germany and the Netherlands) the main centre-right party is a secular one.
- In France (80 per cent Catholic) almost half the Catholics voted for a centre-right party in the 1980s, compared with fewer than one in seven of the Protestants. In 1998 only 29 per cent of church-going Catholics voted for the right.
- In the 1950s, more than 90 per cent of Dutch Catholics voted for the Catholic People's Party (KVP), the second largest in the country. By 1998, 61 per cent were doing so.
- The ISSP social survey of twelve western countries in 1998 shows that whereas religious groups in Europe used to be in rather different political camps, the evidence now is that they are moving together in their social and political attitudes. In most countries (but not all) church-going Catholics and Protestants generally lean towards the political right. The least religious generally (not always) lean to the left.

Briefing 12.1

Main voting systems

■ Plurality–majority

1. *Simple plurality/First-past-the-post* (FPTP) The candidate with most votes (a simple plurality) wins the seat no matter how many candidates and how small the winning margin. Usually used in conjunction with **single-member districts**, so the combination of single member and simple plurality is often known as the SMSP system. Its advantage is simplicity and direct democratic accountability, because each district is represented by *one representative*. SMSP is likely to produce single-party governments with stable majorities, and this also favours clear lines of *political accountability*. The disadvantage is **disproportionality** in election results. The SMSP system favours large parties and discriminates against small ones, which are often seen as a 'wasted' vote.

Single-member districts One elected representative for each constituency.

Proportionality The ratio of seats to votes. The more proportional the closer the ratio.

Multi-member districts (MMP) These have two or more elected representatives for each constituency.

A variation on SMSP is the *block vote* which combines first-past-the-post counting with **multi-member districts**.

Plurality–majority countries include: Bolivia, Canada, India, Jamaica, Mauritius, the UK and the USA. Italy adopted a mainly SMSP system in 1994.

2. *Second ballot* The second-ballot (SB) system tries to avoid the disproportionality problem of SMSP systems by requiring the winning candidate to get an *absolute majority* of the votes (i.e. 50 per cent + 1) in the first round – or if not, a second run-off ballot is held between the two strongest candidates. The advantage is simplicity, the disadvantage the need for a second ballot shortly after the first. The French use this system in presidential elections.

3. *Alternative vote* (AV) Voters mark their first and subsequent preferences among the candidates for their own constituency. If no candidate receives an absolute majority of first-preference votes on the first count, the candidate with the smallest number of first-choice votes is eliminated, but their second-choice votes are redistributed among the remaining candidates. This process continues until one candidate has an absolute majority.
   The system is simple to understand, but its results are no more proportional than the SMSP system, and it can produce unpredictable results. It is used only in Australia.

■ Proportional representation

Proportional representation (PR) tries to ensure the proportionality of votes to seats. The three main forms are:

- The list system
- The single transferable vote
- The mixed-member proportional system.

1. *List PR system* One of the simplest ways of ensuring proportionality is to distribute seats on a *national basis* or on a large regional one. Parties rank their candidates in order of preference, and they are elected in proportion to the number of votes for that party, starting from the top of the list. A party getting 25 per cent of the poll will fill 25 per cent of the seats from the top of its list. The advantage is simplicity and proportionality. The disadvantage is that voters cast a preference for a party, though they may prefer to vote for an individual candidate. The system also gives power to party leaders, who decide the rank order of candidates on their lists. Because list PR voting requires multi-member districts it also breaks the direct and simple link between representatives and their districts. List PR is highly proportional and can encourage small parties and fragmentation of the party system. An **electoral threshold** can overcome this problem, but this increases disproportionality.

> **Electoral thresholds** A minimum percentage of the poll required to be elected (to discourage small parties).

Many democratic countries have adopted the list PR system, including: Argentina (compulsory voting), Belgium, Chile, Costa Rica (compulsory voting), Cyprus (compulsory voting), the Czech Republic, Denmark, the Dominican Republic (compulsory voting), Estonia, Finland, Greece, Israel, Italy (before 1994), Latvia, the Netherlands (compulsory voting before 1970), Norway, Poland, Portugal, Slovakia, South Africa, Spain, Sweden and Switzerland.

2. *Single transferable vote* (STV) Voters rank candidates according to their order of preference, and elected candidates must either get a specified number of first preferences or else

the second preferences are taken into account. If no candidate has an absolute majority, the third preferences are counted, and so on until all seats are filled. STV must be used in conjunction with multi-member constituencies. The advantage of the system is its proportionality and the avoidance of 'wasted' votes. The disadvantage is the complexity of the STV formula (although this is now easily and quickly done by computers) and the fact that multi-member constituencies do not create a direct link between constituencies and a single representative. The system is used only in Australia, Estonia (1989–92) and Ireland.

3. *Mixed-member proportional* The mixed-member proportional system runs two voting systems at the same time. Plurality–majority districts are used to keep the link between representatives and constituencies, but a list PR system is added for a certain number of additional seats (usually 50 per cent) in order to compensate for any disproportionality that arises from the plurality–majority system. In Germany, half the additional seats are allotted at district and half at national level, and citizens have two votes, one for their district and one for the national list. MMP is found in Germany, Hungary, New Zealand (since 1996) and Uruguay.

■ Semi-PR

1. *Parallel systems* Like the MMP systems these use the plurality–majority system with a PR system but, unlike MMP, the PR system does not compensate for disproportionality resulting from the plurality–majority system. Used in Japan (from 1994), Lithuania and South Korea.

2. *Single non-transferable vote* (SNTV) The SNTV system combines multi-member constituencies with simple majority vote counting, and one vote for each elector. Used in Japan (before 1994) and Taiwan (for 78 per cent of seats).

and accountable government, and the list PR system, which results in more proportionate election outcomes (see table 12.1).

Voting turnout

Voting is the most basic and simple duty of the citizen, so **voting turnout** is often treated as a good measure of the basic health of a democracy. Unfortunately, there are two problems with this:

Voting turnout The number of citizens casting a valid (i.e. not a spoiled ballot) vote expressed either as a percentage of those eligible to vote (adult citizens), or as a percentage of those on the electoral register.

Protest vote Voting for a party not to support it, but to show opposition to another party or parties, usually those in government.

• First, does low turnout indicate an alienated and dissatisfied electorate, or, on the contrary, one that is satisfied and happy to let politicians get on with it? History suggests that sudden and large increases in turnout indicate widespread dissatisfaction. The sudden jump in voting turnout in Germany in 1933, when Hitler's Nazi Party won, was the result of alienated people deciding to cast a **protest vote**. Equally, the arrival of an unusually popular candidate or party can mobilise voters (the USA in 2008).

Table 12.1 Liberal democracies: voting systems, 1990s

	%
Non-PR	
Simple plurality	44
Second-ballot	5
AV	1
Sub-total	50
PR and Semi-PR	
List PR	36
Additional member	8
STV	3
Limited vote (semi-PR)	2
Sub-total	49
Total	**99**

Source: Derived from J. Denis Derbyshire and Ian Derbyshire, *Political Systems of the World* (Oxford: Helicon, 1996).

- The second difficulty of using turnout as a indicator of democratic health is that there are two different measures of turnout, and a lot turns on which one is used:
  - Voting as a percentage of the voting-age population, usually all adult citizens, or
  - Voting as a percentage of those on the electoral register.

Some countries make it easy to register, and some even register people automatically when they register themselves as residents or pay their taxes. Other countries make it more difficult, or even discriminate against certain groups. As a result, the percentage of all adults on the register can vary quite significantly between countries. There can, therefore, be a big difference between turnout figures according to which of the two measures is used. It is thus important to make it clear which baseline – adult population or registered electorate – is used. It is also important to use one or the other consistently when comparing countries. There is the further complication that some countries make voting in national elections **compulsory**. Although this may be observed in theory more than practice, it does complicate comparisons (see fact file 12.1).

Compulsory voting The legal obligation for citizens to appear at polling stations on election day.

Declining turnout?

Although it is common to lament a decline in turnout, especially when it is interpreted as a sign of disillusionment with democracy, the facts suggest otherwise. In the established democracies (countries that have been democratic for twenty years or more) turnout as a percentage of the voting-age population rose from around 70 per cent in the 1940s to around 75 per cent in the 1950s. This figure remained fairly constant over the 1960s and 1970s and then declined slightly to around 70 per cent by 1997. This does suggest a slight fall, but only to the previous lower level, and it is not clear how much this decline is due to changing socio-demographic patterns, or to growing apathy, alienation or political satisfaction. Some groups in the population with a typically low turnout have tended to increase in size – the old, the ill, students, immigrants and ethnic and language minorities. In short, turnout across the democratic states has not declined very much, and even this may be the result of socio-demographic change as much as disillusionment with democracy and voter apathy.

Determinants of election turnout

There are considerable variations in voting turnout in the democracies (see table 12.2). In Italy, Iceland and South Africa it is above 85 per cent, but in the Dominican Republic, Poland, Switzerland and the USA it is below 50 per cent. Why is this? Many factors seem to affect turnout, and they may be conveniently grouped under two categories: system and individual influences.

System variables
We can distinguish nine of these:

Democratic deficit A term used to convey the idea that the institutions of the European Union are not fully democratic, or as democratic as they should.

1. *The importance of the election* Citizens are more likely to vote if they think the election is important. They turn out in larger numbers for national than for local government elections, and for the election of executive presidents and lower chambers rather than upper chambers and weak assemblies. The **democratic deficit** of the institutions of the EU, especially the European Parliament (EP), is said to be partly responsible for the low turnout in the EU.
2. *Democracy* Turnout in established democracies with entrenched political freedoms and civil liberties is higher than in non-democracies.
3. *Electoral system* PR voting systems have a higher turnout than other systems (see briefing 12.1). Countries with automatic or easily used registration systems also have a higher turnout than others.
4. *Close, competitive elections* Close elections, where every vote counts, tend to have a higher turnout, as do competitive elections (where the largest party wins less than 50 per cent of the vote).
5. *Left parties* Elections that manage to mobilise sections of the population with a low voting turnout will usually register a higher turnout – for example, where left-wing parties appeal to working-class voters.

Table 12.2 Voting turnout as a percentage of those registered, selected democratic countries, 2004–2008

	Parliamentary election	Presidential election
Argentina	73.1	71.8
Australia	94.8	
Austria	81.7	71.6
Belgium	91.1	
Brazil	83.3	81.0
Canada	64.9	
Czech Republic	64.5	
Finland	65.0	74.0
France	60.0	84.0
Germany	77.7	
Greece	74.1	
Hungary	64.4	
Ireland	67.0	46.7
Israel	63.5	
Italy	80.5	
Japan	58.6	
Latvia	61.0	
Mexico	58.9	58.6
Namibia	84.8	85.5
Netherlands	80.4	
New Zealand	72.2	
Norway	77.4	
Peru	88.7	87.7
Poland	53.9	51.0
Portugal	64.3	61.5
Slovenia	63.1	58.4
South Africa	98.4	
Spain	75.3	
Sweden	82.0	
Switzerland	82.0	
United Kingdom	61.4	
USA	47.5	61.7

Source: International Institute for Democracy and Electoral Assistance (www.idea.int/vt/survey/voter_turnout4.cfm).

6. *Frequency of election* Citizens who are often called out to vote seem to suffer from 'election fatigue'.
7. *Founding elections* It is often believed that 'founding elections' (the first democratic elections after authoritarian rule) have high turnouts. One thinks of the long queues at polling stations in the first democratic election in South Africa in 1994. An examination of election statistics, however,

shows that this turns out to be true of central and eastern Europe, but not generally of other parts of the world.

8. *Presidential and parliamentary elections* In parliamentary elections in the second half of the twentieth century turnout was a good 20 per cent higher than presidential turnout, but by 1997, the two were virtually identical. At the same time, presidential elections increased from 30 per cent of all elections to more than 50 per cent in 1999, so it is not clear whether presidential turnout has changed, or whether presidential elections are now held in a different set of countries affected by different turnout factors.

9. *Community characteristics* Socially homogeneous communities (predominantly in terms of class, religion, language or ethnic group) with a sense of solidarity often have high levels of social and political participation.

Individual characteristics
We can distinguish four of these:

Social stratification The hierarchical layering of society into socially and economically unequal groups.

1. *The standard model* The standard model of political participation, described in chapter 9, applies to voting turnout as well, but as with political participation its influence on voting behaviour is also declining. The higher an individual's position in the social stratification system, as measured by caste, class, status, income or education, the more likely they are to vote.

Party identification The stable and deep-rooted feeling of attachment to and support for a political party.

2. *Age, gender, length of residence and race* The standard model of voter turnout may be modified by other variables. Young and old people are less likely to vote, so also are women and members of minority groups – unless minorities are mobilised by their own political organisations or political issues relevant to them. Long-term residents with roots in the community are more likely to vote than more mobile people.

3. *Party identification* Individuals with a strong party identification (**party ID**) are more likely to vote.

4. *Values* Post-materialist values, it is said, promote participation and civic responsibility.

■ Party voting

Although there is a great deal of variation in party voting across the democratic world, it is also possible to advance some generalisations about voting patterns and the way they are changing with respect to economic issues and social stratification, race and religion, and urban–rural cleavages.

Economic voting and stratification

Economic issues are intimately linked with some of the most basic conditions of daily life – not just money but housing, health, education and family prospects. Therefore there is often

> **Class** A form of social stratification that is determined by economic factors, notably occupational hierarchy, income and wealth.

a link between the economy and voting, as in the commonly observed tendency for working-class and poor social groups to vote for parties of the left, and for wealthier groups to favour the centre or right. There is also a tendency for voters to punish governments that perform badly on economic matters. But, and it is an important but, economic voting is dependent on four other factors.

1. Non-economic cleavages may override economic ones. A large working-class, left-wing party has not emerged in India, in spite of widespread poverty, because of the strength of race, religious, language and regional cleavages. In contrast, class voting was particularly strong in the UK and Australia, when class was the dominant cleavage and there were few other cleavages.
2. The extent to which voters reward or punish their government for its economic performance depends on how clear it is that the government is responsible for economic performance: government coalition partners blame each other for failures; higher levels of government blame lower levels and vice versa; presidents blame legislatures and vice versa; and poor government performance may count for little if voters believe that opposition parties would do worse.
3. Voters learn about government economic performance in different ways, at different times and with different effects. They are more likely to forgive the poor performance of parties they identify with and vote for (the 'home team' effect).
4. Class is a largely objective way of grouping people based on income and occupation, but status is more subjective, based on how people spend their money and how others see them, judged according to such things as their behaviour, education, manner of speech, clothes and life-style. People who believe

> **Status** A form of social stratification determined by social prestige rather than economic factors or occupation.

they are middle class may behave politically as the middle class does, even though economically they are not the same. People from high-status backgrounds who have fallen on hard economic times can retain their high status even though they are impoverished, and equally those from poor backgrounds who have made a lot of money may be regarded as vulgar and nouveau riche. A combined measure of class and status is referred to as 'socio-economic status'.

For much of the late nineteenth and the twentieth century class voting was common in western Europe. It is argued that by 1920 the party systems of

Briefing 12.2

The left–right dimension in politics
At the heart of the left–right dimension in politics lies a profound difference between (1) the left, which favours the welfare state and government intervention in society and the economy in order to achieve a degree of equality of opportunity, and (2) those on the right, who favour less government intervention and a market economy, although they often favour strong government in the interests of domestic law and order and national security. The left–right dimension is becoming less important with the decline of class differences in many democracies, but more important in some industrialising democracies, where a rapidly growing urban working class is combining with poor agricultural workers.

most of these countries had frozen around their main class cleavage and largely remained that way until the 1970s. During this period the left–right dimension was the most important in their politics (see briefing 12.2). However, when economic changes brought about a change and weakening of class structures, other social divisions became more important for voting. One of the most important is religion.

Religious voting

Religion has been a major source of political conflict for most of the world's history, and it remains a major, if not the major, social and political division in some democratic countries. In India, conflict between Muslims and Hindus is an acute political issue and Hindu fundamentalism is the basis of the Bharatiya Janata Party (BJP), which became the governing party in 1998. Religious issues and voting patterns were strong in much of Europe and are still strong in the USA. Religion, ethnicity and language are frequently closely associated, but sometimes the same ethnic group and language groups can be divided along religious lines.

While it is not surprising that religion is a basic foundation of political life in religious societies, it also continues to be a major influence on voting behaviour even in the secular parts of western Europe, where churches and the state came to a formal settlement centuries ago (see chapter 1). In fact, as class voting tends to decline, so religious voting, which has maintained its strength, emerges as being relatively more important (table 12.3). Religious voting tends to be more complex than class voting, since there is no simple working-class–middle-class/left–right cleavage. Instead there is a more complex set of divisions between many different churches and faiths – including the formation of secular parties in opposition to religious ones, in some countries.

What makes the existence of persistent religious differences all the more interesting and important is that politicians in secular societies usually try

Table 12.3 Class, religious and value voting, 1990s

Correlation with party preferences	Class voting	Religious voting	Materialist–postmaterialist voting
0.37		Netherlands	
0.30		Belgium	
0.29		Denmark	
0.27		Finland, Italy, Norway	
0.26		Austria	Netherlands, Finland
0.25		Spain	Denmark
0.22	Norway	France, West Germany	
0.21	Denmark		Britain, (West) Germany
0.20	Austria	Sweden	
0.19	Iceland		France, Iceland
0.18	Britain, Netherlands		Italy, Norway
0.17		Iceland	Spain
0.16	Belgium, Finland, Sweden	Ireland	
0.15	France, Italy, Spain	Japan	Sweden, Austria
0.14	Ireland		East Germany, Japan
0.13	(West) Germany		Belgium, Canada
0.12		Britain, Canada	
0.11	Japan		Ireland
0.10	Canada, USA		
0.09			USA
0.08		USA	

Note: [a] Table 12.3 shows the strength of the statistical association (the correlation) of party preference with social class, religion and post-materialism in the 1990s

Source: Russell J. Dalton, Citizen Politics (London: Chatham House, 1996, 2nd edn.: 171, 180, 190).

to push religious issues, such as abortion or matters of faith, off the political agenda. These are highly charged moral and emotional issues of the kind that politicians try to avoid. Nevertheless, religious cleavages that usually emerged a long time ago, even before the creation of democratic elections and party systems, are still relevant.

Perhaps the most conspicuous example of the connection between religion and politics is the emergence of Christian Democratic parties and unions (see chapter 13) – some small and weak, others large and powerful – in thirty of the democracies of the world from Finland to Chile and Canada to South Africa. Christian Democracy is noticeably absent from Asian politics, where other religions are important.

Other voting patterns

Few things rival class and religion as the major influences on party voting across the broad sweep of modern democracies, but other factors can play a significant role:

- Most countries have urban–rural differences, for example, and more especially regional variations in party voting. The latter are particularly likely to be associated with ethnic, religious, class, or language differences, as they are in Belgium, Canada, Italy and Spain. India stands out in this respect as well.
- There is a slight gender gap in some societies, although it is rarely of great importance compared with religion or stratification.
- Race and ethnicity, important in some of the newer democracies, has also gained in importance in the older ones as a result of global migration patterns.

Chile in the nineteenth and twentieth centuries demonstrates many aspects of the relationships between social cleavages and politics, particularly insofar as inequality, religion, class and region are concerned. The Spanish conquest of the country created a dominant white, Catholic, ruling class and a coerced labour force consisting of the indigenous population that worked on farms and in mines. As the economy and society developed in the nineteenth century it created social and economic groups, including a middle class, and a set of regional, anti-clerical and economic elites. But Chile has long had a tradition of constitutional and multi-party government, and it succeeded in gradually accommodating these interests into the political system in a largely peaceful manner (see briefing 12.3).

New party voting patterns

Social and economic changes (some brought about by government policies) have had a strong influence on voting patterns. In the industrialising democracies, the decline of the agricultural sector and the growth of the cities populated by the working class and the poor have had a profound impact on the strength of parties and the nature of old social cleavages based on urban–rural differences, regions and ethnic concentrations. In the older democracies of western Europe, the old pattern of class politics, and the left–right party system associated with it, shows clear signs of 'unfreezing'. Class is less important than it was and there is evidence that **class (and party) de-alignment** and **partisan de-alignment** has caused voting patterns to show more **volatility**.

Class de-alignment Decline in the class-based strength of attachment to class-based political parties.

Partisan de-alignment Decline in the strength of attachment to political parties.

Volatility The opposite of stability, volatility involves change in voting patterns from one election to another. Some refer to it as 'churning'.

Cleavages and politics: Chile

Republican political institutions were able to take root in Chile in the nineteenth century before new social groups demanded participation. Contenders from the middle and lower classes were gradually assimilated into an accommodating political system in which most disputes were settled peacefully, although disruptions related to the demands of workers often met a harsh, violent response. The system expanded to incorporate more and more competing regional, anti-clerical and economic elites in the nineteenth century. The middle classes gained political offices and welfare benefits in the opening decades of the twentieth century. From the 1920s to the 1940s, urban labourers obtained unionisation rights and participated in reformist governments. In the 1950s, women finally exercised full suffrage and became a decisive electoral force. And by the 1960s, rural workers achieved influence with reformist parties, widespread unionisation and land reform.

As Chile's political parties grew, they attracted followers not only on the basis of ideology but also on the basis of patron–client relationships between candidates and voters. These ties were particularly important at the local level, where mediation with government agencies, provision of public employment and delivery of public services were more crucial than ideological battles waged on the national stage. Over generations, these bonds became tightly woven, producing within the parties fervent and exclusive sub-cultures nurtured in the family, the community and the workplace. As a result, by the mid-twentieth century the parties had politicised schools, unions, professional associations, the media and virtually all other components of national life. The intense politicisation of modern Chile has its roots in events of the nineteenth century in spite of later twentieth-century developments including military coup, dictatorship and democratisation.

(For a more detailed analysis of Chile's cleavage politics, see http://workmall.com/wfb2001/chile/chile_history_historical_setting.html)

The reasons for changing voting patterns, therefore, are many and varied but they include several common developments:

- Industrialising societies have often mixed old stratification factors based on caste, religion and ethnicity with new class and status distinctions. Post-industrial societies, in contrast, have tended to increase their proportion of middle-class people, while fragmenting both working- and middle-class strata into smaller sub-groups. This has weakened class voting.
- Urban–rural differences have declined with a shrinking agricultural sector, particularly where the urban and rural poor have formed a political alliance in industrialising countries.
- Education has created a more independently minded electorate that is less bound by class identities. Social mobility between classes has strengthened this.
- The mass media, especially television, have become more important.

- New parties have emerged and old parties have shifted their policies in an attempt to broaden their appeal and to respond to the demands of new social groups. In some cases, the old parties have stolen policies from the new parties and social movements in their attempt to maintain their electoral appeal.
- The basic bread-and-butter issues of poverty, work, health, housing and education have become even sharper in industrialising democracies, whereas the environment, nuclear issues, gender and minority rights, and (in Europe) European integration, have often cut across the old politics of class in post-industrial societies.

The result of these far-reaching changes in socio-economic patterns is increased volatility and unpredictability in voting patterns in both new and old democracies. Nevertheless, talk of revo-lutionary and radical transformation is often exaggerated. Changes are usually gradual and involve fusions of the old and the new, and shifts of degree rather than kind. In some cases, even **partisan re-alignment** can be observed. Social stratification and religion remain the basic sources for politi-cal mobilisation, even if the nature of the stratification is shifting.

> **Partisan re-alignment** When social and economic groups change their old party identifi-cations in favour of new ones.

Tradition and change in Mexico

We can see the interplay of tradition and change in the electoral politics of Mexico, where economic inequalities of class are superimposed on old ethnic divisions. The Mexican social and political elite is composed of the *criollos*, people of pure Spanish ancestry dating back to the invasion of Mexico in the sixteenth century by the Spanish conquistador, Hernán Cortés. The middle layer of society is made up of people of mixed blood, the *mestizos* with Spanish and indigenous Mayan and Aztec backgrounds. For sixty years, Mexico had an authoritarian system of government based on electoral manipulation and the the ability of the Institutional Revolutionary Party (PRI) to unite the interests of these groups and those of the lowest class, the *indigena*, by bringing them together in a corporatist structure (see chapter 10). The structure however, largely excluded the interests of the very poorest section of society, the rural farmers who were concentrated in the south of Mexico and consisted mainly of people of Mayan background.

On New Year's Day 1994, the revolutionary National Liberation Front (NLF, the Zapatistas) burst into armed guerrilla activity that shook the founda-tions of the state and the governing PRI. Zapatista demands were economic, regional and ethnic. They wanted a better economic deal for poor farmers, who were mainly of Aztec origin and concentrated in Chiapas in the south of Mexico. Two remodelled parties emerged to challenge the hegemony of the PRI, both representing class interests. The Democratic Revolutionary Party (PRD, founded in 1989) is supported mainly by poor urban and rural people, and the National Action Party (PAN, founded in 1939) mainly by upper-income groups. PAN captured the presidency in 2000.

The Mexican case illustrates several points about changing voting patterns:

- Change is usually mixed with tradition.
- Voting is based on a mixture of factors involving social stratification and inequality, ethnicity and regional and urban–rural differences. Religious differences are not important in Mexico because it is 90 per cent Catholic.
- History is important. The Zapatista movement is the result of the subjugation of the Mayan and Aztec populations in the sixteenth century, and the 1990s movement named itself after the revolutionary leader Emiliano Zapata (1879–1919), who fought for the rights of poor farmers. Politics is important. Poor farmers lived in Mexico for centuries, but it was the charismatic leader 'Subcomandante' Marcos who organised a rebellion in 1994, which had a subsequent influence on the formation of new parties.

■ Theories of voting

There are the three main approaches to the explanation of voting behaviour:

- Sociological/political sociological
- Psychological/social psychological
- Rational-choice/economic.

Sociological approaches: the Columbia school

Paul Lazarsfeld (1901–76), a sociologist at the University of Columbia in New York, carried out an early American election study in 1944 which showed that people vote according to their membership of social groups, and that social groups vote for the party that best serves their interests. This makes class, religion, race, language, urban–rural differences and sometimes gender, generation and occupation the most important determinants of voting behaviour.

The strengths of the sociological school are that it relates politics to broad social and economic patterns and, as we have seen so often in this book, there is often a close connection between society and its government and politics. Indeed, research shows a close relationship between voting and factors such as class, religion, age, gender, education and ethnicity. However, the theory is not good at explaining the causal links between politics and society. To understand why, for example, the working class votes for left-wing parties, we have to introduce political elements – such as values, ideology and party policy – into the explanation. Working-class people do not vote for working-class parties naturally or automatically, any more than members of a religious group generally vote for a given party because of instinct. They do so because they see a link between the interests (material or ideal) of their social group and the things that the party stands for.

The sociological approach works very well in some cases – religion and voting in Northern Ireland, for example – but there are always exceptions to the social patterns, and some of them are so large they cannot be overlooked. Working-class people do not always vote for left-wing parties, just as some middle-class people do not vote for right-wing ones. Ethnic groups are rarely 100 per cent solid in their voting patterns. Sometimes they are split between two or more parties, sometimes divided down the middle. And, as we have already seen, the sociological model seems to be losing some of its power, with the emergence of the 'new' politics based not on group membership but on values and issue areas.

The cleavage model is a more complex version of the sociological approach. It also argues that voting is organised around social groups, but points out those cleavages are not the automatic outcome of social divisions. Indeed, many social divisions, such as age or gender, do not normally take on the importance of political cleavages. Social divisions become politically potent only when political interests (elites, parties, movements) manage to give them a political and symbolic significance, and build organisations around them. In other words, parties do not merely respond to cleavages; they play upon them and develop them in their attempts to win support. Parties would find it difficult to mobilise voters without cleavage groups to appeal to, but social cleavages would have little political significance without parties to mobilise them and articulate their interests and values.

While cleavage theory can explain the historical origins of parties and party systems, it is less successful in explaining changing political alignments. The theory tends to take cleavages as given, and works out their political implications from there. It is rather less interested in why different societies have different cleavages or how and why they reconfigure themselves over time. Since the old cleavages appear to be fading a little, and new ones emerging, this is important to contemporary politics.

Psychological approaches: the Michigan school

Starting with Angus Campbell (1910–80) and his collaborators, the Michigan school of election studies emphasises the psychological orientations of voters. Whereas the sociological school emphasises social groups, psychological approaches concentrate on individual characteristics, particularly the role of party identification (party ID). This is a relatively stable and enduring feature that individuals acquire as a result of childhood and adult socialisation. Party ID is more than identification with a party, because it acts as a prism through which individuals perceive politics and interpret policies, issues, parties and candidates. It affects voting, and it also helps to mould the way in which citizens relate more generally to government and politics.

Campbell and his colleagues develop what they call 'the funnel of causality', in which all the variables affecting voting behaviour are organised according to the theoretical order of their influence. At the 'wide end' of the funnel are a set of the most general constraints on voting, such as social background and socialisation. As the funnel narrows so variables constrain the voting decision more tightly. At the narrowest point are factors closest to the circumstances of particular elections, including attitudes towards party policies, candidates and election issues. This is a useful way of organising the many different variables that seem to affect voting behaviour, but at the same time it is a complicated model that is difficult to test as a whole.

The psychological school introduces specific political elements (party ID) into voting studies that are lacking in the sociological approach. It picks out the significance of political issues (unemployment, public services, economic development), party programmes (left–right dimensions, ethnic, religious, language and regional parties) and the images and appeal of political leaders as influences on party ID. There is also a close relationship between party ID and party voting. However, this is scarcely surprising since party ID and party voting are almost the same thing: if people are asked in surveys which party they identify with, they are likely to think of which party they vote for. In the long causal chain of explanatory variables explaining voting patterns, party ID and the vote are practically next door to each other, so of course we find that they are closely correlated. The problem is not to understand the causal links between ID and voting, but to understand who develops what sort of ID, and why. In addition, survey research shows that the strength of party ID is fading in many western countries (party de-alignment), although it is alive and well in countries such as South Africa, where black South African identification with the African National Congress (ANC) is widely and strongly held.

Rational choice

The rational-choice theory of voting originates with Anthony Downs' (1930–) book, *An Economic Theory of Democracy,* published in 1957, a work that starts with the assumption that citizens are rational and vote on the basis of a calculation of which party is most likely to satisfy their own self-interested preferences. Voting decisions are similar to those of consumers (voters) in the economic market who calculate the costs (taxes) and benefits (public services) of choosing one commercial product (political party) rather than another. Voting for a party is rather like choosing a basket of goods in a supermarket, in that voters select the 'package' of party policies that best fits their preferences at a price they can afford. Similarly, parties are like business competing for customers in the market place. They try to locate themselves and their policies close to the **median voter**, who represents the position of the typical

Median voter The median voter is in the middle of the distribution with equal numbers of voters to the left and right, and is, therefore, a typical, middle-of-the-road voter.

middle-of-the-road voter. Rational choice, in short, claims to explain the behaviour of individual voters and the strategies and policies of political parties in terms of an economic theory of the consumers (voters) and producers of public policies (parties).

Rational-choice theory – sometimes known as formal modelling because it can be expressed in terms of symbols and formulae – is said to have opened up many promising lines of research by virtue of its deductive and logical powers. It claims, first, that candidates in elections must locate themselves close to the median voter, in order to maximise their chances of election vistory, and second, that most citizens have little incentive to vote because among millions of others their vote counts for virtually nothing. For this reason, voters also have little incentive to inform themselves about election issues.

Rational choice has problems with explaining why people bother to vote at all. Logically, the most rational course of action for the voter is not to bother, not to vote, join a party or participate in collective actions because the costs in time and effort of acquiring the necessary information and then following up with action exceed whatever benefits are produced. Better by far to stay at home in warm and comfort watching the TV, leaving others to do the work – what is known as **'free-riding'**. However, people do vote, and they vote in large numbers even when the election result is a foregone conclusion and the winning candidate is expected to win by a very large majority. The reason is that voting seems to be a symbolic act in part, and people feel obliged to perform their citizen duty. This is not a matter of the rational calculation of self-interest, but a collective sense based on the value of democracy and the importance of exercising the right to vote. The voting act, then, needs explanations rooted in norms, values and social expectations.

Free ride To extract the benefits of other people's work without making any effort oneself. The free-rider problem is acute in collective action when individuals can benefit from a public good without paying taxes or making any effort of their own.

The claim that all voters act in their own self-interest can easily be circular, non-falsifiable or tautological. How can we tell when people are not acting in their own self-interest, and what counts as non-rational behaviour? Are middle-class socialists running against their own class interests? Were the Christians who chose to be thrown to the lions rather than recanting their religious beliefs defying their own self-interests? Perhaps not: some people define their preferences in terms of the public good and are prepared to lay down their life for others and their own beliefs. But then it is difficult to see what 'self-interest' means, other than what individuals say it is. In this case whatever they do, no matter how altruistic or concerned with the public interest, is a rational calculation of self-interest.

Rational-choice has helped stimulate an interest in **issue voting**, which occurs when voters choose one issue rather than a total party programme as the basis of their voting decision. Traditional issues are unemployment and the economy ('it's the

Issue voting Voters choosing one issue rather than a total party programme as the basis of their voting decision.

economy, stupid'), but it has also been suggested that race, human rights, the environment and peace have emerged in many countries as the focus of single-issue voting. However, research shows that the importance of issue voting may not be as great as some have suggested and that, in any case, voters do not always choose the party with the best policies on the issues they think are important. The voting decision is a trade-off, a package deal that is not simply the net balance of issue-based calculations but involves, in addition, a broader set of values and ideological considerations: voters use their hearts as well as their heads. Rational choice tends to avoid issues of the heart, or takes them for granted.

■ What have we learned?

This chapter deals with elections, which are vital in every democracy. It argues that:

- Democratic elections require a large number of preconditions. They should not be taken for granted even in advanced democracies.
- Election turnout in the post-war period has declined a little in the democracies, probably because of socio-demographic change as much as increasing voter apathy or disillusionment with democracy.
- The voting decision is the result of an interplay between social (group membership), economic (class and inequality) and political (party appeals and policies) factors. Inequalities based on class, status and caste are often tangled up with race, religion, language, education and region, and sometimes with age and gender as well.
- Although economic and political factors play important roles, voting behaviour is also based on normative, social considerations and ideologies (left–right placement).

■ Lessons of comparison

- Although every country has a unique electoral system, they fall into three main types: plurality–majority, proportional representation and semi-PR systems. The first two are the most common.
- There is no simple answer to the question: What is the best voting system? Each has its advantages and disadvantages. It is necessary to decide what one wants from an electoral system and choose accordingly.
- History matters. Once again we see that history and tradition cast a long shadow over contemporary events, and changing voting patterns are usually a mixture of the old and new rather than a transformation.
- Institutions matter. The electoral system of a country and, more broadly, its system of government, has an impact on voting behaviour. We will see in the next chapter how voting systems can affect party systems.

Projects

1. Was turnout in the last national election in your country high or low by national and international standards. What sorts of factors explain this level of turnout?
2. What is the best voting system? Why do you prefer it to other systems?
3. What are the strengths and weaknesses of (a) the rational-choice approach to the explanation of turnout and party voting, (b) the sociological approach (Columbia school) and (c) the psychological approach (Michigan school)?

Further reading

D. M. Farrell, *Electoral Systems: A Comparative Introduction*, Basingstoke: Palgrave, 2001.
A comprehensive account of electoral systems.

M. Gallagher *et al.*, *Representative Government in Modern Europe,* New York: McGraw-Hill, 2nd edn., 1995.
The best short introduction to cleavage systems, voting and coalition governments in western Europe.

R. J. Dalton, *Citizen Politics,* Chatham, Chatham House, 3rd edn., 2002
Compares electoral behaviour in France, Great Britain, the USA and West Germany

P. Norris, *Democratic Phoenix,* Cambridge: Cambridge University Press, 2002.
Discusses the rising level of political interest and activity in the established democracies, with chapters on voting turnout around the world.

L. LeDuc, R. G. Niemi and P. Norris (eds.), *Comparing Democracies: Elections and Voting in Global Perspective,* Thousand Oaks, CA: Sage, 1996.
A good comparative study of voting and elections, covering a wide range of the literature.

C. van der Eyck and M. Franklin, *Voters and Elections*, Basingstoke: Palgrave Macmillan, 2009.
A broad overview of electoral behaviour and the role of elections in democracies.

Websites

http://electionresources.org
Links to internet sites around the world which provide detailed information about national and local elections, as well as other election resources.

www.fairvote.org/turnout/intturnout.htm

For data on electoral turnout.

http://dodgson.ucsd.edu/lij

Website of the Lijphart Election Archive, which is a research collection of district-level election results for approximately 350 national legislative elections in twenty-six countries.

www.idea.int/publications/vt/index.cfm

An excellent account of voter turnout in over 170 countries.

13   Party government

Democratic government is party government: electoral competition is largely party competition; parliamentary politics is invariably party politics; and government is rarely anything but party government. For better or for worse, **political parties** pervade all aspects of government and politics in democracies. They help to integrate the political system from top to bottom, and to integrate from side to side across a wide span of political interests and social segments of society. From top to bottom they create two-way lines of communication between the mass of ordinary citizens at the bottom of the political pyramid, and the political elites and decision makers at the top. Large parties are also a 'broad church', bringing together a wide variety of people with similar political interests but different social backgrounds. They help to integrate across lines of class, gender, religion, ethnicity and region and they form alliances with a variety of voluntary associations and pressure groups. Parties do this is in different ways according to their times and circumstances, so the first task of comparative studies is to identify the different types of party and the ways in which they operate.

In recent decades the old parties have been challenged by new ones and by other forms of political organisation. It was even said that the newcomers would replace the old parties with broader, looser, less bureaucratic and more flexible 'rainbow coalitions' of political interests. The old parties are still with

Political parties Organisations of politically like-minded people who seek political power and public office in order to realise their policies.

us, however. It is also notable that the parties in any one country often bear a striking family resemblance to those in other countries – that is, one can find socialist parties with similar policies and appealing to similar social groups in many countries across the globe, and similarly conservative, liberal, nationalist, Christian and green parties operate in many countries.

Parties compete with each other for government power. Sometimes a single party wins enough votes to take control of government on its own, but more usually a combination of parties must form a coalition to form a government. This generally involves a good deal of bargaining and 'horse-trading' to get an agreement on a set of policies for the new governing coalition, and to decide which partners in the coalition are to hold which positions in the cabinet. There is also the problem that, according to some political scientists, coalition government is inherently frail and unstable, a claim that is strongly contested by others, who argue that coalitions can not only form durable governments but more democratic and effective ones as well.

The major topics in this chapter, therefore, are:

- Party organisation
- New parties and movements
- Party systems and party families
- Coalition government
- Coalitions and government effectiveness
- Theories of parties.

■ Party organisation

Parties in democracies have two central purposes: to gain power by winning elections; and once in power, to implement their **(public) policy**. For both these purposes, organisation is vital. It is essential to capturing government power, and it is the backbone of a united government that can carry out its policy programme.

> **Public policy** A general set of ideas or plans that has been officially agreed on and which is used as a basis for making decisions.

Parties have passed through three main stages of organisation since their appearance in anything like a modern form:

- *Caucus parties* (also known as elite parties) In the nineteenth century, when few people had the vote, political parties were little more than loose alliances (a **caucus** or a clique) of like-minded people. They were usually led by a few elite 'notables', aristocrats, or wealthy public figures.

  > **Caucus** A small but loose-knit group of politicians (notables) who come together from time to time to make decisions about political matters.

- *Mass parties* In the twentieth century, with the coming of the universal franchise, parties broadened their electoral appeal by turning themselves into mass parties, with a large membership and a bureaucratic, centralised and hierarchical form of organisation.

- *Catch-all parties* Since the 1970s, the 'unfreezing' of old cleavages and the development of 'new politics' have pushed parties towards **'catch-all'** organisations, or rainbow coalitions that try to appeal to a wide variety of social groups and interests. Catch-all parties are widespread in Latin America where, though run along democratic lines now, they have something in common with the clientalist parties of authoritarian governments which bought support from a mixture of different social groups with money, contracts and jobs.

> **Catch-all parties** Parties that try to attract a broad range of supporters by advocating rather general policies.

It is suggested that parties are now moving towards a fourth stage in which they are described either as media parties, cartel parties or electoral–professional parties:

- *Media parties* The spread of the mass media and computer technology means that party leaders can appeal directly to voters. This reduces the need for a mass membership, a cumbersome organisation and mass meetings. State funding also relieves financial pressures. Media parties do not need such deep roots in society, and it may even be that ordinary party members with views of their own about politics make life more difficult for leaders who want to respond rapidly and flexibly to fast-changing political developments in the world.
- *Cartel parties* Political parties in the late twentieth century adapted to declining participation and turned themselves from mass, competitive parties into cartel parties that collaborated with each other for state resources (money and patronage) as well as career stability and continuity for their leaders. Parties are increasingly a part of the machinery of state. Politics used to be a more 'amateur' affair for people who combined it with ordinary jobs in law, teaching and other forms of public service, or who moved from business and professional life into politics. Now parliaments are full of career professionals who have done nothing but politics all their life. They listen mainly to other career professionals, rather than the general public, and try to secure their own political jobs by colluding with each to exclude the smaller and newer parties.
- *Electoral–professional parties* Drawing from Michels' 'iron law of oligarchy' (chapter 9), it is argued that modern parties have been 'captured' by professional career politicians who run highly centralised and technically skilled party operations and election campaigns.

Party policy and organisation, it is said, are now as much a technical and professional matter as an ideological one. They involve opinion polling, focus groups, spin-doctors, carefully planned public relations and money-raising campaigns, computer technology and mastery of the mass media. Party conferences are no longer policy-making events, where the party faithful debate party policy to reach a decision, but stage-managed public relations events organised around photo-opportunities and sound bites designed to confirm

the policy of the leaders. At the same time, parties still need a core of supporters and workers to get the vote out on election days and to raise money.
Party organisations, albeit in new forms, and grass-roots members are still
required, even in the media age.

■ New parties and movements

New forms of organisation are not the only change that modern parties
have experienced. We have already seen how old voting patterns in western
Europe, based on class cleavages, have changed to some extent, causing the
old party system to 'unfreeze'. The result has been the appearance of new parties and movements that differ from the old parties in three main ways:

- They are based on the 'new' issues of the environment, peace, feminism,
  nuclear weapons and energy, animal rights, community participation and
  minority group rights.
- They are supported mainly by the young, well-educated and relatively
  affluent sections of the population, so are found mainly in the most affluent democracies rather than in industrialising countries.
- They use different political methods, often direct and grass-roots community action, protests and demonstrations and sometimes even violence.

Sometimes the new parties are known as 'anti-party parties' or 'anti-politics
movements', because they oppose the ideas and methods of the traditional
and conventional parties and pressure groups. The first flowering of such
parties is often said to have been in 1968 when a new generation of student activists, intellectuals and some workers took to the streets in many
western countries to protest against conventional politics. According to some
analysts, the new parties are closely associated with the emergence of post-
materialism (chapter 9) and they also overlap with the New Social Movements
(chapter 10).

Originally there was speculation that the new parties and movements
would cause a crisis in democratic politics by replacing the old party and
pressure groups, or at least undermining them, so destabilising conventional
politics. This has not happened, partly because the new parties have usually
remained quite small, and partly because the old parties have adapted to
them by stealing some of their new policies. In fact, some of the old parties have long advocated aspects of the 'new' policies, though they have not
always put them at the very top of their agendas. They have now polished
them up and pushed them closer to the front of their political stall to try to
outflank the new organisations.

The result, as we saw in terms of voting in chapter 12, is not the replacement of the old politics by the new, but rather a fusion of the two. Few of the
old parties have disappeared, although they have adapted their policies and
organisation to fit new conditions, and they have sometimes declined in

power. At the same time, few new parties seriously rival the old, although some have forced old parties to shift their political agenda. There has been a tendency for **party systems** to fragment as new parties have entered the arena, and some increase in electoral volatility as the electorate changes its voting habits. But in general the pattern is one of change with continuity rather than the total transformation of the old system.

Party system The pattern of significant parties within a political system, especially their number and the party families represented.

In large part this is because parties set out to appeal to sections of the population according to their social, economic and political interests. Since the social and economic structure does not change rapidly nor do the political parties, and since the social and economic structure of advanced societies are often rather similar, so also are their political parties. This leads us to a discussion of party families.

■ Party systems and party families

Most democracies have many parties, and each country has its own unique combination of them. Nonetheless, the parties of democratic countries have two major features in common:

Party families Groups of parties in different countries that have similar ideologies and party programmes.

- They often group into **party families**.
- They form party systems which can be explained with a few simple rules.

Party families

Although parties come in all shapes and colours, they often fall neatly into types, because parties of the same sort in different countries often bear a striking family resemblance to each other. Because the main parties are built around the main social cleavages in society, and because urban–industrial societies tend to have similar cleavages, one can usually find a few main parties that appeal to similar social groups, and have similar core values and policies that express similar goals. There are seven main party families and, to simplify our task of classifying parties even more, most can be arranged fairly neatly on a left–right scale. We shall look much more closely at the beliefs and programmes of party families in chapter 14; here it is enough simply to identify the types and show how they fit into government coalitions. Starting with the left the families are:

1. Socialist parties are found around the world from Chile to New Zealand and from Canada to Japan, and virtually everywhere in between. They include social democratic, Labour, new-left, left-socialist and ex-communist parties.

2. Christian Democratic parties and Christian Socialist parties are found mainly in Europe and Latin America.

3. Agrarian parties, variously called Farmer, Peasant, Agrarian or Centre parties are mainly found in Europe (and India), and are of declining importance. In other places agrarian and rural interests are often organised into powerful interest groups with close links to government ministries.

4. Liberal parties, often known as Radical, Progressive, Liberal or Freedom parties. Liberalism is strong in Europe, Canada, Australia and New Zealand, but weak in Africa and Asia and most of Latin America.

5. Conservative parties often go under the name of Conservative, National or Moderate parties.

6. Nationalist, regional or minority ethnic parties. These take all sorts of political positions from radical parties of the left and the right. Some want complete national independence for their region, some want more independence from their central government. Regional parties are strong in India, for instance.

7. Green parties come in different left–right colours but are often centre-left and all stress environmental protection and sustainability.

Briefing 13.1 lists these types, and provides examples of the parties in each family and the countries in which they are found. As stated, their ideological positions and policies are discussed in chapter 14.

Party systems

Party families are closely linked with party systems because both are based on the same features of the social and economic structure of society:

1. Since large parties are built upon cleavages, there is a connection between the number of cleavages and the number of parties. Countries with one main cleavage – usually class – tend to have two main parties, one on the centre-left and one on the centre-right. Countries with two main cleavages – class and religion, for example – tend to have three main parties, one to represent the middle class and its main religion, and two others to represent the working class and its different religious or secular values. This association between the number of cleavages and parties is sometimes expressed by the simple formula:

    $P = C + 1$

    where P stands for the number of parties and C for the number of cleavages.

2. Because there is usually room only for one major party to articulate one side of a cleavage, we rarely find more than one large party on the same side. A large social democratic party is not often found alongside a large communist party, and a large Christian democratic party is unlikely to be opposed by a large conservative party, or a major agrarian party found

with a major liberal party. This, of course, is only another way of formulating the $P = C + 1$ rule.

Briefing 13.1

Party families

Family	Country	Example
Socialist	Brazil	Democratic Labour
	Canada	New Democratic Party
	Czech Republic, Denmark, Estonia, Finland, Germany, Iceland, Japan, Lithuania, Sweden, the Netherlands	Social Democratic Party
	Australia, Ireland, Mauritius, New Zealand, Norway, UK	Labour Party
	Argentina, Austria, Belgium, Chile, France, Greece, Hungary, Japan, Portugal, Spain, Uruguay	Socialist Party
	Costa Rica	National Liberation Party
	Dominican Republic	Dominican Revolutionary Party
	Jamaica	People's National Party
	Peru	Peruvian Aprista Party
	South Africa	African National Congress
Christian Democrat	Argentina, Australia, Chile, the Czech Republic, Germany, Hungary, Latvia, Lithuania, the Netherlands, Portugal, Slovenia, Sweden, Switzerland Romania, South Africa	Christian Democratic Party National, Peasant or Christian Democratic Party
	Denmark, Norway	Christian People's
	Belgium	Flemish Christians, French Christians
Agrarian	Estonia, Finland, Norway, Sweden	Centre Party
	Latvia	Farmers Party

	Australia	Country, National Party
	Poland	Peasants' Party
Liberal	Canada	Liberal, Social Credit Party
	Sweden	People's Party
	Finland, Japan, Taiwan	Progressive Party
	UK	Liberal Democratic Party
	France	Left Radical Party
	Germany	Free Democrats
	USA	Democratic Party
	Philippines	Liberal Party
	South Africa	Democratic Alliance
Conservative	Canada, Denmark, Norway, UK	Conservative Party
	Japan	Democratic Liberal Party
	New Zealand	National Party
	Sweden	Moderate Party
	Finland	National Coalition
	France	Gaullist Party
	Austria	Freedom Party
	USA	Republican Party
Regional, Ethnic parties	Finland	Swedish People's Party
	Belgium	Flemish, Flemish Nationalist Party
	Spain	Basque Nationalist Party, Catalan Nationalist Party
	UK	Irish Nationalist (Unionist, Social Democratic and Labour Party), Scottish, Welsh
	Italy	Northern League
	Canada	Quebec Nationalist Party
New parties	Australia, Austria, Belgium, Canada, Finland, France, Ireland, Italy, Israel, Japan, Poland, South Africa, Sweden, Switzerland	Green Party
	New Zealand	Values, Greens and Alliance Parties

3. Most social cleavages are old, so many of the main parties date back to the late nineteenth and early twentieth centuries, when the modern industrial system was formed and voting rights extended.

4. Across western nations the social democrats are usually the largest single party because the working class is the largest, though their strength has declined a little. They are followed by the conservatives, Christian democrats, liberals and agrarian parties, in that order.

Dominant one-party system A party system in which one party dominates all the others.

Two-party system Party system in which two large parties dominate all the others.

Multi-party system Where several main parties compete, often with the result that no single party has an overall majority.

Most discussion of party systems distinguishes between dominant one-party, two-party and multi-party systems. **Dominant one-party systems** are relatively rare, **two-party systems** more frequent and **multi-party systems** the most common (see fact file 13.1). The party system has a great significance for the kinds of governments that are formed in most democracies.

One-party and coalition government

Democratic accountability in democracies is supposed to be maintained by the fact that free elections allow voters to choose their political representatives. They can either reward good governments with another term of office or kick them out. The overwhelming majority of representatives are elected as party candidates, and it is the party distribution of seats in a parliamentary system that determines the composition of the government. As long as the government can muster the support of a majority of elected representatives in the assembly, it can continue in government.

In dominant one-party systems government formation is straightforward – there is no alternative to the dominant party (see briefing 13.2). In two-party systems, it is usually also straightforward because the majority party will form the government if it has an absolute majority of seats in parliament, and if it does not it can probably govern with the legislative support of one or more of the other parties, usually minor ones. As a result, two-party systems generally produce one-party government in which the other party forms the opposition. However, one-party government is the exception rather than the rule in most democracies.

Most government in most countries is by **coalition** simply because they have electoral and multi-party systems that make it unusual to have a single-party majority in the assembly. This makes it important to understand the process of government formation and maintenance in multi-party systems with **coalition** government.

Coalition A set of parties that comes together to form a government.

Fact file 13.1

Party systems, government formation, coalitions and electoral systems

■ Party systems

- Dominant one-party systems have occurred in India (Congress Party), Japan (Liberal Democratic Party), South Africa (African National Congress) and Sweden (Social Democratic Workers' Party).
- Few countries have a two-party system. Canada, New Zealand (until 1966), the USA and the UK are the main examples.
- Multi-party systems are the norm and are found in most parts of the democratic world.
- The multi-party systems of most western European nations since 1945 are associated with coalition government.

■ Government formation and coalitions

- About 10 per cent of all governments formed in western Europe between 1945 and 1995 were single-party governments, about a third were MWC (see p. 279), another third minority governments and one in six were surplus majority.
- Coalition government is common in the Nordic and Benelux countries, Germany, Switzerland, Israel and India. In some countries coalition has been the response to national crisis or war.
- Electoral coalitions in presidential campaigns are common in Brazil, Chile and Costa Rica, and legislative coalitions are not unusual either, although multi-party systems and loose-knit catch-all parties make coalition stability a problem.
- Grand coalitions have often ruled in Austria and Switzerland, and sometimes in Germany.
- MWCs have survived well in Austria, Germany and Norway, and minority governments have done well in Ireland, Sweden and especially Denmark.
- Coalitions of all kinds have fared poorly in Belgium, France (1945–58), Portugal and Finland.

■ Voting and party systems

- Of 73 democracies in the 1990s, 36 had PR electoral systems and 37 non-PR systems. Of the 36 PR countries, 81 per cent were multi-party and the remaining 19 per cent were either two- or dominant one-party systems. Of the 37 non-PR countries, 50 per cent were either two- or dominant one-party systems, and 13 per cent were multi-party.

■ Coalition government

If no single party is large enough to form the government, then a party coalition will have to be formed. Most democracies have quite a few parties that are important enough to claim a position in government, either because their size makes it difficult to overlook them, or because their place in the party system gives them a pivotal role in government formation. The creation of such a coalition often involves long, hard and complex negotiations between party leaders. In some cases, alliances are negotiated before elections (electoral coalitions), but more normally coalitions are constructed after elections, when the parliamentary strength of the parties is known (see briefing 13.2). This process of bargaining between possible coalition partners is usually a hidden form of 'horse-trading' taking place in smoke-filled rooms, but there are some rules governing the process:

1. Normally, the leader of the largest party in parliament/assembly has the first chance at trying to form a governing coalition, and as such is known as the *formateur* but if this fails the job passes to the leader of the second largest party.
2. Some constitutions give the head of state the right to nominate the *formateur*, though there is often little choice given the first rule.
3. The job of the *formateur* is to find agreement among coalition partners on government policy and the division of cabinet posts between the parties. Policy agreements can be very specific indeed and result in thick and detailed policy documents. This may take months of hard bargaining.

Briefing 13.2

Government formation: parliamentary systems

Party system	Assembly	Government
One-party dominant	One-party majority	Dominant party government – Japan, Sweden, South Africa
Two-party system	One-party majority or near-majority	One-party government with swings between the two main parties – Greece, Norway, Spain (1982–95), the UK
Multi-party system	Multi-party assemblies	Coalition government
Electoral alliance		Coalitions formed before election
No electoral alliance		Coalition government formed after election Minority government – common in Denmark and not uncommon in Finland, Italy and Sweden MWC – quite common in many coalitions Oversized coalition – quite common in Finland, Italy and The Netherlands 'Grand' coalition – Austria, Bulgaria, Canada, Switzerland, (West) Germany, Portugal

4. Cabinet positions in a coalition are usually distributed roughly in proportion to the strength of the coalition partners in the assembly, and the leader of one of the largest parties usually becomes the prime minister. Which politicians end up with which cabinet posts is usually a matter of tough negotiation, and pivotal parties in the coalition can drive a hard bargain.

5. If a governing coalition is formed it is then formally invested in office by the head of state, and sometimes parliament must give its formal assent as well.

6. A coalition government that loses a **vote of confidence** in the parliament/assembly is normally required to resign, but remains in office as a caretaker government until a new government is formed.

> **Vote of confidence** A vote of confidence (or no confidence) tests whether the government of the day continues to have the majority support of members of the assembly.

Early theory predicted that coalition governments would usually take the form of **minimum winning coalitions (MWC)** because these are the smallest that can count on a majority of votes in the assembly. Anything larger than a MWC has more votes than strictly necessary, and the more coalition partners there are the greater the chance of difficulties between them. Anything smaller than a MWC means that the government cannot count on a majority of votes in the assembly.

> **Minimum winning coalition** The smallest number of parties necessary for a majority of votes in parliament.

However, an examination of coalition governments shows that a large proportion is either smaller or larger than a MWC. **A minority government,** often consisting of one party, is quite common. The reason is that opposition parties can sometimes exercise a great deal of influence within parliament through its committees, or outside it through affiliated pressure groups (trade unions, business organisations). In such systems, it is not essential to have a position within government in order to wield political influence. In other cases, minority governments persist simply because the opposition majorities are not sufficiently unified to be able to remove the minority from power.

> **Minority government** A government or coalition that is smaller than a MWC.

Quite a few coalitions are larger than necessary. **'Oversized' coalitions** often exist where the 'surplus' parties have policies that are similar to those of the other parties in the coalition. Drawing from similar parties in this way includes all like-minded groups in the government, and reduces the chances of conflict and instability caused by excluding people who might easily be allies if included, enemies if excluded. Surplus majorities may also help to keep the minority parties within them quiet because they know that they can be ejected from the coalition if they make trouble, without risking the government's majority. In some cases, **'grand' coalitions** are formed, consisting of all the most important parties. These are not common and are usually created in the face of a crisis.

> **'Oversized' coalition** A coalition that is larger than an MWC.

> **'Grand' coalition** Oversized coalitions that include all parties or the largest of them.

It is easier to form and maintain a government if the coalition partners have a similar outlook and policy. Most coalition governments therefore contain parties that are quite 'close' in policy terms. This gives centre and moderate parties an advantage because they can form an alliance with the moderate left or the moderate right. Sometimes, however, the strength of parties in the assembly makes it difficult to achieve a minimum ideological spread, and then politics makes for strange bed-fellows and greater instability.

■ Coalitions and government effectiveness

It used to be thought that two-party systems were the best because they tended to result in stable, moderate and accountable government. They often produced clear and stable working majorities in parliament. If only one party was in power it could be held clearly accountable for government actions. In two-party systems, there was a strong incentive for both parties to try to hold to the middle ground and hence moderate policies. The inter-war Weimar government in Germany, and the frequent collapse of coalition governments in the Fourth French Republic and in post-war Italy were often wheeled out as examples to make the point about the instability of coalition government.

It is also claimed that the process of forming coalition government gives too much power to politicians and their wheeler-dealing and secret horse-trading. The outcome of their bargaining may not reflect the preferences of voters, it may also give too much power to pivotal parties, whose support is necessary for successful coalition formation, even if they are rather small and unrepresentative. Experience, however, suggests that coalitions can be as stable as one-party government. Germany, The Netherlands, Scandinavia and Switzerland have all had long periods of coalition government that have been effective, stable and moderate.

It is true that unstable coalitions sometimes require the reconstitution of government between elections – that is, the formation of a new coalition: hence some countries have more governments than elections. But the consequences of instability need not be severe or chaotic. The presence of the same party (or parties) in successive coalitions often gives continuity, and the cautious, inclusive and consensual nature of much coalition government discourages rapid swings of policy from one single-party government to the next. It is also easy to exaggerate the instability of coalition government. While single-party governments are generally the most long-lasting, MWCs survive well in some countries, just as surplus majority ones do in others (see fact file 13.1). By and large, coalitions made up of a small number of parties, and of parties that are quite close on the left–right continuum, are most stable. Finally, coalitions are not unrepresentative of electoral opinion. They often have to be moderate to stay in power, and their frequent inclusion of a centre party as a partner means they tend to be representative of the middle ground of politics.

■ Parties and democracy

Competition between parties for governing power is at the very heart of democracy. All stable democracies, even those with dominant single parties, have organised oppositions ready to step into office if they are electorally successful. The peaceful transfer of power between parties at election time is a hallmark of a successful and stable democracy. Parties were also crucial in the second and third wave of democratisation where leaders acted on their willingness to accept (many or most of) the democratic rules of the game. Authoritarian governments and dictators often try to hold on to power at any price. Democratic politicians comply with election outcomes that are peaceful and fair.

Nevertheless, party politics is often attacked as harmful and unnecessary in a democracy (see controversy 13.1), especially when they are corrupt or where party leaders handle themselves and public affairs badly. There can be much truth in these criticisms, but there is also much truth in the counterargument that there seems to be nothing better than parties. It is probably true that if parties did not exist, someone would have to invent them.

It remains the case, however, that parties across the democratic world, and especially in the older democracies, are losing members and that fewer people are identifying with them. This means that parties are more dependent on sources of money other than individual subscriptions, which has raised the issue of whether to allow them to raise more from private (business?) sources or to subsidise them with public funds. This is a highly controversial matter much discussed when parties run into severe financial problems or find themselves in the hands of wealthy donors to party funds.

■ Theories of parties

The 'iron law of oligarchy'

In *Political Parties,* published in 1911, and one of the most influential books on the subject, Robert Michels (1876–1936) argues that parties are, and always will be, run by minorities. Michels' famous 'iron law' claims that all large-scale organisations – parties, pressure groups, trade unions, churches, universities – are controlled by a few leaders, no matter how democratic they try to be. There are several reasons for this:

- Organisationally, leaders are best informed about the business of the organisation and control its internal means of communication. They are also likely to have better organisational skills than ordinary members.
- Psychologically, the masses rely upon leaders because they have neither the time nor the ability to master the affairs of the organisation, and because they feel the need for leadership 'direction and guidance'. Leaders generally have better pay and status than followers, so they try to hang on to their jobs.

CONTROVERSY 13.1

Parties and democracy

Parties are bad for democracy because:
- Parties involve faction and conflict, and politicians should search for consensus and national unity.
- Parties represent the interests of particular sections of society (classes, religious groups, regions, ethnic groups, and the like).
- There is no need for party politics because common sense tells us there is only 'one way to lay a sidewalk'.
- Parties are inherently undemocratic, being run by small cliques and elites of self interested and untrustworthy politicians.
- Therefore, society should be run and important decisions taken not by factious, self-interested politicians but by a small group of wise people with the public interest at heart – the 'philosopher kings' advocated by Plato, or the 'good and the great' of society, or a group of experts and technocrats.

Parties are good for democracy because:
- Faction and conflict are unavoidable in politics. Disagreement and incompatible interests are the reason for politics in the first place, and democracy is a way of settling these differences in the most peaceful and least unsatisfactory manner.
- Society is, whether we like it or not, divided according to class, religion, region, gender, age, ethnicity, and so on. Democracy involves parties representing group interests trying to resolve their differeneces.
- There is not 'only one way to lay a sidewalk'. There is not and never has been anything but a variety of approaches to all public matters. And why use scarce resources on sidewalks at all when the money should be spent on education or health or housing or art or public transport or … ? The 'one way' argument is used by people who believe theirs is the only 'true' way.
- We can rarely agree on who are the best people to run society and make important decisions, so we have elections. Therefore, we have political parties of like-minded people to run for office.
- Parties perform vital political functions: interest articulation and interest aggregation, the communication of opinion and information between masses and elites, providing party cues and political information for those who need them in elections; the mobilisation of citizen and voters at appropriate times; the co-ordination of the machinery and policy of government; recruiting citizens for political office and training party activists for high positions of government; the formal organisation of a political competition for power at election time.

Not all parties are good. Some are anti-democratic. But a competitive party system stands the best chance of producing a stable democracy based on majority voting.

A more recent version of Michels' theory of **oligarchy** is the electoral–professional interpretation of modern political parties discussed earlier in this chapter.

Oligarchy Government by a few.

Oligarchy in organisations would not matter so much if it were not also believed that leaders inevitably betray their organisation, using their position either for their own interests – personal power, glory, or money – or following policies that are not approved by rank-and-file members. They may do the latter not because they are corrupt or untrustworthy, though this may be true in some cases, but because being leaders of their organisations who come into contact with leaders of other organisations, they take a wider view of matters. They may also follow longer-term and more strategic policies.

Max Weber (1864–1920), a contemporary of Michels in Germany, argued a similar case when he said that 'for the time being the dictatorship of the official and not that of the worker is on the march' (see chapter 8). Michels and Weber argue that full-time, experienced and trained professionals will always dominate part-time, untrained and inexperienced amateurs. Although Weber applies his theory to the power struggle between bureaucrats and politicians, rather than party leaders and followers, the principles are the same.

There are two possible responses to the Michels–Weber thesis. The first argues that the law, though it may be generally true, is not 'iron' because there are examples of private organisations that are not oligarchical. The second claims that it does not particularly matter if organisations are internally oligarchic if competition between them produces democracy. Business associations and trade unions may not be particularly democratic, but competition between them may be.

Duverger's law

The 'iron law' deals with the internal organisation of parties, while another classic 'law', of the French political scientist Maurice Duverger (1917–), is concerned with the relationship between electoral systems and party systems. He argued that states that have non-proportional elections (specifically single member, simple plurality systems) favour two parties, while proportional elections favour multi-party systems. Non-proportional elections usually discriminate against small parties because they fail to turn their votes into a proportional number of seats. The electorate knows this, and is less inclined to vote for small parties because it may be a 'wasted vote'.

Many years of debate about Duverger's law have tended to concentrate on two issues:

- First, what is cause and what is effect? Belgium, Denmark, Germany and Norway were multi-party systems before they opted for PR, and they may have done so because it was in the interest of small parties to have PR, or because it was the only electoral system that was acceptable to most parties, including the small ones. On the other side of the coin, the USA and the UK seem to keep their SMSP system because it is in the interests of the two main parties that are the only ones with power enough to change them. Since governing parties gain power through SMSP they are unlikely to change it for a different electoral system that might lose them this advantage.

- Second, in spite of exceptions to the 'law', there is in general a good deal of truth in it. The most proportionate voting systems are much more likely to be multi-party than the most disproportionate (see chapter 12).

Coalition theory

The early and influential work on coalition formation by William Riker (1920–93) predicted that coalitions would be just big enough to ensure a majority in the assembly, but no bigger or smaller. It was assumed that politicians were motivated primarily by a desire for power or prestige, in which case there was no sense in sharing cabinet posts among more parties than was strictly necessary. Consequently, coalitions would be MWCs.

A different assumption is that politicians seek office not exclusively for power, prestige or government office, but in order to influence public policy. Such politicians might consider a course of action that gave them influence over public policy even if it fell short of government office. Minority governments may thus be successful if there are politicians outside government who are prepared to support their policy. Similarly, surplus majority governments may be formed if they help to achieve policy goals. If it is policy, rather than office-seeking that counts, one might assume that the limits on coalition formation will be set not necessarily by coalition size but by the ideological 'closeness' of parties. If so, according to the theory proposed by Maurice Axelrod in his book *Conflict of Interest* (1970) coalitions might be the smallest ideological span necessary to drive policy in a particular direction. Coalitions will be formed by the closest set of parties capable of forming an effective alliance.

Evidence over the post-war years in the democracies provides support for both the Riker and Axelrod theories, but there is not overwhelming support for either:

- The largest group of government coalitions are MWC, but it is also true that minimum coalitions are outnumbered by oversized and minority governments.
- It is also the case that nearly a half of all coalitions are MCW, but this means that half are not.
- In short, most situations that could result in MWCs have not produced them, although, of all kinds of coalition, the MWC are most numerous.

Giovanni Sartori (1924–) argues that both the number and the ideological distance between parties are important for understanding how multi-party systems work and how governments are formed. He distinguishes between moderate and polarised pluralism. The moderate type usually has three to five main parties, which tend to compete for the centre ground, and therefore tend to be moderate. Polarised systems normally have six or more main parties, which tend to move to the extremes in order to find votes in an overcrowded political arena. This makes it difficult to form and sustain coalition cabinets.

Perhaps the only safe conclusion to draw from this discussion of coalition theory is that politicians are not exclusively self-interested (office-seeking), and that they may opt for either surplus majority or minority governments, if this helps them, or they may opt to work outside the government if the system allows them to influence policy in this way. This conclusion is consistent with the conclusion that voters are not always self-interested, but pay some regard to the public interest. It does not follow that politicians are not interested in power and office, but it does seem to be the case that they are not interested in these things all the time.

Majoritarian and consensus government revisited

At the end of chapter 7, we presented Arend Lijphart's account of majoritarian and consensus government, but did not complete the discussion, having covered only the formal institutions of government at that point. We can now deal with the rest of the majoritarian–consensus typology, having also discussed its other characteristics in chapters 9–12 dealing with electoral systems, party systems, government formation and pressure groups.

Majoritarian governments tend to concentrate power in the hands of the political executive and are associated with the fusion of executive and legislative powers, a unicameral legislature, unitary government, and government control over central banks and courts with no special powers to review constitutional matters or legislation. In the classic 'Westminster system', built around the principle of parliamentary sovereignty, these features of government fit together in a logical and consistent manner, given the initial purpose of concentrating a good deal of political power in the hands of the party that represents a majority of citizens. The remaining four key features of majoritiarian democracies also fit the pattern well:

1. *Majoritarian and disproportional electoral systems* Majoritarian democracies tend to favour single-member districts and first-past-the post voting systems. This favours large over small parties and magnifies the size of the winning party's majority of seats compared with its votes.
2. *Two-party systems* The winner-takes-all nature of parliamentary systems, as well as their electoral discrimination against small parties, encourages the formation of two large parties that alternate in government.
3. *Single-party government* The winning party with a majority of seats becomes the government. All other parties form the opposition.
4. *Pluralist pressure group systems* Pressure groups in society are loosely integrated in the decision-making structure of government, sometimes forming policy communities but more usually taking the form of competitive policy networks.

Consensus democracies try to represent not the electoral majority and its party but as many people as possible, including minorities. They therefore try to distribute executive power more broadly and are associated with the separation and balancing of executive power, bicameralism, federalism, independent central banks and judicial review. The other four key features are consistent with the goal of broad representation and the distribution of power:

1. *Proportional electoral systems* These systems distribute seats in more or less the same ratio of votes.
2. *Multi-party systems* Multi-party government and proportional electoral systems do not discourage small parties.
3. *Coalition governments* The formation of broad coalition governments can involve sometimes oversized or 'grand' coalitions.
4. *Corporatist pressure group systems* Major pressure groups are formally incorporated into the decision-making machinery of government, where they cooperate on policy issues.

This twofold typology does not simply describe the political systems of democracy, it also helps to explain their performance in five interesting and important respects:

1. *The distance between governments and voters* Consensus democracies have governments that are closer to the policy preferences of citizens than majoritarian systems.
2. *Citizens' satisfaction* The citizens of consensus democracies are more satisfied with the democratic performance of their countries than those of majoritarian democracies. In part, this is because the losers in consensus systems are more satisfied than the losers in majoritarian systems, in part because they acknowledge that the electoral system is fairer and they have not been discriminated against and because, even as electoral minorities, they still have influence over government policies.
3. *Turnout* Consensus democracies have a higher voting turnout (by about 7.5 per cent) than majoritarian ones.
4. *Women in parliament* Consensus democracies have about 6.5 per cent more women in the main legislative chamber.
5. *Effective number of parties* Consensus democracies not only have a larger number of parties contesting elections but, because of their proportional voting systems, they also have a larger number of effective parties – that is, parties that are large enough to play a significant role in the assembly.

On the basis of this evidence, Lijphart concludes that the majoritarian and consensus systems have extremely important practical implications for the performance of democracies. The performance of consensus democracies is superior.

■ What have we learned?

Politics is about the struggle for power, and this chapter deals with how parties are at the very centre of this struggle in their attempts to win elections and gain government office. It argues that:

- Parties have passed through three main phases of organisation – caucus, mass parties and catch-all parties. Now they are said to be moving into a new phase of media parties, or cartel parties, or electoral–professional parties, which have strong leaders and few members.
- Just as old patterns of voting have tended to persist, albeit with some changes, so the old parties, formed in the late nineteenth and early twentieth centuries, have persisted, albeit with changes induced by new parties and movements. The result is continuity of historical patterns with change, in which the new has combined and fused with the old, rather than a transformation of party systems.
- Democracies have one-party, two-party or coalition government, but coalitions are most common.
- Contrary to early theories, most coalition governments do not take the MWC form. Minority governments, surplus majority governments and (occasionally) 'grand' coalitions are more common.

■ Lessons of comparison

- There is not much evidence to support the claim that coalition government is unstable, unaccountable, or unrepresentative compared with single-party governments.
- Although there are significant exceptions, proportional voting is associated with multi-party systems and coalition government. Non-proportional voting is associated with a dominant party or two main parties.
- The evidence suggests that politicians are not exclusively interested in prestige or the power that goes with government office (office-seeking). They may support surplus majority or minority governments, and they may choose to work outside government if this helps them influence government policy.
- The evidence suggests that the democratic performance of consensus democracies is superior to that of majoritarian systems.

Projects

1. Collect a list of all the main political parties in your country and try to sort them into the seven main categories discussed in this chapter. What difficulties do you meet in trying to classify your parties, and why do you think your country produces parties that do not fit the scheme?
2. Are you persuaded that the democratic performance of consensus democracies is superior to that of majoritarian systems?
3. Are parties good or bad for democracy?

Further reading

A. Ware, *Political Parties and Party Systems,* Oxford: Oxford University Press, 1995.
A broad survey of the literature on parties.

P. Webb, D. Farrell and I. Holliday, *Political Parties in Advanced Industrial Democracies,* Oxford: Oxford University Press, 2002.
A stystematic account of how parties have changed and adapted to new circumstances.

R. Gunther, J. R. Montero and J. J. Linz (eds), *Political Parties: Old Concepts and New Challenges,* Oxford: Oxford University Press, 2002.
An expert survey and review of recent literature on political parties.

S. B. Wolinetz (ed.), *Political Parties,* Aldershot: Ashgate, 1997.
Essays reviewing most of the current topics on political parties.

P. Webb and S. White (eds), *Party Politics in New Democracies*, Oxford: Oxford University Press, 2007.
Examines the development and performance of parties in the new democracies of Latin America and central Europe.

R. S. Katz and W. J. Crotty (eds), *Handbook of Party Politics*, London: Sage, 2006.
A broad array of essay on parties and party research.

Websites

http://sosig.esrc.bris.ac.uk/roads/subject-listing/World-cat/polparties.html
An extensive list of web resources on parties and politics in the regions of the world.
www.gksoft.com/govt/en/parties.html
Provides links to political parties in the nations of the world.
www.wordiq.com
Lists political parties by region, country and ideology.
www.politicalresources.net/
Website of political sources on the net with links to all the parties of the world by country.
www.psr.keele.ac.uk/parties.htm
Website with links to party constitutions.
www.psr.keele.ac.uk/sseal/index.htm
The updated Seventh Seal website with links to many political parties and movements.

PART IV

Policies and performance

Most ordinary people are not very interested in political institutions and proc-esses. What interests them about politics is what governments do to them and for them: How much tax do they pay? What sorts of public services do they get? How well does the government handle financial crises? Do their children get a good education? Is the nation well protected against its enemies?

Part IV of the book is about the policies and performance of governments. A 'pol-icy' is a general set of ideas formulated into a plan that has been officially agreed, and which is used as a basis for making decisions. Although ideas and plans are important, what most people care about is performance. By 'performance' we mean the actual results that governments get – is inflation low and economic growth good? Is crime under control? Are schools well staffed and equipped? Is hospital care effective? Plans are no good if they do not achieve their goals, and perform-ance is no good if it is based on muddled or dangerous plans in the first place. Citizens want good plans and good performance together, but they care most about performance.

Part IV of the book has chapters on both the policies and performance of demo-cratic states. Since plans and policies are what parties and governments start with, chapter 14 examines the 'isms' of politics – competing ideas about what govern-ments should do, and how they should do it. These are known as 'ideologies', and there are four main ones in western politics: socialism, liberalism, Christian democ-racy and conservatism. Each is built on rather different basic values and assump-tions about important concepts such as individualism and collectivism, liberalism and the role of the state, equality and freedom. Different attitudes towards these basic concepts and values are what define the 'isms' of politics and the fundamental difference between parties.

Chapter 15 then focuses not on the theory but on the practice of making government decisions and implementing them. This can be seen as an endless cycle, starting with a general plan of action and ending with an evaluation of the results achieved by implementing it. We will see that for all the variation in the details of their policy-making processes, states tend to follow one of two general logics. Some incorporate their main social and economic interests into a formal structure of cooperative decision making. Others lean towards conflict and competition between different groups.

In chapter 16 we examine the defence and security of the state, and the way states defend themselves against domestic crime and foreign aggression. Security of the state and its individual citizens, however, does not end here because modern life is beset by any number of other dangers ranging from atomic radiation to badly designed toasters, and governments are expected to do something about these as well. The chapter looks at how the democratic state handles all these threats to the safety and security of its citizens.

Chapter 17 looks more closely at a different form of citizen protection – namely the social security and welfare system. It deals mainly with welfare and social security, pensions and health, and with the way that the state raises money to pay for these services. Of course, government is involved with a far wider range of public services than defence, national security, social security and welfare. We have chosen the fields of national security and social welfare because they cover two of the oldest of all functions of the state (to protect itself from internal and external enemies) and one of the newer (to provide its citizens with a decent standard of living and security against poverty, unemployment, ill health and the difficulties of old age). These areas of policy making highlight the problems that governments face when it comes to making decisions and implementing public policy. Chapter 18 draws some brief conclusions about the future of the democratic state.

The chapters in part IV, therefore, examine the key aspects of government policies and performance:

- Political ideologies
- Decision making
- Defence and security
- Welfare.

14   Political ideologies: conservatism, liberalism, Christian democracy and socialism

Politics is confusing. A casual look at the daily news shows a great profusion of fast-moving events, with many conflicting and incompatible interpretations of them. How can we ever make sense of such a bewildering and incomprehensible business? The answer lies partly in how we organise our ideas, preconceptions and assumptions about politics. We develop a framework of ideas known as an **ideology**, which helps us to understand and interpret politics. This system of ideas, values and assumptions enables us to fit events into a pattern that we can understand.

> **Ideology** A more or less systematic, well-developed and comprehensive set of ideas and beliefs about politics consisting of both (empirical) statements about what is, and (prescriptive) statements about what ought to be.

Ideologies are about more than understanding, however. If politics is a struggle for power, then ideologies are part of that struggle. Party politicians in democracies know that they must win the tacit support, if not the 'hearts and minds', of most of their citizens if they are to continue in power. Ideologies are the tools – perhaps even among the most important tools – by which they do this because ideologies are built around the basic interests of the most important groups in society.

Because people have contrasting interests and ideas, and because they see politics in radically different ways, there are naturally different ideological world views, including liberalism, conservatism, anarchism, Marxism, Maoism, socialism, Christian democracy, social democracy, fascism, nazism and libertarianism, among others. Fortunately, there are only four main ideologies to be found in democracies, which helps to simplify the life of comparative political scientists to a great extent. These are conservatism, liberalism, Christian democracy and socialism/social democracy. There are also three other systems of thought – nationalism, Green political thought and populism – but their status as ideologies is disputed so we will discuss them after the main four.

In this chapter, we present an account of the main party ideologies in democracies. The chapter also analyses the nature of ideology itself and discusses the future for ideological thinking in a world where ideology is said by some to have come to an end. The main topics in this chapter, therefore, are:

- The nature of ideology
- Four main democratic ideologies
- Three other types of political thought
- Theories of ideology.

■ The nature of ideology

Ideology is a confusing concept that has been given different meanings in its history. Some have used it as a weapon in the struggle for power, and as a term of approval or disapproval, saying that while they have truth, reason, or science on their side, their opponents have only dogma and ideology. But the term is used here in its social science sense, as a tool of analysis, not as a weapon in the political struggle. Ideologies may be defined in terms of their four main characteristics:

1. *Complexity and abstraction* Ideologies are relatively complex, abstract, comprehensive and integrated systems of beliefs about politics. They are based on fundamental ideas and assumptions about human nature, society and politics, and on a set of basic values relating to the central concepts of political life including justice, liberty, equality, freedom and democracy. Ideologies are, therefore, far more than a loose bundle of beliefs about politics; they offer a systematic and well-articulated view of the political world and a consistent and generalised interpretation of it. This means that an ideology must be specific enough to fit particular circumstances, but abstract enough to be able to endure and travel widely across the globe.

2. *Empirical explanation* Ideologies claim to explain the political world. They pick out what they think is important from the mass of political details and events and offer coherent explanations of what is happening and why. This does not mean that they are right or wrong, only that they try to explain the facts of the political world as they see them.

3. *Normative prescription* Ideologies offer a vision of how political life could be and ought to be. They present a vision of what good government should be. In this sense ideologies are **normative statements** and prescriptive.

> **Normative statements** Statements based upon faith, values or evaluations. Sometimes referred to as prescriptive, or evaluative statements. They are neither scientific nor unscientific, but nonscientific.

4. *A plan for action* Ideologies spell out a set of beliefs about how political goals should be achieved. They claim to answer Lenin's (1870–1924) question: 'What is to be done?' Since there is often agreement in democracies about political goals – who is against liberty, justice, democracy and progress for all? – ideological differences are commonly about political means, rather than goals. Is it legitimate to use violent or illegal politics, or should we stick to the ballot and persuasion? Should we form political alliances with this or that group, or remain 'pure' and separate? Should we support this policy or a slightly different one? Should we vote for this democratic party or another?

Some writers are suspicious of ideologies, claiming that they are closed systems of thought that are not amenable to reason or disproof. They point to Marxism as an example, although there are many others like it. The Marxist claim that the capitalist system will collapse under the weight of its own contradictions has been repeated many times since the publication of *The Communist Manifesto* in 1848, but somehow capitalism has survived. As one cynic puts it: 'The imminent collapse of capitalism is the longest running show in the west.' Marxists, or rather crude Marxists, always have a Marxist explanation for this, and so they always manage to preserve their own belief system in the face of evidence that seems to disprove it. Whatever argument is used to criticise a closed ideology of this kind, and whatever evidence is used against it, is somehow treated as evidence to confirm it.

According to Karl Popper (1902–94), a philosopher of the social sciences, ideologies are to be distinguished clearly from scientific theories that can, in principle, be tested and falsified against the available evidence. In his book *The Open Society and Its Enemies*, published in 1945, Popper argues that some ideologies (not all, by any means) can be turned into closed and totalitarian systems of thought that can always justify themselves in their own terms. Scientific theories are falsifiable, closed systems of ideology are not.

There is a lot of truth in this point. In some respects, some ideologies are constructed rather like religions that seek to explain everything, and can be manipulated to fit the facts, whatever these are. Equally, it can be difficult to avoid this closed and dogmatic way of thinking. If we are to have a comprehensive and systematic view of the political world then our ideology must be broad and flexible to cover a wide variety of circumstances but not so broad that it can explain even those things that seem to contradict the ideology. Although this can be difficult to achieve, it is not necessarily true that ideologies turn into closed and totalitarian belief systems. An ideologist such as

John Stuart Mill (see below) proposed an open and self-critical belief system, and lived up to these standards in his own life.

Some analysts reserve the term 'ideologies' for a highly abstract, integrated and comprehensive set of values, beliefs and ideas. In this case, relatively few intelligent and well-educated people, with a strong interest in politics, have an ideology. Sometimes such people are referred to as 'ideologues' (see chapter 9). Others want to use the term more generally to cover more loose-knit, but still relatively coherent systems of ideas and values. Used in this way many ordinary citizens have an ideology.

Ideology is not the same as political culture, however. Ideologies are more or less explicit, whereas much of political culture is implicit and built on assumptions and deep-seated values that are taken for granted (see chapter 9). The language of ideologies consists of abstract concepts – including liberty, equality, fraternity, rights, justice and liberalism. Political cultures are built on assumptions about trust, happiness, political salience, national pride and political competence. To oversimplify, one is socialised into and assimilates a culture in the family, at school and in the community, but one learns an ideology by thinking, arguing and reading in a more self-conscious way.

Before we start our exploration of the main democratic ideologies, two last general points should be made:

1. Ideologies are an **essentially contestable concept**, which is a 'shorthand' way of saying that there is often little agreement about them, or about what they mean and what sort of action they entail. This is why even members of the same political party sharing the same ideology will often argue interminably with each other.

> **Essentially contestable concept** A concept that is inevitably the subject of endless dispute about its proper use (e.g. art, democracy, justice, beauty, goodness).

2. Closely related to this point is that fact that each major ideology has many variations within itself, and each different ideology has points in common with rival ideologies. It is difficult to draw a clear line around any ideology, or its variants, and difficult to summarise them in a clear and simple way.

■ Four democratic ideologies

In chapter 13, we organised party families along a left–right continuum according to their general views about the central issue of state intervention in society and the economy. We can do the same with ideologies, from conservatism on the right, to liberalism and Christian democracy in the centre and socialism and social democracy on the left. The three other schemes of thought (nationalism, Green political thought and populism) do not fit neatly on the left–right continuum, and so they will be discussed separately.

Conservatism

Because conservatism is pragmatic and flexible, some argue that it is not an ideology so much as a loose collection of ideas defending the status quo.

However, conservative thought can be based on a systematic set of funda-mental ideas. Two are particularly important. The first concerns social and political life, the second economic matters.

Social and political affairs

- *Organic society* Conservatism places great value upon the preservation of the status quo and its traditional institutions. It is a pragmatic ideology that argues that old institutions survive and work well because they are built on the accumulated wisdom and experience of the past. Society is like a natural organism that has changed slowly but surely over a long period. Moreover, it is composed of a complex set of interdependent parts, and reform that moves too fast will almost certainly destabilise the sys-tem and do more harm than good. Reform should be piecemeal, slow and cautious.

- *Pessimistic view of human nature* Conservatives tend to be pessimistic about human nature, arguing that the worst aspects of human nature – greed, selfishness and irrationality – will inevitably rise to the surface unless there is a clear social hierarchy to locate citizens in the social order, and a strong state to maintain it. Consequently, conservatism generally rejects competing ideologies that assume the natural goodness or 'perfectibility of man'. Instead it argues for a strong police force to maintain the social order, and a strong army to protect the state from its external enemies.

- *Representative democracy* Many conservatives believe that liberal democracy is best preserved in the hands of a relatively small, educated elite. The masses are not naturally democratic and it is dangerous to give them too much power. Hence conservatives often prefer indirect and representative democracy to direct, participatory forms.

- *Inequality* Many conservatives believe that people are inherently unequal in their intelligence and abilities, and that some economic and social inequality is natural and inevitable. Some conservative thought goes on to emphasise the social responsibilities of the rich and powerful for the poor and weak. Since this style of conservatism fits well with a religious emphasis on the importance of the family and traditional social values, it is often aligned with traditional Christian beliefs. Other conservatives, however, do not emphasise the importance of social conscience but argue, instead, that wealth produced by a small minority of energetic and able entrepreneurs will 'trickle down' to the poor.

Economics

- *The invisible hand of the market* The second fundamental tenet of conserva-tism is a belief in the market, and the claim that economic competition will result in efficiency and the achievement of the public interest. The 'invisible hand of the market' (see briefing 14.1) means that the best way

Briefing 14.1

Conservative thinkers

■ Edmund Burke (1729–97)

A British writer and MP, he formulated many of the social and political principles of modern conservatism. He argued that society was like a complex organism that was easily ruined by attempts to reform it too quickly, and pointed to the disastrous experience of the French Revolution to support his claim. He believed in a 'natural aristocracy' in society, and that the mass of ordinary people could sustain a democracy only with the guidance of a political elite. Above all, he claimed that practical experience and wisdom are always to be preferred to abstract rationalism.

■ Adam Smith (1723–90)

The Scottish philosopher and economist, Adam Smith laid the foundations of classical economics in his book *The Wealth of Nations* (1776). He claimed that individual self-interest on the part of 'the butcher, brewer, and baker' led, by way of the 'invisible hand' of the market, to the satisfaction of the general good. The butcher and the baker do not provide a good service because of their concern for others, but because the workings of the market economy makes it in their own self-interest to do so. The state should leave this invisible hand to play its part by setting up the right conditions for laissez-faire economics and a free market.

■ Joseph Schumpeter (1883–1950)

An Austrian economist and political scientist, Schumpeter is best remembered for his book *Capitalism, Socialism and Democracy* (1942), in which he argues for an elitist form of democracy. Contrary to Marxist theory, and other theories that place faith in the 'will of the people', Schumpeter claimed that the masses are capable of little, other than stampeding. Democracy should be limited to elitist, representative forms, in which the masses have the power only to vote at regular intervals for representatives who compete for popular support.

■ Friedrich von Hayek (1899–1992)

Another Austrian economist, von Hayek is best known for his book *The Road to Serfdom* (1944), which argues that state regulation and collective action of all kinds tends to limit the freedom of the individual, even if it is moderate and well-intended.

of optimising the general interest is to allow each individual to act in her own economic interests. Economic competition will force businesses to produce the best goods and services at the lowest price in order to keep their customers happy. If they do not then customers will shop around for a better deal. Individual competition and self-interest will thus paradoxically, result in efficiency, innovation and the public good. Attempts to

improve or modify the workings of the market will result only in inefficiency and poor **performance**. For this reason
one of the main planks of conservatism is the
belief that the state should intervene as little
as possible in the economy, although the left

> **Performance** Actual activities and results;
> how well government is doing or how success-
> fully it is meeting citizen demands.

and right wings of conservative thought argue about how much or how
little this should be.

Liberalism

Liberalism is an ambiguous term. In classical political theory its essence is
the belief that individual liberty is the highest political value and can be preserved only by limiting the powers of the state. In modern politics, especially
in the USA, a 'liberal' is, on the contrary, someone who believes in more
rather than less state intervention. This is because the term 'socialist' is not
politically acceptable in the USA, so those who advocate even modest government action refer to themselves as 'liberals' to distinguish themselves from
conservatives. In what follows the terms 'liberal' and 'liberalism' are basically
used in their classical sense.

Early liberalism emerged in the seventeenth century in opposition to traditional government by kings, aristocracies and elites, and to the social order
and hierarchy they imposed. Liberals rejected the constraints of traditional
government, emphasising instead the importance of individual freedom (see
briefing 14.2). This idea continues to lie at the heart of modern liberalism
and distinguishes it fundamentally from conservative ideas. It has five main
characteristics.

Limited state power

Classical liberalism was built around the principle that the state should be
limited to the 'night watchman' function of protecting individual rights and
property, and should not pretend to any other function. The modern version
of this belief claims that 'government is best that governs least'.

Parliamentary government and the division of powers

Because of their concern with individual rights and duties liberals have traditionally placed great importance on parliament, and on the checks and balances of
divided government that protect citizens from arbitrary power. But though early
liberals believed in parliamentary government, they did not necessarily believe in
democracy, because they feared that giving power to the mass of uneducated and
unsophisticated citizens would threaten democratic practice and values. They
feared that the 'tyranny of the majority' would
replace the tyranny of monarchs and aristocracies.
In the twentieth century, however, liberals came
to accept mass democracy, hence the term '**liberal
democracy**'.

> **Liberal democracy** The form of democracy
> that tries to combine the powers of democratic
> government with liberal values about the free-
> dom of the individual.

297

FOUNDATIONS OF COMPARATIVE POLITICS

Briefing 14.2

Two concepts of liberty

Freedom (or liberty – the two terms are used interchangeably here) may be defined as the absence of restraint. According to this simple definition, we are free when we are not prevented from doing what we wish. In political matters, however, this definition does not get us very far. I may be free under the law to set up my own political party or pressure group, or free to start my own newspaper, but these formal freedoms are no good to me if I am living in poverty, hunger, fear, disease and ignorance. Formal freedom under the law, and substantive freedom – freedoms that people can actually use – are quite different. As the saying goes, both the rich and poor are free to stay at the Ritz Hotel or to sleep under a bridge. Having the formal freedoms to vote, to speak one's mind and to associate with others is not the same as having subsantive political freedom, which entails a life without poverty, disease, fear and ignorance.

Along these lines, the British political theorist Isaiah Berlin (1909–97) distinguished between two concepts of liberty, 'liberty from' and 'liberty to'. Liberty from, or negative liberty, is the absence of restraint. Those who believe in it will argue for a minimal state as a matter of principle. Liberty to, or positive liberty, is concerned with the actual capacity to do things. For example, to play their role as citizens people need to be educated and informed enough to make sensible judgements about political issues. Since the economic market typically makes a good education available only to the small number whose parents are able and willing to pay for it, but rarely for those who cannot afford it, the state must provide free public education for all. The implication of the positive notion of freedom – freedom to – is that the state must ensure that citizens are able to make use of their formal freedoms. This may require state action to lift the restraints on liberty imposed by poverty, hunger, disease and ignorance. This, in turn, means that the state must tax to provide education for all, which means restricting the liberty of people to control their own money.

The two main schools of liberal political thought take different views of liberty. Classical liberals, neo-liberals and libertarians favour freedom from state regulation to maximise individual freedom. Radical or progressive liberals and liberal democrats argue for enough state regulation to overcome the main social and economic obstacles to substantive freedom. According to them the state can intervene as a liberator, not as an oppressor.

Optimistic view of human nature

Unlike conservatism, liberalism takes an optimistic view of human nature, assuming that mankind is rational and reasonable when left to its own devices. Liberals also assume that individuals should be formally equal before the law – not that they are equal in capacities, abilities or intelligence but that they have equal rights and duties.

Slow reform by individual action

Because classical liberalism assumes that most citizens are rational and responsible, they also tend to argue for slow reform brought about by the individual action of free people, rather than the radical collective action favoured by socialists or conservative reaction.

298

Free trade

Like one school of conservative theory, classical liberalism believes strongly in laissez-faire economics and free trade. Its defence of market economics is logically consistent with its strong belief in a limited state, and of the rights of individuals to make their own economic decisions.

As liberal thought developed in the eighteenth and nineteenth centuries, it divided into two schools. One continued to hold to the classical position of individual rights and a minimal state, especially in economic matters, but a second took the view that some freedoms require a degree of state action to eliminate the obstacles to real or substantive freedom (see briefing 14.2). According to this view, the state can intervene as a liberator, not an oppressor, if it creates the conditions necessary for individuals to be able to develop their potential and use their natural rights. For example, early social liberals argued for the state to raise taxes to pay for education, public health and housing for the poor, on the grounds that poverty, disease and ignorance were incompatible with human freedom. Known as radical, progressive or social liberals, this school sits somewhere between conservative and socialist thought, arguing not for or against state intervention in principle, but for it when it is necessary, and against it when it is not.

The ideas of classical liberalism were revived in the late twentieth century by neo-liberals who believe that the powers of the state should be drastically reduced and the economy deregulated and privatised. At the same time, the state should be strong enough to protect itself from all internal and external enemies, which requires a strong army and firm rule of law at home. Neo-liberalism of this kind exercised a strong influence over some conservative politicians, notably Margaret Thatcher in Britain and Ronald Reagan and Geroge W. Bush in the USA. Many other countries, as diverse as Bolivia, Chile, India, Mexico, New Zealand, South Korea and Taiwan have implemented neo-liberal economic policies to a greater or lesser extent.

Some ideologists take neo-liberal ideas even futher. Known as libertarians, they argue for the abolition of almost all state regulation, even of such things as pornography, drugs and prostitution, on the grounds that all regulation infringes liberty, and that responsible adult citizens should be free to make up their own minds about such matters (briefing 14.3).

Christian democracy

Pope Leo XIII (1810–1903) laid out the basics of Christian democracy in the encyclical *Rerum Novarum* (1891). This was partly in reaction to the (classical) liberalism of the times, which tended to be secular or anti-clerical, to anti-religious socialism, which was gaining rapidly in popular support, and to monarchism and extreme conservatism. But it was also an attempt to incorporate Catholic thought into a practical ideology. Christian democracy is neither liberal, nor socialist, nor conservative, but somewhere in between. It has five main characteristics.

Liberal thinkers

■ John Locke (1632–1704)

The British political theorist John Locke wrote that natural law guarantees to every individual the right to 'life, liberty, and estate' (private property). Citizens enter into a 'social contract' with their government to protect themselves against those who would try to infringe their rights. The proper role of government is limited to upholding natural rights. It has no other function.

■ John Stuart Mill (1806–73)

The British political theorist John Stuart Mill drew a distinction between self-regarding and other-regarding actions. Self-regarding actions have no impact on others, and should not be subject to any restraint by government or any other power. According to Mill 'the only purpose for which power can be rightfully exercised over any member of a civilized community, against his will, is to prevent harm to others. His own good, either physical or moral, is not a sufficient warrant.' Other-regarding actions are a different matter and may be constrained by the force of the law. In some ways Mill's distinction between self-regarding and other-regarding actions opens up the possibility of broad intervention by the state, on the grounds that there are very few purely self-regarding actions and many examples of them are trivial. The state can therefore often claim the right to regulate social life. Since Mill modified classical liberal theories in different ways, his thought can be interpreted as standing between liberalism and socialism.

■ John Rawls (1921–2002)

John Rawls is among the most influential liberal thinkers of the twentieth century. In his book *A Theory of Justice* (1971), he introduced the idea of 'justice as fairness' and strongly defended the idea that equality and liberty should be closely related. In his view all social primary goods – liberty and opportunities, income, wealth and the bases of self-respect – should be distributed equally unless an unequal distribution of any or all of these goods is to the advancement of the least favoured. So, for Rawls, the unequal treatment of individuals is acceptable only if it improves the situation of those who are in the worst social position. He is not, however, willing to accept limitations on basic liberties: each person is to have an equal right to the most extensive liberties and this principle precedes any other principle. Just as John Stuart Mill can be considered a socialist or a social democrat through his emphasis on social equality and the relationship between equality and freedom, so also can Rawls. In fact, libertarian philosophers such as Robert Nozick (1938–2002) have criticised Rawls for his willingness to consider restrictions on individual freedom. Nozick strongly defended the idea of a 'minimal state'.

Natural law
Christian democracy starts from the premise that natural law is the basis of society and its rules of conduct. Natural law is not given by the state (that is, by kings, or courts, or parliaments, or electoral majorities), but by God. It is revealed to human beings by their capacity to reason.

Family, church, community
Christian democracy rejects the conservatism of traditional social orders, the atomistic individualism of classical liberalism and the 'tyranny of the masses' advocated by the political left. In place of these, it stresses the importance of 'natural' groups in society, above all, the family, the church and the community.

Subsidiarity
Natural groups should be allowed to run their own affairs in their own way, which means subsidiarity (chapter 6). Christian democrats assert the importance of the autonomy of 'natural groups' in society to run their own affairs, without interference or regulation by the state. Private and semi-private agencies are morally superior to public ones, because they give individuals the opportunity to exercise their Christian conscience. They are also more effective in meeting human needs. The state should, therefore, intervene only when it has to, and only in order to restore the natural community to its proper functioning. In this way, it argues, solidarity and harmony in society will be preserved.

Protection of the weak and poor
Christian morality requires that the state protects the weakest and poorest members of society. In turn, this means a moderate welfare state with special support for the family (family allowances), education (financial support for schools, many of them church schools) and the community (to alleviate poverty and protect people against illness and unemployment).

Harmony, integration, consultation
Christian democracy emphasises social harmony and integration. This means the reconciliation of class, religious and other differences by means of formal social institutions that enable social groups to consult and discuss with one another, something known as the 'concentration of interests'. This involves an elaborate consultative machinery in which government, business, trade unions and other interests participate.

Christian democracy is a middle way between conservatism and unbridled capitalism, secular liberal individualism and atheistic socialism. It is neither for nor against state intervention in principle, but argues for enough of it to protect human dignity in accordance with natural law. Some forms of it are close to socialism, others to conservatism.

Socialism and social democracy

It is important, first of all, to distinguish between the communism found in China and the former Soviet Union, and the socialism and social democracy found in the democratic world. Communist countries have undemocratic regimes controlled by Communist parties, and their dominant ideologies are better known as 'Marxism' or 'communism'. Socialist and social-democratic ideologies are strong in democracies. To distinguish themselves clearly from Marxism and communism, some socialist parties prefer to call themselves social democratic (see briefing 14.4). Social democracy has five distinguishing features.

Optimistic view of human nature
Human nature is naturally reasonable, rational and sociable. It is capitalism and its allies (religion, capitalist education, capitalist media) that makes people greedy and keeps them in ignorance.

Equality of opportunity
Inequalities between individuals are a product of their social environment rather than their inborn talents. The function of the state is therefore to eliminate inequalities of opportunity and release natural abilities.

Participatory democracy
Democracy is built upon the free and equal participation of all, and on participatory rather than representative democracy.

Mixed economy
At the heart of socialist ideologies is the belief that some of the most important parts of the economy should be owned or regulated by the state in order to eliminate the worst forms of inequality, exploitation and social injustice. Capitalism produces unacceptable and inefficient inequalities of wealth and opportunity, and market failure means that capitalism is unable even to support itself as an efficient form of production. Economic inequality means injustice, poverty and economic inefficiency. Market failure is a capitalist inevitability and it means periods of economic depression, monopolies and oligopolies and underinvestment in collective goods, including health, housing, education, welfare, research and communications. Socialism, however, differs from communism in that it rejects total state control (the command economy) in favour of a mixture of public, private and joint enterprise (**the mixed economy**).

> **Mixed economy** An economy that is neither wholly privately owned (a capitalist market economy), nor wholly publicly owned (a communist command economy), but a mixture of both.

Briefing 14.4

Socialist thinkers

■ Karl Marx (1818–83)

The German philosopher Karl Marx, with his friend and collaborator Friedrich Engels (1820–95), had an immense impact on western politics, and discussions, amendments and attacks on his work form a whole library of books in themselves. Marx argued that capitalism would inevitably produce an extremely polarised society consisting of a few immensely rich and powerful capitalists, on the one hand, and a mass of poor wage-slaves, on the other. The result was that the workers, encouraged by their overwhelming weight of numbers, and with 'nothing to lose but their chains', would organise themselves, rise up in revolution to capture power and overthrow the capitalist state and economic system. In power they would set up a socialist state in which the means of production would be collectively owned, allowing wealth to be equally distributed. The state would then wither away and a stateless communist society would replace it. The Russian Revolution of 1917 was initially driven by Marxist principles, but these did not last long, and the communist systems of the Soviet Union and its central and eastern European dependencies soon ceased to be Marxist. Outside the Soviet Union, Marx's main impact has been through socialist and social democratic movements, and the revisionist thinkers who guided them.

■ Karl Kautsky (1854–1938) and Eduard Bernstein (1850–1930)

Both leading members of the German Social Democratic Party (SPD), Kautsky and Bernstein were influential revisionist thinkers and politicians who argued for evolutionary rather than revolutionary socialism, on the grounds that the working-class movement could and should gain power through peaceful, parliamentary means.

■ John Maynard (Lord) Keynes (1883–1946)

The British economist John Maynard Keynes was perhaps the biggest influence on social democratic economic thinking after Marx. He argued, against the conventional wisdom of the time, that governments should reduce taxes and public expenditure in times of economic recession in order to balance their budgets. Keynesian policies of economic demand management appealed to many governments because they offered a way of controlling the business cycle of 'boom and bust' without centralised socialist planning and without total state control of the economy. Consequently, Keynesianism was the dominant economic orthodoxy in many western states from 1945 until the 1970s. It was replaced by neo-liberal, free-market ideologies at least until the economic crisis and collapse of 2008, when variants of Keynesian thinking regained favour.

Peaceful reform
By gaining power through the ballot box, socialist and social democratic governments can change the capitalist system to produce a more just mixed economy.

Socialism, like most other 'isms', takes many forms. Most are to be distinguished not by their political goals, for most socialists agree that the aim is to achieve general values such as justice, liberty for all and equality of opportunity. Socialists argue mainly about how best to achieve these sorts of goals: the far left argues for revolution, the moderate left for evolution. Moderate and evolutionary forms of democratic socialism have had most influence in democratic states, where socialist and social democratic parties have often been elected to power, sometimes with the support of sections of the middle class, and centre and centre-right parties.

■ Three minor schools of thought

Conservatism, liberalism, Christian democracy and socialism are well-defined and systematic ideologies with a specifiable content. Three other ways of thinking about democratic politics are looser and less specific; nationalism, Green political thought and populism. Some writers reject their claim to be ideologies, but they do have things in common with ideologies.

Nationalism

Nationalism has been an extraordinarily potent force in politics. Its enduring strength can be seen in the fact that the French Revolution of 1789 set off a train of nationalist movements in the name of freedom. The twentieth century was also the age of nationalism because even more states were born then (see chapter 1). Yet it is hard to capture the ideas of nationalist ideologies in a few short paragraphs because they vary greatly from one place to another and have been advocated by communists and conservatives, fascists and democrats, imperialists and anti-imperialists alike. Because nations differ tremendously, so also do nationalist ideologies. For this reason, some analysts reject the idea that nationalism is an ideology, claiming that it is an empty bottle into which one can pour any doctrine. At the same time, nationalist thought has features in common with ideologies based on the three main features of modern states: territory, people and sovereignty.

Ethno-nationalism and territory
All nationalist ideologies believe that a common national identity is more important than any differences of class, race or religion that might exist within the area. Usually, this common identity is formed by the ethnic, linguistic, religious, cultural or historical characteristics that distinguish the

population of a given territory. Nationalism, territory and ethnicity are thus often linked under the concept of ethno-nationalism – in Belgium, Canada, Northern Ireland and Spain, among many other countries.

National independence

Nationalists believe that common identity should be turned by separatist movements into national self-determination. Sometimes this takes the form of full-blooded independence and sovereignty, sometimes the devolution of power from the centre. In this sense, there is a difference between political nationalism demanding full independence and sovereignty, and cultural nationalism that is satisfied with greater autonomy for a region within a state to preserve its own language, run its own TV stations and teach its own history and culture. Nationalism was given great impetus by the dissolution of empires after 1918 and 1945, and then by the collapse of the Soviet empire in 1989, events caused, in part, by the strength of nationalist movements in the first place. Having gained independence, the new nations then added to the nationalist culture of the world with their own flags, national anthems, leaders, full UN membership, national airlines and football teams.

Nationalism does not manifest itself only in the new states of the world, however. On the contrary, it is so much a part of the fabric and structure of everyday politics in 'old' states that it is often taken for granted. Nationalism is all around us, not just when our country happens to be playing in the World Cup or participating in the Olympics. Most people simply presume that the territory of the globe should be divided between states – and that the borders of our own state are somehow natural and inevitable. As a result much nationalist ideology is taken for granted.

Some people claim that the long era of nationalism is coming to an end. Their theory is that modern society will bury the state and nationalism in the 'borderless world' of the 'global village'. The more integrated the global economy, the wider the spread of McDonalds and global TV stations, the more powerful transnational corporations (TNCs), and the more urgent the need to take global action against natural disasters, terrorism and global warming, the less relevant is the nation-state. The argument may be appealing on theoretical grounds but, as we have seen in chapter 2, nation-states are still powerful, still popular and their number is still growing. Nationalism seems to have a lot of life in it yet, a claim we shall return to in chapter 18.

Green political thought

Green political thought is the most recent ideology of the seven discussed here. Also known as the environmental or the ecological movement, it emerged as a political force in the late 1960s as part of what has been termed the 'post-materialist' ethos. As we saw in chapters 9 and 12, this stresses the importance of the quality of life, self-fulfilment and the protection of the environment, rather than money, obedience and material possessions. Greens often stress their opposition to all the 'isms' of conventional politics, and argue that they are trying to create entirely new kinds of political organisations with entirely new political aims.

There are many forms of green political thought including green socialism, green Marxism, green anarchism, green feminism, green libertarianism and even green capitalism, which favours the use of state power and financial inducements to push production and consumption in a 'green' direction. The environmental movement includes those who want to use the traditional means of influencing government policy, and radicals who advocate direct and revolutionary action. There is a tendency for Green parties and movements to fragment into smaller splinter groups because of disagreements about means and ends. Like nationalism, some argue that Green thought is so diverse that it cannot count as an ideology, but like nationalism, it has common themes that are of an ideological nature.

Sustainable development

One is the importance of achieving 'sustainable development'. The term reached a wide audience in 1987, when the *Report of the World Commission on Environment and Development: Our Common Future* (also known as the Brundtland Report) laid out the case for environmental action and the means of achieving it. The affluent parts of the world, it was argued, would have to adapt their way of life to ecological demands, by reducing energy consumption, for example. In addition, the existing institutions of government and international relations that are based on nation-states would have to give way to a broad, integrated and comprehensive approach involving popular participation and international cooperation.

Decentralisation

Another Green theme is localism and decentralisation. This means the local production of goods and services for local consumption, which reduces the power of large MNCs and the need for long lines of transportation and communication, which degrade the environment and the local ecology. It is also argued that local production improves the satisfaction of people,

Ecology The study of the relationships between organisms and their environment.

who can see the fruits of their labours. Local markets are said to be more responsive to local demands, and deliver fresher produce. Politically, localism means community participation and self-regulation, hence the slogan 'Small is beautiful'.

Direct participation and democracy

Greens oppose the traditional centralised and hierarchical organisation of political parties, and favour direct participation and the rotation of elites.

Some Green parties have tried (not always successfully) to ensure that no one stays in a leadership position for long, and that no one is paid more than the average wage or more than a given multiple of the average wage. Some critics argue that Green thought is inherently anti-democratic when it puts the utmost importance on taking action to protect the environment now, before it is too late, irrespective of public opinion and the slow processes of democracy. Others claim that the decentralist and participatory thrust of Green thought guarantees its democratic credentials.

The core of Green support lies among younger, better-educated and secular sections of the middle class. Green parties also attract those who are alienated from conventional politics, including feminists and gays. In elections, Green parties are usually quite small, rarely getting more than 10 per cent of the vote and, if anything, support seems to have waned since the 1980s and early 1990s. At the same time, it seems that more people support Green objectives than join Green movements or vote for their parties. Some with Green sympathies vote for the socialists. Some of the older parties have also taken Green ideas, and built them into their own programmes.

Populism

There is some doubt about whether **populism** is an ideology at all, and if it is, about its democratic credentials. It is mentioned briefly here because it can have democratic tendencies and has appeared, strongly at times, in some democracies, especially in Latin America. Like nationalism, populism is a loose and varied approach to politics with many different contents. It is characterised by political **demagogues** who appeal to the prejudices and emotions, particularly of citizens who believe that the elites of society are misleading, oppressing or exploiting them. Populism can take a left-wing Marxist form and a right-wing fascist one. In some places it is mixed with extreme nationalism, religion and racism, while in others it is based on attempts to improve living standards and education in poor areas. Populism in one form or another is often found in the catch-all parties of Latin America, and in countries with a large percentage of poor, rural people. It has appeared as a strong political force in Mexico, Peru, the Dominican Republic and Argentina.

> **Populism** A demagogic style of politics that appeals to political prejudices and emotions, particularly of those who feel exploited and oppressed by the rich and powerful.

> **Demagogues** Political leaders who use impassioned appeals to the emotions and prejudices of citizens to try to gain political power.

■ Theories of ideology

We have seen that ideologies themselves mix empirical and normative statements. **Empirical statements** are 'is' or factual statements about the world, and normative statements are value

> **Empirical statement** Factual statement about or explanation of the world that is not necessarily true or false, but amenable to falsification.

judgements about how it ought to be. Some writers have treated the concept of an ideology in an ideological way, claiming that ideologies can be 'true' or 'false', 'good' or 'bad'. In analysing ideologies as political scientists, however, we must be careful to avoid ideological statements of the 'ought' kind. We must try to stick to social science and make no value judgement about them, so far as this is possible, but providing a full and fair account of what different theories have to say.

Marxist and neo-Marxist theories

Marxist theory

Marxists theorists distinguish between the sub-structure and the super-structure of society. The sub-structure consists of the material conditions of society (**materialism**), especially its economic conditions, and the super-structure includes ideas and ideology, art, philosophy and culture. Marxists then argue that the material sub-structure fundamentally determines the super-structural world of ideas. According to Marx himself: 'It is not the consciousness of men that determines their being, but, on the contrary, their social being that determines their consciousness.' This is the essence of the Marxist materialist theory of political ideas and ideology.

> **Materialism** The theory that ideas are rooted in the material or physical conditions of life, as opposed to spiritual ideals and values which are constructs of the mind which can be independent of material and physical conditions (see Idealism).

According to Marxist theory, ideologies are systems of ideas that justify the interests of the ruling class. Under capitalism, the bourgeoisie uses its power to delude and manipulate other classes into believing that capitalism is not only natural but in the best interests of everybody. According to Marxists, therefore, an ideology is a false set of beliefs, a mystification of the real world, a myth or a lie. Those who believe it suffer from false consciousness (chapter 9). In contrast, Marxists claim that their own theory is not ideology but scientific and 'true'.

According to Marxist theory, religion is no more than the 'opiate of the masses'. It justifies the social order as God-given. Nationalism is a way in which the ruling class prevents the working class from seeing its common interests with workers in other countries. Wars are a way of fighting for capitalist advantage, markets and profit. Respect for the aristocracy, deference towards economic elites and love of the monarchy and the national football team are means by which the ruling class divides and rules, and conceals the nature of capitalist exploitation. Belief in parliamentary government obscures the fact that real power lies with the owners of property. In this way, Marxist theory tries to explain away other ideologies and religions as false beliefs designed to maintain capitalism.

Neo-Marxist theory

Marxist ideas of ideology were especially developed by the Italian Antonio Gramsci (1891–1937), who spend much of his life as a prisoner of Mussolini's fascist government. Gramsci was struck by the fact that the ruling class in western society managed to maintain its economic and political power, without exercising much overt force. He concluded that it managed this by virtue of its ability to infuse its own values throughout society. It maintained its hegemony (see chapter 9) not by naked power but by more subtle and indirect control over what people thought. It won 'the hearts and minds' of people, and gained their willing consent by use of religion, education and the mass media.

Gramscian ideas have been developed more recently by the French structuralist theorist Louis Althusser (1918–90), who argued that the ideological state apparatus was important for maintaining the capitalist system. The main institutions of this ideological apparatus were the churches, schools and universities, families, the legal system, the means of mass communications, culture and parties and trade unions.

Marxist and neo-Marxist theories of ideology have been important for introducing realist and materialist theories of ideologies into the social sciences, which focus on the relationships between social and economic conditions and what people think about politics. This aspect of their approach is commonly accepted or assumed in contemporary theories. Nonetheless, criticisms of Marxism and neo-Marxism abound. Four important questions need to be asked:

- To say that a person does not know what is in their own best interests opens up the possibility of forcing them to do things against their own will, because they do not know what is in their own best interests. Do you suffer from false consciousness? If not, why do you think others do?
- Is it plausible to argue that most of the major institutions of modern society are instruments of a hegemonic ruling class? Is this true of schools and universities, parties, trade unions, families, the legal system and TV and newspapers?
- Is Marxism a science? Are all ideologies a matter of false consciousness and Marxism alone a scientific theory?
- Is it possible to distinguish between the material sub-structure and the ideological superstructure? Do ideas help to shape the social and economic structure?

Beyond these criticisms there also lies a deeper argument about the role of ideas in politics and history that involves a confrontation between materialist theories on the one hand and idealist theories on the other. A third school of thought claims that both material and ideal interests play their own role in history.

Material and non-material interests

Born in the year that Karl Marx finished the first volume of *Capital*, Max Weber (chapter 1) was a German professor who managed for most of his life, as he said, to avoid the 'drudgery' of university life. Weber much admired the work of Marx and declared it to be profoundly true, but he also tried to show that Marx's materialist interpretation of history was insufficient. Weber argues that modern capitalism could not have developed without the ideas of the *Protestant ethic*. Capitalism is the renewed pursuit of profit, and the Protestant ethic entails a commitment to the sort of hard and systematic work that is capable of producing renewed profit. Moreover, capitalism and Protestantism are linked, because some Protestants came to believe that economic success was a sign of God's favour.

The link between capitalism and Protestantism was entirely unrecognised and unintended by the leaders of the Protestant Reformation, Luther and Calvin. They were interested in religious matters, not economic ones. Nevertheless, their ideas, Weber argues, were necessary to start capitalism on its successful world-wide career. Once in the saddle the capitalist system would ride forever because its own logic and imperative would force others to copy it, or perish economically, but it took the ideas of the Protestant ethic to launch it in the first place.

> **Idealism** The theory that ideas have a life of their own as the products of consciousness or spiritual ideals and values that are independent of material conditions. In international relations, idealism emphasises the role of ideas and morality as a determinant of the relations between states.

Weber did not try to replace Marxist materialism with the opposite theory, known as **idealism**. Rather his work has been described as a 'debate with the ghost of Marx', in which he argues that it is not material conditions but material and ideal interests that drive the behaviour of individuals. Ideal interests – related to ideological beliefs – are no less important than material ones. In this case, if politics is a struggle between competing forces, ideas and ideologies play an important role in the struggle.

The end of ideology and the end of history

In the 1960s, the end of ideology was widely proclaimed by social scientists such as Daniel Bell (1919–) in *The End of Ideology* and Seymour Martin Lipset (1922–2006) in *Political Man* (both published in 1960). They argued that the appeal of ideologies, especially communism, fascism and other utopian theories, were exhausted. The main problems of the industrial revolution had been solved and the main issues of the class struggle resolved. As a result, there was a non-ideological consensus about the virtues of liberalism, democracy, the welfare state, decentralised power, pluralism and the mixed economy. This amounted to the exhaustion of political ideas during this period.

The 'end of ideology' thesis depended on the idea that only extreme and utopian systems of thought counted as ideologies. In this sense there may well have been some truth in the thesis. But, as we have argued, the term applies also to liberal democratic ideas as well. Defenders of these faiths are as 'ideological' as anyone, perhaps more so if they believe that their ideas are pure 'common sense' and are unable to see the ideological nature of their own thought. Moreover, the theory has apparently been overtaken by the events of the late twentieth century, which saw the revival of classical liberal ideas about free markets and minimal government, and the emergence of post-materialist and Green thought, to say nothing of the argument about the clash of civilisations – 'the west versus the rest'.

In the late 1980s, when the Berlin Wall came down, and when western liberal democracy had triumphed over communism, the 'end of ideology' thesis was presented again by the American Francis Fukuyama (1952–) in his book *The End of History and the Last Man* (published in 1992). He did not suggest that from now on nothing would happen or that everything would remain as it is. In his view, most of the globe seemed to have reached the point where liberal democracy was regarded as the only acceptable form of government. With this decided, there was little need for further ideological disagreement. History, seen as the struggle between competing ideologies, had come to an end, as almost everyone had agreed upon the fundamentals of the political order. This theory, too, seems to have been confirmed by the collapse of communism in 1989 but later overtaken by events, most notably by conflicts within and between states, particularly the international flashpoints in eastern Europe and the Middle East, and between poor and wealthy nations. In these conflicts, a revival and strengthening of nationalist ideologies can be observed.

The moral of the story seems to be that while some social scientists will, every now and again, proclaim the 'end of ideology' or 'the end of history', new (and old) ideological differences will continue to play their usual role in the power struggle within and between states.

■ What have we learned?

This chapter deals with the frameworks of ideas known as ideologies, which help people to understand and interpret politics.

- The term 'ideology' is used here to mean a broad and systematic set of ideas that mix empirical and normative statements about politics with a programme for political action.
- Once again we find that the political world is simpler than it might seem at first glance. Although every ideology is different in thousands of particular ways, we can see that there are four general democratic ideologies – conservatism, liberalism, Christian democracy and socialism/social democracy – and three more minor ones – nationalism, Green thought and populism.
- Conservatism is distinguished by its core beliefs that: society is an organic entity that has evolved slowly and should not be reformed rapidly; the natural failings of human beings are best restrained by a strong state that maintains social order and the social hierarchy; some inequality in society is inevitable; there is representative democracy; and the market is the best way to achieve the public economic good.

- Classical liberalism is distinguished by its core belief that individual rights and freedoms can be maximised only by limiting the powers of the state. Neo-liberals hold to the negative definition of freedom and argue for limited state intervention, but social or progressive liberals argue for some state intervention to secure positive freedom.
- Christian democracy incorporates Catholic thought into a practical ideology that emphasises community, family and church; the devolution of power; institutions to bring different interests in society together to achieve social integration and reconciliation; and state services to protect the weak and the poor and to prevent the failure of key private institutions.
- The distinguishing features of socialism and social democracy are: an optimistic view of human nature; a participatory form of democracy; the legal and peaceful attainment of parliamentary power through popular election; a mixed economy, with state power to control or regulate key elements of the economy: a guaranteed minimum standard of living for all; and equality of opportunity.

■ Lessons of comparison

- Families of ideologies correspond in general terms to families of political parties (chapter 13) because both are associated with social, economic and political conditions as well as historical developments.
- Political ideas are related to social and economic life.
- Materialist theories, notably Marxism and neo-Marxism, argue that ideologies are the products of social conditions, but other theorists claim that both material and ideal interests are crucial for understanding ideologies.
- Comparison of different places and different historical periods shows that neither ideology nor history seems to have come to an end. The world is divided by ideological clashes as much as ever it was.

Projects

1. Collect the programmes of the two main parties in your country. Summarise the ideological points in these programmes in a systematic way (that is, search for normative and empirical statements about politics and related proposals for action). Enumerate the distinguishing features of each programme in order to decide to which of the seven democratic ideologies discussed in this chapter these parties belong.
2. Similar ideologies are usually used by various organisations (for instance, in many countries we find social-democratic unions, parties and other organisations). Try to find at least two

organisations in two or more countries for each of the seven democratic ideologies mentioned here.

3. With growing international dependencies, parties in different countries but with similar ideologies often try to cooperate and establish a common international organisation. Which parties with what ideologies do you think are most likely to cooperate successfully? Can you support your expectations with examples?

Further reading

A. Heywood, *Political Ideologies: An Introduction,* Basingstoke: Palgrave, 1997.

Three general introductory works on political ideologies.

R. Eccleshall *et al., Political Ideologies: An Introduction,* London: Routledge, 2nd edn. 1994.

R. Eatwell and A. Wright (eds.), *Contemporary Political Ideologies,* London: Pinter, 1993.
A short account of ideologies.

S. D. Tansey, *Politics: The Basics,* London: Routledge, 2nd edn., 2000: chapter 4
A shorter account of ideologies.

For books on families of ideologies and political parties see the following.

A. Arblaster, *The Rise and Decline of Western Liberalism,* Oxford: Basil Blackwell, 1984.
D. Hanley, *Christian Democracy in Europe: A Comparative Perspective,* London: Pinter, 1994.
Elie Kedourie, *Nationalism,* London: Hutchinson, 1966.
N. O'Sullivan, *Conservatism,* London: Dent, 1976.
A. Wright, *Socialisms: Theories and Practices,* Harmondsworth: Penguin, 1987.

Websites

Virtually all political philosophers have websites dedicated to their life and work. Simply submit a name (for instance 'Edmund Burke') to any major search engine and you will easily find these sites. Useful websites are:
http://berlin.wolf.ox.ac.uk
A virtual library of the work of Isaiah Berlin and many links to related websites.
www.jsmill.com
A website with all information and publications of John Stuart Mill.
www.marxists.org/archive
A very extensive website with all information and publications of Karl Marx, Friedrich Engels, Rosa Luxemburg and many other Marxist authors.
www.nationalismproject.org
A very extensive website about Nationalism.

www.nationmaster.com/encyclopedia/Christian-democracy

General website with a brief overview of Christian democracy and many links to related websites.

www.nationmaster.com/encyclopedia/Social-democracy

General website with a brief overview of Social democracy and many links to related websites.

www.nationmaster.com/encyclopedia/Green-parties

General website with a brief overview of Green political ideas and many links to related websites.

www.nationmaster.com/encyclopedia/Conservatism

General website with a brief overview of Conservatism and many links to related websites.

www.nationmaster.com/encyclopedia/Liberalism

General website with a brief overview of Liberalism and many links to related websites.

www.nationmaster.com/encyclopedia/Nationalism

General website with a brief overview of Nationalism and many links to related websites.

15   Decision making

Government exists to solve problems. To do this it must take decisions. In one sense, the whole process of government is little else than a ceaseless process of decision making: how to respond to the latest international crisis; whether to increase taxes or cut services; how to balance economic development against environmental needs; how to handle an economic crisis; what to do about traffic congestion. Politics never sleeps, and governments can never pause for a rest. They are assailed from all sides by endless cycles of demands and events, and they must constantly make decisions about options, priorities, policies and courses of action.

   This chapter deals with public policies and decision making. A policy is a general set of ideas or plans that has been officially agreed on and which is used as a basis for making decisions. *Public policy* is a more specific term. It refers to the long series of activities, decisions and actions carried out by officials of government in their attempts to solve problems that are thought to lie in the public or collective arena. In that sense, we speak of 'environmental policies' if government shifts from coal and nuclear power to oil and wind-powered generators, and of 'educational policies' if the school leaving age is raised or money is redirected from primary to secondary education. How can we analyse such public policies in general, when there are so many decisions made and each one has its own specific circumstances? How do governments make decisions and which political and governmental structures are relevant for public policies? How do governments respond to public demands?

The four main topics of this chapter are:

- Public policies: their nature and importance
- The public policy cycle
- Public policy structures
- Theories of decision making.

Public policies: their nature and importance

Goals and results

Public policy (chapter 7) is designed to achieve specific goals and produce particular results. Public policies are supposed to solve public problems, or at least improve them. In this sense, public policies are the main **outputs** of the political system – the actions it takes in response to the demands made upon it and the problems it faces. Two points follow from the idea that public policy and decision making aim to improve the world:

Outputs Policy decisions as they are actually implemented.

- *Public policy is important* Almost everything we do is affected by public policies, sometimes in many trivial ways, but also in many crucial ones. They determine which side of the road we drive on and whether we carry identity cards. They also decide whether we receive a free university education, have to pay for health care, pay a lot or a little tax and, in the extreme, whether we are sentenced to death if we are found guilty of murder.
- *Public policy is conflict-ridden* Because public policies are so important, they are the focus of fierce and constant political battles. Which policy is adopted depends on the competing and conflicting political forces that operate on the state from both within and without – the executive, legislative and judiciary, the state bureaucracy, other states and international organisations, sub-central governments, parties and pressure groups, public opinion and the mass media. A public policy is the 'end product' of the battle between these political forces. Consequently, public policies and political decision making tell us a lot about how political systems actually work, and about who is powerful. If politics is to be about who gets what, when and how, then the study of public policy making can tell us a lot about who gets what, when and how they obtained it.

The nature of policy-making processes

Discussions about public policies usually start with the cliché that public policy making is extremely complex and difficult to analyse. This is certainly true. Yet, paradoxically, we all know about decision making because we do it all the time. Take a simple decision: at this minute you are reading chapter 15 of this book, but you might have made the decision to go to the cinema, drink with friends, read a book for another course or catch up on sleep instead. If you analyse your decision to read the textbook, you know well enough that you are not completely free to do what you want. Perhaps you have an essay deadline tomorrow, or not enough money to go to the cinema. So the first thing to notice is that your decision is subject to constraints. Second, your decision is also partly in response to the decisions of others. You made your own decision to go to college and study this course, but your teachers put on the course and set essays, and your friends may have decided to work today, and go to the cinema tomorrow. In other words, your decision is closely tied up with the decisions of others. And, third, you know that today's decision has implications for future decisions you might make – what you do tomorrow, and if you write a good essay, what courses you study in the future, even what kind of job you get. In other words, today's decisions are influenced by a long chain of decisions that reaches back into the past, and has implications for decisions in the future.

These three simple aspects of decision-making processes can be used to characterise public policy making:

Constraints
Policy making is beset on every side by constraints. No government can do what it likes. It is always faced with shortages of time and resources, or by pressure from foreign governments and economic forces. It is subject to the conflicting demands of public opinion, the mass media, pressure groups and opposition parties. It must meet the requirements of the law and the courts. The permanent officials of the state bureaucracies may have views and powers of their own, and so may sub-central units of government. Indeed, governments themselves are invariably composed of factions that push and pull in different directions. Politics is the art of the possible, and what might appear to be the most obvious or most sensible course of action is often ruled out by circumstances.

Policy processes
The repeated use of the term 'policy processes', in the plural, is deliberate because there is no single 'policy process' – there are many of them. Governments are not integrated, coordinated and centralised machines: they are fragmented and disjointed, with different departments and units that compete, overlap and work unknown to each other. The agricultural ministry may want to preserve farmland, the transportation department may want to cover it with a road and the military may want it as a training ground. One of the big problems for the huge and sprawling apparatus of the modern state is how to produce 'joined-up' government, where public policies are more or less coherent and push in roughly the same direction. This may be an impossible ideal. Even within the same ministry, there are likely to be different views on any given matter, and each matter may well involve parties, pressure groups, international government agencies, the mass media and public opinion – each with its own decision-making processes.

Unending policy cycles

Policy processes consist not of discrete decisions, distinct from one another, but of a continuous and unending cycle of decisions and policies which merge into one another without a break:

- In the first place, no policy decision is independent of the decisions that have gone before. A government that has decided to invest heavily in nuclear power will frame its current power policies with this in mind.
- In the second place, every policy has knock-on effects that require a further round of decisions. Bigger and better roads have been built in an attempt to solve traffic problems and reduce accident rates, only to discover that this has increased sales of cars, which makes the traffic problem worse than before. Successful promotion of economic growth in the post-war years has resulted in much higher standard of living, which has led to all sorts of environmental problems. Higher standards of living and improvements in public health have also produced an aging population, which has generated severe problems for state pensions (see chapter 17).

Almost every public policy has its unintended and unanticipated side effects, which then become another problem for public policy. The result is an endless cycle of policy and decision making that tries to solve both the new problems of the world and also the side effects of old policies.

■ The public policy cycle

It is helpful to imagine policy processes as consisting of six stages. Analytically, each policy process starts with selecting the most urgent problems to be dealt with (agenda setting). Then decisions have to be taken about the course of action (decision making) and appropriate means to be used (choice of means). The next stage consists of putting the plan into action (implementation), which results in specific consequences (outputs and **outcomes**). Finally, the effects and costs of the policy are assessed and conclusions are drawn for future actions (evaluation and feedback). This last stage leads directly back into the first stage, so it is helpful to think of the process as a continuous and unending cycle, not as a one-way flow with a clear beginning and end (see figure 15.1). In real life the different stages of the cycle are not separate and distinct. On the contrary, they merge and overlap with one another, and sometimes the stages get mixed up, but nevertheless they are helpful analytical categories.

> **Outcomes** The impacts, or effects, of outputs.

Agenda setting

The world is full of political problems and it is impossible to give much attention to more than a small number of them at any given time. You can think of the list of problems to be dealt with as a kind of 'agenda' with the more urgent concerns at the top of the list receiving the most attention. An

Figure 15.1: The six stages of the policy cycle

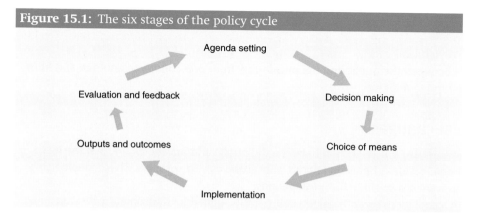

important part of the political struggle is the attempt by different groups and interests to put their issues at the top of the agenda, or at least to push them up the agenda, so they have a better chance of being considered. This struggle is called 'agenda setting' (chapter 11). Being able to control or influence the agenda is an important source of political power. The struggle is endless because as the world changes so priorities and agendas also change. For example, according to post-materialist theory (see chapter 9) the public agenda is shifting from safety and security, money and material advantages, to the quality of life, self-fulfilment and environmental protection. Although new political parties, such as the Greens, have rarely played a direct role in government, they have had a political influence to the extent that they have shifted the political agenda.

One important aspect of the public agenda is the divide between what is thought to be the proper concern of the state, and what is outside its sphere of action, and therefore off the public agenda. What is thought to be a public matter varies considerably from one country to another, and from one historical period to another (see briefing 15.1). In fact, political conflicts frequently concentrate on the question of whether government should deal with specific problems (such as providing day-care for young children or banning genetically modified (GM) food), or leave it to private action. The shifting divide between the public and the private reminds us that the nature of politics itself is constantly contested.

As we have seen in chapter 11, the mass media play an important role in public debates and therefore also in agenda setting. The argument is that although the mass media cannot do much to influence what people think, they can exercise a good deal of influence over what people think about. Television, with its unquenchable thirst for new issues and stories, is constantly engaging in 'feeding frenzies' involving issues such as road rage, football hooligans, new diseases, genetic engineering, crime, drug crazes, political corruption, the sexual abuse of children and terrorism. Known as 'moral panics', these matters hit the headlines for a time, focus public attention

Briefing 15.1

The public–private divide
The boundaries between the public and the private vary from one country to another, and from one historical period to another.

■ Historical changes

As we saw in chapter 14, the distinction between the public and private sphere is at the heart of the battle of political ideas between liberals, conservatives and socialists. These ideologies have waxed and waned over three historical periods.

The dominant liberal ideology of the nineteenth century argued for a minimal, 'night watchman' state with responsibility for little beyond the defence of the realm, law and order, the protection of private property and the necessary conditions for a market economy.

As the welfare state grew in scope and activities during the late nineteenth and in the twentieth century, so the public sphere expanded. Taxes increased, more public services were delivered and the role and scope of the state grew rapidly, especially in western Europe after 1945 (see chapter 17).

In recent decades the neo-liberals have been successful to some degree in rolling back the frontiers of the state, by privatisation and deregulation and tax/service cuts. In other words, the boundaries of the public sector were first pushed out a great deal in the mid-twentieth century, and then contracted somewhat at the end of the millennium.

■ Country differences

Since we often take the boundary between the public and private for granted in our own country, a few examples will help to illustrate the idea:

- In some Catholic countries in western Europe the names that parents can give their children are restricted to a state-recognised list of Catholic saints' names. There is no such restriction in Protestant or secular countries.
- In north European countries the sale of alcohol is often closely controlled by the government, sometimes through state monopoly shops. In the south, it is not.
- Norwegian municipalities own cinemas and spend the profits on public services. In most countries cinemas are in the private economy.
- In some countries shops can open when they like. In others, their opening hours are restricted.
- In some countries all citizens must carry ID cards. In others there is no such requirement.
- A good indicator of the breadth of the public sector is what proportion of total national production is spent by all public authorities. Countries vary enormously in this respect, as figure 15.2 shows. At the top of the league (right side), half the nation's wealth is spent by government in Sweden and France. At the bottom (left side), it is less than a third in Korea, Australia, Switzerland and Ireland.

■ The public–private mix

There is no clear line to be drawn between the public and private. They can overlap a good deal in some policy areas, where private or semi-private groups and organisations cooperate closely with government to provide services, with financial and other help from the state. For example, in Germany the state collects taxes for the Catholic and Protestant churches, which provide social and other services with the money. Scandinavian housing associations are neither public nor private organisations, but

> **Public–private partnerships** Formal cooperations between government and private groups to obtain specific goals.

public–private partnerships (PPPs) (see below) that cooperate closely with public agencies and receive resources from them. Many politicians have turned to PPPs since the 1980s as the best solution to a wide range of problems.

Figure 15.2: General government expenditure as a percentage of GDP, OECD countries, 2007

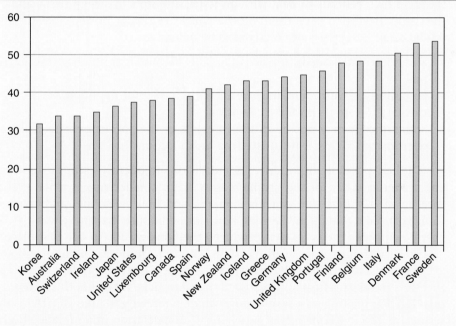

Source: OECD, National Accounts Statistics

upon them, but then disappear in favour of another issue, perhaps before anything has been done about the matter, or perhaps prompting hasty and ill-considered action from policy makers.

Decision making

Having decided upon the priorities of the political agenda, decisions must then be taken about them. A major decision is usually the end product of a series of decisions leading up to it, each preceding decision being made by different individuals and bodies that feed into the process. In democracies, major policy decisions should be taken by publicly accountable bodies, normally the elected executive or the legislature, or both. Nonetheless, many other public and private organisations and officials may have an impact on a particular decision, and they, in their turn, will have to make many decisions in order to exercise influence.

Decision making is by far the most popular research topic of the six stages of the policy cycle and there is a huge literature on the topic. Decisions represent the most important output of the political process, not only for practical politics, but also because they reveal how political forces mix together to produce a policy. Remember, however, that *not* making a decision counts as decision making as well, because the decision not to make a decision is itself a decision. A **non-decision** has its consequences and reveals the interplay of political forces just as much as a decision to do something. In fact, refusals to deal with an issue, attempts to sweep them under the carpet (trying to keep them off the political agenda), or decisions to put off decisions, are tactics often favoured by politicians:

Non-decision The decision not to deal with an issue, perhaps not even to consider it.

- Sometimes the issue is 'too hot to handle' because it is a highly emotional one.
- Sometimes government may be faced by powerful opponents with the capacity to veto its preferred decision.
- Sometimes it may not be in the interests of the government to make a decision or to leave it until after the next election.

For all their possible importance, non-decisions frequently escape attention and academic study for the simple reason that a non-decision is a non-event that involves things that did not happen, and how does one study something that did not happen? Besides, how can we be sure that there was ever a need to consider the issue that produced the non-decision in the first place? 'Conspiracy theorists', as well as those who hold minority opinions about a flat earth, unidentified flying objects and such like, are always claiming that governments refuse to investigate their favourite theory. Is this a case of non-decision making or a case of governments refusing to take silly theories seriously? The methodological problems of non-decision making have been heatedly discussed by community politics studies and no firm conclusions have been reached.

Choice of means

Choosing the best means available to bring about the goals selected is the next step confronted by policy makers. This may seem a straightforward job after issues have been selected and priorities set, but it is not simple at all. There is usually a wide variety of possible policy instruments available to achieve a given end, and deciding which to use is no easy task. The options include:

- *Taxing specific products or services* to change the costs of action – excise duties on cigarettes and alcohol, for example, or lower duties on lead-free petrol to encourage more environmental motoring.
- *Imposing regulations* – shop opening hours can be restricted, dog owners required to have a dog licence, toxic products banned, or industrial plants regulated.
- *Encouraging citizens* to do certain things – some governments carry out intensive and expensive publicity campaigns to persuade people not to smoke, to use condoms, to eat healthily, not to drink and drive and to take exercise.
- *Offering subsidies or grants* – many countries subsidise food production and some offer tax reductions to home owners, or child benefits to increase the birth rate.
- *Direct provision* of services by the state itself – education, health services, transport, etc., especially if the private provision of these services is problematic.
- *Encouraging private organisations to regulate themselves* – governments are often reluctant to intervene directly in, for example, the conduct of the mass media where the principle of the freedom of the press is involved.
- *Passing new laws* – not only to make things legal or illegal but to introduce one of the measures mentioned in the list above. Changing the law may appear to be the obvious method, but it can be cumbersome and ineffective because it usually takes a long time, and the effects are uncertain.

In most cases, decision makers choose a combination of these, since it is unlikely that any single one will work well.

Implementation

As we saw in chapter 7, policy making is supposed to be the responsibility of elected and accountable politicians, whereas implementation (chapter 8) is mainly a matter for state bureaucracies. In practice, the distinction between policy making and implementation is not clear because policy goals cannot be separated from the means of implementing them, and vice versa. Besides, in political life policies often get changed in the process of implementation:

- Sometimes, this is for very good practical reasons (economic pressures, bureaucratic procedures, the avoidance of unforeseen side effects) that may not have been recognised when the policy was formulated.
- Sometimes it is because implementing agencies have their own interests, and bend the policy to their own wishes as much as they can.
- And sometimes it is because legislation deliberately gives agencies discretion over how to implement a policy because of difficulties in deciding in advance.

Private organisations and pressure groups may also try to influence implementation in their own interests. One way or the other, therefore, there may well be slippage between what policy makers intend and what is actually implemented.

The book *Implementation* (1973) by Jeffrey L. Pressman and Aaron Wildavsky is one of the classic studies of policy in practice. It reveals its main message in its sub-title: 'How Great Expectations in Washington are Dashed in Oakland: Or, Why it is Amazing that Federal Programs Work at All'. They found that federal policies in the USA were distorted as they passed down through a long chain of 'clearance points' between the committee rooms and debating chambers in Washington, and local street-level bureaucrats who made decisions on the ground 4,500 km away.

Outputs and outcomes

After a policy has been applied, its results or consequences become clear. Political scientists find it useful here to distinguish between outputs and outcomes:

- By 'output' we mean the political decisions taken, the laws passed and the money spent. So the decision to build another 10,000 km of roads in order to ease traffic congestion and reduce road accidents is an output.
- The term 'outcome' is used to refer to the results or consequences of the outputs. The new roads are intended to reduce accident rates and traffic congestion, but if their effect is to increase car usage they may well increase congestion and the accident rate as well.

The distinction between outputs and outcomes reflects the often unintended and unrecognised nature of policy effects, and the differences between policy decisions and what is actually achieved. Since society is exceedingly complex, and since decision making is no less difficult, governments quite often fail to achieve their intended goals, and sometimes even have an opposite effect.

Evaluation and feedback

Once the policy has been in operation for some time, its effects can be reviewed. Policy evaluation provides a feedback loop, enabling decision makers to learn from their experiences. Policies should be evaluated for their efficiency (using the least resources to the maximum effect) and effectiveness (achieved what was intended). Since all but the most trivial public policy decisions have knock-on effects – intended or unintended – there is almost always something to be learned from evaluation, and it can be a nasty lesson. It is this feedback loop that creates an endless policy cycle. Even if no explicit evaluation takes place, the outcome will often be evident and will play a role in future policies. To say that 'the outcome is evident' is not to say that the evidence is perceived correctly. Citizens and governments alike may entirely misconstrue the actual effects of a policy for their own political reasons: they may choose to believe that a policy was not successful simply because they did not like it in the first place, or the may believe biased accounts of the policy impacts or they may simply get the story wrong. At any rate, one policy decision simply leads to another, or serves as a background context for new decisions. In this sense, there is no such thing as a decision, but only a ceaseless and unbroken flow of them.

In practice, evaluation and feedback are the 'Cinderella elements' of policy processes, for several reasons:

- Policies should be evaluated in terms of their objectives but policy makers may deliberately leave their objectives vague in order to avoid political controversy, or in order to avoid responsibility for failing to meet them.
- Policy makers rarely want their failures evaluated.
- Policy makers may pay little attention to the evaluation, no matter how well it was carried out, because the public agenda has already changed.
- Often little money is set aside for proper evaluation of government programmes.
- Governments often evaluate their own policies, although they normally insist, for obvious reasons, that other organisations are evaluated by independent agencies.
- Efficiency in the public sector is difficult to measure. Some services are taken into the public sector because they are not amenable to the usual market measures of efficiency.

In this brief overview of the policy cycle we have emphasised the complexity of the whole process, and the difficulties of making decisions, implementing them and evaluating them. We have frequently used the phrase 'unrecognised and unintended effects'. However, in spite of all this, public policies are often drawn up and implemented more or less effectively. That is to say, children are educated, health systems operate, transport is available, welfare benefits paid, pensions schemes funded and so on. No doubt no policy works quite as well as it is supposed to, but many of them work nonetheless and, for the most part, they manage to avoid the worst disasters.

■ **Public policy structures**

Policy and decision making is full of conflict between groups and organisations with different and often incompatible interests. Sometimes this conflict is protracted and bitter, because the stakes are high or the moral issues of great importance. At the same time, the public policy process is rarely a free-for-all battle between warring interests. Few human activities are without structures and rules to organise them. Even war is supposed to be conducted according to international agreement and conventions, and even the freest of all free-market competition is tightly regulated and controlled by government regulation and international trade agreements, or by economic interests themselves, which try to limit unrestricted competition in one way or another. Public policy and political decision making are no different. It occurs within 'structures and rules of the game' that try to ensure that public policy making is relatively smooth, ordered, regulated and predictable (see chapter 4).

The structures of public policy making can be differentiated according to two main types: corporatism and **pluralism**. Corporatism is the more top-down, state-centred arrangement, whereas pluralism is a more 'bottom-up' and decentralised system.

> **Pluralism** A situation where power is dispersed among many different groups and organisations that openly compete with one another in different political arenas.

Corporatism

In some countries special policy making and implementation structures and institutions have been created in order to minimise conflict, maximise consensus and ensure a smoothly executed policy cycle from agenda setting to implementation and evaluation. The term 'corporatism' (chapter 10) has been invented to describe these sorts of structures. To avoid confusion with the Fascist theory of 'state corporatism', corporatism in democratic states is also referred to as 'neo-corporatism', 'liberal corporatism', or 'social corporatism'. In this chapter, however, we will use the simple term 'corporatism', on the understanding that this is a democratic form of political decision making.

Modern corporatist theory evolved in the late nineteenth century as a reaction to socialism, on the one hand, and laissez-faire capitalism, on the other. It argued that society is an organic entity consisting of different functional parts – genders, classes, economic sectors and interests – that should work together in harmony. In this sense, corporatist theory owes a lot to Christian democracy (see chapter 14). To create social harmony and a common purpose it is necessary to create collective institutions in which all major social and economic interests can participate in order to formulate mutually acceptable policies, and implement them effectively.

In modern industrial society, corporatist policy making rests on a set of specific conditions and formal structures, without which it cannot work:

- A small number of hierarchically organised peak associations or federations that speak authoritatively for all their members. For example, there should be no more than a handful of organisations to speak for the major economic interests – labour, industry, commerce, the financial sector and farming – and ordinary members of these organisations should accept the agreements reached. Usually, a few peak associations are recognised, licensed, or even created by the government as a way of ensuring that the government deals with only a small number of dependable official representatives.
- An elaborate structure of government decision making, consultation and negotiation in the form of consultative committees, advisory bodies and social and economic councils. The most important groups and interests

are formally co-opted into this machinery and have a recognised place in it.

- An ability to produce policies that are binding on all parties, and implemented by them. This means that the system is hierarchical and centralised – there is only one decision-making centre in any policy area. Its decisions are passed down and implemented by centralised and hierarchical groups.
- All participants in corporatist arrangements must be prepared to compromise. They cannot get everything they want, but they can get some of it, by 'playing by the rules'. It may be much better to stay within the system, where one can be heard, than to be on the outside.

In modern societies, corporatism has generally worked best in economic policy making where business interests, trade unions and government have been brought closely together in specific institutions in order to consult and negotiate with each other. Countries vary considerably in their degree of corporatism. There is, however, a good deal of agreement among experts about which are the most corporatist countries, and the least. The northern European countries Denmark, the Netherlands, Norway and Sweden are among the most corporatist countries, but Austria also belongs in this category. Corporatism, however, is by no means restricted to western Europe, as the account of Mexican corporatism in briefing 15.2 shows. On the other hand, decision making in the Anglo-Saxon democracies of Australia, Britain, Canada, New Zealand and the USA do not have much in common with the corporatist model (see table 15.1).

Corporatism developed in the 1970s and 1980s, especially in western Europe, as a method of promoting and managing economic growth. Its achievements in this respect were substantial. According to the research of Markus Crepaz (see further reading below), corporatist countries had lower rates of unemployment, lower inflation, less working time lost from strikes, but no better rates of economic growth. Although its main goal – promoting exceptional economic growth – was not reached, the successes of corporatism were evident and widely recognised.

In spite of these successes, however, corporatism began to break down in the 1980s:

- Corporatism is easier to work in periods of economic growth (the 1960s and 1970s), when there are additional resources to distribute, than in harder economic times (the 1980s), when some groups lose.
- Corporatism works best with issues that are amenable to bargaining, compromise and incremental change, such as those between management and workers over pay, hours and conditions of work. The issues raised by new pressure groups and New Social Movements – peace, rights, environmental protection – in the 1970s and 1980s have often been moral issues that are not easily handled by corporatist negotiation and bargaining.
- The shift from heavy industry and manufacturing to service industry has fragmented business organisations and trade unions, making them less

Briefing 15.2

Mexican corporatism: rise and fall

In the 1920s President Calles reorganised Mexican government along corporatist lines. Given the factious, unstable and violent nature of politics his first priority was to produce an inclusive, peaceful and stable system. He created new 'umbrella organisations' that brought together the disparate parts of the broad functional sectors of society and then gave them state subsidies to encourage their dependence upon the state and their links with Calles' ruling party. The trade unions were organised into one organisation run by a friend. The civil service was expanded to handle the corporatist machinery and disperse state funds.

A successor of Calles in the 1940s – Cárdenas – built on these foundations, expanding the social base of the ruling party to include and incorporate the four sectors or 'legs' of Mexican society – the working class, the peasants and rural workers, the military and middle-class civil servants and businessmen. Their organisations were legally recognised and incorporated into the machinery of public policy making. The system, in its general form, remained in place for the next forty years. In the 1980s the corporatist structures created by Calles and Cárdenas began to break down and with it the stable politics of one-party government. Public subsidies to the four organisational sectors were cut back and government programmes reduced, which meant a weakening of the old clientelist arrangements of previous decades. State ownership and regulation of industry gave way to more competitive and privatised forms. Subsidies for consumer goods and services were reduced and the economy opened up more to international trade. Internal schisms developed within the ruling party between a traditional wing favouring the old system and a more technocratic faction that eventually broke away. The old one-party corporatist state gave way to a more open and pluralist one.

amenable to corporatist centralisation and hierarchy. Trade union membership has fallen in many countries, making it difficult for peak organisations to speak authoritatively for their members.

- Globalisation has made it more difficult to control national economies, and to impose regulation upon them.
- Keynesian policies have tended to give way to a belief in market competition (see chapter 14).
- Demands for more political participation have tended to erode the closed circles of corporatist policy making. Groups that are excluded from the cosy circles of corporatist policy making (students, immigrants, peace and anti-nuclear campaigners, the Greens and minority groups, as well as extremist right-wing and racist organisations) may use direct and unconventional forms of political participation to make their voices heard.

Pluralism

The Anglo-Saxon democracies in table 15.1, and others like them that rank low on the corporatism scale, make policy in a more fragmented and less

Table 15.1 Corporatism in eighteen democracies, 1950s–1970s

Country	Corporatism rating
Austria	2.9
Norway	2.8
Sweden	2.7
Netherlands	2.4
Denmark	1.9
Switzerland	1.9
Germany	1.9
Finland	1.8
Belgium	1.6
Japan	1.4
Ireland	0.8
France	0.7
Italy	0.6
Great Britain	0.5
Australia	0.3
New Zealand	0.2
Canada	0.0
USA	0.0

Source: Derived from Arend Lijphart and Markus Crepaz, 'Corporatism and consensus democracy in eighteen countries', *British Journal of Political Science,* 21, 1990: 235–56.

centralised/hierarchical manner. In these countries, power is dispersed among many different groups and organisations that openly compete with one another in different political arenas. Because there are supposed to be many competing interests and organisations, and many centres of power, this sort of policy process has been labelled 'pluralism' (see chapter 10). There may be consultation and consensus-seeking in pluralist systems, but the absence of fully-fledged corporatist structures makes it difficult to reach binding agreements. Even if such agreements could be hammered out, the absence of centralised and hierarchical interest groups means that the peak organisations could not ensure the compliance of any or all of their constituent interest organisations and members to implement the agreement.

A lack of corporatist structures does not mean that policy and decision making is an unorganised free-for-all struggle for power. There are two main ways of organising and integrating policy making to make the power struggle more predictable and manageable: tri-partite arrangements and policy communities (chapter 10).

Tri-partite arrangements
Pluralist systems sometimes use what are known as tri-partite arrangements in which the three 'corners' of the economic 'triangle' (business, unions and

government) try to cooperate through both formal and informal channels. The formal channels include a variety of official committees and consultative bodies and the informal can include quite close personal relations between the elites of government, business and even unions. Such arrangements existed in France, Italy, Japan and the UK, especially in the 1960 and 1970s, but less so in the 1980s and 1990s. Tri-partism (chapter 10) is most often found in economic policy making, including matters such as employment policy, the control of inflation and unemployment and agricultural policy. The three-cornered relations are known as 'iron triangles' (chapter 10).

Policy communities

Outside the economic sphere pluralist policy making can also be organised and given a degree of integration by what are known as policy communities (chapter 10). These are small and exclusive groupings of government officials (both elected politicians and appointed bureaucrats) and pressure group elites, who agree on many of the broad issues in a particular policy area. They meet often, sometimes in formally constituted public bodies (committees, councils and consultative bodies) and sometimes informally. These groupings are generally influential and sometimes very powerful in their particular policy area, though not necessarily outside it. Policy communities tend to form around food and drink policies, education, health, defence matters and technical issues of government policy making. They often involve the most established of the 'insider' groups drawn from the world of professional and business organisations.

Policy communities have some strong advantages:

- They keep government and those most directly affected by its policies in close contact.
- They exchange information on both policy and technical matters.
- They help to formulate and implement policy in the most effective and efficient manner.

Policy communities also have their disadvantages:

- They are exclusive, keeping 'outsider' groups and interests at a distance from policy making.
- Close and constant contact may also result in government officials and group representatives ending up in each other's pockets. Officials may 'go native' and be unable to represent the public interest properly. Group representatives may be 'captured' by government officials, and unable to represent the interests of their organisation properly (see chapter 10).

Nevertheless, by containing group conflict, limiting participation in policy-making and establishing close working relations between public officials and private interests, policy communities can contribute to the stability and continuity of decision making. In pluralist systems, this form of policy making is most usually found in Canada, India, New Zealand and the USA – the more decentralised countries among the Anglo-Saxon democracies.

Policy networks

Policy networks (chapter 10) are looser and less exclusive than policy communities. They consist of all the organisations, groups and actors that cluster around a concern in a given policy area and that participate in public discussion about it. Their advantage is that they are more open and less exclusive than communities, so they are less likely to create resentment on the part of groups and interests that are outside the system. At the same time, because they are more open to all sorts of interests they are also likely to be more conflictual, and therefore decision making involving networks is likely to be less smooth and predictable.

■ Theories of decision making

Decision-making theories often mix analytic and prescriptive elements, in the sense that they try both to help us understand how decision-making processes actually work, and to say how decisions should be made. Generally speaking, two broad approaches have been developed, one based on economic theory and rational behaviour, another based on more pragmatic considerations of actual policy making processes.

The rational-comprehensive model

The rational-comprehensive model draws from economic theory about how rational individuals make decisions in complex situations. Analytically the four main characteristics of decision making according to this model are that:

- First, rational participants collect all the information relevant to a decision, and carefully analyse it. They rank and define their policy objectives, and systematically survey all the means appropriate to achieving these goals, choosing the most efficient and effective.
- They then calculate the consequences of their actions, and compare their costs and benefits with alternative strategies.
- The most cost-effective strategy is implemented.
- Finally, rational individuals evaluate their policies so that they can learn from the experience and improve things in the future.

Applied to public policy making, such a model assumes a single, centralised and coordinated decision making body, and a smooth and efficient government machine that implements decisions in the specified way. It should be kept in mind, however, that the rational-comprehensive model of decision making is like the Weberian ideal-type of bureaucracy (see chapter 8). It is not an account of how decisions are actually made but an abstract model for judging reality.

The rational-comprehensive model may approximate to the kind of decision making that is possible, even if rarely found, in relatively small and highly effective decision-making organisations, especially those concerned with technical problem solving. Something like it was used in the USA by the National Aeronautics and Space Administration (NASA) to land a spacecraft on the moon in 1962. But the model is usually far removed from the reality of decision making by large governments, as the fate of the centralised command economies in former socialist states demonstrates only too clearly. So far as decision making in large-scale government is concerned, the rational-comprehensive model is mainly of use as an abstract ideal by which to measure actual decision making. In real life, decision makers:

- Rarely have even adequate, much less complete information
- Often handle crises with little time to think or prepare; they have to 'rebuild the ship at sea', sometimes in a Force 10 gale
- Are surrounded by powerful political constraints
- Rarely have adequate resources
- Sometimes are pushed by powerful political forces to make policy decisions that are incompatible or downright contradictory
- May already have invested heavily in other policies that they feel should not be compromised by a later one, even if the latter would be better
- Have limited control of the bureaucracies that implement central policies, especially if state and local government, which has its own democratic legitimacy, is involved
- Have to deal with unknown and unintended consequences that blow their policies off course
- Have their own blind spots, prejudices and ideological preferences.

Some techniques have been devised to help rational decision making, most notably Cost-Benefit Analysis (CBA). CBA involves the attempt to calculate all of the costs of a policy and the benefits it will bring at an early stage of decision making. It assumes that all the important factors to be taken into account can be quantified and that the costs (not just financial, but everything including social, environmental and aesthetic) can somehow be weighed against all the benefits. Advocates of the method argue that it forces decision makers:

- To think carefully and systematically
- To take a broad range of factors into account
- To question assumptions
- To make decisions transparent.

Critics have called CBA 'nonsense on stilts': how would you calculate the costs and benefits of, say, building a new motorway through a beautiful and untouched mountain pass? CBA sometimes involves trying to estimate labour costs for a particular project by getting workers on the project to apportion the time they spend on it. This is notoriously difficult and imprecise where, as often happens, office and managerial staff work on different projects at the same time, or where capital costs are shared between different projects.

The incremental model

'Muddling through'

If the rational-comprehensive model is an ideal, the incremental model is a realistic and pragmatic account of how decisions are actually made. Since political problems are so complex, and since policies have all sorts of unintended and unrecognised effects, it is better to minimise risk by proceeding cautiously, a small

> **Incremental model** The theory that decisions are not usually based upon a comprehensive review of problems, but upon small, marginal changes from existing policies.

step at a time (incrementally). The result is piecemeal, gradual, *ad hoc* decision making, not a fundamental reappraisal of all goals and means. Since public policy is a political matter, it is also characterised by political bargaining, negotiating and compromise. This is especially true in fragmented and decentralised political systems where many different actors and organisations can get in on the act – that is, in pluralist systems. These can make centralised, rational decision making very difficult to achieve.

According to the American political scientist Charles Lindblom (1917–), in real life decision makers respond to problems, rather than anticipating them or creating new goals. Instead of formulating some idealistic model of rational behaviour, Lindblom describes the behaviour of decision makers as follows:

- They consider only a few alternatives for dealing with a problem
- They pick those that differ marginally (incrementally) from existing policies
- They evaluate only a few of the most important consequences
- They continually review policies, making many small adjustments
- They do not search for the best single solution but recognise that there are many alternatives and pick those that are politically expedient and have political support.

This, says Lindblom, is the science of 'muddling through'. Though widely accepted as a rough and ready account of how decisions are made, the model has also been criticised for being:

- Too conservative and too reactive: it concentrates on existing problems and solutions, instead of widening the search for new solutions.
- Unable to deal with emergencies and crisis situations, requiring radical solutions.
- Unable to bring about fundamental re-thinking: the accumulation of incremental decisions over a long period of time can result in a 'policy morass', consisting of all sorts of conflicting and incompatible policies. In such a situation, fundamental re-thinking may be absolutely necessary. Sometimes it actually occurs.

Bounded rationality and advocacy coalitions

Nobel prize laureate Herbert Simon (1916–2001) emphasises the boundaries to rational decision making created by the personal values of decision makers, the culture and the structure of the organisations they work in and the complexity and unpredictability of political events. These constraints mean that decision makers 'satisfice' – a word Simon coined to describe policies that are not perfect but satisfactory and suffice (are sufficient) for the time being. Decision makers will not continue to search for the very best policy but accept one that is adequate under the circumstances.

The importance of organisational cultures and structures is emphasised by Graham Allison (1940–) in his book *The Essence of Decision*. He found that American decision making about the Cuban missile crisis was the result of bargaining and negotiating between a small group of key decision makers representing departmental interests. Decisions were made not by a single, rational process, but by departments and departmental coalitions engaging in a political power game of 'pulling and hauling', amid a lot of noise, confusion and lack of information.

This idea is developed further by Paul Sabatier (1944–) and Hank Jenkins-Smith (1956–), who argue that policy areas create 'advocacy coalitions' consisting of interest groups, politicians, professionals, journalists, researchers and others, who compete, bargain and compromise with each other. They also learn as circumstances change, so that policies also change.

■ What have we learned?

This chapter deals with public policies and the way governments decide on those policies. It argues that:

- Governments try to deal with many problems, interests, and demands. They develop public policies: long series of activities, decisions and actions carried out by officials of government in their attempts to solve problems that are thought to lie in the public or collective arena.
- Non-decision making is just one form of decision making (the decision not to make a decision) that is favoured by politicians who do not want to face an issue. Non-decision making may be important but it is difficult to study it empirically.
- Policy making is a ceaseless, cyclical process that analytically consists of six overlapping phases: 'agenda setting', decision making, choice of means, implementation, outputs and outcomes, and evaluation and feedback. The last phase leads back into the first to create an endless cycle.
- Policy making is also a ceaseless process because many policies have unintended and unanticipated consequences, some of which are thought to be bad, and have to be 'cured' by a further round of policy making.

■ Lessons of comparison

- The scope of public policy making depends on the demarcation between the private and the public. Where the line is drawn is itself a matter of political controversy and varies from one country to another.

- Policy-making processes are structured in various ways in different countries. Corporatist structures are mainly found in northern Europe. Corporatism involves close cooperation between a few umbrella groups, mainly of business, trade union and professional interests, within a formal government apparatus in order to formulate and implement binding public policies.
- Policy making is much less structured in many Anglo-Saxon countries, which are characterised by more open, loose-knit and competitive policy making.
- Approaches to policy making can be broadly divided into models emphasising rational behaviour (systematically selecting alternatives and strategies, optimising costs and benefits) and those stressing the limitations of the process ('satisficing' instead of 'optimising') and the relevance of cultural and political factors.

Projects

1. Visit your local community council and make a list of the ten issues at the top of the public agenda. Did any issues 'disappear' from the public agenda in your community? Which groups are involved in the present top three issues, and which groups find it difficult to get their issue high on the agenda?
2. Select a Scandinavian country and an Anglo-Saxon country, and search for information to compare the influences on public policies. Is their influence explained by the corporatist–pluralist nature of the political system?
3. Suppose you decided to spend a term abroad while a student. Present a clear description of your complete policy cycle for this decision.

Further reading

Among a number of good general introductions to policy making and the study of policy making processes are:

T. R. Dye, *Understanding Public Policy,* London: Prentice-Hall, 10th edn., 2001.

C. Lindblom, *The Policy-Making Process,* Englewood, Cliffs, NJ: Prentice-Hall, 1968.

J. E. Anderson, *Public Policymaking,* Boston: Houghton Mifflin, 4th edn., 2000.

S. S. Nagel (ed.), *Handbook of Public Policy Evaluation,* London: Sage, 2001.

A more advanced level set of case studies of policy making.

B. G. Peters, *European Politics Reconsidered,* New York: Holmes & Meier, 1991: 165–92.

A general account of the nature of corporatism, and of its rise and fall in western Europe.

J. L. Pressman and A. Wildavsky, *Implementation: How Great Expectations in Washington are Dashed in Oakland,* Berkeley: University of California Press, 1973.
A fascinating and classic study of policy implementation.

Markus Crepaz, 'Corporatism in Decline?: An Empirical Analysis of the Impact of Corporatism on Macroeconomic Performance and Industrial Disputes in 18 Industrialized Democracies', *Comparative Political Studies*, Vol. 25, 1992: 139–168.
A good analysis of the impact of corporatism on public policy.

Websites

www.uoregon.edu/~vburris/ whorules/policy.htm
Extensive website on policy research with a number of links to different organisations and projects.
www.aspanet.org
Website of the American Society for Public Administration.

16   Defence and security

What would happen if everybody did just whatever they liked? Why do we need police, courts, and armies? Can't people take care of their own business without violence and oppression? Do citizens need protection against the consequences of GM food, atomic energy, or toxic paint? Is the exercise of force compatible with democracy's claim to peace and justice?

Living together is based on mutual understanding and the acceptance of certain social rules, conventions and habits, yet these are not enough on their own to maintain peace and harmony. In the end, severe conflicts of interest can be resolved only by force. Therefore, the traditional tasks of government include the enforcement of rules and the regulation of social life. Governments preserve law and order by protecting their citizens from internal disorder (internal security), and their country from foreign aggression (external security). Increasingly they also offer protection against potentially harmful products such as unsafe cars, dangerous food additives and toxic substances. Governments also regulate the construction and operation of many other things – from atomic plants to electric toasters – to protect their citizens against the dangers of modern life.

In this chapter, we examine the efforts of governments to protect citizens from assault, interference and physical danger of many kinds. The provision of social security to protect citizens against the consequences of illness, poverty and unemployment is discussed in chapter 17. Meanwhile, this chapter deals with national defence and domestic law and order – that is, with measures to secure the life and property of citizens against threat, especially crime and foreign aggression. The main topics in this chapter are:

- The state and security
- Defence and national security
- Internal law and order
- Other forms of protection
- The limitations of state security
- Theories of security and conflict.

■ The state and security

In 1651, the British philosopher Thomas Hobbes (1588–1679) published a classical defence of the need for security in society. Starting from the premise that completely free and independent people are naturally selfish and self-seeking, he concluded that only the provision of collective security could banish the risk of injury or violent death. What was needed was a third party commanding enough power to make sure that each citizen respected the security of everybody else. This is where the state – or the 'King' or 'Leviathan' as Hobbes preferred to call it – comes in. According to this line of reasoning the state's main task is to provide physical security for its citizens. Without this protection, everybody is under threat and life becomes, as Hobbes put it 'solitary, poore, nasty, brutish and short' (briefing 16.1).

Hobbes' argument still underpins the case for a state that wields a monopoly of the legitimate use of physical force in order to protect itself and its citizens. People were never free and independent in the way the romantic idea of a 'state of nature' suggests, and the need for protection and the enforcement of rules is self-evident. Without them, peaceful social life is impossible. Even the mafia and terrorist cells insist on obedience to their own rules and, as we have seen in chapter 1, there is a close connection between the development of the modern state and the need of early capitalism for the protection of property, including its investments and markets at home and abroad.

Briefing 16.1

The life of man [is] solitary, poore, nasty, brutish and short

Whatsoever therefore is consequent to a time of Warre, where every man is Enemy to every man; the same is consequent to the time, wherein men live without other security, than what their own strength, and their own invention shall furnish them withall. In such condition, there is no place for Industry; because the fruit thereof is uncertain: and consequently no Culture of the Earth; no Navigation, nor use of the commodities that may be imported by Sea; no commodious Building; no Instruments of moving, and removing such things as require much force; no Knowledge of the face of the Earth; no account of Time; no Arts; no Letters; no Society; and which is worst of all, continuall feare, and danger of violent death; And the life of man, solitary, poore, nasty, brutish and short.

(Thomas Hobbes, Leviathan, *Harmondsworth: Penguin, 1968 [1651]: 186)*

Defence and national security

Protecting the state and its citizens from outside aggression is probably the most conventional task of any government. Of course, many contacts between states or their citizens result in cooperation, collaboration or peaceful exchange, but disputes and conflict cannot be avoided, and so the need for regulating the relations between states is evident. In the final analysis, international conflict of values and interests can be settled only by force – war if necessary – because war, in the words of Karl von Clausewitz (1780–1831) is nothing more than the continuation of politics by other means.

Conflict resolution

Conflicts involving states can be classified according to the degree of *violence* involved. At one end of the continuum are non-violent conflicts that entail no more than a clear expression of different interests. Such mild conflicts can, however, easily escalate when participants start to press their case by means of diplomatic pressure, economic sanctions, or threats of violence. Usually some arrangement is reached between conflicting parties to settle their disputes, so many conflicts between states and other groups remain at a non-violent level. Arrangements can be formalised in treaties or pacts, with special agencies to enforce them and avoid further conflict.

By reaching agreements with other parties, states try to protect the interests of their citizens as well as their position in the world. Notice that the term 'non-violent conflicts' does not mean that there are no real victims, for the use of economic sanctions and blockades in non-violent conflicts can results in deep misery or death for thousands (see briefing 16.2).

Severe conflicts cannot be solved easily by exchanging views and trying to reach agreement. In cases where there is little trust, those involved may use

Briefing 16.2

Economic sanctions or genocide?

The death sentence for hundreds of thousands of Iraqis was pronounced on August 6, 1990. With Resolution 661 the UN Security Council imposed a full-scale economic embargo against the country, four days after Saddam Hussein's army had invaded Kuwait. The brutal dictator was not overthrown by the sanctions; the Iraq people, however, has had to endure almost inconceivable suffering in the last twelve years. According to a Unicef study, by 1999 the sanctions caused the death of about half a million people. Due to shortages of food and medicine, or due to polluted drinking water, about 5,000 to 6,000 Iraq children died each month…In a report to the UN Commission on Human Rights, the Belgian international lawyer, Marc Bossuyt, wrote: 'The sanctions against Iraq intentionally generates living conditions that aim to destroy a group (of people) physically – this is a literal definition of genocide'.

(Sanctions: who gets punished?, *Amnesty International Switzerland*)

third-party **mediation** (or **conciliation)** to try to find common ground – turning to an 'honest broker' who can break the deadlock. Alternatively, conflicting states may bring their case to the Security Council of the UN or to the International Court of Justice (ICJ), or to some other authoritative international body. The problem here is that states are sovereign (see chapter 1): they can accept or reject the legal decision, just as they can accept or reject mediation in the first place. Instead of trying to reach a peaceful settlement, states can, and do, use force to reach their goals.

> **Mediation** Attempt by a third party to reach an agreement between disputing parties on the basis of an investigation of the facts of the dispute.

The **Charter of the United Nations** (UN) starts with the statement that the purpose of the UN is: 'To maintain international peace and security' (Art. 1.1) and it obliges member states 'To settle their disputes by peaceful means' (Art. 2.3). The Charter clearly bans the initial use of force and spells out the peaceful means that are available as an alternative:

> **Charter of the United Nations** Founding treaty of the United Nations (UN) that defines the purposes of the UN and confers certain powers on it.

> The parties to any dispute, the continuance of which is likely to endanger the maintenance of international peace and security, shall, first of all, seek a solution by negotiation, enquiry, mediation, conciliation, arbitration, judicial settlement, resort to regional agencies or arrangements, or other peaceful means of their own choice.
>
> *(Art. 33.1)*

The use of violence between states is – measured by the number of conflicts – rather limited. As can be seen in figure 16.1, violent conflicts between states since 1945 show a modest increase in the late 1970s and into the 1980s whereas a further rise can be noticed recently. Of the total of thirteen wars fought in 2003, only one was between states (the war of the USA and its allies against Iraq). What has been growing constantly, however, is the number of violent disputes within states. All six wars in 2007 were internal ones. After the Second World War, internal violence increased steadily to reach the figure of about thirty to thirty-five conflicts each year. In short, the clear decline in wars between states in the last two decades must be balanced against an equally clear increase in violent conflicts within states in the same period – most of them in Africa and Asia.

Two factors should be kept in mind when we look at the historical and geographical changes in violent conflicts between states:

- First, many used to take place in Europe. After the Second World War, European integration was seen as an important way of avoiding these conflicts, especially the age-old clash between France and Germany. The development of the European Union and its continuous expansion can be seen as a successful attempt to prevent wars in Europe, and many other kinds of conflict between states as well.
- Second, the spread of democracy around the world (see chapters 2 and 3) seems to have reduced international wars. The 'democratic peace'

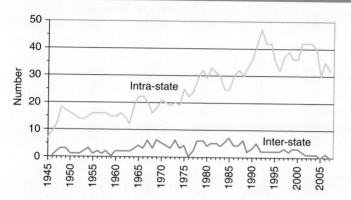

Figure 16.1: Intra- and inter-state conflicts of high intensity, 1945–2007

Source: Konfliktbarometer 2007: 3 (www.konfliktbarometer.de).

theory states that democracies do not go to war with each other. This does not mean that democracies are not warlike – as the examples of the USA and Britain clearly show – for democracies do make war against non-democratic states. Yet the fact that democracies do not go to war with each other means that the increasing number of democratic states in the world reduces the incidence of war.

Just wars

In the international community, violent action is accepted only if (1) force is used in self-defence, or (2) the action is authorised by the UN. Straightforward as these principles may seem, they are highly disputed in any given case. Self-defence against aggression seems relatively unproblematic, but what about pre-emptive strikes against an anticipated attack? Apart from the ethical and diplomatic problems that go with attacking first, the danger is that pre-emptive strikes may overestimate the aggressive intentions of the other country and thereby intensify the conflict. On the other hand, it is difficult to see how one can deny the right to pre-emptive strikes, especially when, in retrospect, history shows that it might have been beneficial in reducing conflict in some cases.

One of the problems is that it is very difficult to reach consensus about the meaning of terms such as 'aggression', 'attack' and 'self-defence', so that the use of violence in self-defence remains highly contested. Nonetheless, three points about self-defence are clear:

- The force used must be proportional to the force used by the assailant. A minor violation of a frontier is no pretext to start a full-scale war. The problem, of course, lies in stating exactly what is 'proportional'.

- Self-defence does not mean a right to reprisal. For instance, an attack on country *A* by terrorists who happen to operate out of country *B* does not justify country *A* attacking country *B* or its residents. The problem, of course, comes when country *A* claims that the terrorists were agents of country *B*, or otherwise aided by that country. Country *A* might then justify its counter-attack in the name of self-defence.
- Self-defence can usually be invoked by states whose territory is violated (see chapter 1). Attacks on its citizens who are living abroad does not entitle a state to use force against another state as an act of self-defence. The problem, of course, lies in defining what is 'home' and what is 'abroad', as the examples of the Gaza Strip, North and South Korea, China and Taiwan, or Georgia and Osetia show.

The self-defence problem is even greater in the case of conflict within a state:

- Is a corrupt government entitled to defend itself against attack by rebels who are clearly supported by the population?
- Are violent separatist movements legitimate if the government suppresses the rights of minorities?
- Does international terrorism or piracy establish general rights of self-defence, including a declaration of war, or is a large-scale violent response excluded by the principle of proportionality of means?

In a world where violent internal conflict is more common, states are increasingly turning to self-defence arguments to justify their own violence, and so the meaning of the term 'self-defence' is becoming increasingly unclear.

Instead of relying on self-defence, states may try to protect their interests by turning to the UN, for both peaceful intervention and peace-keeping by force. Since the 1990s, the UN has increased its armed peace-keeping activities by sending military forces to areas of conflict all over the world. By the end of 2007, twenty peace-keeping missions were active (see table 16.1), with a total of 83,000 soldiers and police officers from 115 countries. The largest contributions came from Pakistan, Bangladesh and India, together accounting for more than 40 per cent of UN peace-keepers. Missions are common in areas with a very high level of violence (for instance in Congo, Israel, Kashmir or Darfur). In fact, since its start in 1948 more than 2,000 of its forces have been killed in UN peace-keeping missions all over the world.

Military expenditure

In spite of the determined attempts to regulate conflicts by peaceful means or to rely on UN action, many states maintain large armies or manufacture large amounts of military equipment. The 'top five' states in the world with the

Table 16.1 UN missions around the world

Mission	Name	Start (or period)	State/Region
BINUB	UN Integrated Office in Burundi[a]	2007	Burundi
MINUCRAT	UN Mission in the Central African Republic and Chad	2007	Central African Republic-Chad
MINURSO	UN Mission for the Referendum in Western Sahara	1991	Western Sahara
MINUSTAH	UN Stabilisation Mission in Haiti	2004	Haiti
MONUC	UN Mission in the Democratic Republic of the Congo	1999	Congo
UNAMA	UN Assistance Mission in Afghanistan	2002	Afghanistan
UNAMID	African Union/UN Hybrid Operation in Darfur	2007	Sudan
UNDOF	UN Disengagement Observer Force Golan Heights	1974	Syria–Israel
UNFICYP	UN Force in Cyprus	1964	Cyprus
UNIFIL	UN Interim Force in Lebanon	1978	Lebanon
UNIKOM	UN Iraq–Kuwait Observer Mission	1991–2003	Iraq–Kuwait
UNIOSIL	UN Mission Integrated Office in Sierra Leone[b]	2006	Sierra Leone
UNMEE	UN Mission in Ethiopia and Eritrea	2000–2008	Ethiopia–Eritrea
UNMIBH	UN Mission in Bosnia and Herzegovina	1995–2002	Bosnia-Herzegovina
UNMIK	UN Interim Administration Mission in Kosovo	1999	Yugoslavia (Kosovo)
UNMIL	UN Mission in Liberia	2003	Liberia
UNMIS	UN Mission in the Sudan	2005	Sudan
UNMIT	UN Integrated Mission in Timor-Leste[c]	2006	Timor-Leste
UNMOGIP	UN Military Observer Group India and Pakistan	1949	India–Pakistan
UNMOP	UN Mission of Observers in Prevlaka	1996–2002	Croatia
UNOCI	UN Operation in Côte d'Ivoire	2004	Côte d'Ivoire
UNOMIG	UN Observer Mission to Georgia	1993	Georgia
UNTSO	UN Truce Supervisory Organisation Middle East	1948	Middle East

Notes:

[a] Successor of the UN Operation in Burundi (ONUB), start 2004.

[b] Successor of the UN Mission in Sierra Leone (UNAMSIL), which started in 1999 and succeeded the UN Observer Mission in Sierra Leone (UNOMSIL), that began operations in 1998.

[c] Successor of the UN Mission of Support in East Timor (UNMISET), which started in 2002 and succeeded the UN Transitional Administration in East Timor (UNTAET), that began operations in 1999.

Source: Konfliktbarometer 2007: 9 (www.konfliktbarometer.de).

largest defence budgets are (in US$ billion in purchasing power parity – i.e. equalising the purchasing power of different currencies):

1. USA
2. China
3. Russia
4. India
5. Britain.

With total spending of about $547 billion a year, the USA's budget is by far the largest. Even before the Iraq War of 2003, the USA's defence budget equalled the total of Britain, China, France, Germany, Italy, Japan, Russia, Saudi Arabia and Taiwan.

The picture of military spending changes dramatically when we calculate it as a percentage of gross domestic product (or GDP). Measured this way, spending in the USA is only about 4 per cent of GDP – and this figure does not even get into the top forty states. The list is headed by North Korea, which spends an estimated 31 per cent on defence, followed by Oman, Qatar, Saudi Arabia, Jordan and Israel. Western European countries such as France or Britain spend only 2.5 per cent of GDP on defence, while Germany, Spain, the Netherlands and Norway are even lower, with less than 2 per cent. Notice, however, that obtaining reliable figures on military expenditure is a tricky business. Many states manipulate information about military expenditure for obvious reasons, so that estimates by independent institutes are usually (much) higher than the official figures.

Selling arms is big business, although it is sometimes difficult to know exactly how big. For leading exporting countries such as Britain, France, Germany and the USA, it is difficult to distinguish between the production of arms for the defence of these countries and for the economic benefit of the private arms industry. Global trading is heavily dominated by US firms. In many countries, military expenditure is mixed up with spending on general research and development (R&D), making it very difficult to disentangle 'pure' military efforts from civilian and applied research. In Britain, France and the USA, substantial proportions of public expenditure on R&D are used for military purposes.

Military budgets have been reduced in most countries since the late 1980s. The main reason is political: when the Cold War between the Soviet Union and the west came to an end, a number of states no longer used conscription but turned to professional soldiers instead. These forces are much smaller and do not concentrate on the defence of national territory, but can be deployed for military tasks all over the world. A second reason is the serious economic problems faced by many countries, resulting in growing financial restrictions on public spending of any kind. Even in prosperous times, military spending is not popular and an easy target for politicians looking for cuts.

States still attach high value to their military capacity for self-defence. Despite their growing military capacities, however, modern states have not been very successful in protecting life (see controversy 16.1). Consequently,

CONTROVERSY 16.1

Is government the greatest threat to human security?

The production of security must be undertaken by and is the primary function of government. As far as empirical – historical – evidence is concerned, proponents of [this] orthodox view face obvious embarrassment. The recently ended twentieth century was characterised by a level of human rights violations unparalleled in all of human history. In his book *Death by Government*, Rudolf Rummel estimates some 170 million government-caused deaths in the twentieth century. The historical evidence appears to indicate that, rather than protecting life, liberty, and the pursuit of happiness of their citizens, governments must be considered the greatest threat to human security. (Hans-Hermann Hoppe, *The Myth of National Defense: Essays on the Theory and History of Security Production,* Auburn: Mises Institute, 2003: 2)

some argue that high levels of military spending are part of the problem of security in the world, and not the solution.

Internal law and order

The dividing line between foreign and domestic security has become increasingly blurred as crime becomes an increasingly multi-national business and with the appearance of international terrorism. For most citizens, however, the protection of life, liberty and the pursuit of happiness starts at home: they expect government to protect their life and property and to punish those who break the law. Punishment for crime is strictly regulated and can be carried out only by order of a proper court.

Law enforcement

Law enforcement and punishment of offenders are among the traditional tasks of the state but, as we saw in chapter 4, the autonomy of the legal system is based on the idea that judges should be independent of the government and final arbiters of the law. Since punishing citizens generally implies a very significant violation of their rights, law enforcement, tracking down of offenders, convicting suspects and punishment are carried out by two or more different branches of government. Their organisation varies considerably between states:

- Usually, a national police force deals with grave offences and threats to the internal security of the state, and usually it has jurisdiction throughout the country and is responsible to the national government. National **police** forces can have a military or semi-military character, such as the *Guardia Civil* in Spain or the

  Police The branch of government employed to maintain civil order and to investigate breaches of the law.

  Carabinieri in Italy. In addition to their national police, many countries also have a local or regional police corps – a *gendarmerie* or civil guard – that is responsible for law enforcement in specific geographical areas. In addition, there are usually national organisations to deal with special criminal activities and intelligence, such as the *Federal Bureau of Investigation* (FBI) in the USA. Police forces are usually part of the Ministry of the Interior (Home Office).

- Deciding who should be prosecuted, of those charged with an offence by the police, is the main tasks of public prosecutors. Here, too, we find substantial differences between countries depending on the judicial system and the division of labour between police and prosecutors. Generally speaking, public prosecutors are part of the Ministry of Justice, and independent of the police.

- Convicting and punishing those found, as well as issuing judgements resolving disputes, are tasks assigned to judges and courts or the judiciary (chapter 4). Their job is to interpret the law and apply it to particular cases. The judiciary has to be protected from political interference and from the temptations of corruption. The police and the judiciary are usually housed in different ministries.

- Finally, convicted offenders may be punished, and it is usually the job of the Ministry of the Interior or the Ministry of Justice to organise this, by running prisons, receiving fines, or organising community work.

- The complicated and lengthy procedures that follow, from notification of an offence to conviction of the offender, differ noticeably between countries, and can involve a set of independent public agencies and departments. Consequently, it is difficult even to estimate the overall costs of law enforcement in any given country, much less compare a range of them. Even apparently simple indicators such as the number of police officers per 100,000 citizens can be misleading if the organisation of regional, national and special police forces is not carefully taken into account.

Crime, punishment and prevention

Citizens in virtually every western country consider crime – especially violent crime – to be an increasingly serious threat to their well-being, and want the government to do something about it. Does this widespread feeling of insecurity indicate real danger? Are crime rates rising? Or is it mainly a matter of the insecurities of modern life, magnified by the popular and sensational mass media?

These questions are difficult to answer, for six main reasons:

- Estimates of the number of crimes are influenced by how the police register crimes, by the ways different sorts of crimes are recorded and counted and by the willingness of the public to report them. Similar countries can have remarkably different crime statistics (see table 16.2), which is at least partly due to differences in crime reporting and counting.

- Feelings of insecurity and threat are difficult to measure, and the figures one gets from surveys depend on the precise question asked.

- Different definitions of delinquent behaviour produce different crime rates. For instance, if corruption and bribery is part of the traditional culture, it will not appear to the same extent in the crime statistics.

- Different ownership rates cause different crime rates. Bicycle theft is especially high in The Netherlands, Denmark and Japan, where cycling is common.
- Different demographic factors can account for differences in crime rates. Since young men are the most crime-prone group, their decline in the population may result in a changing pattern of offences.
- Instead of focusing on feelings of threat and insecurity, information from victims of various crimes can be used to analyse crime and crime rates. Research in this area – *The International Crime Victims Survey*, for instance – shows that the pattern of crimes differs across countries, with Spain (Catalonia) and Portugal having a crime problem with cars and Finland an unusually high number of sexual offences.

The conventional way to deal with crime is to search for offenders, bring them to court and punish them for their behaviour. The most common measure against grave breaches of the law is to send offenders to jail. Prison figures appear to be highly dependent on national and demographic characteristics. Several studies even conclude that there is no relationship between the size of the prison population in a country and its level of recorded crime. The main factors influencing the size of the prison population are the length of sentences imposed and the number of serious offences recorded by the police. Among some democratic states, especially in the USA, imprisonment is very high, with more than 730 prisoners per 100,000 of the population (see briefing 16.3). Comparative figures for western European countries are much lower, ranging from 130 in Portugal and Britain to as little as 50–60 in Scandinavia. In fact, the number of prisoners per 100,000 citizens is below 150 in about 61 per cent of all states in the world. Nevertheless, growing feelings of insecurity are reflected in steadily increasing numbers of prisoners held in many countries.

Table 16.2 Criminal offences, selected countries, 2001, per 100,000 inhabitants

	Murder	Sex offences	Assault	Theft	Fraud	Other	Total
Belgium	5.97	41.99	552.99	4258.40	85.86	366.74	**5311.95**
France	3.91	60.58	199.20	4310.32	621.70	160.66	**5356.37**
Germany	3.21	64.31	146.30	3682.05	1125.95	306.09	**5327.91**
Italy	3.75	4.24	53.17	2257.74	67.44	62.44	**2448.78**
Netherlands[a]	10.87	42.42	242.77	5302.51	112.22	64.18	**5774.97**
Norway[b]	2.14	72.77	70.38	4329.84	265.00	1128.45	**4742.27**
Spain	2.90	16.80	21.23	1940.92	43.45	44.20	**2069.50**
UK	18.51	237.95	242.40	12130.41	1049.43	999.42	**14678.12**
USA	5.61	–	318.55	3804.58	–	–	–

Notes:
[a] 1998.
[b] 2002 – Missing data.

Briefing 16.3

The world prison population

- More than 9.25 million people are held in penal institutions throughout the world, mostly as pre-trial detainees (remand prisoners) or as sentenced prisoners. Almost half of these are in the United States (2.19m), China (1.55m plus pre-trial detainees and prisoners in 'administrative detention') and Russia (0.87m).
- The United States has the highest prison population rate in the world, some 738 per 100,000 of the national population, followed by Russia (611), St Kitts & Nevis (547), the US Virgin Islands (521), Turkmenistan (c.489), Belize (487), Cuba (c.487), Palau (478), the British Virgin Islands (464) and Bermuda (463). Almost three-fifths of countries (61 per cent) have rates of 150 per 100,000 or below.
- Prison population rates vary considerably between different regions of the world, and between different parts of the same continent. For example:
  - In Africa the median rate for western African countries is 37 whereas for southern African countries it is 267.
  - In the Americas the median rate for South American countries is 165.5 whereas for Caribbean countries it is 324.
  - In Asia the median rate for south-central Asian countries (mainly the Indian sub-continent) is 57 whereas for (ex-Soviet) central Asian countries it is 292.
  - In Europe the median rate for southern European countries is 90 whereas for central and eastern European countries it is 185.
  - In Oceania (including Australia and New Zealand) the median rate is 124.5.
  - Prison populations are growing in many parts of the world.

(World Prison Population List, 7th edn., 2007;
www.kcl.ac.uk/depsta/law/research/icps/downloads/world-prison-pop-seventh.pdf)

In the last few years, prison populations grew in about 73 per cent of the countries, but especially in America and some Asian countries.

Law and order is an expensive business. Even if the police and public prosecutors give priority to serious crimes and pay less attention to minor ones – bicycle theft, parking violations and small tax evasions – large bureaucracies are required to trace and prosecute suspects, while securing their individual rights. Prisons are also expensive, but even long sentences do not seem to act as a deterrent so the preferred solution of many politicians to the crime problem does not seem to work. The crime rate seems unaffected by sentencing policies, and many of those who go to prison return for the crimes they commit after their release. As a result, prison space remains scarce because in spite of additional facilities being built, the prison population appears to expand to fill the space available.

As Hobbes forcefully argued, citizens want governments to protect their property and rights, more than they want punishment for those who have violated their rights. Most people would prefer their car was not stolen in the first place rather than the thief was punished for stealing it. Policy makers are therefore increasingly looking to **prevention** as an alternative to punishment, especially since many politicians realise that imprisonment is an

Prevention Attempt to hinder or deter delinquent behaviour.

expensive and ineffective way of reducing crime. Prevention programmes are often based on the fact that adult crime is linked to the social and behavioural problems of criminals when they are young, and so early intervention is preferred.

■ Other forms of protection

Besides trying to protect citizens against crime governments are involved in another huge area of public activity concerned with protecting citizens from harm. They regulate the production and sale of an extraordinarily wide range of goods and services, from food, cigarettes and alcohol, to dental, legal and insurance services, and from the manufacture of cars, electrical goods and building materials to the construction and operation of tools, factories and engines – from nuclear power stations to electric toasters, in fact. They do so to protect citizens against the dangers and harmful effects of modern life.

Government activity in this area takes four main forms:

* Information
* Certification
* Permission
* Product safety.

Information

Governments try to protect their citizens by requiring the producers of goods and services to inform consumers about what they are buying – nutrition values and risks of food is labelled, the effects and side-effects of medicines are described, operating instructions for machines are provided, the details of contracts are presented in simple language.

Certification

Governments issue rules not only for the standardisation of products (electric plugs should be the same size and shape) but also for safety standards, and they then certify the products as suitable for public use. The European Union is very active in this area of consumer protection.

Permission

In many countries, potentially harmful products such as medicine, industrial equipment, chemicals and guns, can be sold only by registered dealers and to people who are licensed to use them by medical prescription, driving licences or gun licences.

Product safety

Information, certification and permission are ways of increasing product safety, based on the idea that individuals can decide for themselves once they are provided with the relevant information and safety guarantees. However, risk and liability looks quite different when we are dealing not with electric shavers or pharmaceutical drugs, but with polluted streams, atomic plants, or GM food. In these cases, government protection is not about individuals who can make informed and responsible judgements about what they consume, but about public goods and collective resources such as clean air and water, or public 'bads' such as noise and exhaust fumes. By definition, public goods and public 'bads' have to be collectively regulated and this is becoming one of the most important and controversial modern functions of government.

Most governments have developed complicated laws and policies to deal with modern technology and its consequences for individuals and the environment. Since all technologies have their dangers, and since these are often hard (or impossible) to estimate given that some may materialise only many years after their introduction, discussions usually focus on the question: 'how safe is "safe enough"?'. The state cannot protect citizens against all risk, any more than it can ban all new technologies. Nor can governments ignore the possibly considerable advantages of atomic energy or GM food: they have to take into account both positive and negative aspects. The result is very difficult and complicated decisions involving the actual and possible risks, both present and future, to individuals and the environment. This inevitably involves unknowns, and a continuous monitoring of the risks. We now know that smoking is a health risk, but what about mobile phones, or GM and irradiated food, or high-tension electricity cables, or hormone replacement therapy (HRT)?

One important principle of democracy is that government intervention can only follow and not anticipate adverse effects. The government can put you in prison for committing a crime, but it cannot sentence you before you have committed the crime on the grounds that you might commit it at some time in the future. Effective environmental protection, however, is not possible if government has to wait until rivers are polluted or billions of Euros spent on nuclear reactors. At the same time, rapid technological innovation means that governments risk running years behind the latest developments if they are too cautious.

■ The limitations of state security

Although governments devote an increasing amount of time and money to protecting the state and its citizens, their powers in this respect are strictly limited:

- In the first place, no government can guarantee a 'no-risk society' any more than it can prevent all crime.
- In the second, punishment may satisfy the desire for revenge and retaliation, but it seems to contribute little to the prevention of crime.
- And in the third, the world is changing in ways that make the problem even more difficult. With growing interdependence and interconnectedness in the world, national borders become less effective and states exercise less control over their own territory (see chapter 1)

Globalisation (chapter 2) presents new challenges to security, the most significant of which are:

- Terrorism
- International crime
- Corruption.

Terrorism

States, democratic or otherwise, have never been safe from **terrorism** but recent events have concentrated attention on the problem as never before. Palestinian suicide bombers, Basque nationalists, Al Qaida and the Shining Path in Peru are only a few examples. Although most terrorist groups take action

> **Terrorism** The use of violence against civilian targets to create fear for political aims. What some regard as terrorism is seen as 'freedom fighting' by others.

against a particular state or government, they also threaten, hijack and kill innocent civilians, if they feel it can increase political pressure. Terrorism, however, can also be seen as the only means available to the poor and repressed of the world to defend themselves against the overwhelming strength of their oppressors (see controversy 16.2).

The demolition of the World Trade Center in New York on 11 September 2001 made it clear that terrorism is not at all the same as conventional warfare, and requires entirely different methods to deal with it. At the same time,

CONTROVERSY 16.2

Terrorism: a fundamental mind-trick?

The poor, the weak and the oppressed rarely complain about 'terrorism'. The rich, the strong and the oppressors constantly do. While most of mankind has more reason to fear the high-technology violence of the strong than the low-technology of the weak, the fundamental mind-trick employed by the abusers of the word 'terrorism' is essentially this: The low-technology violence of the weak is such an abomination that there are no limits to the high-technology violence of the strong that can be deployed against it.

Not surprisingly, since Sept. 11, 2001, virtually every recognised state confronting an insurgency or separatist movement has eagerly jumped on the 'war on terrorism' bandwagon, branding its domestic opponents – if it had not already done so – 'terrorists'. (John V. Whitbeck, 'A world ensnared by a word', *International Herald Tribune,* February 18, 2004) the end of the Cold War and the decline of wars between states have left quite a few western countries with defence and intelligence capacities that are 'surplus to requirements'. One response has been to re-deploy defence and intelligence staff to fight the 'war on terrorism'. In addition, some countries have created new anti-terrorism units; the USA has created an enormous federal agency to coordinate its anti-terrorist efforts, and justified the war in Afghanistan (2001) and Iraq (2003) in these terms.

International crime

Crime does not stop at national borders. On the contrary: the most profitable crimes are organised internationally. Drugs, women, body parts, art and weapons are exported to places with the highest profits. Organising this business is extremely lucrative, and the chances of arrest are lower because of international legal and policing arrangements. In other words, international crime is running ahead of national and international capacities to deal with it.

Corruption

Political power is crucial for the distribution of resources and the protection of interests, so it comes as no surprise that politicians are under constant temptation to succumb to corruption. Lobbying is an integral part of democratic decision making, but as we saw in chapter 10, the line between legitimate and democratic pressure and less savoury activities is difficult to draw. Clientelism, patronage and outright bribery and **corruption** are by no means unknown in democracies, although they can be defined and evaluated very differently. In some countries they are seen as inevitable, even good or 'functional', in others they are unambiguously rejected and prosecuted. Since it makes sense to try to corrupt only the strong and influential, and since these are often powerful politicians, it is also difficult to root out such abuse. For this reason, it is seen more and more as a major threat to democratic politics. The NGO Transparency International (TI) has been set up to investigate and draw attention to the problem.

> **Corruption** The use of illegitimate means (bribery, blackmail, or threats) to influence or control the making of public decisions, or the secret use of public offices or resources for private purposes.

The limits of state power

Concerns about international crime, terrorism and corruption draw fresh attention to the old problem of the limits of state power. For modern democracies, however, the question is whether they are particularly vulnerable to these threats. Their strict rules about individual rights and freedoms make it easier for criminals and terrorists to work within and across their borders,

CONTROVERSY 16.3

The price of security?

The claim that if you want security you must give up liberty [has] become a mainstay of the revolt against freedom. But nothing is less true. There is, of course, no absolute security in life. But what security can be attained depends on our own watchfulness, enforced by institutions to help us watch – i.e. by *democratic institutions* which are devised (using Platonic language) to enable the herd to watch, and to judge, their watch-dogs. (Karl R. Popper, *The Open Society and Its Enemies, 1: The Spell of Plato,* Princeton: Princeton University Press, 1961 [1943]: 315, emphasis in the original)

and more difficult to take effective measures against them. Hence the claim that 'if you want security, you must give up liberty' (see controversy 16.3). Debate about this claim is likely to persist.

Meanwhile, as a reaction to the risks of modern life, businesses and wealthy citizens are turning to private security arrangements. They live behind walls and gates in protected communities, employ private bodyguards and armed watchmen and install closed circuit TV (CCTV) and expensive alarm systems. This, in turn, means that the state no longer has a monopoly of physical force, a point we will return to in chapter 18.

■ Theories of security and conflict

Over the centuries social scientists, philosophers and military experts have tried to understand war and formulate general theories about it. Their attempts have not been very successful, so far. This is partly because it often seems that each war is the product of very specific and particular circumstances, especially if the focus is on the more spectacular phases of violent confrontation rather than the protracted negotiations to avoid war, or the long chain of events that leads up to war. Violent conflict is also a special interest of modern historians who are often interested in the unique aspects of each case. As a consequence, research on conflicts and peace tends to be fragmented and not cumulative.

Theoretical work is perhaps more successful when it focuses on the role of the state in protecting its citizens. In fact, this is one of the most important arguments for the existence of states and their legitimate use of political power (see chapter 1). According to one view, states should be little more than 'night watchmen' with the job of protecting life and property. Notice that such a 'protectionist' approach says little about the social and historical origins of states, or why they function as they do. It is a normative theory (chapter 1) concerned with what states ought to do, and with the limitations that should be placed upon them. Thomas Hobbes' famous account of the Leviathan is widely recognised as a basic attempt to legitimise strong government in order to protect freedom.

The origins of conflict

More empirical approaches to conflict and security have been formulated in several social science disciplines. Three are particularly well known:

- *Animal behaviour theories* focusing on biological aspects of animal and human behaviour, especially on the aggressive and competitive instincts that are said to be inherent in human nature.
- *Social–psychological theories* examine the inter-relationships between individuals either within small groups or in large ('anonymous') masses. Social psychologists tend to stress the importance of socialisation, especially in childhood, in the development of character, norms and values. They emphasise human 'cultures' rather than 'instinct'.
- *Structural–functional theories* emphasise neither culture nor instinct. They start from the structures and institutions of society and the functions they perform in maintaining social stability and continuity. Societies are seen as an organic 'system' in which each part performs a set of functions, so that to change any one part may have consequences for all the others. If one part of society does not perform its function adequately, the result is likely to be some sort of conflict, until society readjusts itself to establish equilibrium once again. Conflict can, therefore, be 'functional' if it draws attention to a social problem that is then rectified.

Each of these approaches has its problems:

- Can we use animal behaviour to explain human behaviour, and to what extent can we explain human conflict in terms of basic instincts?
- Are human beings 'animals' in this sense, and how can we know what is 'instinctive' or 'hard-wired' into our genetic make-up?
- Equally, how do we know what is learned in society and therefore cultural?
- Can we understand conflict as the product of how people are socialised into their cultures, or perhaps the result of inadequate socialisation? And is it not rather odd to say that conflict is functional?
- If it persists over a long time, as it often does (think of religious and racial conflict), is it functional?
- Is serious conflict more functional than less serious conflict?
- Would it not be much better if there was no conflict to start with?

Realism and idealism

Such theoretical problems have pushed students of international relations to take a different approach towards international conflicts which concentrates neither on individuals and their instincts or socialisation, nor on society and its organic nature, but on states and their reasons for operating in the international system as they do. As so often, there are two opposing theories:

- *Idealism* On the one hand, the idealist approaches that dominated before the Second World War saw politics as the struggle between competing ideas and ideologies (see chapter 14). The behaviour of states in the international system was guided, so far as possible, by ideals and morality, and by the possibility of peaceful coexistence.

- *Realism* **Realism**, which can be seen as a reaction to idealism, sees politics as a struggle between competing material interests. The basic assumption is that international politics is shaped by relatively autonomous actors (especially states, but also other organisations such as MNCs) who act more or less rationally to promote their own interest. These actors are confronted with an unpredictable international system, where few common norms or values exist, and where no single body rules, as states rule the countries of the world. The logic of the international system is for each state to further its own interests by means of economic and military power. Unfortunately, this rational behaviour of state actors results in the continuing insecurity and unpredictability of the international system. Rather than the ordered Westphalia system (chapter 1), we have a 'dog-eat-dog' world that could be described as a 'west failure' system.

> **Realism** In international relations, realism refers to the view of politics that emphasises the role of self-interest as a determinant of state policies and hence the importance of power in these relations.

Policy communities

Defence policy and the arms trade are often used as a prime example of the policy communities that operate in some areas of public policy, and policy community theory has had some success in explaining decision making in government (see also chapter 15). Policy communities:

- Are relatively small and stable groups of people representing the main interests involved in a policy area
- Work closely together in both the formal decision-making bodies of government (committees, consultative groups and official working parties) and in various informal and private ways
- Usually have common interests, and develop a consensual approach to the policy area
- Will do their best to exclude outside groups and interests that try to disturb their close working relations with different ideas and interests. Policy communities are closed.

In the case of defence policy and the arms trade, two closely related issues, there is likely to be a single policy community bringing together three sets of people:

- Senior government ministers and their most senior civil service advisors
- Military leaders in the army, navy and air force
- The business interests that finance, manufacture and sell arms at home and abroad.

Although their interests are not identical, they are likely to overlap to a great extent and they will have a common interest in keeping out other groups that want to get involved. While policy communities build up a great deal of expert and inside knowledge, and can work smoothly, efficiently and consistently over time, the danger is that they can become a closed conspiracy against the public interest. In some cases, those who are responsible for the public interest (elected politicians and public servants) may be 'captured' by private interests (the businessmen) in the community.

The military–industrial complex

In his (1956) book on the power elite, C. Wright Mills (1916–62) goes a long way further than policy community theory, arguing that the military–industrial complex (chapter 10) controls all important decisions in American government. The national and financial issues of foreign and defence policy are so important in terms of national security and profits that a tiny group of politicians, top military officers and businessmen forms a tight political elite that makes all key decisions – social, political, economic, domestic and foreign policy.

This elite is united by a common social background and the same financial interests. Members attend the same schools and universities, join the same exclusive clubs and are related by intermarriage. Most of them are from enormously wealthy families and inherit large fortunes and business interests. This gives them the same vested interests in big business and 'big' government, and in protecting these interests at home and overseas. The elite is not interested in the middle levels of power, which it leaves to pluralist competition between whoever wants to get involved, but it keeps tight control of all 'key' decisions.

Critics of the power elite thesis argue that never once does Mills actually show how the elite makes any given decision, nor does he tell us how many people are in the closed circle – 50, 500, 5,000, 50,000? Another problem concerns how the elite maintains its unity – do the army, navy and air force not have different interests, each fighting for a larger share of the defence budget, and are the financial interests of oil companies always the same as those of, say, finance capitalists or the electronics industry? And even if Mills is right about the USA, does the same model apply to Denmark, Namibia and Peru?

■ What have we learned?

This chapter deals with the defence and security of the state. It argues that:

- Traditional tasks of governments include the defence of the state against its external enemies, the maintenance of domestic law and order and the protection of citizens and their property. In fact, many theories of the state and political power are based on the idea that security and protection are the ultimate reasons for the existence of states and governments.

- Wars between states have declined in recent decades. Armed conflict within states has increased since the Second World War, but does not seem to have increased further recently.
- States have the right to defend themselves, subject to certain conditions (proportionality of response, taking action against attackers and not reprisals against innocent third parties, the maintenance of territorial integrity), but pre-emptive strikes are a different matter.
- International terrorism, organised crime and corruption are very difficult to handle, partly because police activity has traditionally been organised at the national level, and states are unwilling or unable to operate at the international level.

■ Lessons of comparison

- Conflicts between states have been common all over the world, but are more recently concentrated in the Middle East, Africa and Central Asia.
- Defence, military power and the arms trade are important economically for many countries, resulting in tightly knit policy making communities consisting of government, the military and arms producers. Some writers have even argued that 'the military–industrial complex' makes all the really important political decisions in some states.
- Crime rates vary highly between similar states. This may be because crime rates really differ, or because of differences in the definition and recording of crime. There are even larger differences in the number of prisoners, ranging from about 700 per 100,000 inhabitants in the USA to 50–60 per 100,000 inhabitants in Scandinavia.
- Since the deterrent effects of punishment and imprisonment appear to be limited and not very cost-effective, states increasingly develop programmes for crime prevention.

Projects

1. Even in countries with high numbers of prisoners, less than 10 per cent of the prison population are female. How many female prisoners are in jail in your country at this moment? Why is the figure so low? Can you imagine reasons for an increase in the number of female prisoners in your country?
2. Make a list of terrorist actions in the world since 2000. What was the main objective of these actions? Which countries – if any – were involved in these actions and what was their main role (victim, supporter, opponent, mediator)?
3. It took the UN a long time to intervene in Darfur. Make a list of countries contributing to UNAMID. Why was it so difficult for the UN to take action?

Further reading

M. Akehurst, *A Modern Introduction to International Law*, London: Allen & Unwin, 1973.
Studies international conflicts from the point of view of international law.

R. Jackson and Georg Sørensen, *Introduction to International Relations: Theories and Approaches*, Oxford: Oxford University Press, 2nd edn., 2003.
Provides a systematic introduction to the main political theories of international relations.

S. Burchill, Andrew Linklater *et al.*, *Theories of International Relations*, Basingstoke: Macmillan, 1996.
An account of the leading approches to international relations.

H. Entorf and Hannes Spengler, *Crime in Europe: Causes and Consequences*, Berlin: Springer Verlag, 2002.
A comprehensive overview of crime and criminological research.

J. van Kesteren, Pat Mayhew and Paul Nieuwbeerta, *Criminal Victimisation in Seventeen Industrial Countries*, The Hague: NSCR, 2000.
The main findings of the western European International Crime Victims Survey of 2000.

H.-H. Hoppe, *The Myth of National Defense: Essays on the Theory and History of Security Production*, Auburn: Mises Institute, 2003.
A provocative challenge of the traditional claim that the primary function of government is to provide security and protection.

Websites

www.cdi.org
Website of the Center for Defense Information. Information and alternative views on security and issues of security policy, strategy, operations, weapon systems and defence budgeting.
www.curia.eu.int
Website of the ECJ, with extensive information about its functions and procedures.
www.echr.coe.int
Website of the European Court of Human Rights (ECHR), with extensive information about its functions and procedures.
http://rechten.uvt.nl/icvs/
Website of the International Crime Victims Survey.
www.icj-cij.org
Website of the principal judicial organ of the UN, the ICJ, with extensive information about its functions and procedures.
www.iiss.org
International Institute for Strategic Studies (IISS). This is the primary source of accurate, objective information on international strategic issues, weapons and strategy.

www.interpol.int

Website of the largest international police organisation in the world. Information about cross-border criminal police cooperation among its 187 member countries spread over five continents.

www.konfliktbarometer.de

Website of the Heidelberg Institute of International Conflict Research. Provides extensive information on conflicts, crises and wars in the world since the Second World War.

www.nato.int

Website of NATO, the major alliance of nineteen countries in North America and Europe to safeguard the freedom and security of its member countries by political and military means.

www.transparency.org

Website of TI, the only international NGO devoted to combating corruption, with information about corruption in many countries.

17   Welfare

Life can be very pleasant in democratic countries. The state provides schools and hospitals, roads and bridges, parks and libraries and sometimes it even subsidises opera and sport. But consider the following:

- Will the state help you through university?
- What happens if you are ill or disabled or unable to find a job? Will the state help you?
- What about those who are too young or too old to work? Should the state support them?
- What of the poor and vulnerable? For that matter, who is poor and vulnerable?

Welfare state policies are based on the redistribution of resources between parts of the population: taxes and contributions are collected from citizens who can afford to pay and the money is used to support those in need. A detailed list of welfare state provisions would be long in most countries, and the administration of even the simplest of them is exceedingly complex. The politics of the 'taking and giving' that the welfare state involves is also highly controversial and the source of fierce political debate. We cannot cover all aspects of welfare state arrangements in one chapter, so we focus on the most typical ones and use them to illustrate the ways in which democratic states try to improve the well-being of their citizens and redistribute resources between them. In this chapter, we examine social security programmes because these are basic welfare programmes, pensions and health programmes because they are common to all welfare states and, third, the ways in which security programmes are funded because their high costs affect a great number of people.

The major topics in this chapter are:

- Welfare states and redistribution
- Social security
- Pensions and health programmes
- Social security and taxation
- Theories of the welfare state.

■ Welfare states and redistribution

Modern states have passed through several phases in their development: after the consolidation of their territory and sovereignty many of them gradually provided citizens with equal civil rights and with services to protect the poorest and most vulnerable parts of their populations (see chapters 1 and 2). Initially, the intention was to provide no more than a minimal safety net for those in the greatest danger, but gradually public services were extended to include larger sections of the population, and then to work towards equality of opportunity for all. The processes of equalisation and redistribution usually involved conflict between social groups, and the social security programmes we find in many democracies after the Second World War were often the result of political fights. A central issue was:

- Which risks were 'private', and therefore the responsibility of individuals?
- Which risks were 'social', requiring government involvement and public policies (see chapter 15 on the private–public distinction)?

Closely related was the issue of how to define and measure poverty and vulnerability. The 'poverty line' shifts from one generation to the next: poverty now is not the same as poverty in 1960, even less in 1900. Similarly, poverty in Taiwan or Nigeria is different from poverty in Sweden or Canada.

For a long time, most states refrained from 'too much' social and economic intervention. The dominant liberal theory of the state held that its purpose was to provide physical security, not protect the poor and vulnerable. But the traumatic experiences of the Great Depression of the 1930s and the post-war economic chaos of the late 1940s changed the traditional **laissez-faire doctrines** that were associated with emerging capitalism in many countries. Gradually, democratic states accepted the idea that markets did not always function well and that government intervention was necessary to correct market failures. Some states began to accept more responsibility for the very young and very

Laissez-faire doctrines The literal translation from the French is 'to allow to do': maximum freedom for the economic forces of the market, and minimum intervention from the state.

old, the sick and disabled and the unemployed and poor. They developed what are called welfare states, particularly in western Europe after the Second World War, but in other areas of the world as well. We can define five major goals of such states, in general terms:

- Reducing poverty
- Promoting equality of opportunity
- Promoting individual autonomy
- Promoting social stability
- Promoting social integration.

Nowadays these general goals are widely shared in many countries; it is mainly when specific policies are under discussion that conflict emerges (see controversy 17.1). This is usually because welfare – desirable and benign from the social, humanitarian and economic point of view – has to be paid for, like any other policy, and this involves the redistribution of resources: taking from some in order to give to others. For this reason, welfare states are also tax states.

Although it is invariably a political issue, the considerable burden of taxes and contributions was accepted with surprisingly little complaint and protest in many countries for a long time. In fact, the rapid expansion of social security programmes in the 1960s and 1970s was widely accepted and fundamental disagreement did not figure very largely in legislative debate. The reasons for this broad support are easy to understand if we look at the many accomplishments of successful social security programmes:

- *Political* Social security programmes do a great deal to ease political conflict between groups, not least by including all of them as citizens of the state with their own rights and duties.
- *Economic* Social security programmes improve the quality of the labour force, and its **productivity** by maintaining a healthy and educated population.

Productivity The average production per labourer in a specific period (for instance, the average number of ballpoints produced per labourer in a ballpoint pen factory in one year).

- *Social* Social security programmes stabilise society by protecting the family and communities on which society itself depends. Conservative forces opposed to socialism in most of its forms place great importance on family and community.
- *Cultural* Social security programmes help to create a fair and just society, which serves to enhance the legitimacy of the state and its social arrangements. Welfare helps to create a culture of support for society and the state.

Social security is in the interest of many diverse groups in society, ranging from big business in search of efficient workers or early retirement schemes to local charities for disabled children. Put somewhat strongly, welfare states are widely accepted because they meet the diverse needs of many different social and economic groups in society, while their costs are spread collectively.

What is a welfare state?

Definition

What is the welfare state? A common textbook definition is that it involves state responsibility for securing some basic modicum of welfare for its citizens. Such a definition skirts the issue of whether social policies are emancipatory or not; whether they help system legitimation or not; whether they contradict or aid the market process; and what, indeed, is meant by 'basic'? Would it not be more appropriate to require of a welfare state that it satisfies more than our basic or minimal welfare needs? (Gøsta Esping-Andersen, *The Three Worlds of Welfare Capitalism*, Princeton: Princeton University Press, 1990: 19)

Decline of the welfare state?

The contemporary state is very much the product of the collectivisation of health care, education and income maintenance. A modern life, in its most intimate and pervasive aspects, is shaped by this collectivising process. The recent welfare backlash and budget cuts affect the welfare society only superficially, even if they cause much individual distress and institutional upheaval. Cut-backs, also, are central interventions and in the end may even contribute to centralisation. (Abraham de Swaan, *In Care of the State: Health Care, Education and Welfare in Europe and the USA in the Modern Era*, Cambridge: Polity Press, 1998: 11)

It does not follow that each and every welfare state provision is universally welcomed, only that the basic principle is widely recognised.

■ Social security

Social security and social expenditure

Provision for the young and old, the sick and disabled and the unemployed and disadvantaged can be organised in many ways. Individuals can, for instance, buy private nursing care for their elderly parents, send their children to private schools and buy private insurance to cover themselves against unemployment. Welfare states, however, are based on the idea that at least some of these services should be collectively provided and funded because some individuals are unable to provide them for themselves, and because the collective costs of not providing them are too high:

- Imagine, for example, how well the economy would work if the state did not provide free, universal education.
- Imagine the public reaction if accident victims were left to die on the roads because there were no public hospitals to take them to.

The total of all payments for public and private welfare expenditures are called **social expenditures**. The Organisation for Economic Cooperation and Development (OECD) (see briefing 17.1) defines these payments as: the

> **Social expenditures** The provision by public (and private) institutions of benefits to households and individuals in order to provide support during circumstances which adversely affect their welfare.

363

Briefing 17.1

The OECD classification of social expenditure

Category	Examples
1 Old age cash benefits	Pensions, veterans' pensions, early retirement pensions
2 Disability cash benefits	Disability pensions, disabled child pension
3 Occupational injury and disease	Paid sick leave, occupational injury compensation
4 Sickness benefits	Inability to work due to sickness
5 Services for the elderly and disabled	Residential care, day care and rehabilitation services
6 Widow and widower pensions	Pensions and benefits in kind for dependants of deceased persons.
7 Family benefits	Children's allowances and family benefits
8 Family services	Day care for children, household and personal services for the disabled.
9 Active labour market programmes	Labour market training, youth training, subsidised employment
10 Unemployment	Unemployment benefits, severance pay
11 Health	Hospital care, home health care, ambulance services
12 Housing benefits	Rent subsidies, sheltered accommodation for the old and disabled
13 Other contingencies	Income support for those below the poverty line, indigenous people, refugees and immigrants

Source: OECD (2004), Social Expenditure Database (SOCX, www.oecd.org/els/social/expenditure)

provision by public (and private) institutions of benefits to households and individuals in order to provide support during circumstances which adversely affect their welfare.

The OECD definition of social expenditures contains a number of elements that require a little more discussion:

- 'circumstances which adversely affect their welfare' are mainly related to old age, illness or invalidity, unemployment, family problems, poor housing and some aspects of poverty.

- 'provide support' can be done in several ways. Most important are (1) **cash transfers** where individuals or households obtain direct financial support, and (2) the **provision of goods and services**. Examples of (1) are pensions and family allowances for children and of (2) are housing programmes and labour market initiatives, such as retraining. Reimbursements – such as compensation for the costs of medicine or sick leave pay – are a special variant of cash transfers.

> **Cash transfers** Providing social security by giving citizens money.

> **Provision of goods and services** A way to provide social security by offering specific facilities such as housing or job training.

- 'provision by public (and private) institutions of benefits' is probably the most complicated aspect of the OECD definition. Some benefits are universal and available to all citizens, but in some countries they may be paid through **means testing**. Some benefits are provided without any obligation, but others are combined with special requirements, such as participating in a job-training programme. In other words, social expenditures are not necessarily free, or unconditional, or universal. Social expenditure does not necessarily cover the full market costs of the goods or services. To give a concrete example, buying a pain killer at a pharmacy at your own expense is not a social expenditure, but getting it through a public health system doctor is, provided that the cost is covered in whole or in part by some public or quasi-public institution. It immediately becomes clear that exactly what counts as 'social' varies enormously from one country to another, depending on exactly who pays for the benefits. The question is not who provides what but how it is financed. If it is financed in whole or in part by a public or private institution, and not by a private individual, it counts as public social expenditure.

> **Means testing** Investigating a person's income and means of support to ensure that they qualify for public assistance and services.

- 'public (and private) institutions' are responsible for social expenditure programmes. Public institutions can be any government agency at any level (national, regional, local), or a special social security fund. Private institutions, on the other hand, are restricted to institutions that operate according to government rules. Private programmes can be compulsory (employed people are often legally required to pay into social security funds) or voluntary (employees may pay for additional benefits such as a higher pension). It is very difficult, therefore, to draw a clear line between different kinds of private institutions involved in social security programmes, because different agencies are 'public' and 'private' to varying degrees. What is clear is that payments within families (from parents to children, for example) and payments from purely private organisations (the Red Cross) are not included, though they count as private social expenditure.

Social security is organised in very different ways in different countries. Some states – Denmark, The Netherlands, or Sweden – have very extensive programmes covering a wide variety of risk. Others – Japan, the UK, USA – offer more restricted cover. Moreover, in some states, such as The Netherlands, the UK and the USA, private sources play a more important role than others. Comparing social security programmes between states is thus a complicated matter.

Comparing social security systems

To compare social security systems we might try to measure the amount of service delivered, or its quality, or its effectiveness, but these are complicated matters to define and quantify. The easiest yardstick for comparison is cost. Even measuring costs requires us to be clear about the differences between (1) levels of social spending in different countries, (2) the composition of these expenditures (how it is divided between health, education, pensions, etc.) and (3) the trends over time of expenditures in one or more countries. All are important, and we will consider them now.

The level of social expenditure

Since prosperous countries can afford more generous social security programmes, the costs are typically related to economic capacity (measured as gross domestic product, or GDP). Even expressed as a percentage of GDP, the differences between states are significant.

As can be seen in the central column of figure 17.1 about 30 per cent of GDP was spent on public social security in Denmark and Sweden in 2001. At the other end of the scale, we find countries such as Mexico (5.1 per cent) and Korea (6.1 per cent). Several European countries – including France, Germany, Italy and Norway – devote about a quarter of their income to social expenditures. The average for 23 member states of the OECD was 20.5 per cent in 2001.

When we look at the level of social security as a percentage of GDP two important conclusions can be drawn. First, some states spend much more than others – compare France and Mexico – and even similar countries vary a lot – compare Denmark and the Netherlands, or the Czech Republic and the Slovak Republic. Second, although variations within western Europe are considerable (compare Iceland and Sweden), Europe as a whole spends more than other parts of the world. All the places in the top half of figure 17.1 are filled by European countries. The first non-European state on the list is New Zealand, which spends less than the OECD average. The bottom half includes some wealthy countries such as Japan (16.9 per cent), Ireland (13.8 per cent) and the USA (14.7 per cent), as well as poorer ones such as Korea and Mexico.

The composition of social expenditure

Figure 17.1 presents information about the composition of social security spending; that is, the way social security is provided (cash benefits versus the

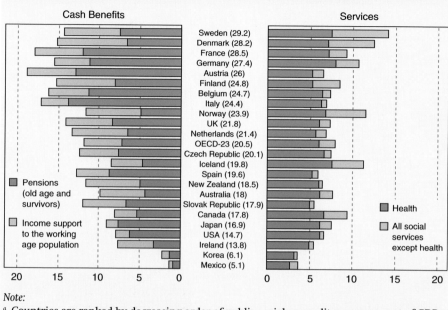

Figure 17.1: Public social expenditure,[a] by broad social policy areas, 2001, per cent of GDP

Note:

[a] Countries are ranked by decreasing order of public social expenditure as per cent of GDP.

Source: OECD Social Expenditure Database (www.oecd.org/els/social/expenditure).

provision of goods and services) and about client groups for these services (the working-age population, pensioners, disabled, poor, etc.). Even though the categories in figure 17.1 are broad, they show how much countries vary. Cash benefits account for a larger proportion of spending than goods and services, but there are exceptions (compare Canada and Iceland). The two types of spending usually balance each other: a state spending relatively large amounts on cash benefits normally spends less on goods and services (compare Italy and the Slovak Republic). The reverse is also true: where cash benefits are comparatively low, goods and services are high (see, for instance, Iceland and Norway).

Differences between states are even more evident in the services they provide. A glance at figure 17.1 reveals astonishing variation, and not just between rich and poor countries, or First and Third World ones. It is no great surprise that Belgium and Mexico have little in common, but what do we make of a comparison of Germany and Italy or the Czech and Slovak Republics?

A closer look at social expenditures is presented in figure 17.2, which shows how total social security expenditures in six selected countries are divided among different programmes. In the first four countries, the largest part is for elderly people. In Greece, about 45 per cent of social security payments are for this group. In European countries, health is usually the second

Figure 17.2: Composition of public social expenditure, selected countries, 2003, per cent of total social expenditure

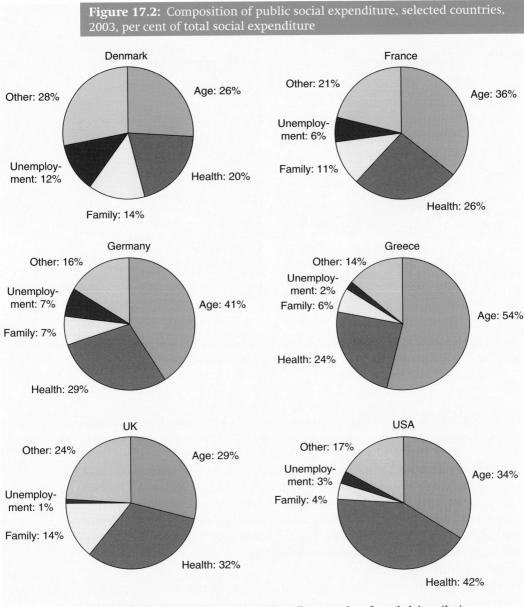

Denmark
Other: 28%
Age: 26%
Unemployment: 12%
Health: 20%
Family: 14%

France
Other: 21%
Age: 36%
Unemployment: 6%
Family: 11%
Health: 26%

Germany
Other: 16%
Unemployment: 7%
Family: 7%
Age: 41%
Health: 29%

Greece
Other: 14%
Unemployment: 2%
Family: 6%
Age: 54%
Health: 24%

UK
Other: 24%
Age: 29%
Unemployment: 1%
Family: 14%
Health: 32%

USA
Other: 17%
Unemployment: 3%
Family: 4%
Age: 34%
Health: 42%

Source: OECD Social Expenditure Statistics (http://stats.oecd.org/brandedviewpilot/default.aspx?datasetcode=socx_det, 2008).

largest, ranging from 20 per cent in Greece to 29 per cent in Germany. The gap between Europe and the USA is evident, since the latter spends no less than 42 per cent of its total social security bill on health. Family-related spending follows a similar pattern of comparisons and contrasts. In Denmark, and the

UK this accounts for 14 per cent of total social expenditure, whereas in the USA it is barely 4 per cent.

The conclusion, once again, is that there are huge differences between countries. Even among western European states the variation is usually large, but the western European average is usually well above other regions of the globe.

Trends in social expenditure

Social security programmes began in Germany and Austria in the 1880s. A second phase of development followed the First World War when other countries took up the idea, and a third phase followed the Second World War when there was a very rapid expansion of a wide variety of programmes in many western countries. These were generally well established by the mid-1970s, but from then onwards until the 1990s there was a fourth phase of stability or reform. We have already seen how the levels and composition of spending varies from one country to another, but to talk about 'phases of development' in a collection of countries suggests that their *trends* over time may be rather similar. In fact we have already seen this in chapter 2, which showed how redistribution of resources was a characteristic of developing democracies in the nineteenth century. We can make two points:

- Could it be that since most industrial democracies are confronted with similar problems as they develop, so they also show similar trends in their social security spending?
- Have democratic countries become more alike (converged) in this respect?

Trends in the level of spending as a percentage of GDP in selected countries are presented in figure 17.3. A first glance confirms our conclusion about the huge differences between countries. Furthermore, the trend lines show more or less similar developments, so that differences between countries do not narrow:

- Social security expanded rapidly in many European countries in the 1960s and 1970s, when the worst damage of the Second World War had been repaired and economic growth provided the necessary finances. In the period between 1960 and 1980 social expenditure rose in Denmark, for instance, from 11 per cent to almost 30 per cent of GDP. On average, the OECD countries doubled their spending from 10 per cent in 1960 to 20 per cent in 1980. This was primarily because social security was extended to larger sections of the population and because higher-quality services were provided at higher cost.
- Expansion reached a ceiling in the 1980s, when few new commitments were added, and spending started to flatten off or even declined slightly. The economic recession of the 1970s made it clear that economic growth could not be taken for granted, and several governments started to curtail social expenditures.

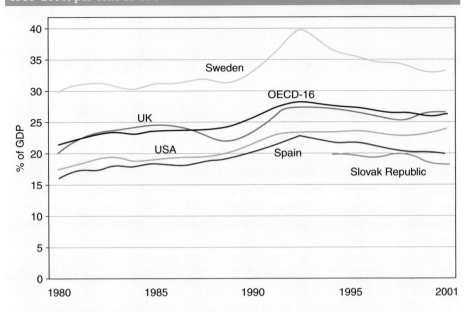

Figure 17.3: Trends in public social expenditure, selected countries, 1980–2001, per cent of GDP

Source: OECD Social Expenditure Database (www.oecd.org/els/social/expenditure).

- However, severe economic problems and rising unemployment at the end of the 1980s and the early 1990s forced some countries to spend more on social security. Increases were evident in Austria, Denmark, Finland, France, Germany, Portugal and Sweden.
- Social spending again declined in many countries in the 1990s, once more for economic and financial reasons – benefits were cut, the people eligible for them restricted and private provision, especially private pensions and insurance provision, encouraged.

The expectation that states converge and become more alike in their social expenditures as their economies develop is not supported by the data. Each country has its own combination of social security programmes and its own approach to reform. What we observe, however, are similar patterns in the time trends, with rising expenditures and attempts to reform social security in economically difficult periods. European countries show such trends since the 1960s, but there is little evidence of convergence.

■ Pensions and health programmes

Pensions and health are the two largest spending programmes in virtually every country. Together, they account for more than three-quarters of all social security expenditures in the USA and about two-thirds in many European countries. We now take a closer look at them.

Pensions

Provisions for the old were one of the first forms of social security in many countries. These included pensions, war veterans' provisions, early retirement pensions and reduced costs for things such as public transport and medicine. The share of these programmes ranges from no less than 54 per cent of all social expenditure in Greece, to 26 per cent in Denmark.

In principle, there are two ways of providing the elderly with benefits:

- *State pensions for the general population* provided to everybody above a certain age – usually sixty-five years and older – with a basic income. Entitlements are based not on earnings nor on contributions to a pension fund, but simply on age and residence, on the grounds that each person is entitled to financial security in their old age. Because it is universal, the high cost of such a pension scheme means that payments to individuals are usually modest. A standard, universal pension, however, does guarantee a minimum income for all.
- *Pension insurance programmes* provided according to contributions to a pension fund. This can lead to severe problems, especially for those who have not had paid employment or who have had it for less than a normal working life. Pension insurance programmes are increasingly found in almost all countries. They tend to reproduce in the retired population the same income inequalities that are found among those with paid employment.

There are also great differences between countries in how pension funds are collected. In all countries the state supports pension programmes with public funds, although this varies from 10 to 30 per cent of the total costs. Both employees and employers are required to contribute to funds in every country. But while general population pensions rely heavily on general taxation, insurance pensions are mostly paid from funds collected from employee and employer contributions.

Whether they are paid from general taxes or specific pension funds, pensions are based on the idea that the current working population pays for the pensions of those who are currently retired. The pensions of those who are currently working will, in turn, be paid by the next generation of workers. The problem with this system is obvious: what happens when, as in many countries now, the population ages, and the smaller proportion of working people cannot afford the pensions of the larger proportion of retired (see controversy 17.2)? The solution often advocated is a capital investment scheme in which each citizen invests their pensions savings during their working life, and lives off the pension income this generates when they retire. The problem with this system is also obvious. What happens if people do not or cannot afford to invest enough for a decent pension income, and what happens

The end of the welfare state?

With few exceptions, systems of social protection are still recognisably the same as they were some forty or fifty years ago. They still revolve around cash support to individuals who are temporarily absent from the labour market, and ensuring that those who are elderly receive an adequate standard of living…long-term trends, which are requiring a new approach to social and health policies, are:

- People are living longer. Dependency ratios will rise.
- The increase in elderly people living alone raises the demand for care services.
- The proportion of children in lone-parent families has risen.
- The increase in dual-earner households, caused by increased female labour force participation, makes childcare and parental leave policies more important for the well-being of families.
- Fertility rates have fallen. Labour market developments appear to strongly influence family formation.
- Low-skilled workers have a higher risk of unemployment, other forms of non-employment, or low wages insufficient to support their families.
- People are leading healthier lives because of declining disability. Demographic changes will nevertheless lead to an increase in demand for health services unless remedial action is taken.
- Previously fatal illnesses are being converted into chronic conditions, implying a need for long-term support.

(OECD, A Caring World: The New Social Policy Agenda, *Paris: OECD, 1999: 15)*

if investments do not generate a good financial return? Stock markets can and do go down as well as up, and people can and do lose some or all of their pension funds.

This brief look at pension programmes underlines the conclusion we reached earlier about country variations. Even for the universal phenomenon of old age, there is a bewildering variety of pension schemes and an even greater variety of different kinds and forms of special provisions and services for the elderly. Nevertheless, an aging population has forced many states to reform their pension system and restrict entitlements. In turn, more private and individual elements are being introduced in many countries and private insurance schemes are becoming increasingly important.

Health

Ill health, like age, is universal, and many people attach supreme importance to good health. Health expenditures now account for about a quarter of social expenditures in welfare states, and as the population ages, and ever more expensive medical technology and drugs are developed, so health costs inexorably rise. In the USA, health expenditures account for as much as 42 per cent of public social expenditure.

As with pensions, health services can be organised as a general and universal benefit ('health care for all'), or as a health insurance matter funded by private contributions. But unlike pensions there is an additional aspect to health insurance: covering the costs of medical treatment, on the one hand, and compensating for income loss while ill, on the other. We need to look at:

- Social security programmes to cover the costs of medical treatment have common characteristics in many countries. These measures are usually a general population programme which offers health care, but entitlements vary: in Britain and Denmark, for instance, health care is available, in principle, to all citizens, whereas in France and Germany, payment into a health insurance programme is required. All countries demand that patients carry some of the costs of medical treatment themselves (often such things as dental costs), but some hospital or medical costs are also charged to patients in some countries. There are clear differences between countries in the way health care programmes are paid for. While Britain and Denmark rely heavily on general taxation, countries such as France or Germany prefer transfers based on contributions. A mixture of taxation and additional contributions is found in Spain and Sweden.
- Compensation for income loss, which is more diverse. The amount paid, and the length of time it is paid for, varies greatly: in Denmark, Germany and Sweden benefits are directly related to income loss; Britain provides a minimum payment and France and Spain occupy a middle position.

Fierce controversies about the rising costs of health schemes have broken out in many countries since the 1980s. Increased spending is mainly due to an aging population and to the costs of high technology medical equipment and drugs, but some critics claim that it is not demographic and technological factors that are responsible so much as the lack of transparent rules about the provision of medical care. On the one hand, demand for care is limitless; on the other, it is difficult to ration because lives, health and well-being are at stake. It is also extremely difficult to lay down general rules about who should and should not receive medical care:

- Should overweight smokers be given the same care as those who have taken trouble to look after themselves?
- If there is only enough money for a hundred operations of a given kind, who should be the hundred and first to go without?

In many cases, and in an increasing number of them, the rationing of medical care is not by general rules, but simply by cost.

Attempts to control costs take three main forms:

- Limiting the public costs of treatment, either by making less available, or by requiring patients to cover more of the costs themselves.
- Limiting compensation for income losses, by lowering payments or restricting the time period of payments.
- Introducing market measures; that is, abandoning the idea of free, universal medical care paid for from general taxation and leaving more to

market mechanisms based on supply and demand. Usually this, too, requires patients to contribute more to their own costs. As with pensions, private medical care and insurance is the result.

■ Social security and taxation

The reasons for the growth of the welfare state and its associated expenditure are well understood in broad outline:

- First, it is generally true that the wealthier the country, the greater the proportion of its income it will spend on welfare and public services. This is partly because services are labour-intensive and labour costs tend to rise faster than the other costs of production, especially the costs of the highly trained professionals employed by the state – teachers, social workers, doctors, administrators, lawyers and so on.
- Second, as society becomes more and more complex so the costs of social coordination rise – the costs of police, transport and communications, education, public health, R&D.
- Third, as technology develops, so the capital and running costs of public services rise.
- Last, of course, with economic development comes higher standards and expectations of public services.

There are also political reasons for the growth of the welfare state, although these are much disputed. As the scope of the state widens so the number of interests organised around its activities grows. The more a state becomes involved in taxing its citizens to pay for public services – especially those that equalise opportunities and resources – the more it becomes involved in conflicts between 'winners' and 'losers' and the more these groups press for additional services. Consequently, the state becomes even more involved in other public services. As it has been said: 'Big government breeds big pressures.' Once this process is started, the circle is hard to break. Each new task of the state produces a new set of interest groups organised around it to put it under pressure to do more, which then attracts new groups, and so on *ad infinitum*. There is always great demand for free public services provided by the state, and also strong resistance to the idea of paying for them.

The growth of the state can be seen clearly enough in the growth of taxation. The average level of total taxation was about 31 per cent in OECD countries in 1970; by 1988, it had grown to 41 per cent. This is not to say, of course, that citizens happily bear their share of the costs of the welfare state. On the contrary, as taxes rise so a larger proportion of the population is drawn into the tax net and taxation becomes more and more controversial. On top of this, the link between the welfare state and the economy as a whole is a highly disputed matter which pervades modern politics across the democratic world.

Taxes increase labour costs, and high labour costs affect the economy in two important ways:

- First, they increase production costs, and if these cannot be passed on to the consumer in the form of higher prices they may result in attempts to reduce employment or move production to countries with lower costs. In both cases, the result will be unemployment.
- Second, individuals will try to reduce their own tax costs. The rich will employ accountants to devise ways of avoiding taxes. Other parts of the population will try to evade taxes by working in the informal 'black economy'. In these instances, social security programmes have the opposite of their intended effect: instead of raising money to pay for services for the poor and vulnerable they reduce the income of the state, but not demand for its services. Notice that this outcome is not the result of political incompetence, corrupt administrators, or poorly designed welfare services, but of the behaviour of ordinary citizens trying to reduce their taxes.

> **'Black economy'** The 'informal economy' in which goods and services are traded for cash, without bills, receipts, or financial records that would enable the authorities to levy taxes on them.

Another reason for the controversial nature of the welfare state concerns what is called dependency, or the 'cycle of deprivation'. This argues that the very success of social security programmes breeds a new generation which is used to living on benefits, and is content to do so. In other words, the children of the poor on social security grow up in a culture of dependency that makes them, in their turn, unable to be self-supporting, and so the process reproduces itself. Critics of this view claim that welfare payments in most countries are not so high that people like living off them and that, in any case, the great majority of people want to work and be indepdendent in order to keep their self-respect. One school of thought claims that welfare cheats get much less money in total than tax cheats, but get much more public and media attention.

A final point about social security and taxation is of a very different nature. Many social security programmes are based on cash transfers as a form of income support. Should these be taxed? Different states answer this question in different ways:

- Some withhold tax at source paying, say, a notional £400 a month in benefits, but actually passing over £300, and keeping £100 in taxes.
- A more generous state might pay the full £400 and cash £100 in taxes afterwards.

This difference is important when it comes to comparing the total cost of welfare services in any two countries, and on this basis some have even challenged the conventional wisdom that the welfare state in the USA is much smaller than its European counterparts (see controversy 17.3).

The American welfare state: unusually small?

Comparing social security programmes is a complicated matter requiring us to take into account different tax systems, exchange rates, costs of living and the value of benefits in cash and in kind. Most analysis is based on *gross payments* (total payments to fund welfare service) or an estimation of income deductions made by the state. A careful estimate of these deductions, however, may change our conclusions about the differences between welfare states:

> I challenge the most commonly made claim about the exceptional nature of the American welfare state – that it is unusually small. This judgement, in my view, is misleading. It is based on an overstatement of the social benefits received in other nations and an underestimate of the social benefits distributed by the United States. The latter results from a narrow focus on just two tools of government action, social insurance and grants, and from a misleading measure of welfare state effort…
>
> In short, the American welfare state may be unusual less for its small size than for its reliance on a wide variety of policy tools to achieve what many European welfare states do primarily through social insurance. While it is hard to be 100 per cent sure of this conclusion, given the difficulties of comparing direct spending, tax expenditures, regulation, loan guarantees, and the like, the evidence certainly suggests that we should be highly suspicious of anyone who declares that the United States has a small welfare state. (Christopher Howard, 'Is the American welfare state unusually small?', *Political Science & Politics*, 34(3), 2003: 411–16)

■ Theories of the welfare state

The question of how and why democratic states gradually came to accept responsibility for their young and old, sick and disabled, unemployed and poor has fascinated scholars. Their interest is related to the fact that welfare systems vary hugely between states, and that social security expenditures, as a form of redistribution between citizens, are most usually the source of serious social, political and economic conflict. The welfare state also involves some fundamental moral issues about social justice, the nature of the modern state and its relationship with its citizens. As a result, theories of the welfare state typically mix normative and ideological approaches (see chapter 14) with empirical research. There are two fundamentally opposed views of the nature of the welfare state, for example:

- *Liberal* approaches regard the welfare state as a left-wing institution that taxes the rich, invades their liberty and encourage laziness and dependency on the part of the workers.
- *Socialist* approaches see the welfare state as a right-wing device that enables the capitalist system to function (that is, to maintain an educated and healthy working population) without having to rely on force or paying too much for it.

We do not wish to cover the ground of chapter 14 again, but shall concentrate instead on empirical theories that explain why very different types of social security programmes arose in various countries and why these expenditures occupy an ever-larger share of GDP. Empirical theories come in four major forms.

Conflict-oriented approaches

These explain the very different paths taken by social security programmes in various countries on the basis of power conflicts between groups in society. A well-known example of this approach is the work of the Danish political scientist Gøsta Esping-Andersen. In his view, the historical role and position of the labour movement was decisive, especially its resources and its ability to mobilise workers. Opposing social elites – capitalists, some churches, and politicians – were forced to compromise on redistribution policies if they were faced by a strong labour movement. Since the division of power varies in different countries according to their historical circumstances, different social security programmes are likely to arise (see briefing 17.2). Other scholars believe that conflicts between political parties are decisive, particularly given the important role that Christian democratic parties have played.

A special version of these theories tries to explain the absence of political conflict between workers and capitalists in Britain in the late nineteenth century. At the time, Britain was the most advanced capitalist economy in the world and precisely the place where Marxist theory predicted a revolutionary working-class movement. British workers, however, were anything but revolutionary. On the contrary, most were comparatively conservative and strongly supported what the Marxists regarded as the 'capitalist' Empire and the First World War, which was fought mainly for capitalist reasons. According to the Russian revolutionary Marxist Vladimir Lenin (1870–1924), this was because late nineteenth-century and early twentieth-century Britain could afford to pay higher wages and finance some rudimentary welfare services out of the huge profits is made by exploiting its colonies. These kept the British workers not just happy and docile but turned many of them into counter-revolutionary supporters of the Empire and of the First World War.

Functionalist explanations

The oldest accounts of diversity in social security systems focus on functionalist explanations. Emerging capitalism requires state intervention to support workers and stabilise families. According to this view, social security differences between countries are mainly the result of different levels of socio-economic development. A recent revival of functionalism argues that welfare policies enable modern societies to shift from industrial to post-industrial economies – for example, to enable coal mines and textile factories to be closed down by pensioning off miners and textile workers, or retraining them for different jobs.

Institutional approaches

These are a rather mixed set of explanations, but they all focus on the importance of institutional structures. Broadly speaking, the idea is that the more

Briefing 17.2

A typology of welfare states

One of the most comprehensive treatments of welfare state policies and the various ways of organising them is presented by the Danish political scientist Gøsta Esping-Andersen (1990). He distinguishes between different types of welfare states according to entitlements to benefits, levels of support, degree of redistribution and success in reducing or reinforcing inequalities. The three major types are:

■ Liberal welfare capitalism

A liberal type of welfare capitalism is found in Anglo-Saxon countries, particularly Australia, Canada and the USA. Benefits are modest and available mainly for low-income groups. Conventional work-ethic norms play an important role and entitlement rules are strict. The state encourages private initiatives to provide social security.

■ Conservative welfare capitalism

A conservative type of welfare capitalism is found in continental Europe, including Austria, France, Germany and Italy. This type is characterised by corporatism – that is, unions, employers' associations and governments collaborate closely to arrange social security programmes (see chapter 15). Because the government relies heavily on the collaboration of trade union and business organisations, the degree of redistribution is usually limited: entitlements are linked to status and class. Because the church plays a major role in corporatist regimes, social security programmes emphasise traditional family values.

■ Social-democratic welfare capitalism

A social-democratic type of welfare capitalism is found in Scandinavian countries. The goal of social security is not 'equality of minimal needs', but equality based on the highest standards. This means, first, that cash benefits are generous and service of a high quality and, second, that every citizen participates equally in the system (the principle of universal entitlement). The ideal is to maximise individual independence, rather than emphasise either the family or the market.

Esping-Andersen's typology was at the core of debates about the welfare state in the 1990s. Although critics point to severe limitations – such as the neglect of gender issues, the special features found in southern Europe and the interdependence of 'welfare capitalism' and negotiations between unions and employers' associations about benefits – his typology is indispensable. As with every good typology, its main advantage is the way it groups a large number of disparate systems into a *few categories* that make sense and are helpful.

See Gøsta Esping-Andersen, *The Three Worlds of Welfare Capitalism* (Princeton: Princeton University Press, 1990).

institutions are involved in policy making, the more difficult it is to create extensive social security arrangements. States with complex federal structures, and those making most use of referenda, are less developed than unitary states where decision-making power is unified and centralised. Institutional inertia may also explain the persistence of welfare states once they are established, because they are surrounded by bureaucracies and institutionalised interests that protect them against reform (see chapter 8 and 10). This does not explain how and why they arose in the first place.

Two versions of the institutional approach can be applied to different countries according to their decision-making institutions in the welfare field. The first involves the idea of policy networks. We discussed policy communities in chapter 15 and again in chapter 16 in the context of military and defence matters. Policy networks are looser and more open than communities, generally involving a wider range of interests and, therefore, more disagreement and conflict. Welfare policy networks involve government leaders and top administrators in welfare departments, a wide range of welfare professionals and employees and a wide range of pressure groups representing welfare service consumers. These come together in the network of committees, working groups and consultative bodies set up within government institutions and private bodies such as think tanks. Policy networks in the welfare field are found in Britain, France and Italy, and in a weaker form in the USA.

In other countries welfare policy making is more highly formalised within corporatist institutions (see chapter 10). Under these arrangements government and a few private interests work closely together within official structures that formulate and implement public policies. Each set of private interests (welfare professionals, for example) is organised into a single peak association that acts authoritatively for all its members and takes decisions on their behalf. This means that all the actors involved at the highest levels of the corporatist structure can bargain and negotiate in the knowledge that the policy outcome will be accepted and implemented by those lower in the system. The advantage is that binding decisions can be made, and stable and predictable policies can be followed. The disadvantage is that the system is more closed and exclusive than policy networks, so that groups outside the corporatist system are excluded from decision making. Corporatism in its most developed form was found in Austria, Luxembourg, The Netherlands, Norway and Sweden between the 1960s and 1980s. Less pure forms were found in Belgium, Denmark, Finland, West Germany, Ireland and Switzerland in the same period.

International and transnational dependencies

Finally, there are approaches focusing on international and transnational dependencies. These explain the variety of social security systems in terms of relations between states, as Lenin's theory of colonialism does. A heated debate has more recently broken out about whether *globalisation* forces states to cut their welfare programmes in order to make their economies more competitive in the world market. New Zealand is sometimes presented as the classic case of a country with a protected economy and a strong welfare state that transformed itself into a market economy with a modest welfare state. Small or vulnerable economies are said to be under pressure to reform welfare policies. In order to protect themselves from the consequences of global capitalism they have to decrease costs, which means cutting their welfare costs; to do anything else risks being priced out of the international market. To this set of explanations also belong theories focusing on the impact of the European Union on the social policies of its member states: in an open market countries with expensive welfare systems are under pressure to reform these systems in order to reduce costs.

At first sight these various approaches seem to be rival explanations. Yet none seems to be satisfactory on its own. A much better explanation involves all of them, because each explains only a part of the puzzle. For instance, the rise of the welfare state has invariably involved acute conflict between workers and employers with different resources and different capacities to mobilise support. At the same time, this conflict has been played out in different institutional contexts, in different legal frameworks and according to different rules. The outcomes are certainly influenced by international circumstances, in which developed economies – especially colonial powers – had greater surpluses to devote to welfare. And none of these explanations prevents the welfare system supporting the family, which may, in turn, fulfil an important function in capitalist society.

It is worth pointing out finally that just as there are different and equally effective ways of setting up a democratic political system, so there are also many different ways of setting up a welfare state. Cash transfers may be better suited to some circumstances or some purposes than others, but cash transfers are not necessarily better or worse than the direct delivery of services. If this is correct, then a variety of welfare state provisions is no more strange than a variety of democratic states: they are simply different ways of getting to the same place.

■ What have we learned?

This chapter deals with the welfare state and its policies of redistribution of resources. It argues that:

- Democratic states that accept responsibility for the young and old, the sick and disabled and the unemployed and poor among their citizens are called 'welfare states'.
- Many democratic states use about a quarter of their GNP for social security programmes, most being spent on pensions, medical care and income support for the sick and disabled.
- Welfare states organise their social security programmes in a variety of ways: they offer different entitlements, with varying restrictions, to

different social groups, and with varying obligations. They raise money to pay for services in different ways, some relying on general taxation, others on contributions to specific funds.

- All welfare states have recently confronted the need to limit the growth of social security spending, resulting in a slight decrease in many countries over the past ten to twenty years. The aging of society will make further reforms unavoidable.

■ Lessons of comparison

- Despite their similar developments, welfare states differ widely in the way they organise and provide support for their citizens. Even relatively similar countries clearly deviate if we look at their welfare arrangements and the way these are paid for.
- In spite of their infinite variety of detail, welfare states come in three general types: liberal welfare, conservative welfare and social-democratic welfare.
- Most welfare states pass through a similar pattern of growth in which welfare spending increases faster than economic growth in the later stages of industrialisation. This period lasted from about 1950 to 1975 in most of the OECD countries.
- Just as welfare states grew in nation-specific ways, so it seems likely that they will be reformed or cut in nation-specific ways. There is little evidence of 'welfare state convergence' among the democracies.

Projects

1. What would happen to you if you could not earn an adequate income? Could you apply for public support? What are the requirements and conditions of support in your case, and how much would you receive and for how long?
2. Many states have tried to reform their welfare policies. Present a systematic comparison of these attempts since 1995 in two different democracies. What was the main aim of these reforms? How successful were they?
3. Why do welfare reform policies differ between countries facing very similar budgetary, financial and demographic challenges?
4. Is the welfare state a capitalist or socialist institution?

Further reading

A. de Swaan, *In Care of the State: Health Care, Education and Welfare in Europe and the USA in the Modern Era*, Cambridge: Polity Press, 1998.

A general overview of the historical development of social security programmes.

Gøsta Esping-Andersen, *The Three Worlds of Welfare Capitalism,* Princeton: Princeton University Press, 1990.
The classic work on European social welfare systems.

N. Jordan, *Social Policy for the Twenty-First Century,* New York: Polity Press, 2006.
A general discussion of the problems and prospects of public expenditure and policy.

F. G. Castles, *The Future of the Welfare State: Crisis Myths and crisis Realities*, Oxford: Oxford University Press, 2004.
Argues on the basis of OECD evidence that the welfare states of the west are not in a spending-cuts crisis, but have achieved a steady state.

Websites

www.oecd.org
Website of the OECD. The OECD groups thirty member states sharing a commitment to democratic government and mixed economies. Statistical information about social expenditures in many countries as well as a number of reports on welfare state policies can be found on this site.

www.who.int
Website of WHO, which offers reports and overviews about health and health-related problems.

www.oecd.org/maintopic/
Much of the literature on welfare, social security and taxation is rather technical and focused on budgetary and financial aspects. The OECD provides very valuable statistical information on social security and many of its reports are accessible for non-specialists.

18   The future of the democratic state

At the start of the third millennium, states and democracy seem to be the big winners in the fierce conflicts and wars that scarred the twentieth century. With only a few special exceptions, every place on earth falls within the territory of a state. The number of states has increased rapidly from about fifty to not much fewer than 200 since the 1950s. States still claim absolute authority and control over their own territory and its residents, and conflicts between them are still hard to handle. Moreover, modern states are not the puny 'night watchmen' of the liberal era at the start of the twentieth century: they now provide an enormously wide variety of services, extract vast amounts in taxes and pervade almost every aspect of daily life.

Democracy also seems to have triumphed in the twentieth century. Three successive waves of democratisation – driven mainly by post-war de-colonisation after 1945 and the collapse of the Soviet Empire in 1989 – have expanded the number of stable democracies to approximately 120 countries, covering more than half of the world's population. Democracy has grown in depth and strength to cover far more than the most basic rights and duties and now includes universal adult suffrage, referendums, a wide range of legal, social and economic rights, direct participation, greater control over government and fewer privileges for elites.

If the forces of statehood and democracy seem to be taking over the world, it may be because they are inseparable twins: states are essential for the democratic organisation of political life and democracy is essential for the legitimation of the state. Only a few utopians and anarchists can imagine democracy without the power of the state to create and enforce democratic rules and structures. In the twentieth century, and especially in the last half of that century, states and democracy developed together so that they seemed to be different sides of the same coin.

It is ironic that the present time – the very heyday of the democratic state – produces widespread predictions of the imminent decline of the state and a crisis of democracy:

- Could it be that widespread and confident announcements about the end of the state and the crisis of democracy show that they are both past their best?
- Should we now start searching for a new understanding of state and democracy in the twenty-first century, with different theories, fresh concepts and original approaches adapted to the 'post-state' and a 'post-democratic' twenty-first century?

'The Owl of Minerva spreads its wings only at dusk', wrote the German philosopher Hegel (1770–1831), by which he meant that we understand reality only after events have taken place. It may be that the democratic state is so popular today precisely because it is an outdated model!

Those who followed Hegel's approach to the state in the nineteenth century focused on the French Revolution, with its emphasis on citizenship and human rights. They substituted the early morning crowing of the French rooster for the hooting of Minerva's owl. Nevertheless, the great revolutions of France and America that have shaped the development of our contemporary democracies are more than two centuries old. Do we need a new approach and new theories for a new world?

In this concluding chapter we return to questions about the contemporary relevance of states and the future of democracy:

- Is the state and its sovereignty 'withering away' and, if so, what will succeed it?
- Can democracy survive?
- What reforms might help to preserve both the state and democracy?

The terms on everybody's lips, of course, are globalisation, internationalisation and the crisis of democracy. The major topics in this chapter are:

- States and sovereignty
- The retreat of the state?
- Democracy without borders
- The future.

■ States and sovereignty

The usefulness of the term 'state' may be limited by two difficulties. First, the concept has to cover a huge variety of different forms of democratic (and undemocratic) political organisations, from the comparatively tiny states of Mauritius and Botswana to the huge land masses of Brazil, Canada and Australia, from the old-established democracies of Denmark and New Zealand to the new ones of the Czech Republic and Serbia, and from ethnically homogeneous Norway to multi-cultural India. Is it helpful to apply the same term to such a wide variety of political systems? Second, the traditional supremacy of the state is now challenged by globalisation and the 'borderless world' which can no longer be understood in terms of national independence and sovereignty. It was one thing to defend your country against soldiers massing on the border, quite a different thing to defend it against the power of MNCs, satellite TV and international terrorists. We shall argue that, in spite of all this, states are still the main building blocks of modern government and politics.

Conventional states, proto-states and supra-national states

States are characterised by their territory, people and sovereignty, and if we are to analyse their development or their decline, it is helpful to do so in terms of these three elements. In fact, we can distinguish three broad types of state, according to how they combine their three defining characteristics:

- Conventional states
- Proto-states
- Supra-national states.

Conventional states

Conventional states have a well-defined territory, a developed sense of nationhood (a 'people') and all the institutions of sovereignty. They are found all over the globe and the fact that they are usually associated with peace and stability seems to have a lot to do with democracy and relationships and the balance of power between democratic states. Conventional states remain sovereign within their own borders. In some cases, outside influences are crucial for their creation and persistence (the USA playing a defining role in this respect), but in the majority of cases the territory, people and sovereignty of conventional states are not disputed, and they conduct relations between each other on this basis.

Proto-states

States in some parts of the world do not have secure boundaries, or a body of citizens who form a 'people', or a single sovereign power with a monopoly of the legitimate use of physical force. They are threatened by putsches, insurrections, separatist movements, foreign intervention, ethnic clashes or civil wars. Sometimes a conventional state divides itself, to be replaced by one or more new ones (the Czech Republic and Slovakia, or Croatia, Kosovo and Slovenia), but the successors are not guaranteed to turn themselves into conventional states. They may be torn apart by chaos and anarchy, with competing factions and warlords replacing sovereign power. In some instances, no ultimate authority, no sovereign power, no state exists (Afghanistan and Somalia). The label 'proto-state' suggests that conventional states may emerge in these places. This often occurs with the help of foreign assistance, as happened in the Balkans in the 1990s when the Republic of Bosnia-Herzegovina was created on the basis of an international agreement in order to end war and genocide. UN peace-keeping forces are still required here because large parts of the population reject the Republic. And although ethnic war has ended, it will take a long time to establish a conventional state with sovereign power, undisputed territory and a united body of citizens. The independence of Kosovo can be seen as a further step towards creating states in this area that come closer to the ideal-type of the conventional state.

Supra-national states

Serious conflicts between states do not necessarily result in state disintegration, separation or chaos. In Europe, the conventional state is in the process of being transformed by cooperation, negotiation and agreement. The member states of the EU are still characterised by their territories and populations, but national borders are becoming increasingly porous and even irrelevant, and the claim of absolute national sovereignty has been given up. Power has not been shifted to other states, however, but to a new supra-national organisation that co-ordinates its member states and lays down binding rules for them. The EU is the only clear example of a supra-national organisation, and to this extent it still remains a risky adventure that is as ambitious as it is experimental. It is a striking fact that the prototype of the post-conventional state is being created in western Europe, the cradle of the conventional state. Nonetheless, we should not forget that many important policy areas – such as foreign politics and defence, taxation and social security – remain firmly in the hands of national governments, despite continuous attempts by the EU to co-ordinate and standardise them. Furthermore, recent enlargement of the EU will make it more difficult to deepen integration. Indeed, attempts to produce a European constitution failed because of divisions among the member states and the rejection of the proposal in Dutch and French referendums. For all this, the EU is a post-conventional state.

Conventional states remain the most common form of organising political power, a situation that will not change overnight or in the near future. It does not follow that every part of the earth, the sea and the sky is subject to the sovereign power of a given state, any more than it means that all political power is state power, but the modern state remains the anchor point for our understanding of modern comparative politics. Apart from anything else, the strongest political power in the world and the only global power of our time is the USA – a conventional state *par excellence*. To the extent that its power is challenged, it is challenged by the supra-national European Union and by the other conventional states of Japan, China and Russia, and in some ways by smaller powers like Iran and North Korea.

Challenges to the state

Although conventional states rule the world, their position as sovereign bodies is challenged by five developments:

- Concentration of commercial power
- Rise of international NGOs
- Globalisation
- Changing nature of conflicts
- Importance of international organisations.

Concentration of commercial power

Some commercial organisations are wealthier than states, and are able to challenge their power. The GDP of Eritrea – one of the poorest countries of the world – was only US\$ 12,234 million in 2005. Even in wealthy Europe, Portugal and Slovenia had GDPs of US\$ 205,450 million and US\$ 41,498 million (in 2005). These figures are far below the worth of the largest business companies in the world, which reach almost US\$ 400 billion. Although economic indicators are difficult to compare directly, not even the total wealth of Portugal puts it within reach of the largest companies, and for that matter, some individuals are worth more than whole countries (see table 18.1). If power follows wealth, and if wealth generates power, then it is no surprise that the big MNCs can influence economic development and set their own terms when dealing with national governments, not least because the mobility of their capital gives them great locational flexibility.

Rise of international NGOs

International NGOs (see chapter 10) are neither branches or agencies of the state, nor are most of them created by states. They include, for instance, Amnesty International, Greenpeace, Médecins Sans Frontières, the Scottish Catholic International Aid Fund and Volontari nel Mondo and their main characteristics are that they are:

- Founded and run by citizens independently of governments and states
- Non-profit or charitable organisations, which
- Reject the use of violence.

Table 18.1 The ten largest corporations in the world, 2008

Corporation	Origin	Main business	Employees	Revenues (US$ million)
Wal-Mart Stores	USA	Retailing	2,055,000	378,799
Exxon Mobil	USA	Oil	107,100	372,824
Royal Dutch/Shell Group	Britain/Netherlands	Oil	104,000	355,782
BP	Britain	Oil	97,600	291,438
Toyota Motor	Japan	Automobiles	316,121	230,201
Chevron Texaco	USA	Oil	65,035	210,783
ING Group	The Netherlands	Finance	120,282	201,516
Total Fina Elf	France	Oil	96,442	187,280
General Motors	USA	Automobiles	266,000	182,347
ConocoPhillips	USA	Oil	32,600	178,558

Source: http://money.cnn.com/magazines/fortune/global500/2008/full_list/

In their modern form, international NGOs were founded in the nineteenth century, but their numbers and importance increased after the Second World War. It is difficult to estimate their numbers, but according to the UN there were 1,083 international NGOs in 1914, which increased to more than 37,000 in 2000. Nearly one-fifth of them were formed in the 1990s. Most developing countries have seen an even sharper increase in the number of domestic NGOs: in 1996, Brazil had 210,000 non-profit making organisations and India had more than 1 million (UN *Human Development Report*, 2002).

NGOs are non-state organisations and for the most part they are privately financed, but some of them receive financial and other support from states or international organisations such as the European Union and the UN. When they are heavily dependent on public money, and when NGO and government activities are closely interwoven, the sharp distinction between 'private' and 'public' vanishes. Governments also find it useful to create organisations that are independent of them, but which provide public services with the help of public finances. Such organisations are known as QUANGOs (chapter 11), and are useful in politically sensitive areas which fall within the public sector but which governments do not wish to control directly (see chapter 10). Public broadcasting is the classic case where QUANGOs operate in the public sector at arm's length from government. Like NGOs it is exceedingly difficult to estimate QUANGO numbers, but they are also rising steeply.

NGOs (and QUANGOs to a lesser extent) are widely believed to be increasingly powerful actors in national and international government. This is not so much because they are wealthy, like the MNCs, but because NGOs often have a powerful emotional and moral appeal. Organisations such as Christian Aid, Greenpeace, Oxfam and the Red Cross use their popular appeal to gain widespread publicity for their activities, and they can use this to 'leverage' political influence. They represent another force that challenges the power of the state.

Globalisation

The 'interdependence' and 'connectedness' of the world today is evident when we look at the environment and the use of natural resources, or at terrorism and the global drug trade. It is most evident in the economic and financial sectors, where capital and production is free to move around the world in pursuit of the highest profits and lowest taxes. Since welfare states are tax states with high labour costs, they are under pressure (they can even be blackmailed) by businesses threatening to relocate investments and jobs. A whole range of mini-states – the Bahamas, Liechtenstein, Luxembourg – serve as international tax shelters and places where companies can be legally registered. Not only does this have implications for the ability of states to control international business, but it reduces government revenues that are used to pay for public services. Some countries (Brazil, for example) encounter difficult problems if large amounts of money are transferred to foreign bank accounts.

Globalisation is also evident in the rapid spread of the World Wide Web and of satellite communications. States find them difficult, sometimes impossible, to control. Similarly, population movements from one side of the globe to another, and especially from poor countries to rich ones, have created huge problems for some states. It is estimated that the illegal population now totals 8–11 million people in the USA and 3–8 million in the EU. The EU's figure is estimated to be growing by half a million a year.

Changing nature of conflicts

As we saw in chapter 16, violent inter-state conflict has not increased in recent decades in spite of an increase in the number of states. Indeed, in most of the established democracies where national borders are no longer disputed, and even less the borders between post-conventional members of the EU, there is no longer even a need to guard them. To this extent, the age-old justification for the military power of the state is reduced. Even one of the most important justifications for the existence of the state itself – that it is necessary to defend its territory against foreign threat – may have been removed. At the same time, new threats to the state have appeared:

- First, violent conflict within states has increased and the role of the armed forces is certainly not reduced in many pre-conventional states (the Caucasus and many parts of Africa and Latin America), and in some conventional ones as well (Spain). This creates a need for highly trained and specially equipped peace-keeping forces, which are provided mainly by the conventional states.
- Second, the threat of terrorism took a dramatic form with the attack on the World Trade Center in September 2001 (see chapter 16). States that are no longer endangered by foreign armies have to deal with a completely different problem that cannot be handled by the conventional armed forces.

Importance of international organisations

States have created a large number of international organisations to deal with relations between them and to try to settle conflicts in an orderly and peaceful manner. These organisations are institutionalised forms of cooperation and collaboration, and although they work at the international level they are still the product of state cooperation and states take their own decisions about whether to join or leave, and to comply with their decisions or to reject them. The main example is the UN and its many subsidiary organisations, but the list includes thousands more, such as the OECD and the Organisation of Petroleum Exporting Countries (OPEC). International organisations such as these are clearly different from states in that each has a clear and limited task:

- The OECD is concerned with economic matters and collecting statistical information for a comparatively small number of wealthy nations.
- The WHO deals with medical matters.
- The IMF fosters global monetary cooperation, stability, trade and employment.

A very few international organisations (the Security Council of the UN and the EU) can give orders to states and can even use military force to back them up (see chapter 16), but most do not have this sort of power.

As the intensity and scope of relations between states has increased so has the number of international organisations. As a result, states are increasingly caught up in a 'web' of directions, advice and instructions. Globalisation and rising numbers of NGOs will further stimulate this process. Even if most of the decisions taken by international organisations are voluntarily accepted by states, their scope for action is still restricted.

■ The retreat of the state?

The combination of MNCs, NGOs, globalisation, the changing nature of conflict and the importance of international organisations casts doubt on the continuing relevance of the state. It seems to be only one actor among many, and one that is rapidly declining in power and importance at that (see controversy 2.1). Should we even drop the concept of the state, and concentrate on the 'real' and important actors in the world today? This suggestion, however, fails to notice that states are still the most important actors on the world stage, and that sovereignty and the legitimate use of physical force within their given territories is still the main form of organised political power. States continue:

- To be the main actors in modern warfare (Afghanistan, Iraq, the Caucasus)
- To create international and supra-national agencies of government such as the EU and the UN, and control them

- To be responsible for the vast majority of public services delivered to citizens
- To raise vast amounts of money in taxes
- To be mainly responsible for the defence of their territory and their citizens and for the maintenance of internal law and order
- To define the rights and duties of citizens in most democracies (with certain EU exceptions)
- To decide who will live and work within their borders (though admittedly with the increasing exception of illegal immigrants)
- To issue passports and travel documents to their citizens
- To control and influence a great many aspects of the daily life of their citizens with their accumulated laws and with literally millions of ordinances, rules, orders, commands, regulations, precepts, decrees, directives, instructions, edicts, dictates, injunctions, promulgations, guidelines, advisory documents, circulars, specifications and requirements
- To be attacked: even international terrorism is mainly directed towards states or their representatives, even when it attacks ordinary citizens.

Arguments about the decline of the state also seriously underestimate the force of another characteristic of our times: the rising strength of nationalism (see chapter 14). While it is true that technology promotes global integration and weakens national boundaries in some respects, in others it makes it easier to sustain nationalism. Communications technology helps to preserve minority languages and culture with local radio and TV stations and desk-top publishing. Moreover, as each ethnic minority creates its own independent state so it is likely to create another minority within its own borders. Nationalism seems to have a lot of life in it yet – and by definition it implies a strengthening of the state. Summarising the confusing and contradictory trends and arguments about the state, the political scientist Susan Strange (1923–98) presents three hypotheses in her book *The Retreat of the State* (1996):

1. Political power has shifted upwards from weak states to stronger states. Strong states are able to influence, even determine, developments far outside their territory. The best example is, of course, the USA, but one can also think of the influence of France in north and west Africa, and of Russia in central Asia.
2. Political power has shifted sideways from states to markets, strengthening the position of giant MNCs and of international organisations such as the G-9, the IMF and OPEC. Some writers prefer to use the term 'governance' rather than government (chapter 4), because the term implies the coordination of many actors in the political system rather than the old 'top-down' system whereby government controlled everything else.
3. Some political power has 'evaporated', in the sense that state power is excercised weakly or not at all. Examples include some areas of the former Soviet Union, and some parts of Africa and Asia (Afghanistan,

Congo, Ethiopia), where legitimate authorities have been replaced by local potentates, warlords and gang leaders.

Although some organisations have successfully challenged the claims of the state to be the sole source of legitimate political power, and although political power has shifted, or even 'evaporated' in some parts of the world, states remain the point of departure and main focus of organised political power. The state is not 'withering away': on the contrary, it seems to be changing and expanding its power to deal with new circumstances and forms of organised power. So the answer to a key question of this chapter – Are states disappearing? – is an unambiguous 'no'. Circumstances are changing, and states with them, but the result is that states are both stronger and weaker in some respects, just as some states have become stronger and others weaker.

■ Democracy without borders

We know that states can do very well without being democratic, but so far it has taken the organised and limited forms of political power of the conventional state to promote democracy (see chapter 2). To put it in a nutshell: no state, no democracy. To this extent, our conclusion that the state is likely to survive, and even grow stronger in some respects, is a comfort for the foreseeable future. But it does not necessarily follow that future developments of the state will continue to promote democracy, even less improve the quality of democratic government. A second key question of the chapter, therefore, is: What is the future for democracy?

The quality of democracy

Neither states nor democracies are created overnight. The first democracies developed over a period of two hundred years or more, and suffered war, civil disturbance and national trauma in the process (see controversy 18.1). In many cases the most important democratic milestones have been relatively recent ones: the French Revolution secured basic rights for every citizen in the late eighteenth century, but French women had to wait until the 1940s for the right to vote; violations of human rights occur in such countries as The Netherlands and Sweden even now. It no surprise, then, that democracy has a fragile presence in many of the states that have recently joined the list of free nations in the world. Besides, democracy itself is not a fixed or given entity. It is constantly changing and developing as citizens make new and greater demands upon it.

The end of the Cold War resulted in a great deal of optimism about the spread of democracy. The 'triumph of liberalism', 'the end of history' and the 'victory of democracy' were announced (see chapter 14). But in 2002 the UN concluded that although a majority of the people in the world lived in nominal democracies, political freedoms and civil rights were limited in more than a hundred countries. Worse still, the spread of democracy had not done much for many people in the world: civil wars claimed 3.6 million lives in the 1990s, and about 2.8 billion of the world's 6 billion people live on less than 2 US$ a day (UN *Human Development Report 2002*). Democracy, it seems, takes more than organising free, multi-party competitive elections at regular intervals.

After a hopeful start, the third wave of democracy seems to have lost its momentum in some countries, because it turns out that it is fairly easy to mix formal democratic processes with political corruption, civil rights abuses and autocratic rule (chapter 3). While only a few countries have slid backwards into military rule (Pakistan 1999), many more seem to have reached a 'stand-off' or 'cease-fire' between democratic and non-democratic forces where elected government has failed to regulate or take control of the most powerful social and economic groups in society. It was easier to introduce free multi-party elections and the semblance of democracy than to guarantee civil and social rights for all. In such cases, it is not too much to claim that elections do less to guarantee political freedom than to legitimise illiberal democracy. In many of the new democracies violations of freedom and human rights are hard to prevent because these countries lack adequate institutional safeguards for minority, or even majority rights. As a result, simple electoral democracy has swept countries such as Russia and Venezuela toward authoritarian rule that has little in common with the broader principles of democracy. Nonetheless, Freedom House continues to record the spread of democracy around the world (see chapters 2 and 3). Happily, these surveys clearly reveal that freedom and liberty are not restricted to wealthy countries, since many poor and developing states have a record of respecting political rights and civil liberties.

Reform of state and government

Democracy, it is worth saying again, involves a never-ending search for improvement. Even the world's most advanced democracies such as Denmark, Finland, the Netherlands, Norway and Sweden, debate reforms. In fact, discussion about how political life should be conducted is in many countries as important as the actual substance of politics in the form of taxation, services and support or opposition for the Iraq war or for the EU (see controversy 18.1).

CONTROVERSY 18.1

Complaints about democracy?
Complaints about states that have emerged from dictatorship but have not effectively democratised lack perspective. It took American democracy 86 years to abolish slavery, 144 years to enfranchise women and 189 to assure black people the vote. After a century and a half, American democracy produced the Great Depression. Democracy is not a rose garden. It is as fallible as human beings.
(Joshua Muravchik, 'Democracy is quietly winning', *International Herald Tribune*, 21 August 2002)

Virtually every institution of democracy discussed in this book is currently the object of disputes about reform and improvement. The most important items on the agenda for democratic reform are:

- *Constitutional reform*   Since constitutions define the major political institutions and their relationships (see chapter 4), proposals for reform are often basic and far-reaching. Some countries have recently added social rights and a ban on discrimination in order to guarantee equal opportunities for all citizens. Because constitutional matters are so basic and controversial it is sometimes difficult to reach agreement about them. The European Union failed to get agreement on its new constitution in 2003.

- *Strengthening parliaments*   Monitoring and controlling the executive is one of the main functions of parliaments in representative democracies (see chapters 5 and 7) and many parliaments have attempted to strengthen their powers in this respect. Some are using parliamentary commissions or committees to investigate specific policy matters, and to hold ministers to account.

- *Freedom of information and open government*   This concerns public access to documents and the use of electronic media to improve communication between citizens and MPs. Some countries have adopted legislation making government information accessible to the public.

- *Decentralisation of power*   Recent decades have seen a wave of attempts across many democracies to decentralise and deconcentrate power to regional, local and community levels of government (see chapter 6). In some countries city and urban authorities have been strengthened and budgetary powers have been decentralised. Within cities, neighbourhood and community councils have been created or strengthened in order to reduce the 'distance' between citizens and government. Some believe that central governments are trying to decentralise power in the interests of democracy, others that this is simply a way of 'exporting financial problems' to lower levels of government.

- *Making bureaucracies more responsive and efficient*   Bureaucratic reforms (see chapter 8) include proposals to improve efficiency by adopting cost-benefit management and book-keeping practices. More far-reaching is the privatisation of public services. Other reforms have tried to make public bureaucracies more responsive to citizens by involving them in the early stages of decision making.

- *Improving citizen participation*   Citizens have been creative in inventing new forms of political participation and new ways of making their voices heard, including boycotts, demonstrations, sit-ins, civil disobedience and attracting the attention of the mass media (see chapter 9). Governments, for their part, have often responded by reforming laws relating to protest activity, expanding opportunities to vote (the EP, neighbourhood councils, referendums) and to participate in public enquires and hearings. Many experiments with public opinion and participation are being conducted, including reforms of electoral and registration systems, greater use of referendums, citizen juries and assemblies of various kinds, experiments with co-governance involving the sharing of power and influence between governments and citizens, and the use of new electronic means of communication.

- *Strengthening the role of associations* Many governments now acknowledge NGOs and are willing to cooperate with them and support their activities, including their participation in decision making, especially at the local and community level (see chapter 10). Some governments are even attempting to 'unlock' policy communities and networks so they include a wider range of interests and organisations.

- *Strengthening the independence of mass media* Many governments are concerned about the concentration of the ownership and control of the mass media (see chapter 11) and are wrestling with ways of dealing with it. Some feel that the answer lies in allowing the 'old' and 'new' communication technologies to develop within an unregulated market, in the belief that they will form a highly diversified and competitive system. Other governments take the opposite view, maintaining or strengthening market and content regulation laws, including anti-cartel and cross-media ownership regulations and a wide variety of laws relating to such things as cigarette advertising and pornography.

- *Protecting and strengthening human rights* As we have seen, some democracies with multi-party elections are not particularly successful in protecting the rights of their citizens. They must guarantee the independence of their courts, but this is difficult because corrupt governments are unwilling to give up their power. NGOs such as Amnesty International try to mobilise opposition, and a range of institutions has been created to prosecute violations of human rights and empower citizens to take action against governments. These include the ECJ, the highest court of the EU, and the ECHR, as well as special courts created by the UN to prosecute war criminals and to regulate conflicts between states.

- *Social security* Social security and welfare continue to be a central issue in democratic countries. Some argue that a healthy, educated and secure population is a precondition of both democracy and economic growth, and that in any case the state is morally obliged to create the conditions of civilised life for its citizens. They argue that a developed welfare and social security system is essential. Others, especially in the late twentieth century, argue that the best way of meeting the material and spiritual needs of citizens is to leave as much as possible to the 'invisible hand' of market economics, in the belief that this is the most efficient way of generating and distributing wealth and freedom. They argue that globalisation makes welfare states uncompetitive and that a return to laissez-faire economics is inevitable and efficient. The debate rages on.

- *The elimination of corruption and patronage* Corruption is not limited to the developing world. It is commonplace in some established democracies

Briefing 18.1

The need for good governance

Political reforms, such as decentralising budgets and responsibilities for the delivery of basic services, put decision-making closer to the people and reinforce popular pressure for implementing the goals. Where decentralisation has worked – as in parts of Brazil, Jordan, Mozambique and the Indian states of Kerala, Madya Pradesh and West Bengal – it has brought significant improvements. It can lead to government services that respond faster to people's needs, expose corruption and reduce absenteeism.

But decentralisation is difficult. To succeed, it requires a capable central authority, committed and financially empowered local authorities and engaged citizens in a well-organised civil society. In Mozambique committed local authorities with financing authority increased vaccination coverage and prenatal consultations by 80 per cent, overcoming capacity constraints by contracting NGOs and private providers at the municipal level.

Recent experiences have also shown how social movements can lead to more participatory decision-making, as in the public monitoring of local budgets. In Porto Alegre, Brazil, public monitoring of local budgets has brought huge improvements in services. In 1989 just under half of city residents had access to safe water. Seven years later, nearly all did. Primary school enrolments also doubled during that time, and public transportation expanded to outlying areas.

(Human Development Report 2003 *(New York: UN, 2004: 2);*
http://hdr.undp.org/en/media/hdr03_overview.pdf)

and developed economies where it poses a threat to democracy and good government, to fairness and justice, and to the efficient conduct of both private and public life. It seems to have a pervasive effect on society, the economy and government.

Reforming democracies is not easy. Strong interests most generally try to protect their position and democratic reform is often entangled with a lot of other complicated matters. This is because democracy is not above social and economic life; it is not something set apart from 'real' social existence. On the contrary, government and politics are an integral part of daily existence that help to mould and shape how we conduct our lives. Often it is not possible to change social and economic patterns without first changing political patterns. The suffragettes in the early twentieth century, for example, did not campaign for 'Votes for Women' because they saw the vote only as an end in itself, important though this was. They also knew that they could not change their social, legal and economic status without first gaining power in government. In this respect, improving government – that is, improving democratic government – seems to be the key to numerous other problems (see briefing 18.1).

■ The future

Although some of the optimism of the third wave of democratisation in the 1990s may have been exaggerated, it is clear that neither national states nor democracies are 'withering away' – at present, at any rate. For most people, the world has become a better place to live in as democracy spreads. Nevertheless, democratic principles constantly challenge the practice. Not only are the newest democracies somewhat fragile and underdeveloped by modern standards, but the best-developed ones continue to develop and improve as they push back the boundaries of democracy.

Can democracy spread and survive in a changing world? As always, prognosis is difficult and uncertain, and conclusions differ. Since democratic institutions are dependent upon a sovereign body to establish and maintain them, anything that undermines the continuity and stability of states seems to threaten democracy, and there seem to be a great many things that threaten both states and democracies at the present time. Nevertheless, we know that both the number of states and the number of democracies in the world has increased steadily over the past hundred years. There is no clear sign that this trend will not be continued in the near future.

We also know that democracy is unstable in many of the newest democracies, and that they can easily slip back into dictatorship and autocracy or simply fail to become fully developed democracies with free and fair elections, individual rights, a free press, low rates of corruption, impartial courts and properly functioning public bureaucracies. It is easier to establish free, multi-party elections in these countries than to guarantee freedom, human rights and government accountability, much less equality of opportunity and a decent quality of life. In the younger democracies, therefore, our studies should not be confined to elections, parties and formal decision making procedures, but broadened to encompass wider social and economic matters.

Democracy is certainly no paradise. And yet even modest success in replacing authoritarian, corrupt and abusive government with more democratic practices is desirable. As the UN concluded:

> When governments are corrupt, incompetent or unaccountable to their citizens, national economies falter. When income inequality is very high, rich people often control the political system and simply neglect poor people, forestalling broadly based development. Similarly, if governments fail to invest adequately in the health and education of their people, economic growth will eventually peter out because of an insufficient number of healthy, skilled workers. Without sound governance – in terms of economic policies, human rights, well-functioning institutions and democratic political participation – no country with low human development can expect long-term success in its development efforts or expanded support from donor countries.
>
> *(UN, The Millennium Development Compact 2003, New York: UN 2004: 3)*

■ What have we learned?

This chapter deals with scenarios for the future of the state. It argues that:

- The state is not 'withering away'. Conventional nations are still widely spread and new ones are establishing themselves, especially in large parts of east Asia and south America. The world's first supra-national state has appeared in Europe in the shape of the EU. 'Proto-states' are found in several regions (Africa, Central Asia and eastern Europe), mainly after the collapse of larger states.

- Developments such as the concentration of commercial power, the rise of NGOs, globalisation, the changing nature of conflicts and the growth of international organisations all cast doubts on the state's claim to be the sole (or the most important) source of political power. The state persists, however, as the body with a monopoly of legitimate physical force.
- Democracy is not fixed or static but a continuous and developing attempt to make government accountable and responsive to the needs of the people it governs. Reforming and developing, therefore, the democratic system is a regular aspect of democratic government.
- The number of democracies in the world is still rising, but some of the newest ones have problems protecting freedom and human rights. Organising multi-party elections seems to be less problematic.

■ Lessons of comparison

- The power of some states has increased in some respects, but in other cases it is shared with other organisations, and in 'proto-states' some state power seems to have disappeared.
- In terms of economic capacities the biggest corporations are much stronger than many states are.
- The numbers of NGOs and QUANGOs have risen rapidly in all countries, but the increase is especially visible in developing countries.
- Democracy differs between states and therefore democratic reforms differ between states, too.
- The number of democracies in the world is still rising, but some of the newest ones have problems protecting freedom and human rights. Organising multi-party elections seems to be less problematic.

Projects

1. Make a list of five countries in the world that have improved their democracy since 1990, and another five that have slipped back. What are the main reasons for these changes? How likely is a change in democracy in these ten countries in the next decade?
2. What democratic improvements have been proposed in your country recently, and which of these have been realised? Present a systematic overview of the most important proposals according to their goals, means and people or groups they affect. Discuss the arguments for adopting or rejecting these proposals.
3. Why has it been so difficult to adopt a constitution for the EU?

Further reading

S. Strange, *The Retreat of the State: The Diffusion of Power in the World Economy,* Cambridge: Cambridge University Press, 1996.
Discusses the various approaches to the changing role of the state.

F. Zakaria, *The Future of Freedom: Illiberal Democracy at Home and Abroad,* New York: Norton, 2003.
A thought-provoking analysis of the rise of democracy that is mainly restricted to electoral procedures.

M. van Creveld, *The Rise and Decline of the State,* Cambridge: Cambridge University Press, 1999.
A detailed account of the rise and decline of the state.

G. Sørensen, *The Transformation of the State: Beyond the Myth of Retreat,* Basingstoke: Palgrave, 2004.
Examines the impact of globalisation on the modern state.

T. V. Paul, G. John Ikenberry and J. A. Hall (eds.), *The Nation-State in Question,* Princeton: Princeton University Press, 2003.
A collection of readings on globalisation in the modern state.

Websites

www.amnesty.org
Website of Amnesty International, the world's largest organisation campaigning for the international recognition of human rights.
www.curia.eu.int
Website of the ECJ with information about its operations and procedures.
www.echr.coe.int
Website of the ECHR with information about its operations and procedures.
www.freedomhouse.org
Provides information about democracy and human rights in each state of the world.
www.icj-cij.org
Website of the ICJ, the principal judicial organ of the UN, with information about its operations and procedures.
www.undp.org
Website of the UN Development Programme that offers extensive information on the relationship between development and democracy.

Postscript: How and what to compare?

Many things are clear without comparisons. For example, to accept that India is a democracy or that democratisation follows several stages needs no comparison of countries. In fact, you can spend a lot of interesting and fruitful time analysing the democratic characteristics and explanations of its success in India alone, so why make everything even more complicated by comparing it with other countries? What can be gained from comparisons?

In the first place, it widens and deepens our knowledge of the political world. A comparison of India and Canada would show not only that both countries are democratic but also that they are large federal systems with mixed ethnic and linguistic populations and that both were parts of the British Empire. Does one of these characteristics account, perhaps, for their democracy? To answer this question we need to compare the two with other countries. We might select Ghana, Nigeria and Pakistan, for example, and they would show that past membership of the British Empire is not a sufficient explanation of democratic development. We might select Denmark and Japan for our comparison and they would show that there is no necessary connection between federalism and democracy. And since Russia and China are both large and with mixed populations they would rule out the connection between large, heterogeneous populations and democracy. From these simple examples it is clear that we can learn a lot from comparisons, not only about a wider range of countries but also about the similarities and differences between countries, and what might play a role in causing democracy. These similarities and differences, in turn, can be used to develop and to test explanations which go beyond specific cases.

When we compare we start to develop ideas about possible explanations and we can then collect the appropriate evidence to test these explanations. So far so good, but we now face the question of what we should compare. Should we compare India with nearby Pakistan, which is similar in some ways, or perhaps with Russia or Denmark, which are very different? In order to explain and generalise our comparisons must be carefully considered. Broadly speaking, comparison can be distinguished in two ways:

- First, we can distinguish comparisons on the bases of the number of countries considered. Do we spread our net widely over a large number of countries in a search for common patterns among them (for instance, to find out whether economically developed countries are also democracies) or do we focus on one or a few countries and try to understand in depth how they work (for instance, whether Hinduism facilitates democracy in India). Both approaches have advantages and disadvantages and so we might also try to devise a strategy using both of them, to get the best of both worlds.
- Second, we can distinguish comparisons not according to the number of cases they are based on but by the strategy they use in their approach to comparison. We could compare similar countries, say India and Pakistan because both are similar in some important respects, or we could compare India and Denmark, precisely because they are very different in some ways, though both are democratic.

In this Postscript we discuss these four kinds of comparison as a way of outlining the most important problems of designing research in comparative politics.

- Comparing many or a few countries
- Selecting comparable countries
- How many countries is enough?
- Comparing apples and oranges.

■ Comparing many or a few countries?

Comparison does not necessary involve cross-national comparison. We can compare different conditions within a country, say the voting patterns of different social groups, or different conditions over time in that country, say political opinions before and after democratisation in East and West Germany. A well-known example of comparative research in a single country is Robert Putnam's (1941–) widely quoted study of the development of democracy and civil society in Italy in his book *Making Democracy Work* (1994), which examines the differences between the twenty administrative regions of the country.

These examples underline the fact that the logic behind systematic comparisons of states is identical with the logic of comparing other entities, such as different points in time, or different social groups, regions or elections. However, as the term has developed in political science, 'comparative politics' usually refers to a comparison of countries. In this sense comparative politics involves two basic approaches:

- Comparing many cases
- Comparing a few cases.

Comparing many cases

Large-n comparison Comparison of many countries, usually based on statistical analyses of strictly comparable evidence about them.

Considering many cases ('**large-n comparisons**') has a lot of advantages at first sight, especially if we want to develop or test broad generalisations across a wide variety of different conditions. It also allows us to identify unexpected or deviant cases that are exceptions to the general rule. These can also throw light on the question we want to answer. While it may be true that many of the ex-colonies of the British Empire are now democratic, it is not always so, and a study of Pakistan might help us understand why. Nor do we need to cover the entire globe in our comparative study. Research on the twenty-three countries of the OECD might be enough, provided we recognised that these are the wealthier countries of the world and our results might not apply to less affluent countries.

There is no exact minimum for a large-n study but most research of this type is based on comparisons of more than twenty or thirty countries. Although this is still a relatively small number, dealing with even as few as this has implications for research:

1. Analysing twenty or thirty cases means that information about them must be both quantified and standardised. By quantified we mean numerical measures of such things as population density, per capita income or percentage turnout in elections. By standardised we mean that these measures are collected on the same basis in every country and are therefore directly comparable. If we wanted a measure of education, for example, it would make no sense to use the percentage of primary school pupils in one country and the percentage of university students in another. Sometimes the measures take the form of a single indicator of a more complex concept. Per capita income is frequently used as an indicator of the multi-variate notion of economic development. In other cases we might use an index in which many figures are combined to form a single and more reliable measure of a complex idea. The Human Development Index devised by the United Nations Development Program combines eight measures to produce a composite index of human development.

2. Large-n comparisons are often called statistical comparisons because information is analysed with statistical techniques. Patterns and tendencies in quantified information (data) can be very efficiently explored with these techniques using computers. Statistical techniques range from a simple calculation of average voting turnouts to sophisticated causal modelling of the combined effects of individual and institutional determinants of turnout or any other measure of political attitudes and behaviour. These techniques have been developed rapidly in the last decades and a number of computer packages are available for statistical analysis. SPSS and Stata are currently the most commonly used.

3. Large-n comparisons are best carried out on large, standardised data-sets. Organisations like the OECD and the World Bank offer a wide range of these covering many countries. Other specialised data archives provide integrated data-sets covering many countries. These include the World Values Studies, Eurobarometer and the European Social Survey. Some data-sets are known as cross-sectional because they provide the same measures in different countries at a given point in time, for example the percentage of the adult populations of a selection of countries expressing satisfaction with their government in a given year. Others are known as time-series because they cover the same events in a country or countries at different time points, for example a series of election statistics.

Quantitative, statistical analyses of standardised data allow us to search for patterns and tendencies in efficient ways. The main goal is to study relationships between various factors or variables. For that reason, large-n comparisons are also called '**variable-oriented approaches**'.

> **Variable-oriented approach** Comparison focused on specific themes, patterns and tendencies in a set of countries.

The apparent advantages of large-n comparisons can turn into serious problems. Not everything that is important or theoretically interesting can be easily quantified, as the complications to measure 'democracy' already make clear. Sticking to standardised quantitative data runs the risk that the data available dictates our research questions. Nor is every important measure adequately standardised, for many are subject to technical problems in the way they are collected or presented, and each country tends to have their own way of doing things, which can mean that their statistics are not exactly comparable with other countries. Furthermore, many statistical techniques are based on correlations, which are no more than measures of association between variables. Correlations tell us if two measures vary together and how closely they do so, but they do not tell us whether one variable is causally related to another. Even if economic development and democracy were always to occur together it would not necessarily mean that economic development causes democracy. The impact might be in the other direction if it is democracy that promotes economic growth. Or perhaps economic development and democracy are consequences of a third factor that is common to both of them, such as Protestantism. Finally, the application of statistical techniques requires a degree of statistical and mathematical understanding that can only be acquired with the appropriate training, and students who do not like such courses are at a disadvantage in comparative politics.

Comparing a few cases

Small-n comparison Comparison of a few countries, usually based on systematic, in-depth analysis and detailed knowledge of them.

Analysing a few cases ('**small-n comparisons**') seems to be an attractive alternative to the limitations of large-n approaches. Instead of looking for patterns and tendencies among a large number of countries it studies only a few, but in a more detailed manner that allows us to understand the complexity of relations. In this way the historical and cultural particularities of each country can be taken into account. If we want to know, for instance, how exactly colonial legacies influence democratic consolidation, a thorough and in-depth examination of the history, institutions and culture of the Indian sub-continent might give us an answer.

How small should a small-n comparison be? No clear line can be drawn between large-n and small-n studies. Typically, small-n studies deal with five or six countries, but they can cover a larger or smaller number of cases. Whatever their number, small-n studies have a common set of characteristics:

1. Since small-n studies focus on exact processes and relationships in a few countries they can include qualitative evidence and methods. There is no need, for instance, for a single index of democratic development in Poland and Russia if we have a detailed understanding of their transition processes. In these comparisons we can discuss the unique role of Solidarność in Poland and the tsarist legacy in Russia.

2. Broadly speaking, the small-n approach can be characterised as heuristic; that is, methods used to explore complex processes and relationships based on trial and error and an intuitive understanding of politics and society. For instance, by exploring and understanding the different nature of the Protestant religion in Denmark and the Hindu, Jain, Sikh and Buddhist religions in India, we might come to an understanding of their relationship with democracy. We cannot gain such a subjective understanding of religion by examining statistical data, though such information might help our understanding.

3. Small-n studies can handle a mass of country-specific information of a qualitative nature without any need to standardise. Any attempt to understand democratic transformation in Poland would certainly pay attention to the rise of Solidarność, but there is no possibility of standardising that information.

Case-oriented approach Comparison focused on specific countries and the themes, patterns and tendencies within these countries.

The main goal of the small-n approach is to understand actual processes in a few countries, and for that reason it is also known as a '**case-oriented approach**'.

The limitations and disadvantages of small-n comparisons are evident. It is interesting to know precisely how Poland became a democracy and why Pakistan failed, but knowing every detail about these countries does not help us to reach general conclusions about democracy across the globe. Furthermore, while small-n comparisons can be carried out without the statistical abilities required for large-n comparisons, they require in-depth knowledge and familiarity with the countries considered. Studying Poland or Pakistan will be fruitful only if the researcher is very well informed about these countries and is fluent in their languages. No one can have this depth of knowledge about more than a handful of countries.

The most serious problem of small-n comparisons is that generalisations cannot be tested rigorously. In an attempt to overcome this limitation Charles C. Ragin proposed a new approach called **qualitative comparative analysis (QCA)**.

> **Qualitative comparative analysis (QCA)** The systematic comparison of a few cases using specific techniques to develop and test generalisations.

QCA focuses on the presence or absence of factors or variables in the cases available. Based on logical rather than statistical associations, Ragin developed a clear and strict strategy to sort out the causal relationships between various factors. QCA methods have improved considerably in the last few years and are now widely used in comparative politics.

■ Selecting comparable countries

What one compares in comparative political science is crucial. Comparing India and Canada will suggest one conclusion about democracy in large, mixed, federal systems, whereas contrasting India and Russia will suggest a different conclusion. But why should we choose to compare India with only one other country when we can perfectly well compare four or five cases? This sounds sensible but it immediately presents problems:

1. *Efficiency* It can be difficult to compare even a small number of countries when it might take many years to master the politics and government of just two of them.
2. *Relevance* There is a far greater range of comparisons available to us than those already mentioned. We might, for instance, compare India with Brazil, which is also a large mixed society, with a developing economy but different colonial backgrounds. This comparison might tell us something about the importance of the British legacy for democracy.
3. *Generalisation* Four or five countries is a rather small number on which to base generalisations and since there are more than fifty members of the British Commonwealth, we have many more possibilities of testing the ex-British colony hypothesis.

These considerations result in conflicting conclusions. Whereas the first point argues for restricting comparisons to as few countries as possible, the last suggests a systematic comparison of fifty cases. However, if it is true that

405

John Stuart Mill on comparisons

1. The simplest and most obvious modes of singling out from among the circumstances which precede or follow a phenomenon, those with which it is really connected by an invariable law, are two in number. One is, by comparing together different instances in which the phenomenon occurs. The other is by comparing instances in which the phenomenon does occur, with instances in other respects similar in which it does not. These two methods may be respectively denominated, the Method of Agreement, and the Method of Difference.

Source: Mill, John Stuart, A System of Logic, *Volume I, London: Harrison, p. 450.*

the selection of cases for comparison is likely to determine or influence the conclusions we draw then the crucial logic of comparison involves not the number of cases, but the purpose of the comparison. What we compare should be determined by what we want to know in the first place. The selection of countries is not a constraint of our comparative strategy but a consequence of the research question we ask. Although efficiency and generalisations are important, it is relevance that finally determines which countries should be included in our comparison, and what is relevant depends on what theory we want to test or what generalisation we are interested in developing.

As convincing as these arguments might sound, designing an appropriate comparative strategy is not just a matter of formulating goals and labelling countries as relevant or irrelevant. The British philosopher John Stuart Mill (1806–73) distinguished between two basic types of comparisons (see briefing 1). Both types aim at testing causal explanations, but differ in the strategies they follow:

- *Method of Agreement*   If a phenomenon occurs in two or more situations then the explanation for the phenomenon must lie in the common features of those situations. In the **Method of Agreement**, therefore, the presence or absence of a common crucial factor or factors (the 'agreement' between the countries) must account for

Method of Agreement Comparison of cases which share the presence of effects or outcomes as well as presumed causes.

the phenomenon we wish to explain. For instance, India and Canada share the impact of some British traditions, which might account for democracy in both countries.

- *Method of Difference*   If two or more situations are similar, but the phenomenon exists in only one of them, its cause must be related to the different features of its situation. If we use the **Method of Difference**, the presence or the absence of a crucial factor

Method of Difference Comparison of cases which share effects or outcomes but differ in the presence of presumed causes.

(the 'difference' between the countries) is presumed to account for the particular phenomenon or outcome in one of them. For instance, India and China are both very large countries; therefore the fact that India is a democracy cannot be attributed to its size because China is large but undemocratic.

Mill stressed that both approaches are useful, but that the Method of Difference provides stronger evidence of causal explanations. In comparative research this method is widely used for regional or area studies. If we group countries under labels such as 'Latin American countries', 'central Europe' or 'the Middle East', we clearly suggest that the countries in these regions have a lot in common. If, for instance, some Latin American countries are democracies and others are authoritarian, the cause of democracy must be sought among factors that have nothing to do with the common Spanish and Portuguese background of Latin American countries. In a similar way, we can compare 'OECD countries' and exclude economic development as a crucial factor for the explanation of something that occurs in some, but not all, of these countries.

The ideas of Mill are fruitful for developing comparisons in systematic ways. For comparative politics a very influential elaboration of the two strategies has been presented by Adam Przeworski (1940–) and Henry Teune (1936–). Whereas Mill applied his methods mainly to the natural sciences, Przeworski and Teune deal with comparative politics. In a little book on *The Logic of Comparative Social Inquiry* published in 1970, they developed two main strategies for comparisons:

- *Most Different Systems Design (MSDS)* This approach follows the logic of Mill's method of agreement. **Most Different Systems Designs** recommend selecting countries that are very different from each other, but which share the characteristic we want to study. Following this approach, comparing India and Denmark is a good choice because both countries have little in common (are most different systems) apart from being consolidated democracies.

  Most Different Systems Design (MDSD) Comparison of countries that have little in common but the effect or outcome we want to explain.

- *Most Similar Systems Design (MSSD)* Following Mill's method of difference, **Most Similar Systems Design** suggests looking at countries that have a lot in common (that is, are 'most similar systems'), but do not show the same phenomenon or outcome we want to explain. In trying to find out whether British colonial legacies are important for democracy, a comparison between India and Pakistan could be useful since these countries have a lot in common, but only India is a consolidated democracy. Something particular to India in this comparison must be the explanation.

  Most Similar Systems Design (MSSD) Comparison of countries that have a lot in common but the effect or outcome we want to explain.

Both MDSD and MSSD are widely used in comparative politics as strategies for the selection of countries, but before we actually select the countries for our own comparative study, two more preliminary steps are required:

- First, a lot of information is required about the countries selected for comparison. Are India and Canada different or similar? What do Latin

American countries have in common? Which aspects of British colonial rule could be relevant to democracy? Should Brazil be considered? We can only start comparison if these questions are answered and if we have a very good background knowledge of India, Canada, Brazil, Latin America and the history of the British Empire.

- Second, and even more important, before we can start to compare countries we have to be able to pick out factors that are presumed to be crucial to our causal explanation, and to distinguish them from irrelevant ones. Should we compare India and Canada because of their common British legacy and size, ignoring their obvious differences in economic development, population, climate and religious composition?

It is very important to notice that these requirements have to be fulfilled before the merits of deciding between an MDSD or MSSD strategy can be considered. It is easy to compile an endless list of differences and similarities between various countries, but that does not help us. For this we need a theory that specifies what we think are the causal factors to look for and that guide our selection of appropriate countries for our comparison and our appropriate research strategies. Although empirical data of either a qualitative or quantitative kind play a prominent part in comparative politics, it is theory that underpins the whole exercise. Theory guides us in what to look for and which comparative strategy to use.

■ How many countries is enough?

The distinction between MDSD and MSSD strategies helps us to answer the question of which countries should be selected for our comparisons, but it does not answer the question of how many countries are needed. Efficiency dictates the reduction of cases whereas generalisation suggests covering as many as possible. How many countries is enough?

In searching for an answer to this question, researchers are confronted with one of the nastiest problems of comparative research. This complication cannot be solved by theoretical specification. In fact, the clear specification of crucial factors in our theories brings the problem to the surface in the first place. Suppose we want to find out if Britain's colonial legacy is relevant for democracy. In the simplest case we have two dichotomous properties (British/non-British and democratic/non-democratic), which produce four possible types. To study each of these combinations in the real world, therefore, we must base our comparisons on at least four countries. If we use less than four countries, we would not even have the opportunity to find an example of each of the four possible combinations.

	Democratic	Non-democratic
Ex-British colony	Type 1	Type 2
Ex non-British colony	Type 3	Type 4

It does not follow that our search will necessarily produce examples of each of the four simply because one of the combinations may not exist in the real world. But it does mean that we must search for all four, and if one is missing, that itself is evidence that we should take into account in drawing conclusions. The nasty problem, however, becomes clear if we make our theoretical explanations more realistic by adding more factors or variables. With two dichotomous properties the minimum number of cases required is 2 x 2 = 4. If we add country size as a third factor to our explanation of democratic consolidation then the minimum number of cases required is 2 x 2 x 2 = 8. If we want to test four explanatory variables we increase the number to 2 x 2 x 2 x 2 = 16, and adding more variables increases the number exponentially (the rate of increase would itself increase). With less than 200 states in the world it is clear that we run out of enough cases even with only eight explanatory factors. This situation is reached even sooner if we do not use dichotomous properties but variables with more categories – for instance, if we use a distinction between democracies, defective democracies and undemocratic political systems. Since either the number of variables (V) is too large or the number of cases available (n) is too small for a comparison, this problem is referred to as the '**small-n/large-V problem**' in comparative politics.

Small-n/large-V problem With each additional explanatory variable (V) the number of cases (n) required for comparisons grows exponentially. Therefore, only a few explanatory variables are often too many for the relatively small number of cases available, in which case an empirical test is not possible.

If we want to test explanations statistically, the number of cases must be much larger than the number of variables. Since in cross-national comparative research the number of cases is very limited almost by definition, it becomes logically impossible to test all but the simplest explanations. Three basic strategies are available to deal with this problem:

- The first one is, of course, to drop the goal of testing general statements. By opting for MSSD strategies we might be able to delete a number of factors from our analyses and concentrate on a more limited number of factors that we think are important. The problem is that we arrive at limited conclusions that are valid only for the group of countries with 'similar systems'. That might be unproblematic if we want, for instance, to analyse democratic consolidation in Latin America, but it does not help if we want to test a more general theory about democracy and economic development in Africa and Asia as well. For variable-oriented approaches this strategy is unattractive.
- A second strategy is to reduce the number of explanatory variables by specifying our theories more rigorously. If we have clear theoretical arguments to link a few phenomena, we can apply an MDSD strategy and compare a relative small number of very different countries. For instance, a well-developed theory resulting in the expectation that British colonial legacies lead to democracy can be tested by comparing India, Denmark, Canada and Pakistan.

- A final strategy is to increase the number of cases. Germany, for instance, has sixteen middle level units of government – the Länder – and Italy has twenty regional units of government. Brazil has another twenty-six states and a federal district. Why should we not consider these as sixty-three different political systems, especially since some of them are larger and more powerful than the smaller nations of the world? By doing so we might avoid the implications of the exponential growth function of the small-n/large-V problem. This solution has its problems, though. Lower levels of government within the same nation share their respective national institutions, and something of a common history and culture. Therefore, there are not sixteen separate cases but sixteen replications of a single German case. Only if we stress the unique aspects of each of these states are we allowed to treat them as different cases in comparative research. Moreover, if our goal is to compare nations it is not very helpful to recommend a comparison of sub-national entities. Simply looking for 'more of the same' does not solve the problem. This is known as Galton's problem in comparative research, named after the British scholar Francis Galton (1822–1911) who pointed out the complications of replicating cases in 1889.

For each of these three strategies it is clear that only by carefully specifying our theory can we deal with the small-n/large-V problem. We have to develop a specific theory stating precisely the causal variables involved and their relationship with the effect we are trying to explain. This is easier said than done. There is, for example, no satisfactory general theory explaining the development of states and democracies, at least not one that works for a wide variety of different cases. In this situation relying on MSSD strategies seems to be the easiest way out (that is, restrict comparisons to groups of similar countries such as Latin America, federal states or the Indian sub-continent). And yet this strategy risks falling back into ad hoc explanations that do not necessarily apply to the circumstances of other places, precisely because more general approaches to the problem are excluded in the first place.

■ Comparing apples and oranges

The difficult task of selecting countries is not the only challenge for comparative research. Each state has its own historical development, national institutions, customs and traditions, and so on. For instance, although the French and Indian presidents have the same title, their position and powers are very different and not much can be gained from a comparison of them. In fact, no two things in the world are identical, and therefore comparative politics runs into a difficulty when it wants to compare the 'same phenomena' or 'similar objects' in different countries. As it happens, the position of the French president is more like that of the Indian prime minister, and it makes more sense to compare them than the presidents of the two countries.

This raises the whole problem of what exactly it is that we want to compare, a question that is ever-present in comparative research. For instance, is the collection of financial support by German voluntary associations 'the same' as 'fundraising' in the United States, even though the American term cannot be directly translated into German? Indeed, if we were to use only the national terms for institutions and practices in our research no comparative work would be possible at all. What the French call their 'president' does not exist in India. Therefore, a fundamental problem of comparative research is finding concepts that can be used in different countries when each is unique. Two strategies to deal with this problem are available to us:

- looking for more abstract concepts
- looking for equivalent concepts.

Looking for more abstract concepts

In one sense the problem of comparative concepts is simple and one that we solve all the time in everyday life: apples and oranges are different but we put them in the same category when we call them fruit. In the same way we can compare the French president and the Indian prime minister by treating them both as government leaders – political executives. Canadian Catholics are different from Indian Hindus, but both are religious. In all these cases we simply use a more general term to cover different sets of objects.

The Italian political scientist Giovanni Sartori (1924–) discussed this procedure in a seminal article on *Concept Misformation in Comparative Politics*, published in 1970. As the title suggests, Sartori sees a number of risks attached to the search for general concepts because this inevitably involves loosing information. There are, for instance, more than 7,500 different types of apples and each has properties that distinguish it from the others, so that the word 'apple' loses information and covers up differences. When we move to the still more general term 'fruit' we lose still more information about the differences between apples, oranges and pears, to take only three examples. Using more general and abstract terms for comparisons implies **conceptual stretching**, which inevitably introduces ambiguity into our concepts because it remains unclear what is to be included and excluded. The advantage of using a more abstract concept is that it makes comparisons of different phenomena possible; the danger is that the actual phenomena we want to study disappear behind a cloud of rather nebulous general concepts and that we lose more information than we gain. The main task of comparativists, then, is to develop general concepts for comparisons which are at the same time precise, clearly defined and well grounded ones but which lose as little information as possible.

> **Conceptual stretching** Broadening the meaning, and thereby the range of application, of a concept or term.

Sartori presents a 'ladder of abstraction' to clarify this procedure. In order to make comparisons we climb the ladder to some higher level of abstraction by using more general terms or concepts. In a similar way, we can also descend the ladder and replace our general concepts by more specific ones. Climbing the ladder makes comparisons easier at the price of losing information; descending the ladder makes more information available but endangers comparisons. Sartori summarised the level of abstraction in three categories:

1. *High-level categories*   Universal concepts that can be used for comparisons across the world no matter how different the circumstances. In comparative politics 'political system' is a high-level concept that applies to all circumstances.
2. *Medium-level categories*   At this level, general concepts are used to compare reasonably similar things. In comparative politics, 'left-wing party' is pitched at this level to cover everything from communist to centrist democratic socialist parties in established democracies.
3. *Low-level categories*   For country-by-country comparisons specific terms can be used, such as the Indian prime minister or the French president.

Developing appropriate concepts is a theoretical task that should precede the selection of countries as well as the collection of information. Once again, we see that finding solutions for problems in comparative politics can only be based on careful theoretical reflection.

Looking for equivalent concepts

A second strategy to handle country-specific information in comparative politics is to focus on specific contexts. Every comparison must start from the idea that even very similar phenomena or objects are not identical. This does not have to bother us all the time. The fact that German and American voluntary associations differ in the way they raise money does not mean that we cannot compare their roles in community politics. Besides, we can also use devices for making different things similar. One example concerns the exchange rate of different currencies. The money used in our country can be readily changed into that of other countries at a given and recognised exchange rate, but this rate may vary according to whether our currency is over-valued or under-valued for some reason. How can we tell whether our currency is over- or under-valued when each country has its own currency with its own purchasing power in another currency? The *Economist* has invented the 'Hamburger Standard' or 'Big Mac Index' to do this. Since Big Macs are made to exactly the same specification in every country, they should, in theory, cost the same amount in every country at the current exchange rates. The difference between the actual price and official exchange rate price tells you how much a foreign currency is over-valued or under-valued (see www.economist.com/markets/Bigmac/index.cfm).

Hence the Big Mac Index is based on the idea that different things (local currencies) can be compared systematically by means of a standard measure (purchasing power) if we can identify what the different countries have in common (a Big Mac). In a similar way, we could analyse decision-making processes among the executive branches in India and France and see that the president in France has a lot in common with the Indian prime minister. Likewise, no matter how voluntary associations are financed or named in the USA and Germany, the fact that they exist in the spaces between the state, commercial and private spheres in both countries is sufficient ground for comparison.

These examples make clear that we can compare apparently very different phenomena in different countries if we know that they have similar positions in those countries or perform similar functions. Instead of identity, comparisons are based on the idea of **equivalence**. Whether or not the phenomena compared have the same or different names is absolutely irrelevant. What matters is that they operate in similar ways or perform similar functions in different situations. It is this contextual correspondence that makes it meaningful to compare them. In other words, it is possible to compare different institutions if they perform the same functions in their respective countries, as the French president and Indian prime minister do. In terms of concepts we cover them with the term 'political executive'. By using information about specific situations in specific countries we can identify similar phenomena without running the risk of losing information by stretching our concepts unacceptably. In fact, only if we rely on specific information can we answer the question of what phenomena can be considered as equivalent.

> **Equivalence** Two objects or phenomena are equivalent if they have the same value, importance, use, function or result.

By looking for equivalence, comparisons do not have to rely on identical indicators and nor do we have to stretch our concepts. Equivalence can be established by careful analyses of the similarities and differences between countries but this, in turn, requires that we know what we are looking for in the first place. This is a theoretical and conceptual challenge that requires careful consideration at the outset of our comparative exercise. This brings us back, once again, to the vital importance of theory and the need to start with good theory before we start any empirical work in searching for equivalents.

■ What have we learned?

At first sight, making comparisons seems to be unproblematic: Why should we not just get on with the business of comparing India, Canada, Denmark and Pakistan? Yet the question 'How and what to compare?' is not easy to answer. The complications arise mainly because comparativists are not only interested in learning about other countries, important though this may be. They also want to generalise about political life and explain in causal terms why it happens. This produces a set of difficult problems:

* Comparing a large number of countries is appropriate for testing general conclusions but depends on quantitative, statistical analyses of

standardised data. This means that information that cannot be quantified and standardised is lost.

- Comparing a few countries in order to acquire a broad and deep understanding of them depends on qualitative information. This means that testing more general theories is difficult.
- The number of cases available for comparisons is almost always too small for the number of explanatory variables used (small-n/large-V problem).
- Comparative studies can be divided in Most Different System Designs and Most Similar Systems Designs. Whereas MDSD searches for causes of similar effects in countries that differ greatly in many ways, MSSD focus on similar countries that differ in one respect that is thought to be important.
- Using more general concepts or terms makes it possible to compare but at the price of losing specific information. Using specific information, however, makes comparisons much more difficult.
- Comparisons can be based on equivalent but not necessarily identical terms.
- Although empirical information about countries plays a very important role in comparative politics, it is only its theoretical underpinning that makes it truly comparative and makes comparison meaningful.

Projects

1. Suppose you want to make a comparison of voting behaviour in sixteen countries. Present the main steps in your comparison using a small-n design or, alternatively, a large-n design.
2. Compare the advantages and disadvantages of MSSD and MDSD strategies. Give an example of each strategy to underline your arguments.
3. Compare and contrast the process of democratic consolidation in your own and two other countries. What conclusions can you reach from such a comparison?
4. Give three examples of conceptual stretching and explain the conditions in which it is appropriate to climb the ladder of abstraction in these cases.

Further reading

T. Landman, *Issues and Methods in Comparative Politics: An Introduction*, London: Routledge, 2008.
An accessible introduction to comparative methods with many examples and explanations

P. Pennings, H. Keman and J. Kleinnijenhuis, *Doing Research in Political Science. An Introduction to Comparative Methods and Statistics*, London: Sage, 2005.
Overview of comparative methods and approaches

G. L. Munck and R. Snyder (eds.), *Passion, Craft, and Method in Comparative Politics*, Baltimore: Johns Hopkins University Press, 2007.
Interviews with the most prominent scholars in comparative politics.

A. Przeworski and H. Teune, *The Logic of Comparative Social Inquiry*, New York: Wiley, 1970.
Seminal text on the goals and major strategies in comparative research.

Websites

www.nd.edu/~apsacp/index.html
The official newsletter of the APSA's Organized Section in Comparative Politics. Provides a forum for discussing trends and innovations and sharing news of general interest to comparativists.
www.u.arizona.edu/~cragin/fsQCA/index.shtml
Information about qualitative comparative analysis (including literature and software).
www.maxwell.syr.edu/moynihan/programs/cqrm/
The Consortium on Qualitative Research Methods (CQRM) promotes the teaching and use of qualitative research methods in the social sciences.

Glossary of key terms

Administration A term with two meanings. Either (1) a term synonymous with government – e.g. the Obama administration in the USA, the Merkel administration in Germany or (2) a term synonymous with the management processes of bureaucracies – e.g. the administration of the state through bureaucratic agencies.

Affirmative action (also known as positive discrimination) Policies designed to redress past discrimination. Affirmative action may require state bureaucracies to increase recruitment from women and minority groups. Also known in some countries as 'positive discrimination'.

Agenda setting The process by which a multiplicity of political problems and issues are continuously sorted according to the changing priority attached to them. In communication research, the theory claiming that the mass media may not exercise much influence over what we think, but can influence what we think about.

Alford index A measure of class voting that calculates the difference between the proportion of working-class people voting for a left party, and the proportion of middle-class people doing the same. The higher the index, the greater the class voting.

Aligned groups Pressure groups that ally themselves with a political party, the best examples being trade unions and left parties, and business organisations and right parties. Many groups try to maintain a non-aligned status if they can, because they want to work with whichever party is in power.

Authoritarian attitudes A system or syndrome of attitudes based upon: prejudice, dogmatism, superstition, low tolerance for ambiguity, hostility to out-groups (anti-semitism and racism) and obedience to authority.

Authoritarian rule Obedience and submission to authority; that is, the concentration of power in the hands of a leader or elite that is not responsible to parliament (or, in turn, to a popular vote). No opposition is allowed to compete for power.

Bill A formal proposal for a law put before a legislature but not yet accepted by it.

'Black economy' The 'informal economy' in which goods and services are traded for cash, without bills, receipts, or financial records that would enable the authorities to levy taxes on them.

Bureaucracy A rational, impersonal, rule-bound and hierarchical form of organisational structure set up to perform large-scale administrative tasks.

Case-oriented approach Comparison focused on specific countries and the themes, patterns and tendencies within these countries.

Cash transfers A way to provide social security payments to citizens by giving them money. An alternative to cash benefits is the provision of goods and services.

Catch-all parties Lacking a clear social basis, catch-all parties try to attract a broad range of supporters by advocating rather general policies.

Caucus A small but loose-knit group of politicians (notables) who come together from time to time to make decisions about political matters.

Cause groups Sometimes known as 'promotional groups' or 'attitude groups', cause groups are a type of pressure group that do not represent organised occupational interests, but promote causes, ideas or issues.

Centre–periphery cleavage The political cleavage between the social and political forces responsible for creating centralised and modern nation-states, which usually became dominant, and other interests, usually on the periphery of the state, which resisted this process. Centre–periphery cleavages are often, but not always, geographical.

Charter of the United Nations Founding treaty of the United Nations (UN) that defines the purposes of the UN and confers certain powers on it.

Checking and balancing power *See* Separation of powers.

Civic culture The term used by Almond and Verba to signify the balance of subject and participant political cultures that best supports democracy.

Civil service The body of civilian officials (not members of the armed forces) employed by the state to work in government departments. In some countries, the term applies to all public officials (local government and teachers), but in most it includes only the officials of central government.

Civil society That arena of social life outside the state, the commercial sector and the family (i.e. mainly voluntary organisations and civic associations) that permits individuals to associate freely and independently of state regulation.

Class Class is a form of social stratification that is determined by economic factors, notably the occupational hierarchy that broadly groups people into working-class (manual), middle-class (non-manual) and upper-class (wealthy property-owning) groups.

Class de-alignment A process of decline in the class-based strength of attachment and sense of belonging to class-based political parties.

Cleavages Cleavages are deep and persistent differences in society where (1) objective social differences (class, religion, race, language, or region) are aligned with (2) subjective awareness of these differences (different cultures, ideologies and orientations) and are (3) organised by political parties, groups, or movements. Cleavages are often the basis of political conflict.

Clientelism A system of government and politics based on a relationship between patron and clients. Public sector jobs and contracts are distributed on the basis of personal and political contacts in return for political support.

Coalition A set of parties that comes together to form a government. Coalition parties are usually represented in the cabinet, but sometimes one party takes all the cabinet posts with the support of a legislative coalition.

Cognitive mobilisation The process by which increasing knowledge and understanding of the world helps to activate people to play a part in it.

Collective responsibility The principle that decisions and policies of the cabinet or council are binding on all members who must support them in public in order to maintain the government's united front. What cabinet or council members say or believe in private is a different matter, but public disagreement should be followed by resignation from the government.

Compulsory voting The legal obligation for citizens to appear at polling stations on election day.

Conceptual stretching Broadening the meaning, and thereby the range of application, of a concept or term.

Conciliation *See* Mediation.

Confederations Organisations whose members give some powers to a higher body, while retaining their own autonomy and independence, including the right to leave the confederation.

Conglomerates Single business organisations consisting of a number of different companies that operate in different economic fields.

Consolidation Process of maturing and stabilising a new political system by strengthening and formalising its basic arrangements.

Constitution A constitution is a set of fundamental laws that determines what the central institutions and offices of the state are to be, their powers and duties, and how they relate to one another and to their citizens.

Content regulation Regulation of the content of the media by public bodies in the public interest – e.g. to limit violence on TV, or ban cigarette adverts. The content regulation of news and current affairs programmes usually aims at accurate, balanced, and impartial political reporting, and fair access for the parties to the mass media.

Conventions Unwritten rules that impose obligations on constitutional actors that are held to be binding, but not incorporated into law or reinforced by legal sanctions. (The term is also used to refer to meetings of political groups or parties – the Republican Party Convention, for example.)

Corporatism A way of organising public policy making involving the close cooperation of major economic interests within a formal government apparatus that is capable of concerting the main economic groups so that they can jointly formulate and implement binding policies.

Corruption The use of illegitimate means such as bribery, blackmail, or threats to influence or control the making of public decisions, or the secret use of public offices or resources for private purposes.

Country Term usually used as a rather imprecise synonym or 'shorthand' for state or nation-state. It stresses the geographical location or territory of a state.

Cross-cutting cleavages Cleavages that are laid across one another, thereby reducing their capacity to divide.

Cross-media ownership/Multi-media conglomeration When the same person or company has financial interests in different branches of mass communication – e.g. when they own a newspaper and a TV channel, or a publishing house and TV network.

Cultural imperialism The use of cultural products, particularly films, books, music and television, to spread the values and ideologies of foreign cultures. The term was often used to describe the cultural power of the west, especially the USA, over other parts of the world.

Decentralisation Where some functions of the state are carried out by sub-central agencies that have a degree of discretion or autonomy from the central government.

'Declaration of the Rights of Man and of the Citizen' The seventeen articles, describing the purpose of the state and the rights of individual citizens, proclaimed by the French National Assembly in August 1789. A similar list had been proclaimed in the USA thirteen years earlier, in 1776.

Defective democracies Systems of government that are neither democratic nor undemocratic, but maintain some democratic characteristics as well as some undemocratic ones that damage and disrupt the institutional logic of embedded democracy.

Delegated legislation Law or decrees made by ministers, not by legislatures, though in accordance with powers granted to them by the legislative body.

Demagogues Political leaders who use impassioned appeals to the emotions and prejudices of citizens to try to gain political power.

Democratic deficit A term used to convey the idea that the institutions of the European Union are not fully democratic, or as democratic as they should be. The criticism is often used to support suggestions that the power of the EP should be increased at the expense of the Commission and the Council of Ministers.

Democracy A political system whose leaders are elected in competitive multi-party and multi-candidate processes in which opposition parties have a legitimate chance of attaining power or participating in power (Freedom House). Terms such as 'liberal democracy' are often used as synonyms for democracy.

Democratisation The continual process of transforming a political system towards more democratic arrangements.

Devolution Devolution occurs where higher levels of government grant decision-making powers to lower levels while maintaining their constitutionally subordinate status.

Direct election Election by the electorate at large (popular election) rather than by an electoral college, the legislature, or another body.

Disproportionality *See* Proportionality/Disproportionality.

Dominant one-party system A party system in which one party dominates all the others. Dominant party systems are found in democratic countries with competitive parties. They must be distinguished from undemocratic one-party systems where only one party is allowed to operate freely.

Door-step response The tendency of those with no opinion or information to respond to polls and surveys with the first thing that comes into their head, often something they think they are expected to say (sometimes known as 'non-opinion').

Dual systems System of local government in unitary states in which local authorities have more independence than in fused systems but still operate under the general authority of central government.

Ecology The relationships between organisms and their environment.

Electoral threshold A minimum percentage of the poll required to be elected (to discourage small parties).

Embedded democracy A consolidated and stable system that is founded on a well-developed civil society, secure civil and political rights, a set of autonomous institutions of government that act within the rule of law, a system of free and fair elections, and a government with effective power to perform its duties.

Empirical political theories Theories that try to understand, by examining the evidence, how the political world actually works and to explain why it works that way. Empirical theory is ultimately based upon evidence and argument that can, in principle, be tested and verified by political science.

Empirical statements Factual statements about or, explanations of, the world that are not necessarily true or false but are amenable, in principle, to falsification (*see* normative statements).

'Episodic' groups Groups that are not usually politically active but become so for a time when the need arises.

Equivalence Two objects or phenomena are equivalent if they have the same value, importance, use, function or result. They may not be called the same thing but they must have things in common that make comparison meaningful.

Essentially contestable concept A concept that is inevitably the subject of end-less dispute about their proper use (e.g. art, democracy, politics and a Christian life).

Etatism Approaches to the relationships between state and society with a very strong emphasis on state power and an accompanying reduction of social and individual rights.

Executive The branch of government mainly responsible for initiating government action, making and implementing public policy, and coordinating the activities of the state.

Externality A cost or benefit that does not fall on those who are responsible for the decision or action that creates the externality, and which they do not take into account when they take the action.

False consciousness The state of mind of the working class induced by the ruling class to conceal the real nature of capitalism and the real self-interests of the workers.

Federal states Federal states combine a central authority (federal government) with a degree of constitutionally defined autonomy for sub-central territorial units of government (states, or regions, or provinces).

'Fire brigade' groups Groups formed to fight a specific issue, and dissolved when it is over.

Framing The theory that the way news stories are set up (framed) influences how audiences interpret them – e.g. the use of human interest stories to illustrate a social problem can deflect attention from government policies that help to cause the problem to the personal inadequacies of individuals who are the subjects of human interest.

Free-ride To extract the benefits of other people's work without making any effort oneself. The free-rider problem is acute in collective action when individuals benefit from a public good (clean air, for example, or public transport) without paying taxes or making any effort of their own.

Fused systems Systems of local government in unitary states in which officials appointed by central government directly supervise the work of local govern-ment and its elected officials.

General competence The power of local government units to manage their own affairs, provided they observe the laws of the land and relatively few legally defined exceptions.

Gerrymandering A form of electoral corruption in which electoral boundaries are drawn to favour a particular party or interest.

Globalisation The growing interdependencies and interconnectedness of the world that are said to reduce the autonomy of individual states and the importance of boundaries between them.

Governance The act of governing; that is, the total set of government's activities in each phase of the policy-making process.

Government A government has a monopoly on the legitimate use of physical force within a state. Securing internal and external sovereignty of the state are major tasks of any government.

'Grand' coalitions Oversized coalitions that include all parties or the largest of them.

Gross Domestic Product (GDP) The value of all final goods and services produced within a state in a given year. In order to compare the wealth of states the meas-ure used is normally GDP *per capita*.

Hegemony Hegemony indicates a class, political interest or country that is so powerful that it does not have to rely upon force or power to maintain its rule because its values and attitudes have been accepted or because people dare not oppose it. Often used now to mean all-powerful – since the collapse of the Soviet Union, the USA has become the 'hegemonic' world power, for example.

Human Development Index (HDI) A UN index of national development that combines measures of life expectancy, educational attainment and wealth into one measure.

Human rights The innate, inalienable and inviolable right of humans to free movement and self-determination in relation to the state. Such rights cannot be bestowed, granted, limited, bartered away, or sold away. Inalienable rights can be only secured or violated.

Hyper-pluralism A state of affairs in which too many powerful groups make too many demands on government, causing overload and ungovernability.

Idealism In political theory, the term 'idealism' refers to the theory that ideas have a life of their own and must be understood as the products of consciousness or spiritual ideals and values that are independent of material conditions. In international relations idealism refers to the view of politics that emphasises the role of ideas and morality as a determinant of the relations between states (*see* Materialism).

Ideal-type An analytical construct that simplifies reality and picks out its most important features, to serve as a model that allows us to understand and compare the complexities of the real world. An ideal-type is neither a standard of perfection (as in 'an ideal husband') nor a statistical average, but a simplified, theoretical abstraction from the real world that helps us compare individual cases.

Ideologues Those with an informed, broad, sophisticated and more or less consistent (systematic) view of the political world.

Ideology A more or less systematic, well-developed and comprehensive set of ideas and beliefs about politics consisting of both (empirical) statements about what is, and (prescriptive) statements about what ought to be.

Immobilism The state of being unable to move (immobilised) or in a political system of being unable to take decisions or implement policies.

Impeachment To charge a public official, usually an elected politician, with improper conduct in office before a duly constituted tribunal, usually the main elected legislative body, prior to removing the official from office if they are found guilty. Not known much outside the USA, and not often used there.

Implementation The process of applying policies and putting them into practice.

Incremental model The theory that decisions are not usually based upon a rational or fundamental review of problems and solution, but upon small, marginal changes from existing policies.

'Insider' groups Pressure groups with access to senior government officials, often recognised as the only legitimate representatives of particular interests and often formally incorporated into official consultative bodies.

Interest aggregation Sorting the great variety of political attitudes and opinions on a political issue, to reduce it to a more simple, clear-cut and agreed 'package' of opinion.

Interest articulation The expression of political demands in order to influence public policy.

Interest groups Sometimes known as 'sectional groups', interest groups are a type of pressure group that represents occupational interests. The main types are business associations, professional associations and trade unions.

Interpellation A parliamentary question addressed to government requiring a formal answer and often followed by discussion, and sometimes by a vote.

'Iron triangles' The close, three-sided working relationship developed between (1) government departments and ministries, (2) pressure groups and (3) politicians, that make public policy in a given area.

Issue voting Voters choosing one issue rather than a total party programme as the basis of their voting decision.

Judicial activism Judicial activism involves the courts taking a broad and active view of their role as interpreters of the constitution and reviewers of executive and legislative action.

Judicial review The binding power of the courts to provide an authoritative interpretation of laws, including constitutional law, and to overturn executive or legislative actions they hold to be illegal or unconstitutional.

Judiciary The branch of government mainly responsible for the authoritative interpretation of law and applying it to particular cases.

Knowledge gap The gap between those with a good education and understanding of the world, which enables them to acquire knowledge and understanding at a faster rate than those with less education and understanding.

Labour productivity The average production per labourer in a specific period (for instance, the average number of ballpoints produced per labourer in a ballpoint pen factory in one year).

Laissez-faire doctrines The literal translation from the French is 'to let to do'. Laissez-faire is the principle of maximum freedom for the economic forces of the market, and minimum intervention from the state.

Large-n comparison Comparison of many countries, usually based on statistical analyses of strictly comparable evidence about them.

Legislation Legislation is the body of laws that have been passed by the legislature. Legislating is thus the act of initiating, debating and passing such laws.

Legislative oversight The role of the legislature that involves the scrutiny or supervision of other branches of government, especially the executive and the public bureaucracy.

Legislature The branch of government mainly responsible for discussing and passing legislation, and keeping watch on the executive.

Legitimacy The condition of being in accordance with the norms and values of the people. The 'legitimate use of power' refers to the use of power that is accepted because it is in accordance with the norms and values of the people it concerns.

Legitimation The process of making something morally acceptable, proper or right in the eyes of the general public according to accepted standards and values.

Liberal democracy The form of democracy that tries to combine the powers of democratic government with liberal values about the freedom of the individual.

Lobby A popular term for pressure groups (based on the mistaken belief that pressure group representatives spend a lot of time in the 'lobbies' or ante-rooms of legislative chambers).

Low information rationality Where citizens do not have a great deal of factual political information but have a broad enough grasp of the main issues to make up their mind about them, or else they take their cues about the issues from sources they trust (sometimes known as 'gut rationality').

Market regulation The regulation of the media market by public bodies, often to avoid cross-media ownership, foreign control of important channels of national communication, or cases of market failure.

Mass society A society without a plurality of organised social groups and interests, whose mass of isolated and uprooted individuals are not integrated into the community and who are therefore vulnerable to the appeals of extremist and anti-democratic elites.

Materialism The theory that ideas are rooted in the material or physical conditions of life, as opposed to spiritual ideals and values which are constructs of the mind which can be independent of material and physical conditions (*see* Idealism).

Means testing In contrast to public benefits that are universally available, means testing involves investigating a person's income and means of support to ensure that they cannot afford to pay for the service themselves. Means testing is often resented by welfare applicants and is politically controversial.

Mediamalaise The attitudes of political cynicism, despair, apathy, distrust and dis-illusionment (among others) that some social scientists claim are caused by the mass media, especially TV.

Median voter The median voter is in the middle of the distribution with equal numbers of voters to the left and right, and is, therefore, a typical, middle-of-the road voter. The support of the median voter is usually necessary to win an election.

Mediation Attempt by a third party to reach an agreement between disputing parties by suggesting terms of settlement.

Meso-government A middle level or tier of government between central and local authorities, and often known as state, regional, provincial or county government.

Method of Agreement Comparison of cases which share the presence of effects or outcomes as well as presumed causes.

Method of Difference Comparison of cases which share effects or outcomes but differ in the presence of presumed causes.

Military–industrial complex The close and powerful alliance of government, business and military interests that is said by some to run capitalist societies.

Minimum winning coalition (MWC) The smallest number of parties necessary for a majority of votes in parliament.

Minority government A government or coalition that is smaller than a MWC.

Mixed economy An economy that is neither wholly privately owned (a capitalist market economy), nor wholly publicly owned (a communist command economy), but a mixture of both.

Modernisation The dual processes of technological and economic development and the societal responses to these changes.

Most Different Systems Design (MDSD) Comparison of countries that have little in common but the effect or outcome we want to explain.

Most Similar Systems Design (MSSD) Comparison of countries that have a lot in common but the effect or outcome we want to explain.

Multi-member districts *See* Single-member/Multi-member districts.

Multi-party systems Where several or many main parties compete, often with the result that no single party has an overall majority.

Nation *See* nation-state.

Nation-state A state based on the acceptance of a common culture, a common history and a common fate, irrespective of whatever political, social and economic differences may exist between the members of the nation-state.

New Public Management (NPM) New Public Management (NPM) refers to the reforms of the public sector in the 1980s and 1990s, based mainly on what were thought to be private sector practice and consisting mainly of privatisation, deregulation, business management techniques and 'marketisation'. Known also as 'reinventing government', it is said to have had the effect of 'hollowing out' the state.

New Social Movements Loosely knit organisations ('networks of networks') that try to influence government policy on broad issues, including the environment, nuclear energy and nuclear weapons, economic development, peace, women and minorities.

Non-decision The decision not to deal with an issue, perhaps not even to consider it.

Non-governmental organisation (NGO) A non-governmental organisation (NGO) is a non-profit making, non-violent private organisation that is independent of government and seeks to influence or control government policy without actually seeking government office.

Normative political theories Theories about how the world should be or ought to be. Normative theory is based upon philosophical arguments, and ultimately on subjective values and judgements. Sometimes it is known as prescriptive theory, political theory, or political philosophy.

Normative statements Statements that are based upon faith, or contain a value judgement or an evaluation. Sometimes referred to as prescriptive, or evaluative statements. Normative statements are neither scientific nor unscientific, but non-scientific (*see* empirical statements).

Oligarchy Government by a few.

Ombudsman A state official appointed to receive complaints and investigate claims about maladministration (improper or unjust action) and to report their findings, usually to the legislature.

One-party systems Government systems in which a single party forms the government.

Outcomes The impacts, or effects, of outputs.

Outputs The policy decisions as they are actually implemented.

'Outsider' groups Groups with no access to top government officials.

'Oversized' (surplus majority) coalitions A coalition that is larger than a MWC.

Parliamentary systems Parliamentary systems are characterised by (1) a directly elected legislative body, (2) the fusion of executive and legislative institutions, (3) a collective and collegial executive that emerges out of the legislature and is responsible to it and (4) a separation of head of state and head of government.

Participatory democracy That form of democracy in which citizens actively participate in government and political processes.

Partisan de-alignment Decline in the strength of attachment to political parties.

Partisan re-alignment A process in which social and economic groups show signs of a long-term change in their old party identifications in favour of new ones.

Party families Groups of parties in different countries that have similar ideologies and party programmes.

Party identification (ID) The stable and deep-rooted feeling of attachment to and support for a particular political party.

Party systems The pattern of significant parties within a political system, especially their number and the party families represented.

Peak associations See 'Umbrella' organisations.

People Group of persons living together on the territory of a state whose common consciousness and identity usually form them into a collective entity.

Performance Actual activities and results; how well government is doing or how successful it is in meeting citizen demands.

Pluralism A situation where power is dispersed among many different groups and organisations that openly compete with one another in different political arenas.

Pluralist democracy A democratic system where political decisions are the outcome of the conflict and competition between many different groups. Some forms of pluralist theory are empirical attempts to describe and explain how the political system actually works, others are normative theories of how a good democracy should work.

Police The branch of government employed to maintain civil order and to investigate breaches of the law.

Policy communities Small, stable and consensual groupings of government officials and pressure group representatives that form around particular issue areas.

Policy networks Compared with policy communities, policy networks are larger, looser, and more conflictual networks that gather around a particular policy area.

Political alienation A feeling of detachment, estrangement, or critical distance from politics, often because the alienated feel there is something basically wrong with the political system.

Political behaviour Term used to refer to all political activities of citizens as well as the attitudes and orientations relevant for these activities.

Political cleavage A political division created when political organisations use social cleavages for their own purposes to mobilise support. Social cleavages are often more important politically when two or more are superimposed on top of one another.

Political culture The pattern of attitudes, values and beliefs about politics, whether they are conscious or unconscious, explicit or implicit.

Political elite The relatively small number of people at the top of a political system who exercise disproportionate influence or power over political decisions. If it exercises enough power in the system, it is a 'ruling elite'.

Political identity The way that people label themselves as belonging to a particular group (e.g. nation-state, class or caste, ethnic group, religious or ideological group).

Political marginality The condition of being on the fringes of politics, and therefore of having little influence.

Political orientation A predisposition or propensity to view politics in a certain way.

Political parties Organisations of politically like-minded people who seek political power and public office in order to realise their policies.

Political socialisation The process by which individuals acquire their political values, attitudes and habits. Childhood socialisation is most important, but socialisation continues in adulthood as well.

Populism A demagogic style of politics that appeals to political prejudices and emotions, particularly of those who feel exploited and oppressed by the rich and powerful.

Power The ability to make other people do what they do not want to do. Power is the ability to apply force.

Presidential systems In presidential systems a directly elected president is the executive, with a limited term of office and a general responsibility for the affairs of state, who governs with a separate and independently elected legislature.

Pressure groups Private and voluntary organisations that try to influence or control particular government policies but do not want to become the government or control all government policies.

Prevention Attempt to hinder or deter delinquent behaviour.

Priming The theory that the mass media can prime us to focus on certain things and in certain ways by highlighting some issues rather than others – e.g.

focusing on foreign rather than domestic policy favours parties that are thought to be better at foreign policy than domestic policy.

Privatisation The process of converting public services and amenities to private ones.

Productivity *See also* Labour productivity.

Proportionality/Disproportionality A measure of the ratio of seats to votes. The more proportional the system, the closer the ratio of seats to votes. In the most proportional voting system a party getting 43 per cent of the votes should get 43 per cent of the seats, or close to this figure, since seats are not divisible.

Protest vote Voting for a party not to support it, but to show opposition to another party or parties, usually those in government.

Provision of goods and services A way to provide social security for citizens by offering them not money but specific facilities such as housing or job training. Cash transfers are an alternative to goods and services.

(Public) policy Some general set of ideas or plans that has been officially agreed on and which is used as a basis for making decisions. A public policy is the long series of activities, decisions and actions carried out by officials of government in their attempts to solve problems that are thought to lie in the public or collective arena.

Public–private partnerships (PPPs) Formal cooperations between government and private groups to obtain specific goals.

Public sector That part of social, economic and political life that is not private but controlled or regulated by the state or its agencies.

Public service model The system of organising radio and TV in which broadcasting licences are granted to public bodies, usually supported by public funds, for use in the public interest rather than for profit.

Qualitative comparative analysis (QCA) The systematic comparison of a few cases using specific techniques to develop and test generalisations.

QUANGOs (Quasi-autonomous Non-Governmental Organisations) Organisations that are partially or wholly funded by the government to perform public service functions but not under direct government control.

Realism In international relations realism refers to the view of politics that emphasises the role of self-interest as a determinant of state policies and hence the importance of power in these relations. In realist theory states (and other actors such as business organisations) are presumed to act more or less rationally to promote their own interests.

Referendum The submission of a public matter to direct popular vote. Sometimes known as a plebiscite.

Reinforcement theory (also known as minimal effects theory) The theory that the mass media can only reflect and reinforce public opinion, not create or mould it.

Reinforcing cleavages Cleavages that are laid one on top of the other, making them potentially more important.

Representative democracy That form of democracy in which citizens elect leaders who govern in their name.

Ruling elite A political elite that is so powerful that it can make all the important decisions in government.

Salient Something that is important, significant, or prominent in people's minds.

Semi-presidential system Semi-presidential government consists of a directly elected president who is accountable to the electorate and a prime minister, who is appointed by the president from the elected legislature and accountable to it. The president and prime minister share executive power.

Separation of powers The doctrine that political power should be divided among several bodies or officers of the state, often between bodies or officers performing different government functions, as a precaution against too much concentration of power.

Single-member/Multi-member districts Single-member districts have one representative each in parliament, while multi-member districts have two or more to make it easier to attain proportionality.

Small-n comparison Comparison of a few countries, usually based on systematic, in-depth analysis and detailed knowledge of them.

Small-n/large-V problem With each additional explanatory variable (V) the number of cases (n) required for comparisons grows exponentially. Therefore, only a few explanatory variables is often too many for the relatively small number of cases available, in which case an empirical test is not possible.

Social capital The features of social organisations, such as trust, social norms and social networks, that improve social and governmental efficiency by encouraging cooperation and collective action.

Social expenditures Social expenditures are the provision by public (and private) institutions of benefits to households and individuals in order to provide support during circumstances which adversely affect their welfare. This is the definition used by the OECD.

Social stratification The hierarchical layering of society into socially unequal groups. It includes peasants and landowners, castes, classes and status groups.

Sociotropic voting Deciding which party to vote for on the basis of general social or economic circumstances. The opposite is 'pocket-book voting' that is based on private interests of the voter.

Soft power In contrast to 'hard power' based upon military and economic force, soft power uses popular culture and the media to influence the way that people think and feel and behave. It is the way of winning the hearts and minds of people (usually in international relations) rather than using force, threats and sanctions.

Sovereignty A state is sovereign when it holds the highest power and, in principle, can act with complete freedom and independence. Internal sovereignty means that, on its own territory, the state can act as it wishes and is independent of other institutions. External sovereignty refers to the fact that the state is seen as autonomous by other states.

Spectrum scarcity The shortage of terrestrial broadcasting frequencies for radio and TV, which meant that there could be only a few channels.

Spin-doctors Public relations specialists employed to put the best possible light on news about their clients. The term often implies people whose job is to manipulate the news.

State An organisation that issues and enforces rules that are binding for the people living in a given territorially defined area.

Status A form of social stratification determined by social prestige rather than economic factors or occupation. It is sometimes said that class is determined by how people make their money, status by how they spend it. Sometimes class and status are combined in the single measure of social and economic status.

Street-level bureaucrats The bureaucrats who regularly come into contact and deal with the public.

Subjective or internal competence/efficacy The extent to which ordinary citizens feel that they can make their views and actions count in the political system. The opposites of the term are 'powerlessness', 'inefficacy' or 'low competence'.

Sub-central/sub-national government All levels of government below national/central government. Sub-national government covers everything below central government from community and neighbourhood government, through local government of all kinds, to the middle or meso-level of state, regional and provincial government.

Subsidiarity The principle that decisions should be taken at the lowest possible level of government – that is, at the level closest to the people affected by the decisions. Usually the term subsidiarity is used in connection with the territorial decentralisation of government, but it is not limited to this form.

Suffrage The right to vote. Hence 'suffragettes' were women who fought for the right of women to vote.

Supra-national government Organisations in which countries pool their sovereignty on certain matters to allow joint decision-making.

System or external efficacy The extent to which ordinary citizens feel that political leaders and institutions are responsive to their wishes.

Territory Terrain or geographical area.

Terrorism The use of violence against civilian targets to create fear for political aims. What some regard as terrorism is seen as 'freedom fighting' by others.

'Third wave' (of democracy) Democratisation across the world is often divided into 'three waves'. The first, from the mid-nineteenth to the mid-twentieth century, saw between twenty-five and thirty states achieve a degree of democratic stability, depending on how 'democracy' is defined. The second, from about 1950 to 1975, was mainly the result of decolonisation. The third, from about 1975 to 2000, was mainly the result of the disintegration of the Soviet Union and the spread of democracy in Latin America and Asia.

Tri-partism A looser and less centralised system of decision making than corporatism involving close government consultation – often with business and trade union organisations.

Two-party systems Party systems in which two large parties dominate all the others.

'Umbrella'/organisations Associations that coordinate the activity of their member organisations.

Unitary states In unitary states the central government is the only sovereign body. It does not share *constitutional* authority with any sub-central units of government.

Values Basic ethical priorities that constrain and give shape to individual attitudes and beliefs.

Variable-oriented approach Comparison focused on specific themes, patterns and tendencies in a set of countries.

Veto-groups Groups with the power to prevent other groups or the government implementing a policy, although they do not necessarily have the power to get their own policies implemented.

Volatility The opposite of stability, volatility involves change in voting patterns from one election to another. Some voting studies refer to it as 'churning'.

Vote of confidence A vote of confidence (or no confidence), to test whether the government of the day continues to have the majority support of members of the assembly. Its importance lies in the normal convention that governments losing a vote of confidence should resign.

Voting system The arrangements by which votes are converted into seats on representative bodies.

Voting turnout The number of citizens casting a valid (i.e. not a spoiled ballot) vote expressed either as a percentage of those eligible to vote (adult citizens), or as a percentage of those on the electoral register.

Welfare states Democracies that accept responsibility for the young and old, the sick and disabled and the unemployed and poor. Welfare states are characterised by resource redistribution policies.

Index of names

Index of subjects

Page numbers in italic indicate briefings, controversies, facts, figures and tables.